Grand Blue Dreaming 4

PRESENTED BY KENJI INOUE & KIMITAKE YOSHIOKA

PREVIOUSLY ON GRAND BLUE DREAMING

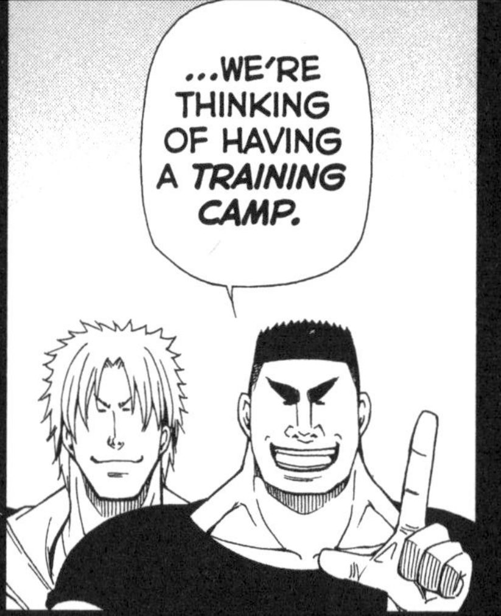
...WE'RE THINKING OF HAVING A *TRAINING CAMP.*

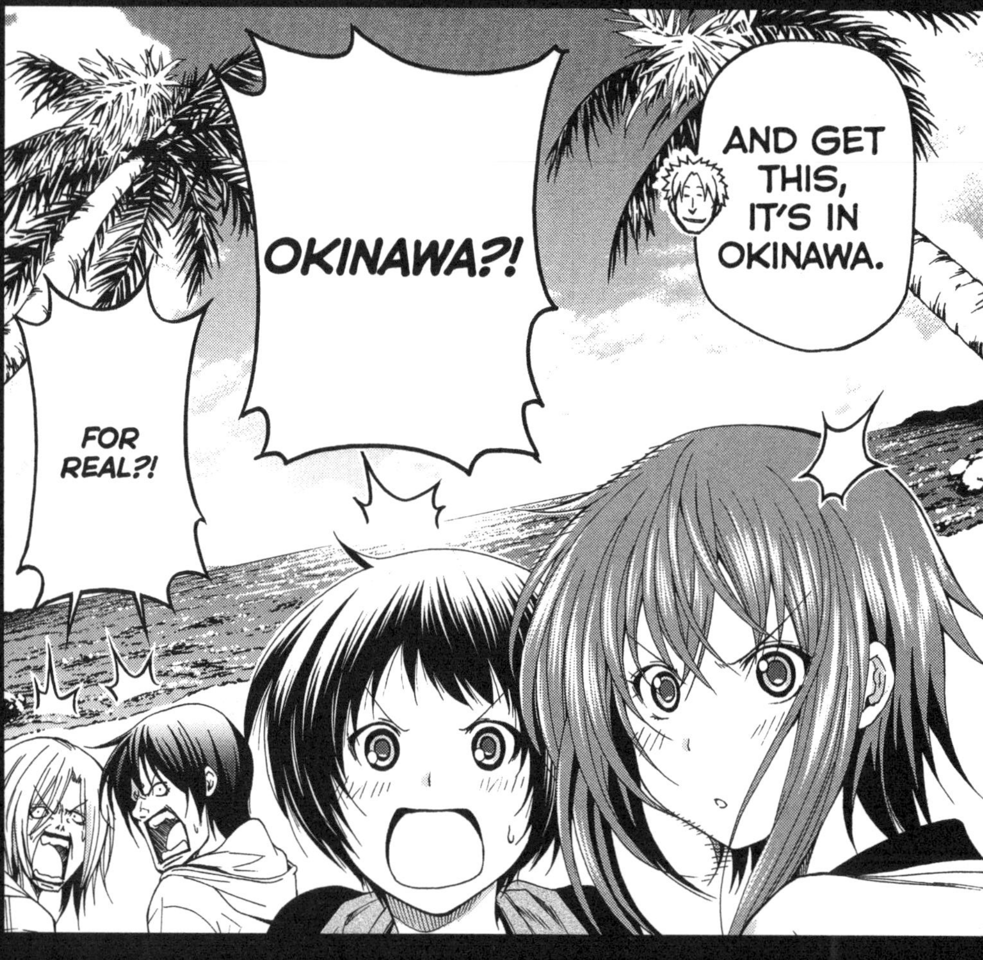
AND GET THIS, IT'S IN OKINAWA.
OKINAWA?!
FOR REAL?!

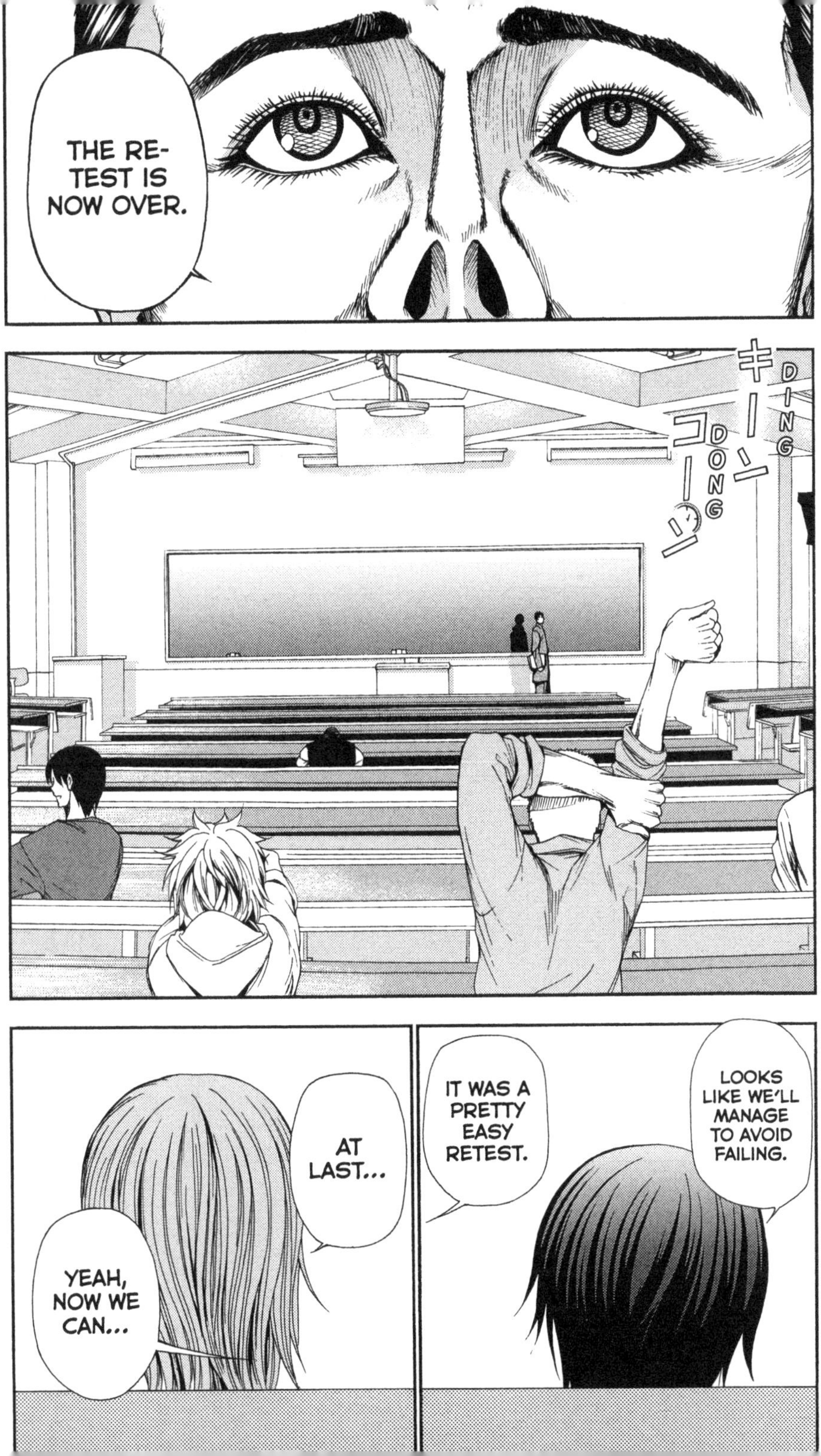
THE RE-TEST IS NOW OVER.
キーン
DING
コーン
DONG
LOOKS LIKE WE'LL MANAGE TO AVOID FAILING.
IT WAS A PRETTY EASY RETEST.
AT LAST...
YEAH, NOW WE CAN...

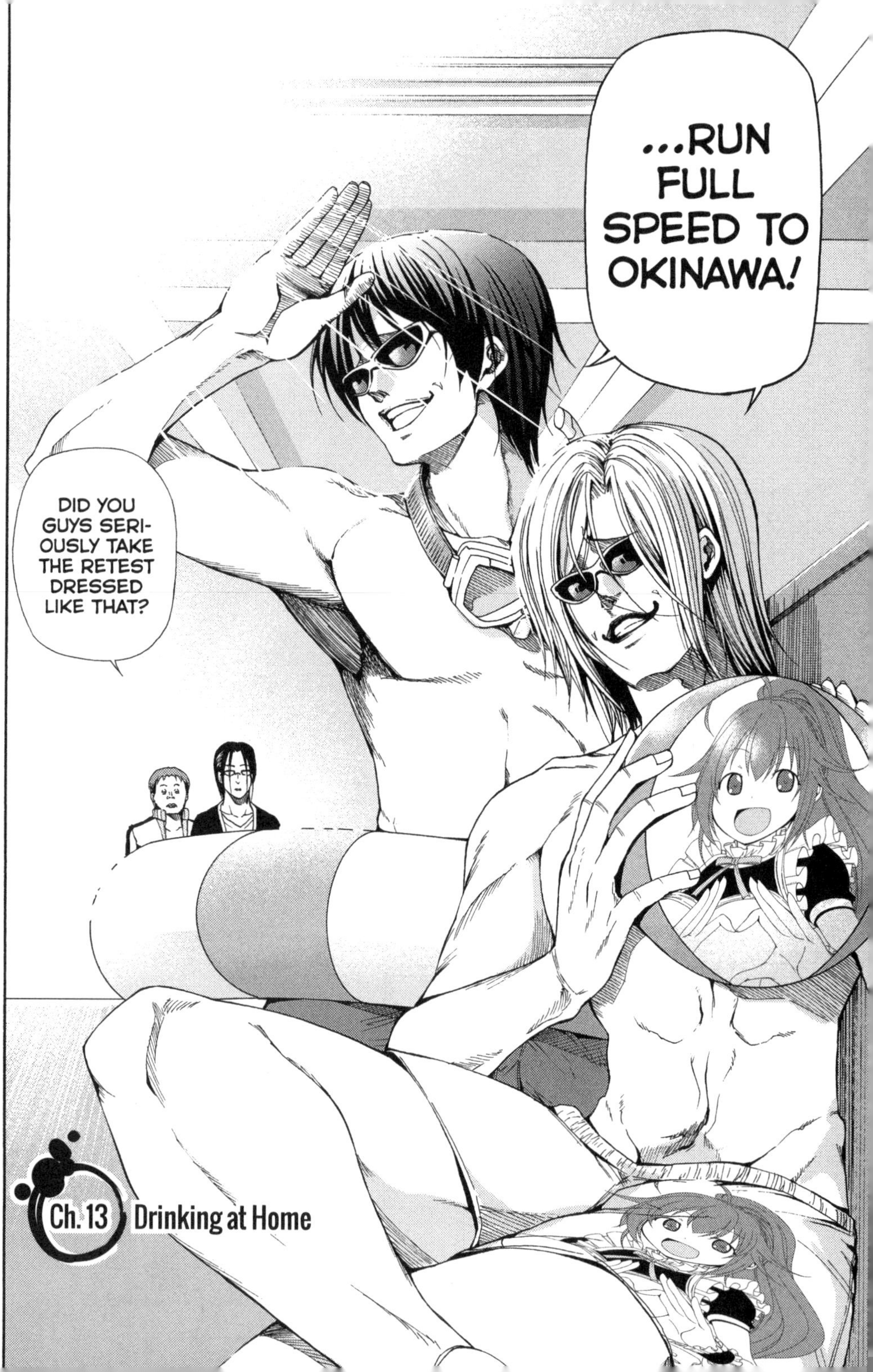
...RUN FULL SPEED TO OKINAWA!
DID YOU GUYS SERI-OUSLY TAKE THE RETEST DRESSED LIKE THAT?
Ch. 13 Drinking at Home

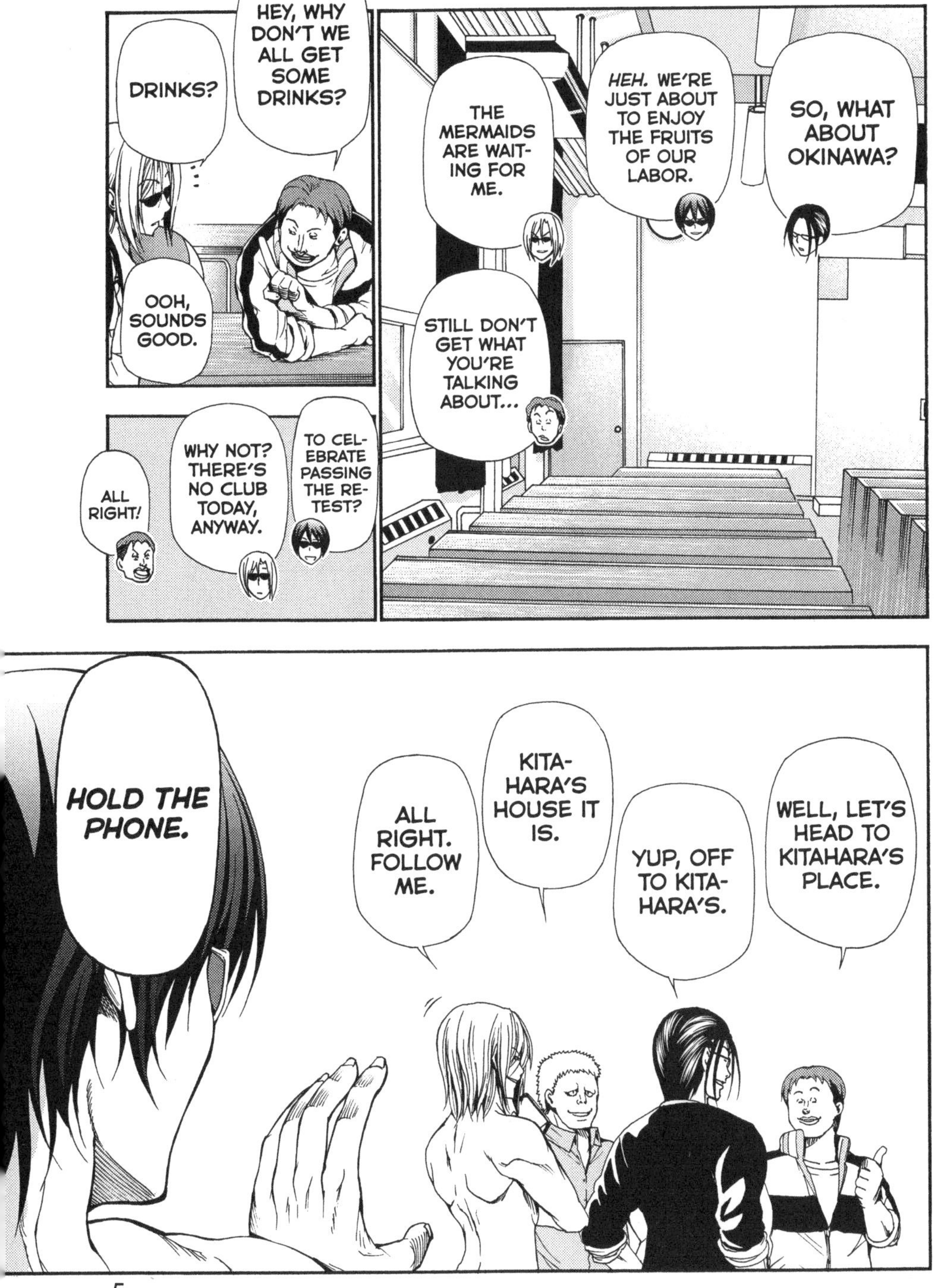
SO, WHAT ABOUT OKINAWA?
HEH. WE'RE JUST ABOUT TO ENJOY THE FRUITS OF OUR LABOR.
THE MERMAIDS ARE WAITING FOR ME.
STILL DON'T GET WHAT YOU'RE TALKING ABOUT...
HEY, WHY DON'T WE ALL GET SOME DRINKS?
DRINKS?
OOH, SOUNDS GOOD.
TO CELEBRATE PASSING THE RETEST?
WHY NOT? THERE'S NO CLUB TODAY, ANYWAY.
ALL RIGHT!
WELL, LET'S HEAD TO KITAHARA'S PLACE.
YUP, OFF TO KITAHARA'S.
KITAHARA'S HOUSE IT IS.
ALL RIGHT. FOLLOW ME.
HOLD THE PHONE.

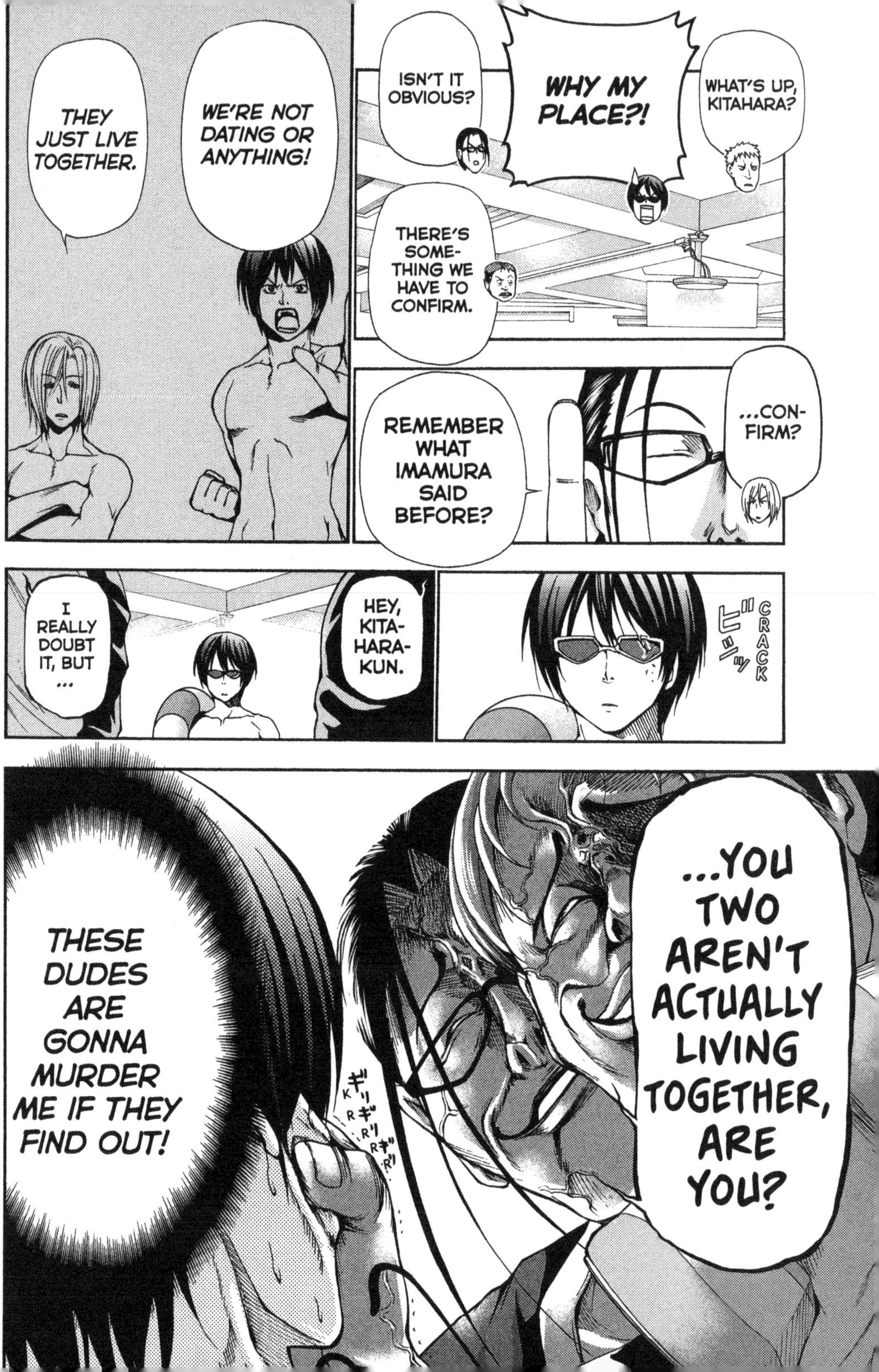
WHAT'S UP, KITAHARA?
WHY MY PLACE?!
ISN'T IT OBVIOUS?
THERE'S SOME-THING WE HAVE TO CONFIRM.
...CON-FIRM?
REMEMBER WHAT IMAMURA SAID BEFORE?
WE'RE NOT DATING OR ANYTHING!
THEY JUST LIVE TOGETHER.
ビッ
CRACK
HEY, KITA-HARA-KUN.
I REALLY DOUBT IT, BUT ...
...YOU TWO AREN'T ACTUALLY LIVING TOGETHER, ARE YOU?
ギリギリギリ
KRRRR
THESE DUDES ARE GONNA MURDER ME IF THEY FIND OUT!

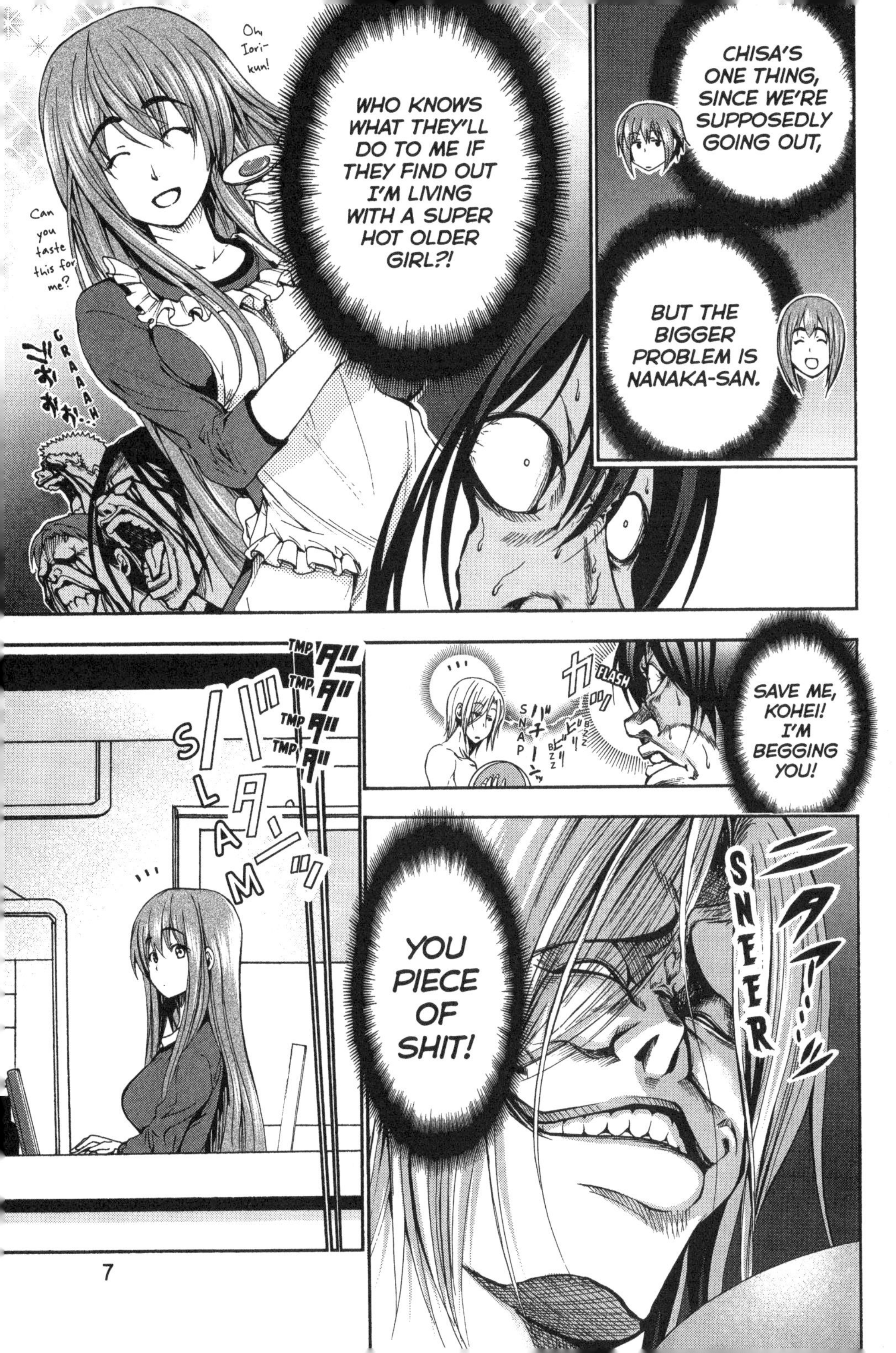
CHISA'S ONE THING, SINCE WE'RE SUPPOSEDLY GOING OUT,
BUT THE BIGGER PROBLEM IS NANAKA-SAN.
WHO KNOWS WHAT THEY'LL DO TO ME IF THEY FIND OUT I'M LIVING WITH A SUPER HOT OLDER GIRL?!
Oh Iori-kun!
Can you taste this for me?
GRAAAAH
SAVE ME, KOHEI! I'M BEGGING YOU!
FLASH
SNAP
BZZ
BZZ
...
SNEER
YOU PIECE OF SHIT!
TMP
TMP
TMP
TMP
SLAM
...

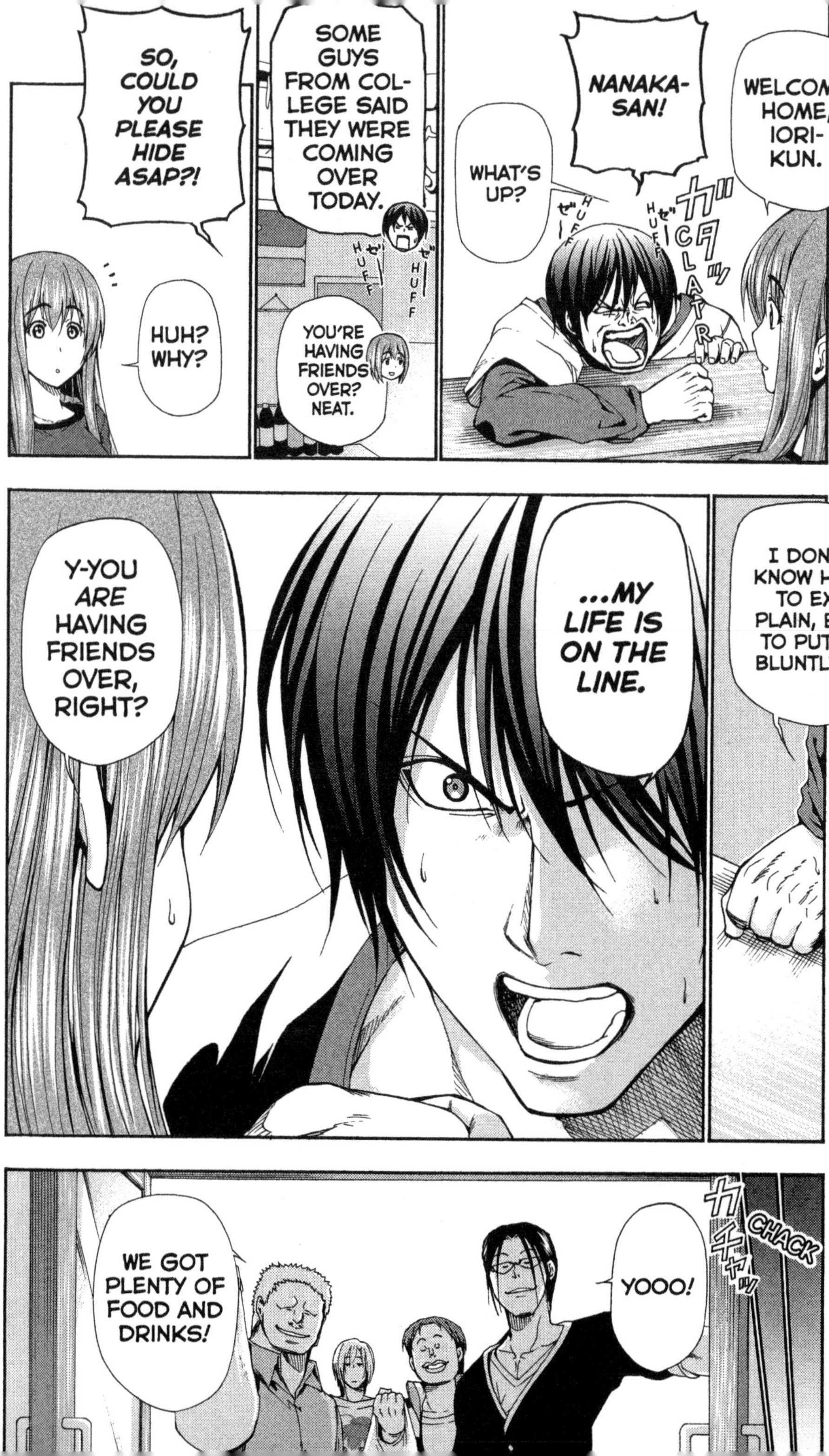
WELCOME HOME, IORI-KUN.
NANAKA-SAN!
CLATR
HUFF
HUFF
WHAT'S UP?
SOME GUYS FROM COL-LEGE SAID THEY WERE COMING OVER TODAY.
HUFF
HUFF
YOU'RE HAVING FRIENDS OVER? NEAT.
SO, COULD YOU PLEASE HIDE ASAP?!
HUH? WHY?
I DON'T KNOW HOW TO EX-PLAIN, BUT TO PUT IT BLUNTLY...
...MY LIFE IS ON THE LINE.
Y-YOU ARE HAVING FRIENDS OVER, RIGHT?
CHACK
YOOO!
WE GOT PLENTY OF FOOD AND DRINKS!

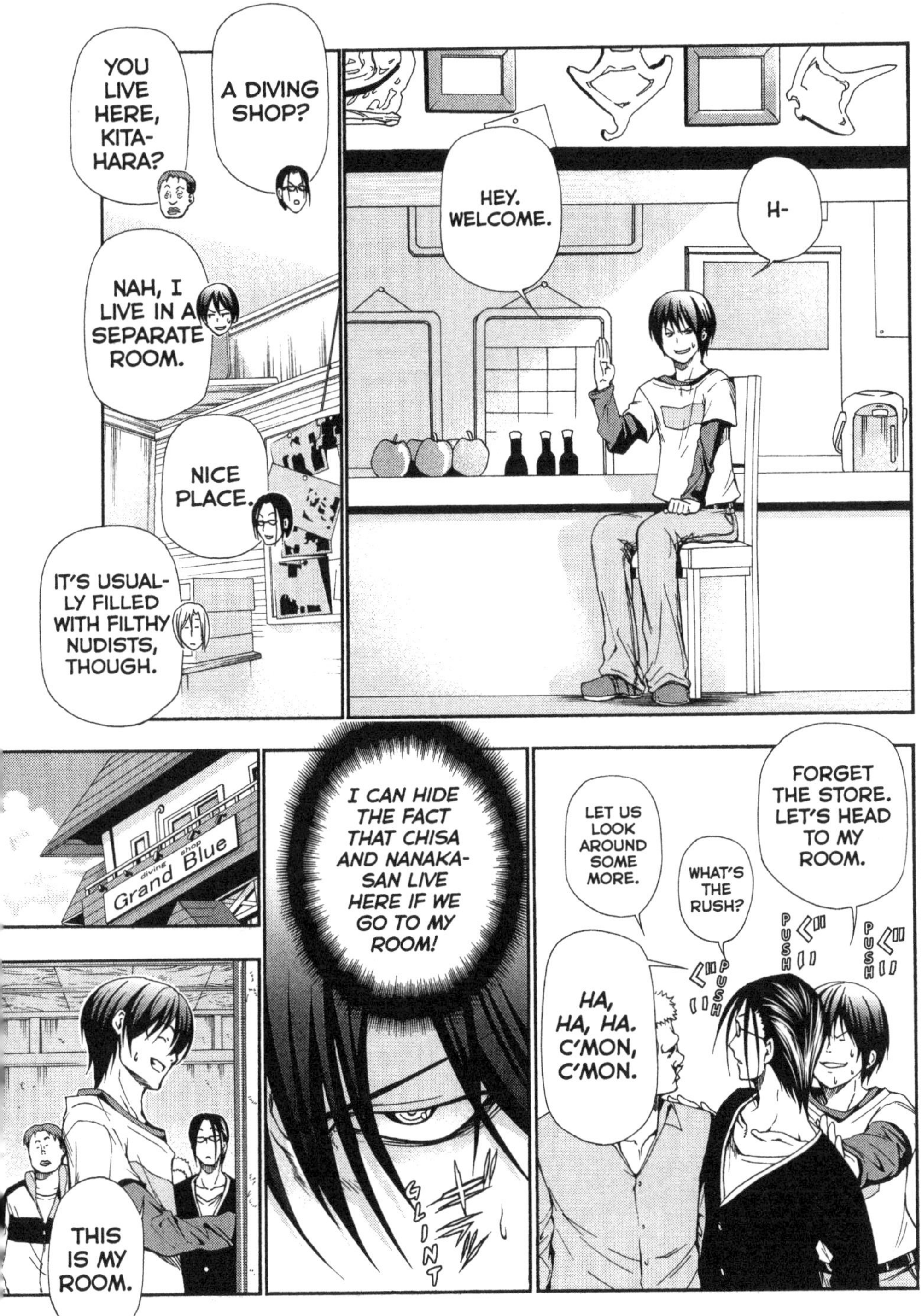
H-
HEY. WELCOME.
A DIVING SHOP?
YOU LIVE HERE, KITA-HARA?
NAH, I LIVE IN A SEPARATE ROOM.
NICE PLACE.
IT'S USUALLY FILLED WITH FILTHY NUDISTS, THOUGH.
FORGET THE STORE. LET'S HEAD TO MY ROOM.
PUSH
PUSH
WHAT'S THE RUSH?
PUSH
LET US LOOK AROUND SOME MORE.
HA, HA, HA. C'MON, C'MON.
I CAN HIDE THE FACT THAT CHISA AND NANAKA-SAN LIVE HERE IF WE GO TO MY ROOM!
GLINT
diving shop Grand Blue
THIS IS MY ROOM.

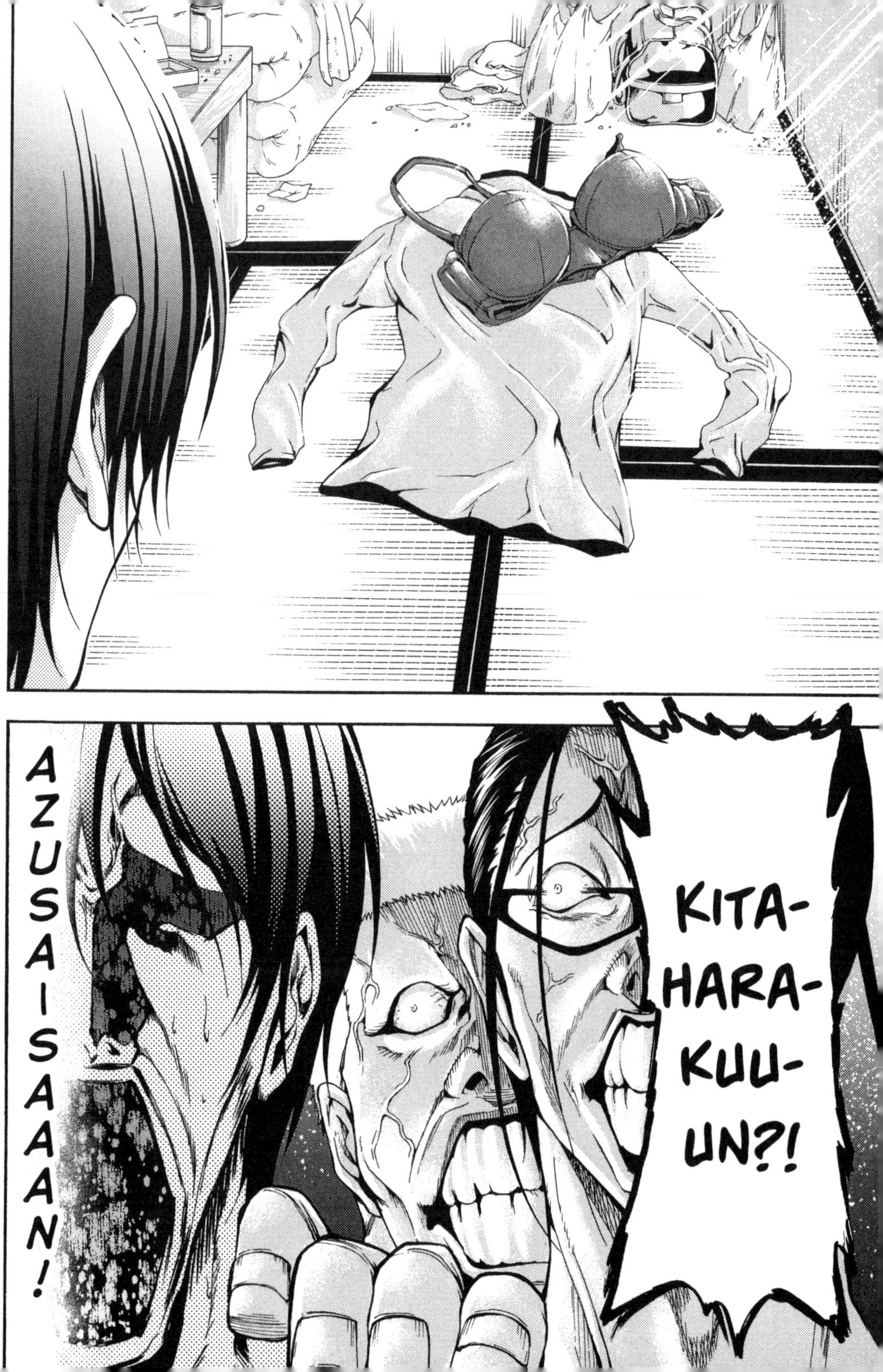
KITA-HARA-KUUUN?!
AZUSAISAAAAN!

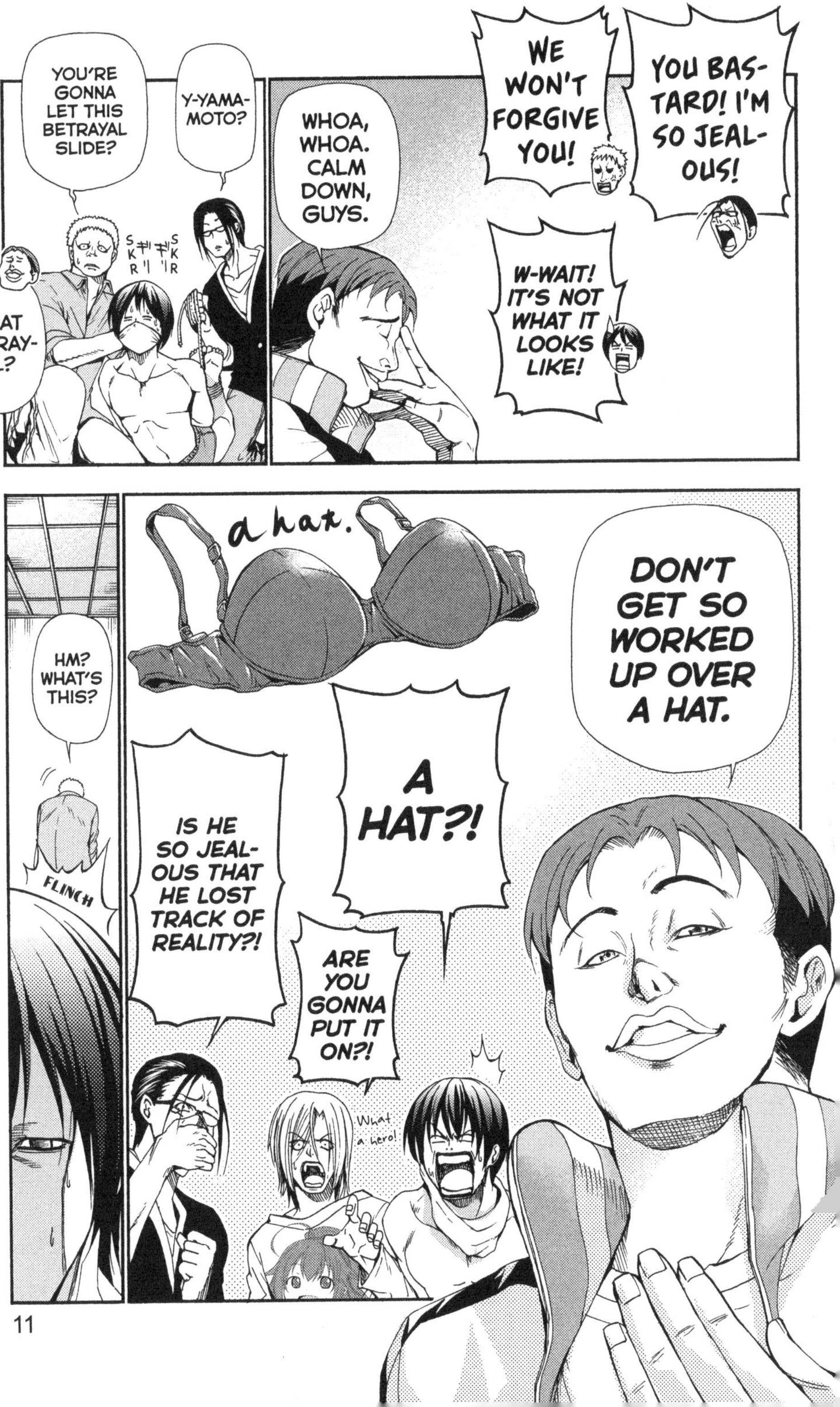
YOU BAS-TARD! I'M SO JEAL-OUS!
WE WON'T FORGIVE YOU!
W-WAIT! IT'S NOT WHAT IT LOOKS LIKE!
WHOA, WHOA. CALM DOWN, GUYS.
Y-YAMA-MOTO?
YOU'RE GONNA LET THIS BETRAYAL SLIDE?
SKR SKR
SKRR SKRR
WHAT BETRAY-AL?
a hat.
DON'T GET SO WORKED UP OVER A HAT.
A HAT?!
IS HE SO JEAL-OUS THAT HE LOST TRACK OF REALITY?!
ARE YOU GONNA PUT IT ON?!
What a hero!
HM? WHAT'S THIS?
FLINCH

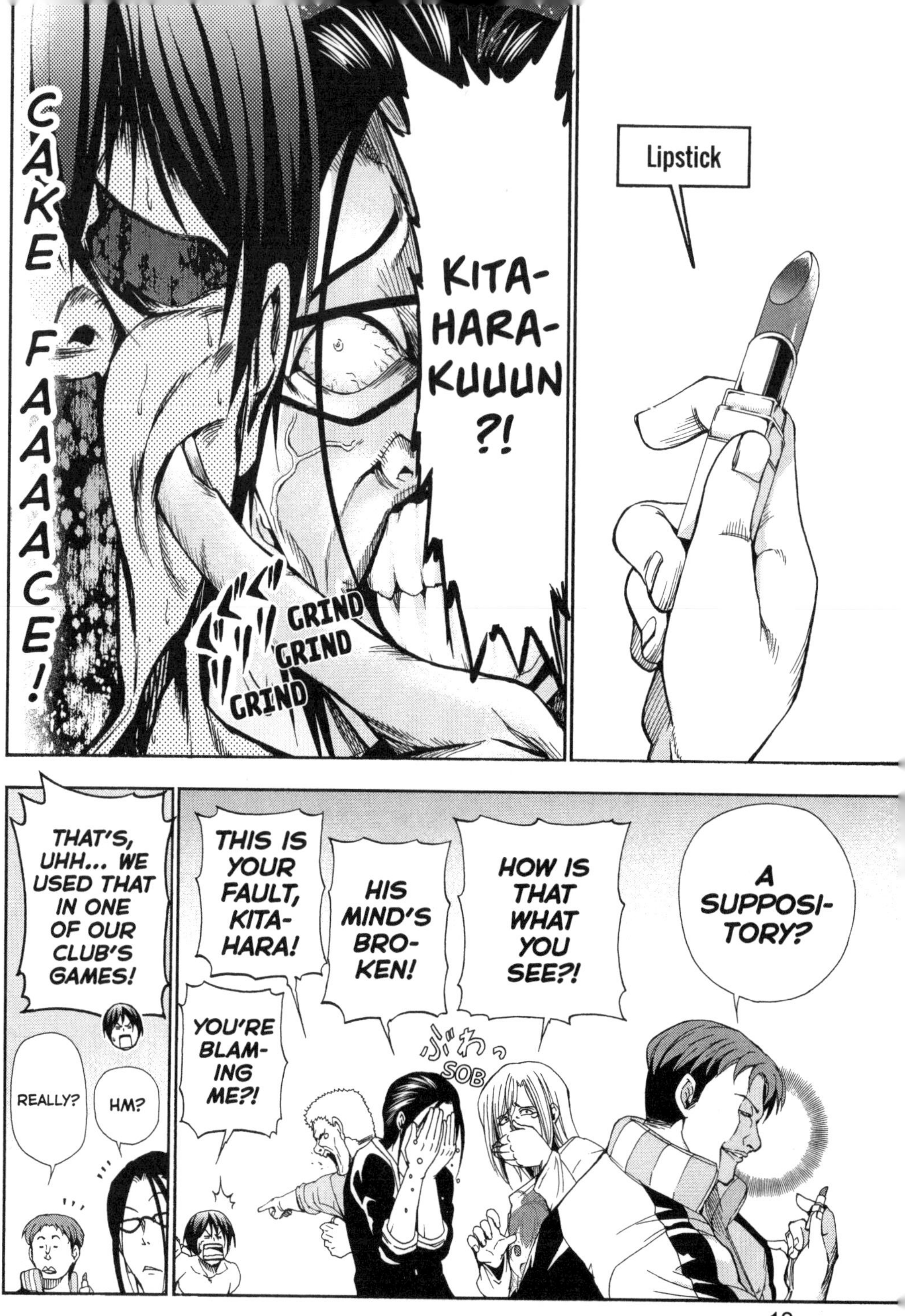
Lipstick
KITA-HARA-KUUUN?!
GRIND GRIND GRIND
CAKE FAAAAACE!
A SUPPOSI-TORY?
HOW IS THAT WHAT YOU SEE?!
ぶわっ SOB
HIS MIND'S BRO-KEN!
THIS IS YOUR FAULT, KITA-HARA!
YOU'RE BLAM-ING ME?!
THAT'S, UHH... WE USED THAT IN ONE OF OUR CLUB'S GAMES!
HM?
REALLY?

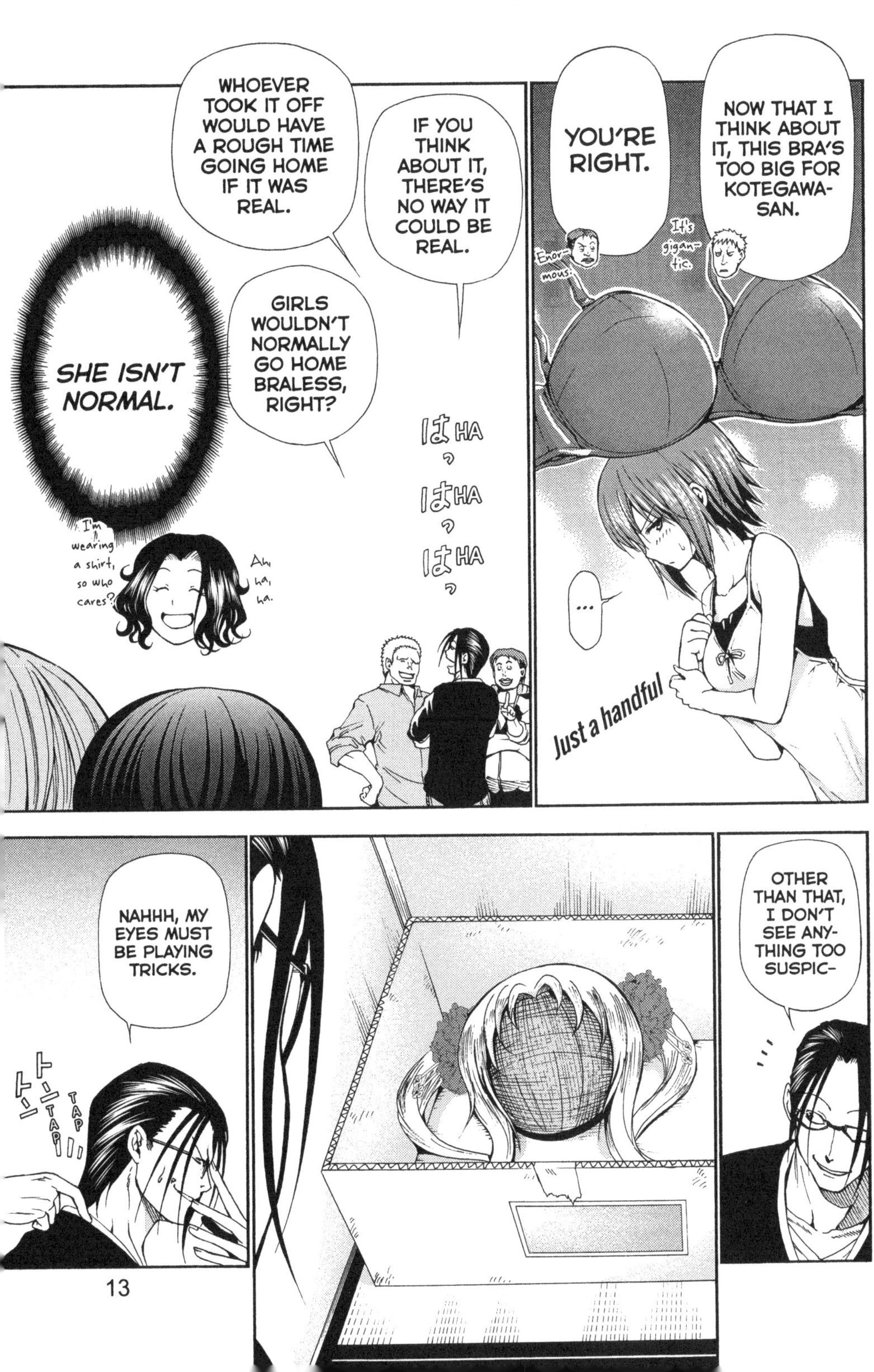
NOW THAT I THINK ABOUT IT, THIS BRA'S TOO BIG FOR KOTEGAWA-SAN.
YOU'RE RIGHT.
It's gigantic.
Enormous.
...
Just a handful
IF YOU THINK ABOUT IT, THERE'S NO WAY IT COULD BE REAL.
WHOEVER TOOK IT OFF WOULD HAVE A ROUGH TIME GOING HOME IF IT WAS REAL.
GIRLS WOULDN'T NORMALLY GO HOME BRALESS, RIGHT?
はっ HA はっ HA はっ HA
SHE ISN'T NORMAL.
I'm wearing a shirt, so who cares?
Ah ha, ha.
OTHER THAN THAT, I DON'T SEE ANYTHING TOO SUSPIC-
NAHHH, MY EYES MUST BE PLAYING TRICKS.
トントン TAP TAP

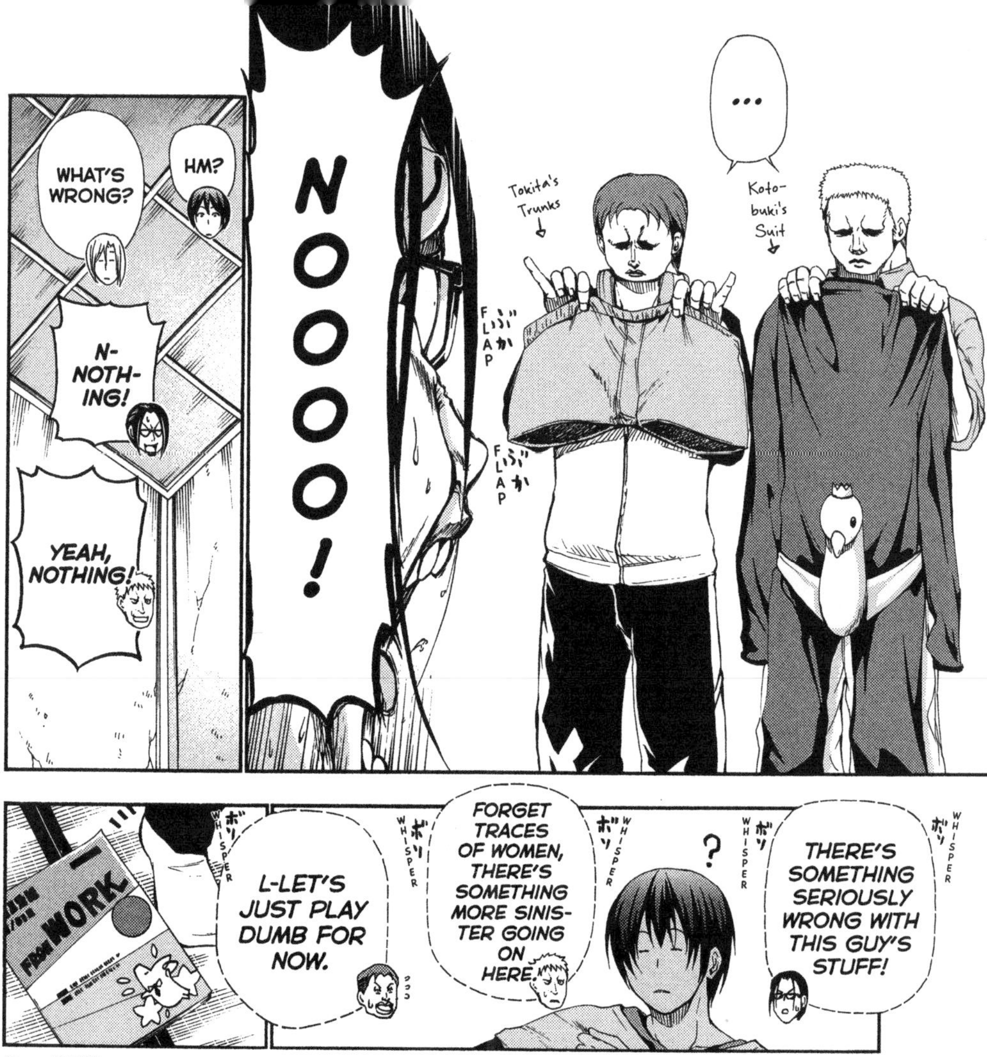
...
Tokita's Trunks
Kotobuki's Suit
FLAP
FLAP
NOOOO!
HM?
WHAT'S WRONG?
N-NOTHING!
YEAH, NOTHING!
WHISPER
THERE'S SOMETHING SERIOUSLY WRONG WITH THIS GUY'S STUFF!
WHISPER
?
WHISPER
FORGET TRACES OF WOMEN, THERE'S SOMETHING MORE SINISTER GOING ON HERE.
WHISPER
L-LET'S JUST PLAY DUMB FOR NOW.
FROM WORK

*Approx. 300 USD.

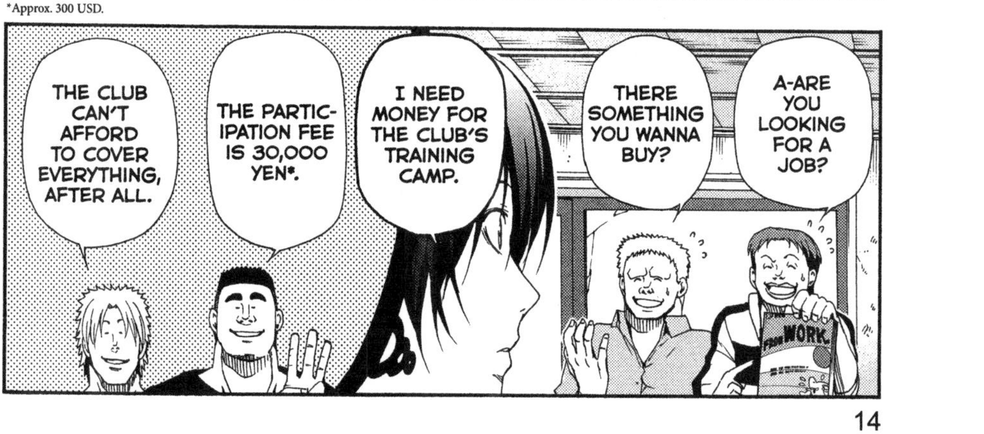
A-ARE YOU LOOKING FOR A JOB?
THERE SOMETHING YOU WANNA BUY?
I NEED MONEY FOR THE CLUB'S TRAINING CAMP.
THE PARTICIPATION FEE IS 30,000 YEN*.
THE CLUB CAN'T AFFORD TO COVER EVERYTHING, AFTER ALL.
FROM WORK

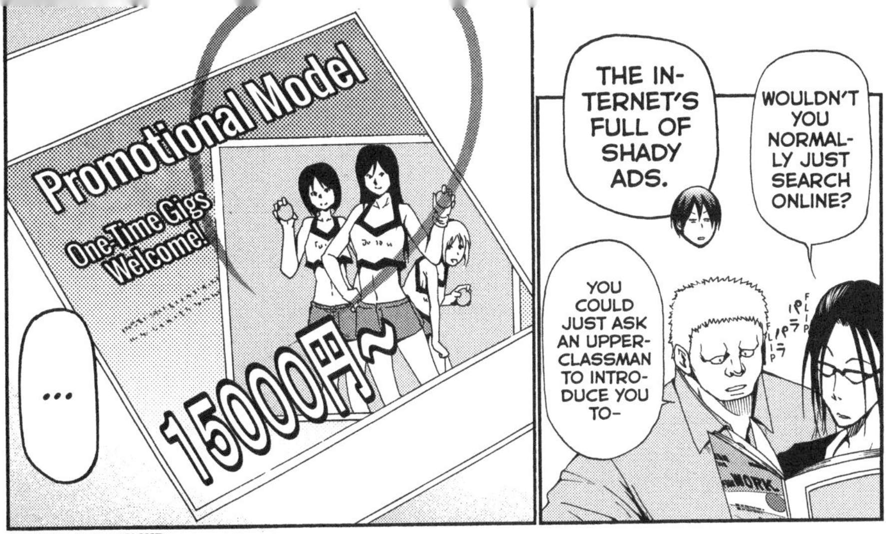
FLIP
PERA
WOULDN'T YOU NORMALLY JUST SEARCH ONLINE?
THE INTERNET'S FULL OF SHADY ADS.
YOU COULD JUST ASK AN UPPERCLASSMAN TO INTRODUCE YOU TO-
Promotional Model
One-Time Gigs Welcome!
15000円~
...

*15000 Yen. Approx. 150 USD.

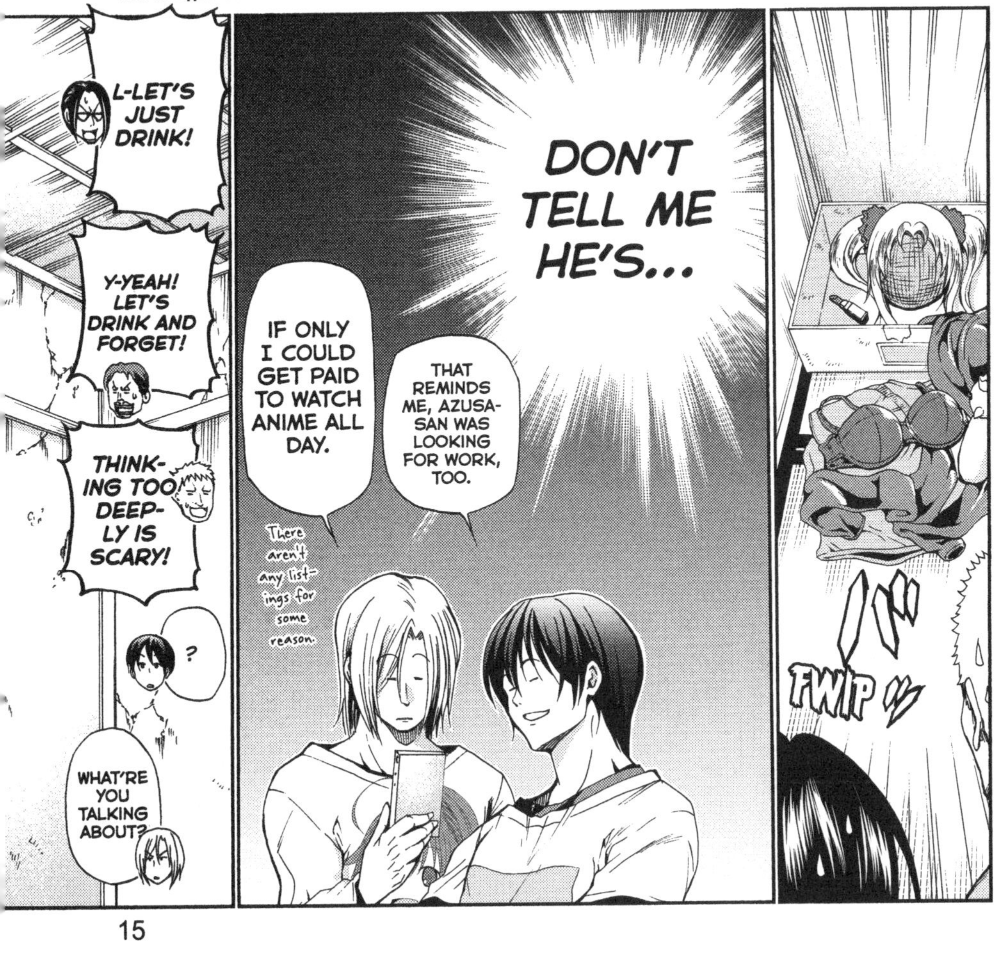
FWIP
DON'T TELL ME HE'S...
THAT REMINDS ME, AZUSA-SAN WAS LOOKING FOR WORK, TOO.
IF ONLY I COULD GET PAID TO WATCH ANIME ALL DAY.
There aren't any listings for some reason.
L-LET'S JUST DRINK!
Y-YEAH! LET'S DRINK AND FORGET!
THINKING TOO DEEPLY IS SCARY!
?
WHAT'RE YOU TALKING ABOUT?

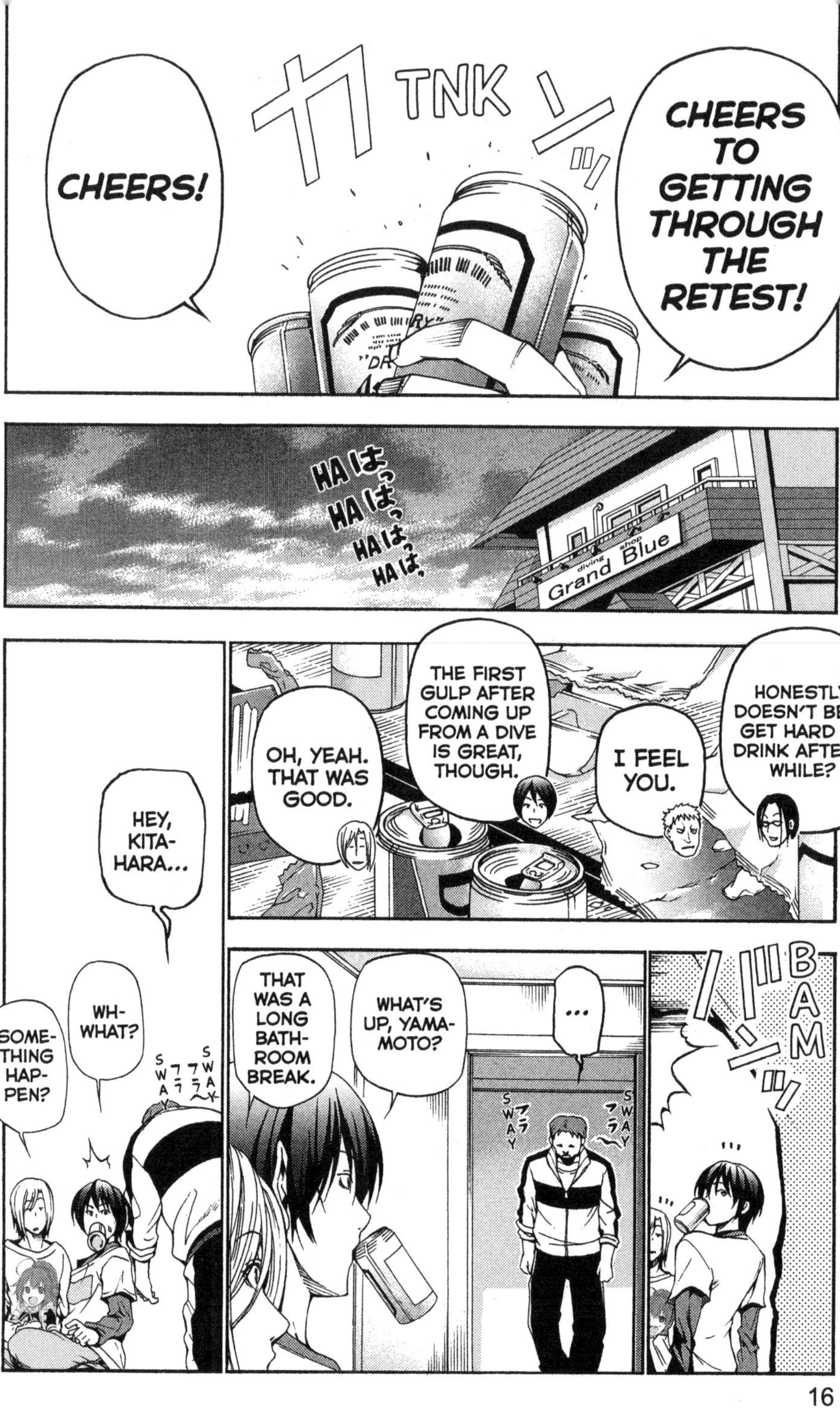
CHEERS TO GETTING THROUGH THE RETEST!
TNK
CHEERS!
HA HA HA HA
diving shop Grand Blue
HONESTLY, DOESN'T BEER GET HARD TO DRINK AFTER A WHILE?
I FEEL YOU.
THE FIRST GULP AFTER COMING UP FROM A DIVE IS GREAT, THOUGH.
OH, YEAH. THAT WAS GOOD.
BAM
...
SWAY
WHAT'S UP, YAMAMOTO?
THAT WAS A LONG BATHROOM BREAK.
HEY, KITAHARA...
SWAY
WH-WHAT?
SOMETHING HAPPEN?

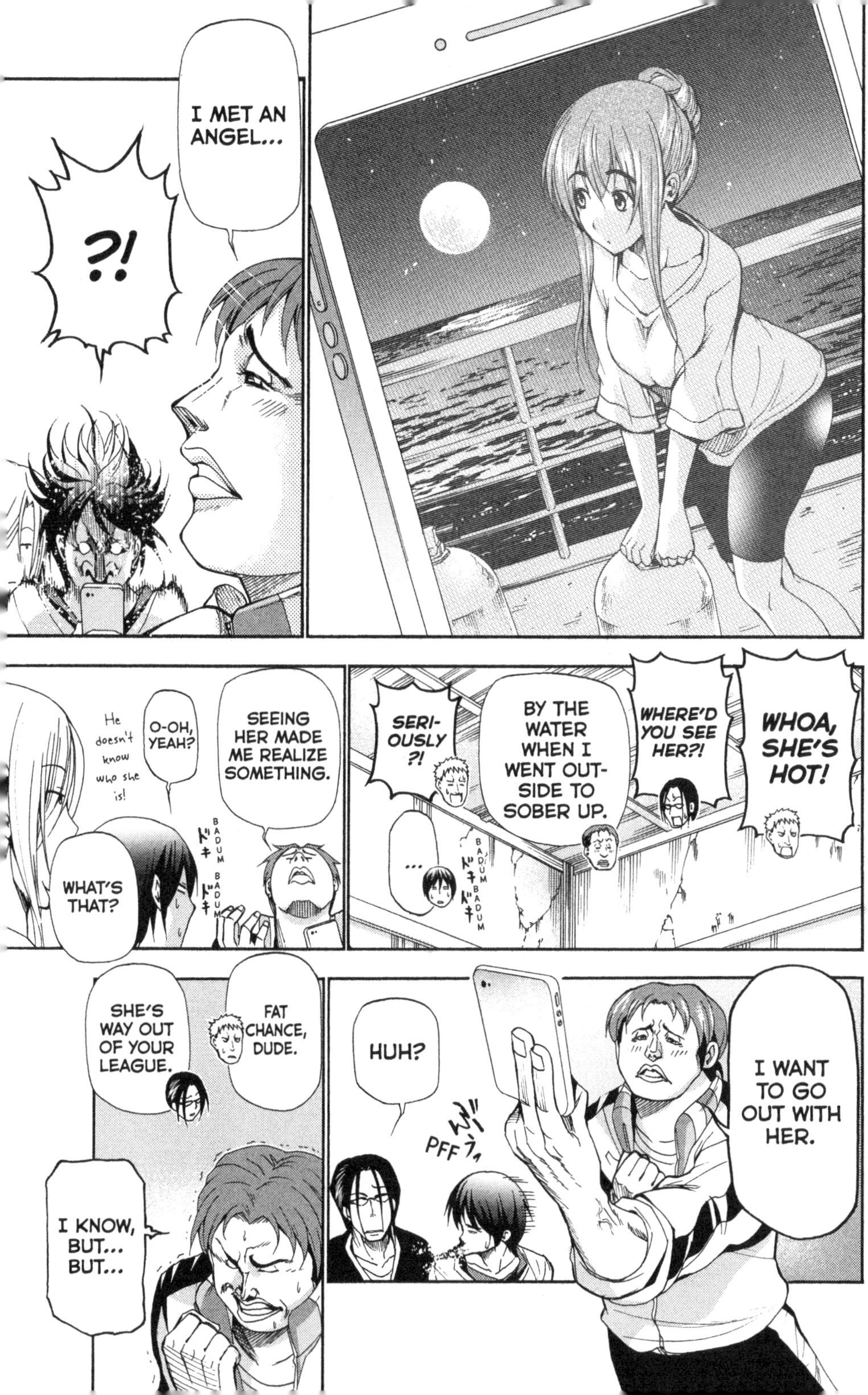
I MET AN ANGEL...
?!
WHOA, SHE'S HOT!
WHERE'D YOU SEE HER?!
BY THE WATER WHEN I WENT OUT-SIDE TO SOBER UP.
SERI-OUSLY?!
...
BADUM BADUM
SEEING HER MADE ME REALIZE SOMETHING.
O-OH, YEAH?
He doesn't know who she is!
BADUM BADUM
WHAT'S THAT?
I WANT TO GO OUT WITH HER.
HUH?
PFF
FAT CHANCE, DUDE.
SHE'S WAY OUT OF YOUR LEAGUE.
I KNOW, BUT... BUT...

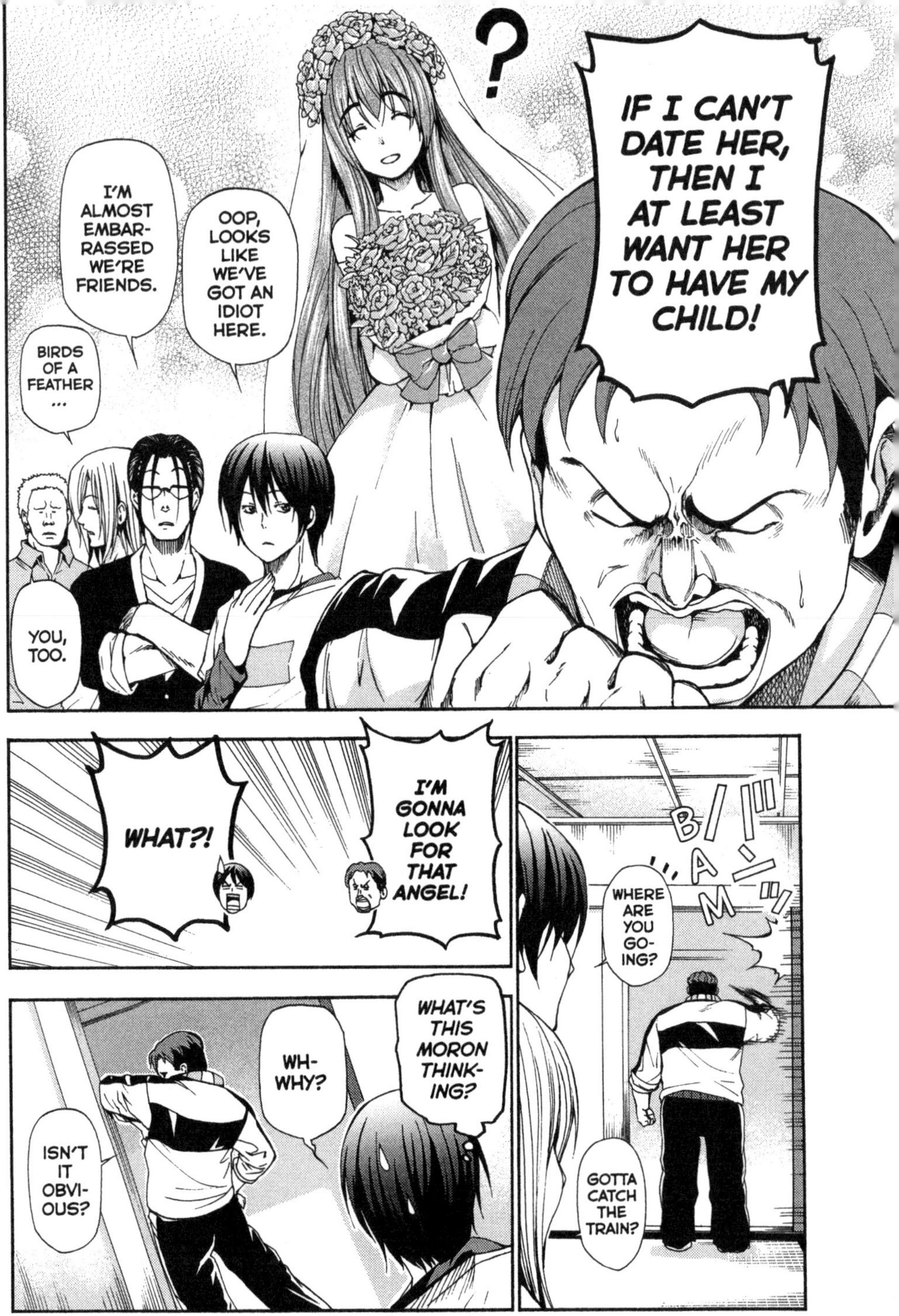
IF I CAN'T DATE HER, THEN I AT LEAST WANT HER TO HAVE MY CHILD!
?
OOP, LOOKS LIKE WE'VE GOT AN IDIOT HERE.
I'M ALMOST EMBARRASSED WE'RE FRIENDS.
BIRDS OF A FEATHER ...
YOU, TOO.
BAM
WHERE ARE YOU GOING?
GOTTA CATCH THE TRAIN?
I'M GONNA LOOK FOR THAT ANGEL!
WHAT?!
WHAT'S THIS MORON THINKING?
WH-WHY?
ISN'T IT OBVIOUS?

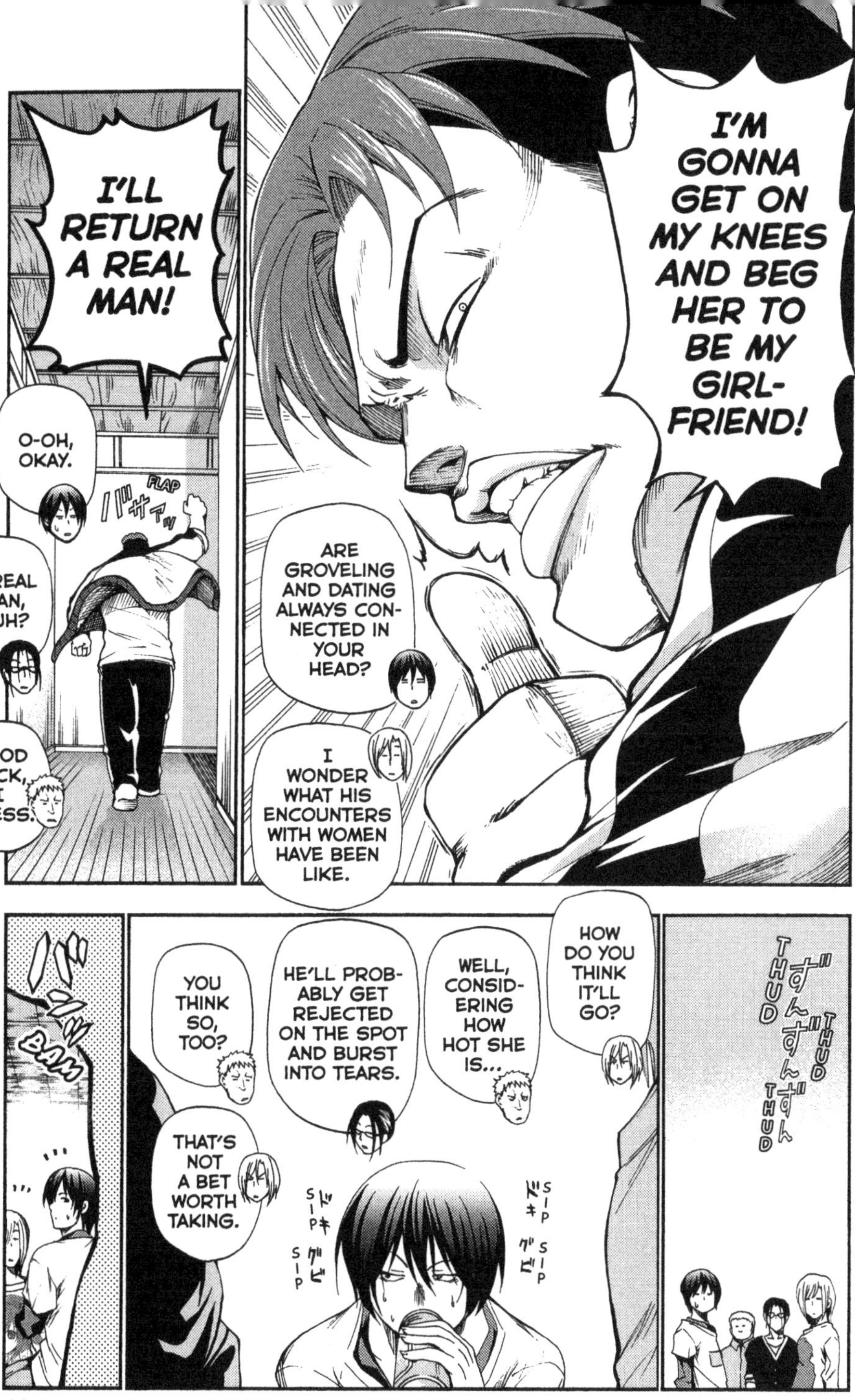
I'M GONNA GET ON MY KNEES AND BEG HER TO BE MY GIRL-FRIEND!
ARE GROVELING AND DATING ALWAYS CON-NECTED IN YOUR HEAD?
I WONDER WHAT HIS ENCOUNTERS WITH WOMEN HAVE BEEN LIKE.
I'LL RETURN A REAL MAN!
O-OH, OKAY.
FLAP
A REAL MAN, HUH?
GOOD LUCK, I GUESS.
THUD THUD THUD
HOW DO YOU THINK IT'LL GO?
WELL, CONSID-ERING HOW HOT SHE IS...
HE'LL PROB-ABLY GET REJECTED ON THE SPOT AND BURST INTO TEARS.
YOU THINK SO, TOO?
THAT'S NOT A BET WORTH TAKING.
SIP SIP SIP SIP
BAM
...
...

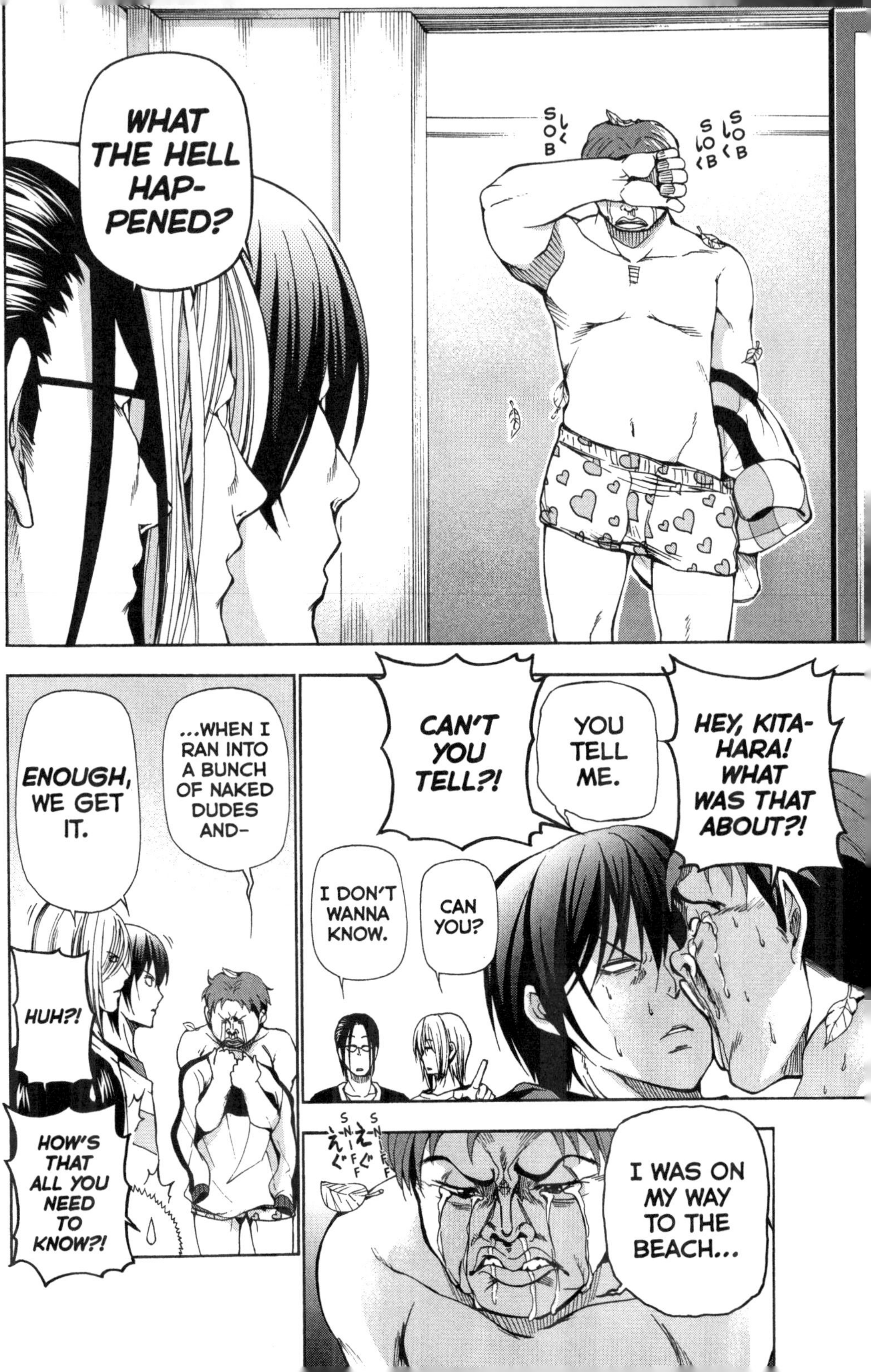
SOB SOB
SOB
WHAT THE HELL HAP-PENED?
HEY, KITA-HARA! WHAT WAS THAT ABOUT?!
YOU TELL ME.
CAN'T YOU TELL?!
CAN YOU?
I DON'T WANNA KNOW.
SNIFF SNIFF
I WAS ON MY WAY TO THE BEACH...
...WHEN I RAN INTO A BUNCH OF NAKED DUDES AND–
ENOUGH, WE GET IT.
HUH?!
HOW'S THAT ALL YOU NEED TO KNOW?!

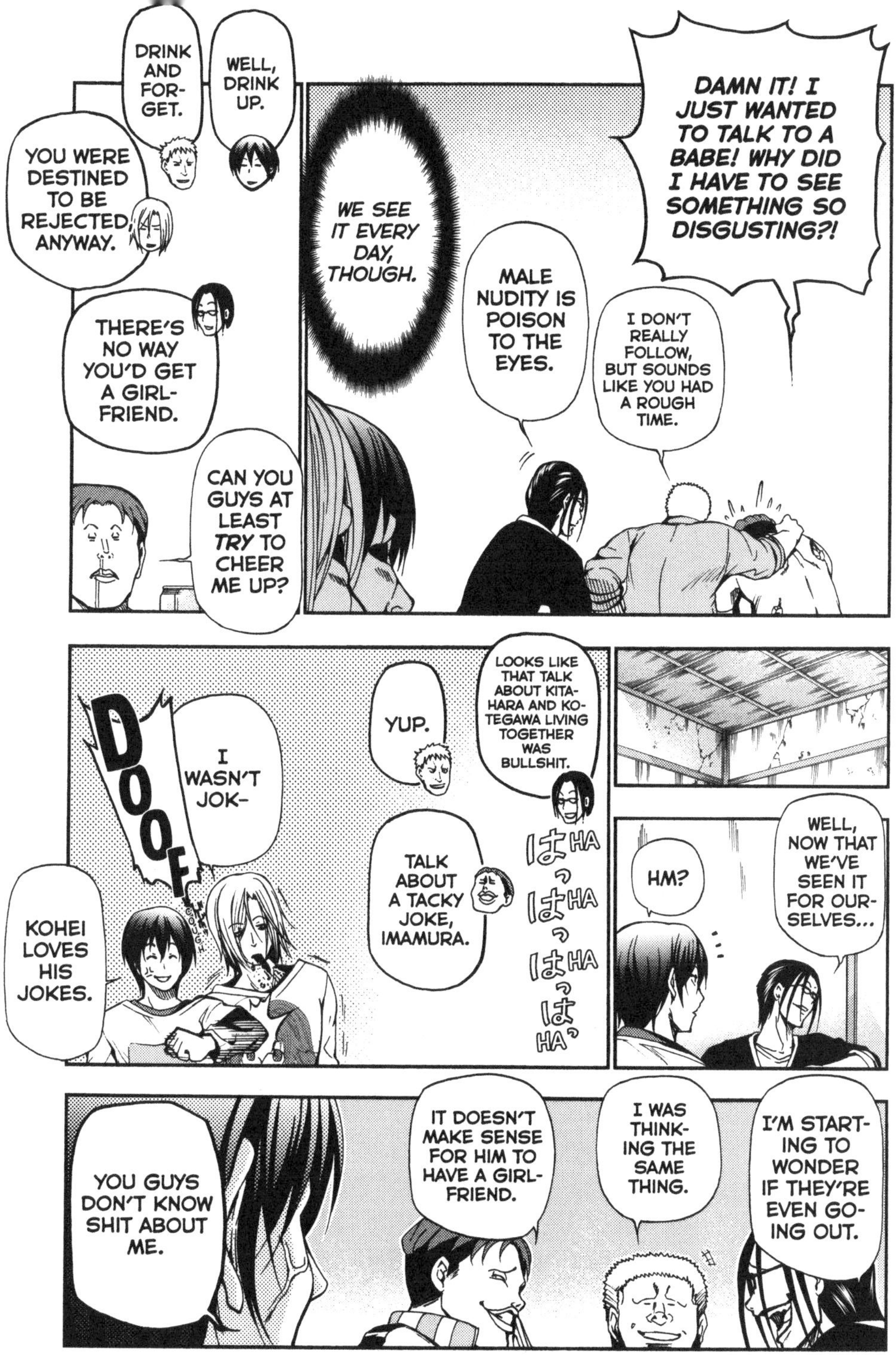
DAMN IT! I JUST WANTED TO TALK TO A BABE! WHY DID I HAVE TO SEE SOMETHING SO DISGUSTING?!
I DON'T REALLY FOLLOW, BUT SOUNDS LIKE YOU HAD A ROUGH TIME.
MALE NUDITY IS POISON TO THE EYES.
WE SEE IT EVERY DAY, THOUGH.
WELL, DRINK UP.
DRINK AND FOR-GET.
YOU WERE DESTINED TO BE REJECTED, ANYWAY.
THERE'S NO WAY YOU'D GET A GIRL-FRIEND.
CAN YOU GUYS AT LEAST TRY TO CHEER ME UP?
WELL, NOW THAT WE'VE SEEN IT FOR OUR-SELVES...
HM?
LOOKS LIKE THAT TALK ABOUT KITA-HARA AND KO-TEGAWA LIVING TOGETHER WAS BULLSHIT.
YUP.
はっ HA はっ HA はっ HA はっ HA
TALK ABOUT A TACKY JOKE, IMAMURA.
I WASN'T JOK-
DOOF
COUGH COUGH
KOHEI LOVES HIS JOKES.
I'M START-ING TO WONDER IF THEY'RE EVEN GO-ING OUT.
I WAS THINK-ING THE SAME THING.
IT DOESN'T MAKE SENSE FOR HIM TO HAVE A GIRL-FRIEND.
YOU GUYS DON'T KNOW SHIT ABOUT ME.

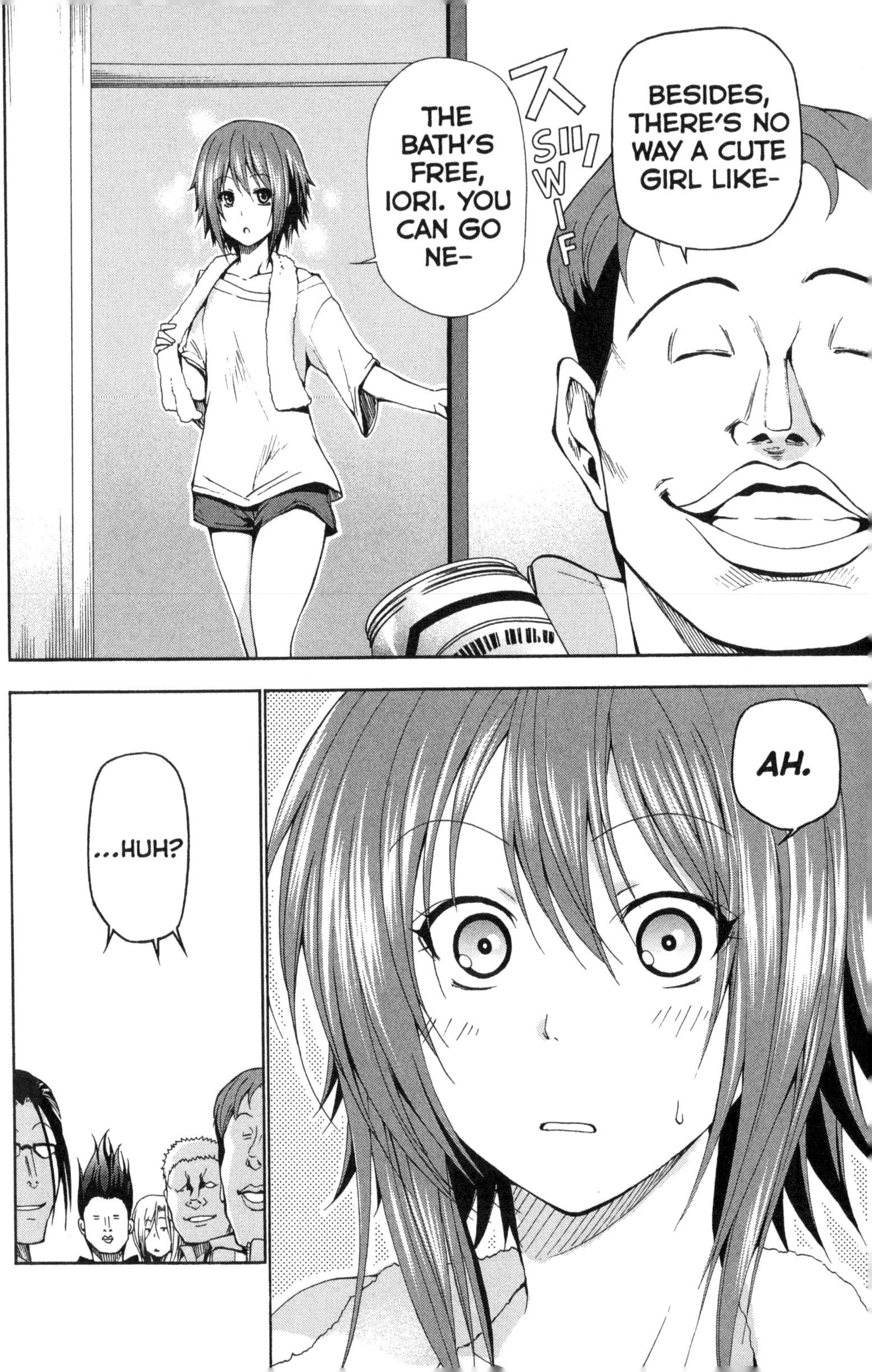
BESIDES, THERE'S NO WAY A CUTE GIRL LIKE-
SWIF
THE BATH'S FREE, IORI. YOU CAN GO NE-
AH.
...HUH?

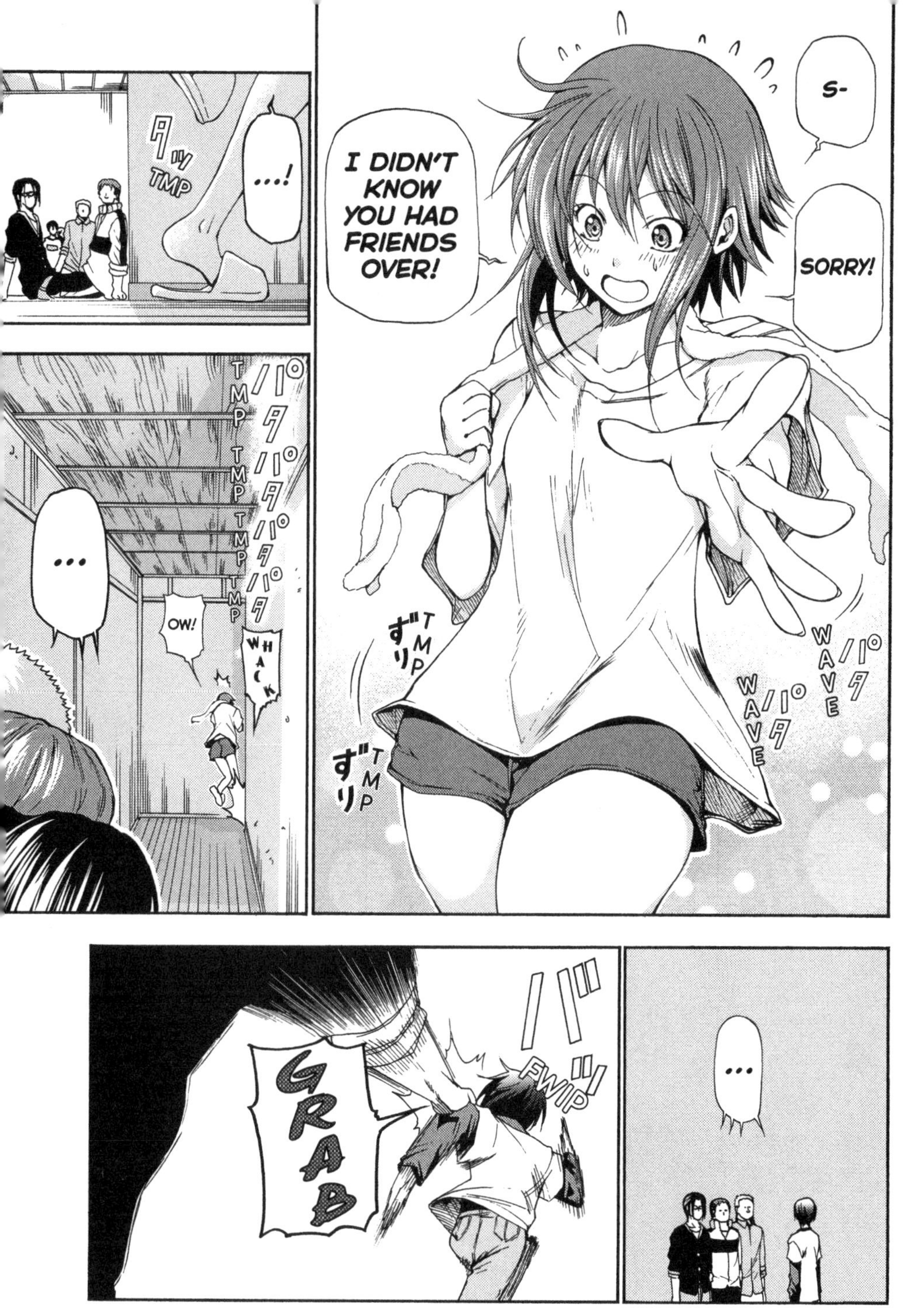
S-
SORRY!
I DIDN'T KNOW YOU HAD FRIENDS OVER!
パタ WAVE
パタ WAVE
ずり TMP
ずり TMP
...!
タッ TMP
パタパタパタパタパタ
TMP TMP TMP TMP TMP
...
OW!
WHACK
...
バッ FWIP
GRAB

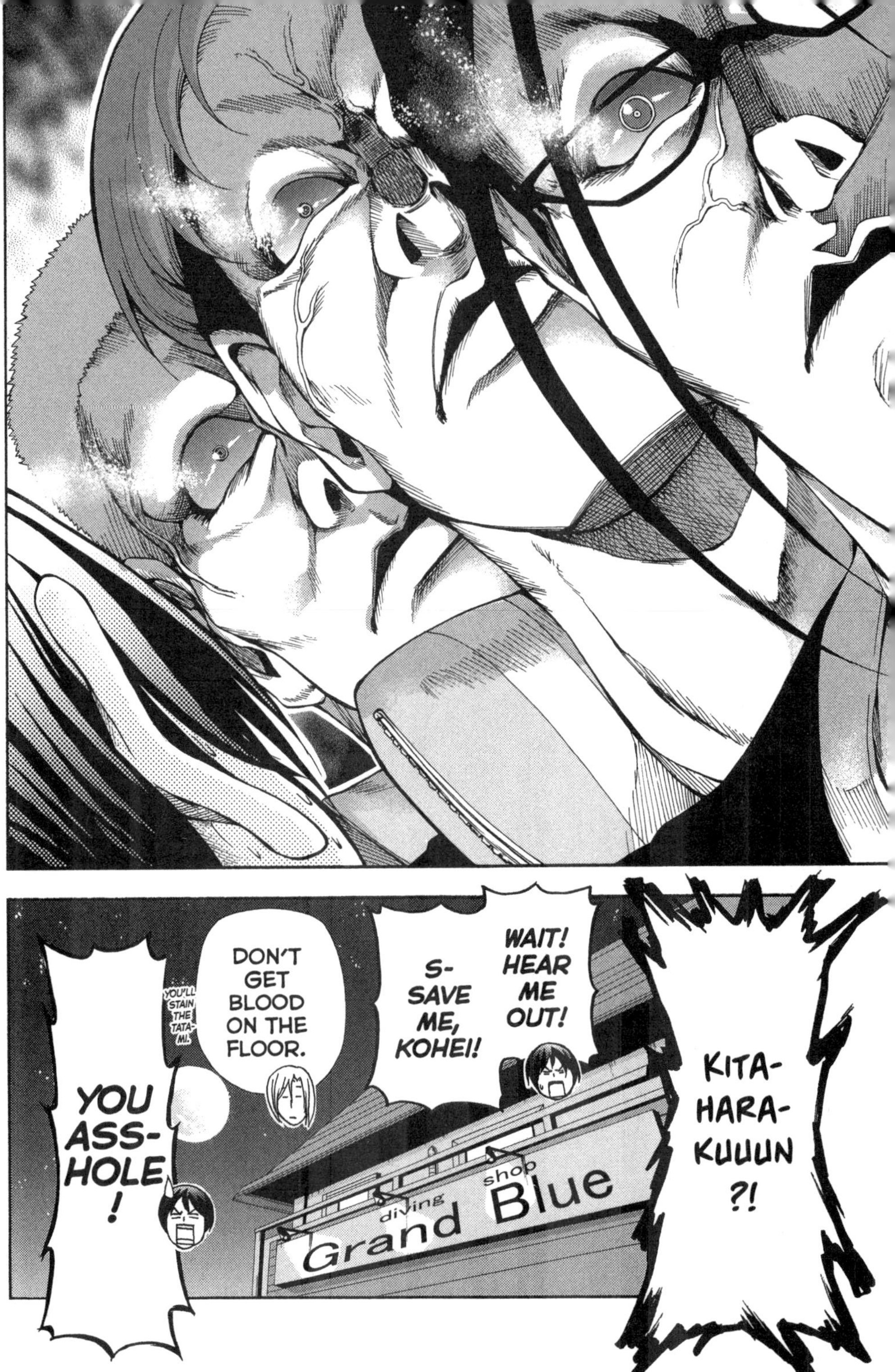
KITA-HARA-KUUUN?!
WAIT! HEAR ME OUT!
S-SAVE ME, KOHEI!
DON'T GET BLOOD ON THE FLOOR.
YOU'LL STAIN THE TATA-MI.
YOU ASS-HOLE!
diving shop Grand Blue

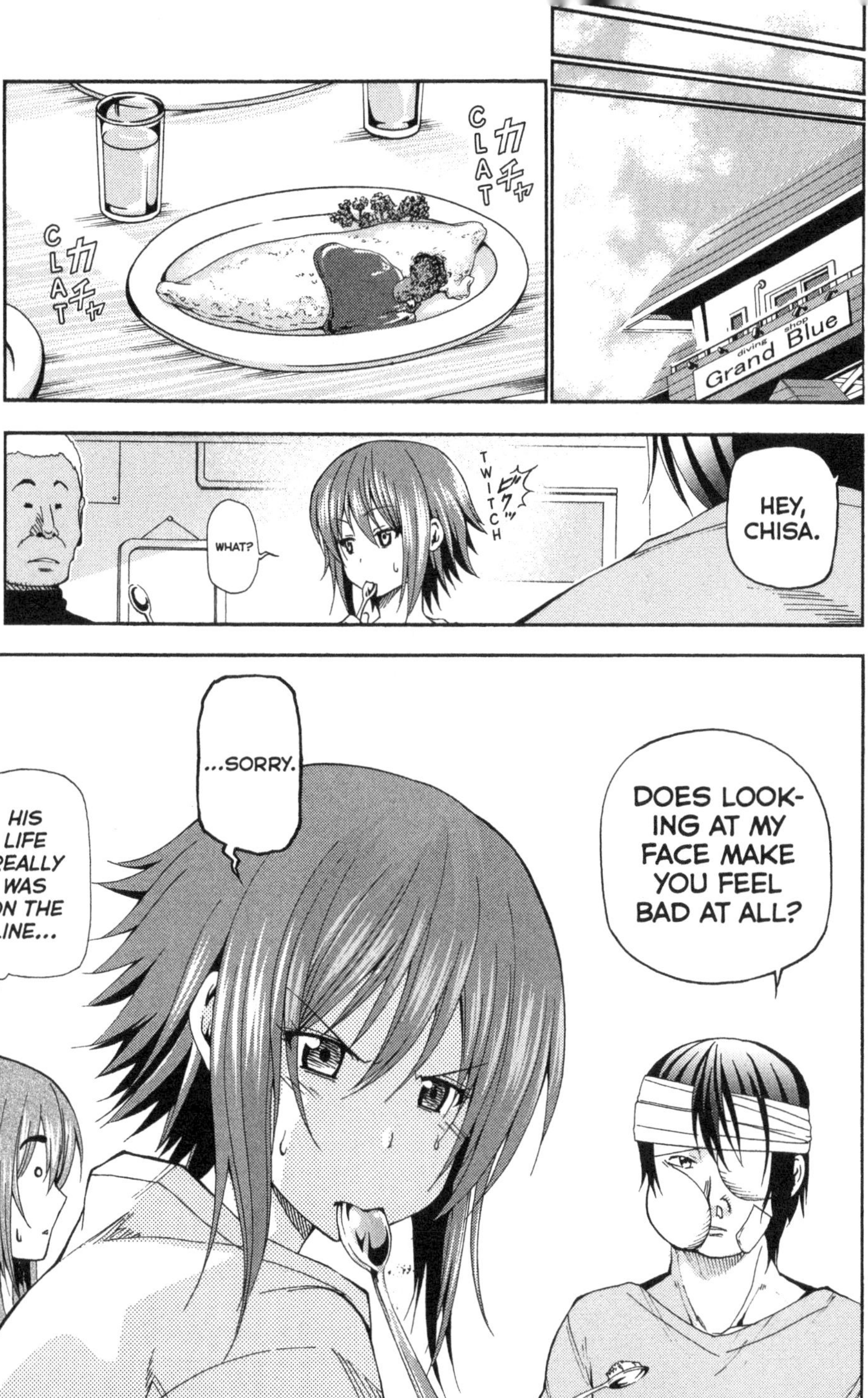
diving shop
Grand Blue
CLAT カチャ
CLAT カチャ
HEY, CHISA.
TWITCH ビクッ
WHAT?
DOES LOOKING AT MY FACE MAKE YOU FEEL BAD AT ALL?
...SORRY.
HIS LIFE REALLY WAS ON THE LINE...

CH.13 / End

Grand Blue Dreaming

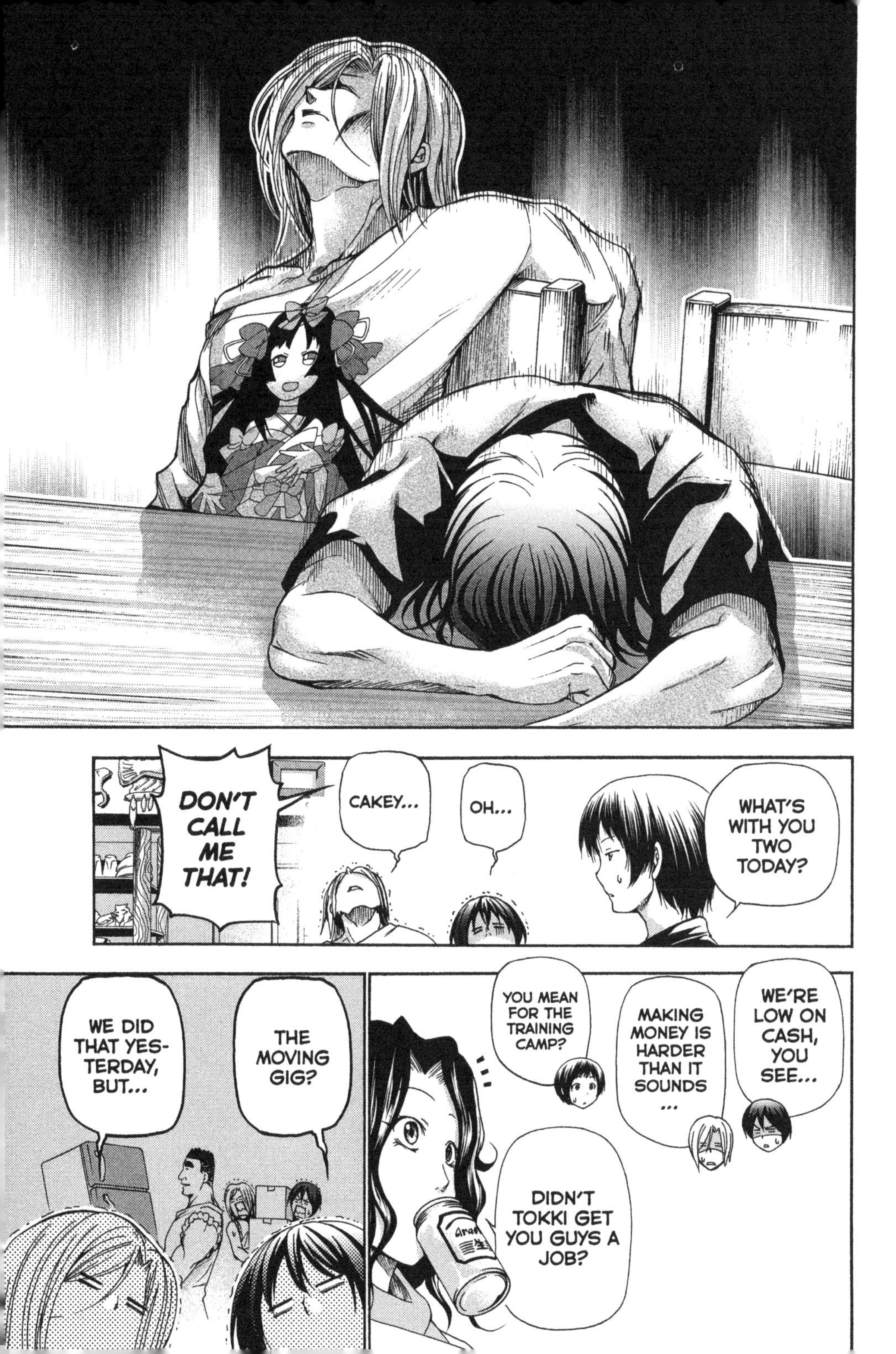
WHAT'S WITH YOU TWO TODAY?
OH...
CAKEY...
DON'T CALL ME THAT!
WE'RE LOW ON CASH, YOU SEE...
MAKING MONEY IS HARDER THAN IT SOUNDS...
YOU MEAN FOR THE TRAINING CAMP?
DIDN'T TOKKI GET YOU GUYS A JOB?
THE MOVING GIG?
WE DID THAT YESTERDAY, BUT...

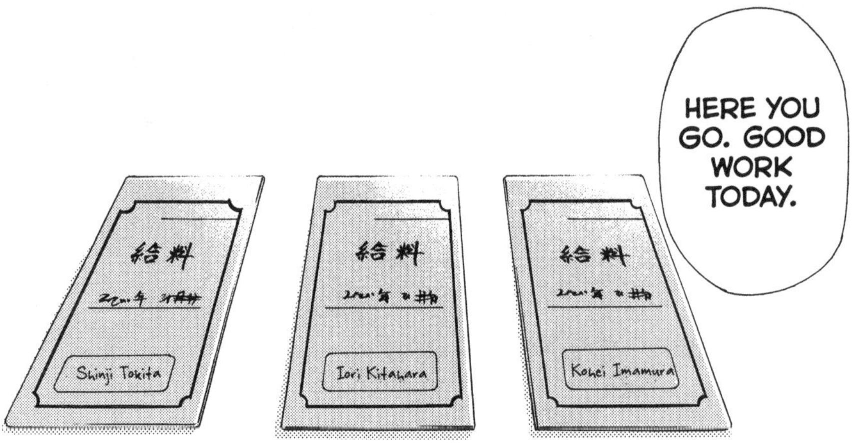
HERE YOU GO. GOOD WORK TODAY.
給料
Kohei Imamura
給料
Iori Kitahara
給料
Shinji Tokita

Wages

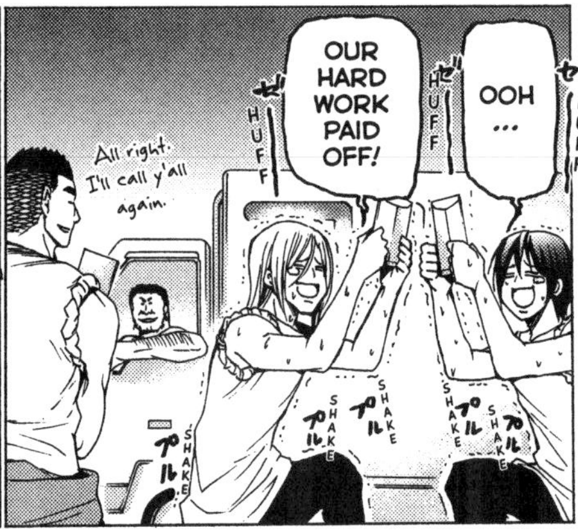
ぜ HUFF
OOH ...
ぜ HUFF
OUR HARD WORK PAID OFF!
ぜ HUFF
All right. I'll call y'all again.
プル SHAKE
プル SHAKE
プル SHAKE
プル SHAKE
プル SHAKE

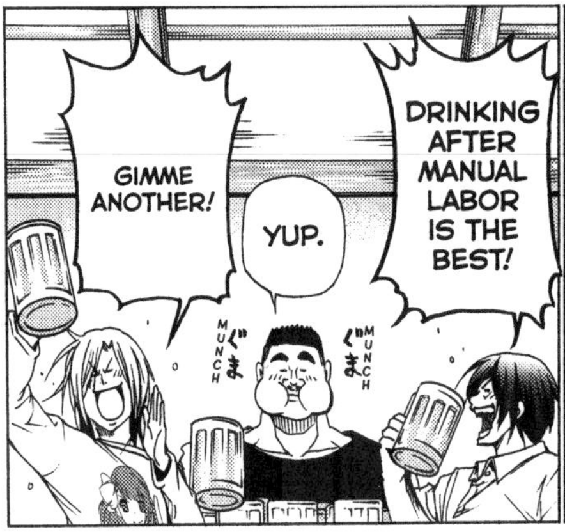
DRINKING AFTER MANUAL LABOR IS THE BEST!
ぐま MUNCH
YUP.
ぐま MUNCH
GIMME ANOTHER!

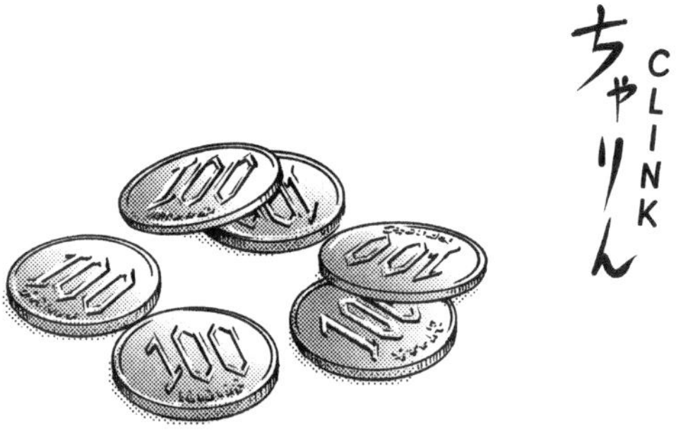
ちゃりん CLINK

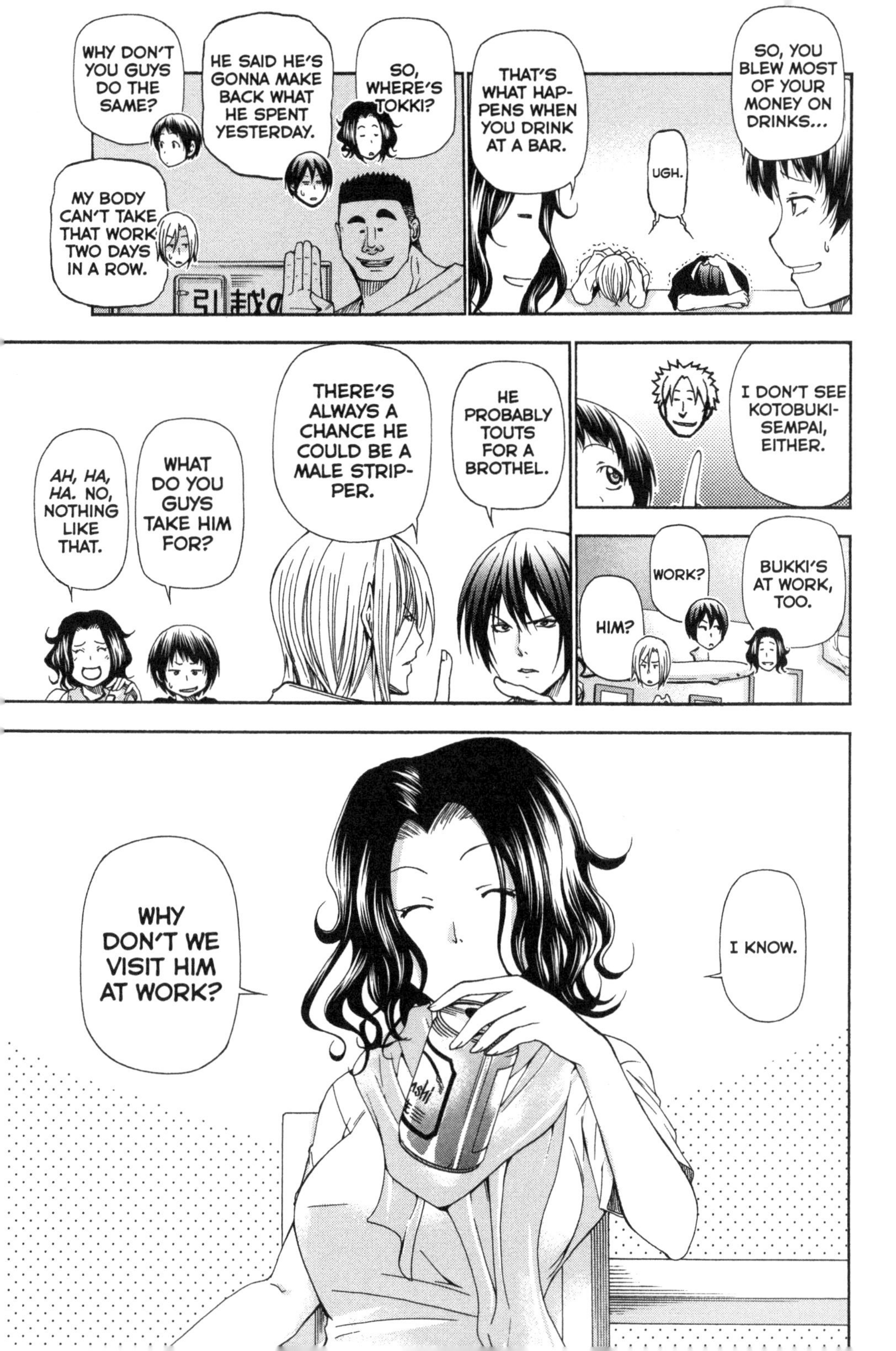
SO, YOU BLEW MOST OF YOUR MONEY ON DRINKS...
UGH.
THAT'S WHAT HAP-PENS WHEN YOU DRINK AT A BAR.
SO, WHERE'S TOKKI?
HE SAID HE'S GONNA MAKE BACK WHAT HE SPENT YESTERDAY.
WHY DON'T YOU GUYS DO THE SAME?
MY BODY CAN'T TAKE THAT WORK TWO DAYS IN A ROW.
I DON'T SEE KOTOBUKI-SEMPAI, EITHER.
BUKKI'S AT WORK, TOO.
WORK?
HIM?
HE PROBABLY TOUTS FOR A BROTHEL.
THERE'S ALWAYS A CHANCE HE COULD BE A MALE STRIP-PER.
WHAT DO YOU GUYS TAKE HIM FOR?
AH, HA, HA. NO, NOTHING LIKE THAT.
I KNOW.
WHY DON'T WE VISIT HIM AT WORK?

Ch. 14 A Man's Cocktail

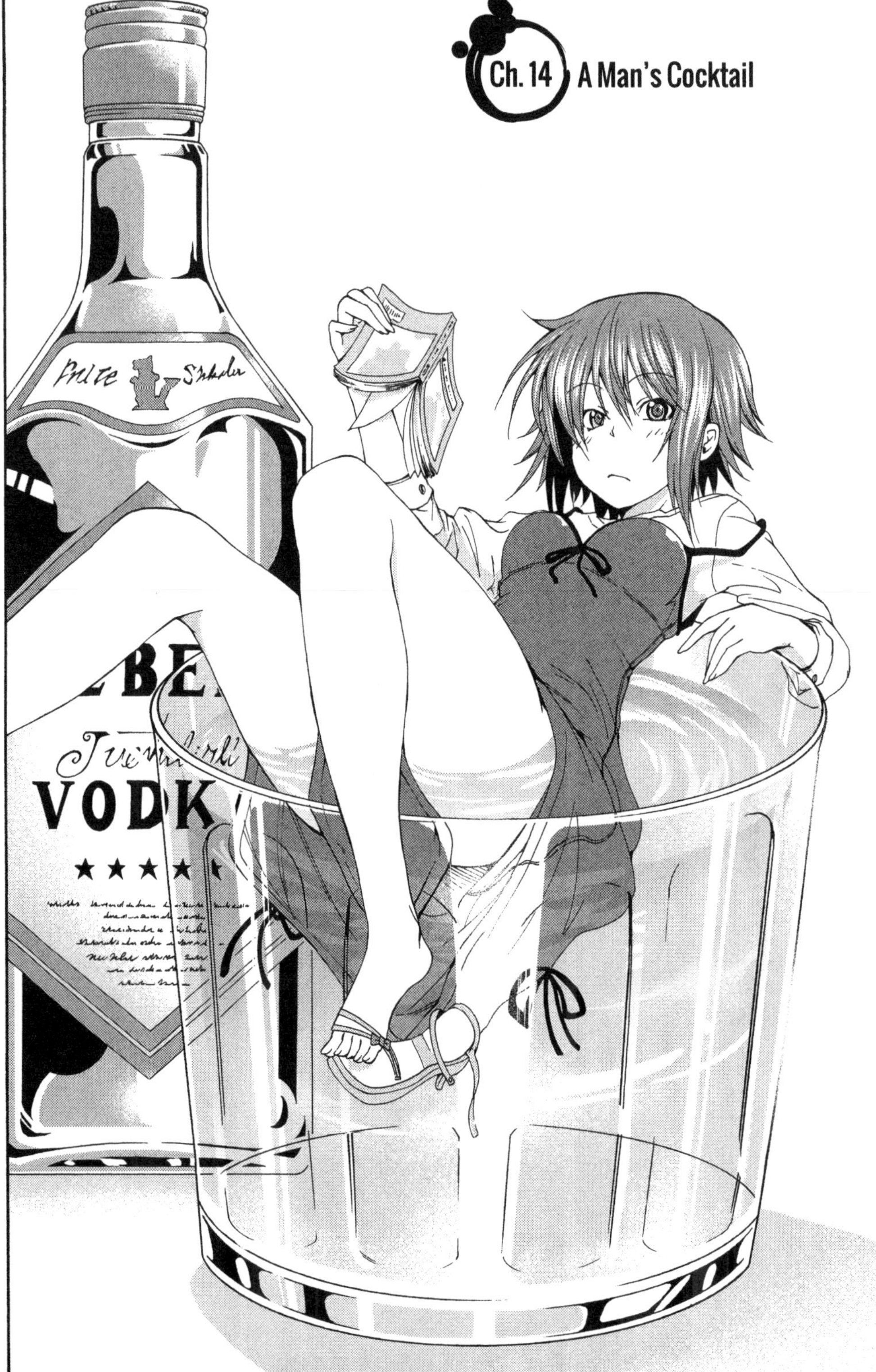

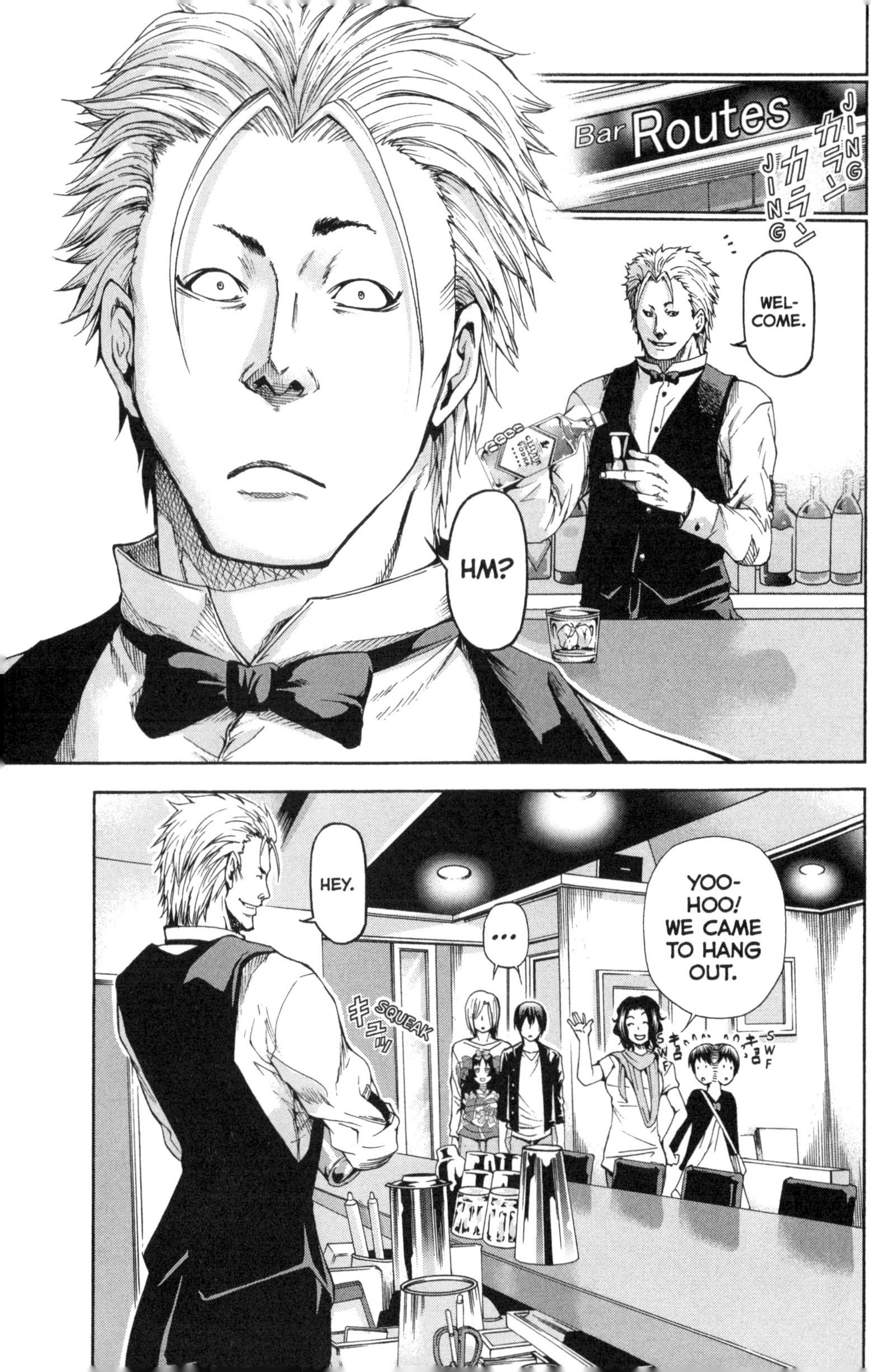
Bar Routes
JING JING
カランカラン
…
WEL-COME.
HM?
YOO-HOO! WE CAME TO HANG OUT.
SWF SWF
…
キュッ
SQUEAK
HEY.

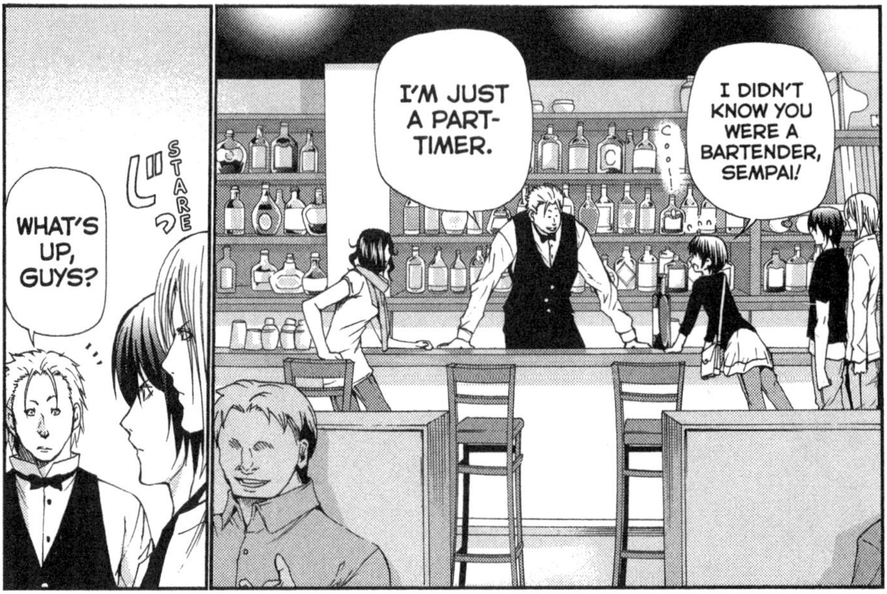
I DIDN'T KNOW YOU WERE A BARTENDER, SEMPAI!
Cool!
I'M JUST A PART-TIMER.
STARE
WHAT'S UP, GUYS?

*Approx. 2,000 USD.

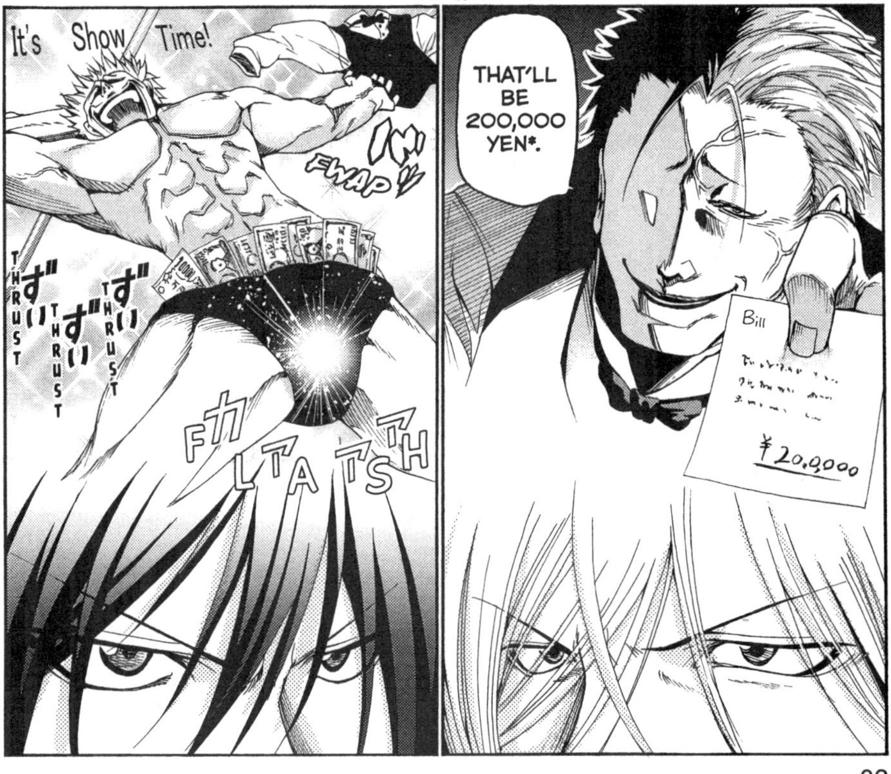
THAT'LL BE 200,000 YEN*.
Bill
It's Show Time!
FWAP
THRUST
THRUST
THRUST

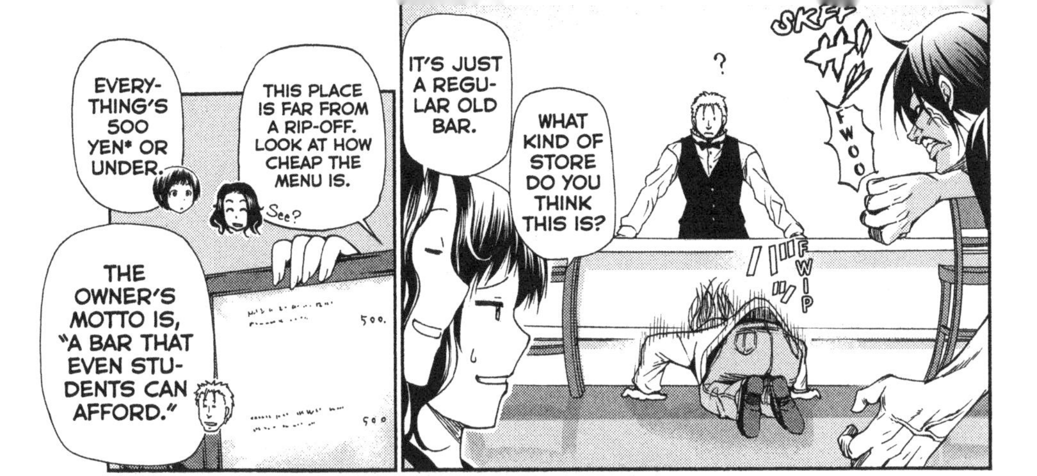
SKFF
FWOO
?
WHAT KIND OF STORE DO YOU THINK THIS IS?
FWIP
IT'S JUST A REGULAR OLD BAR.
THIS PLACE IS FAR FROM A RIP-OFF. LOOK AT HOW CHEAP THE MENU IS.
EVERYTHING'S 500 YEN* OR UNDER.
See?
THE OWNER'S MOTTO IS, "A BAR THAT EVEN STUDENTS CAN AFFORD."

*About $5

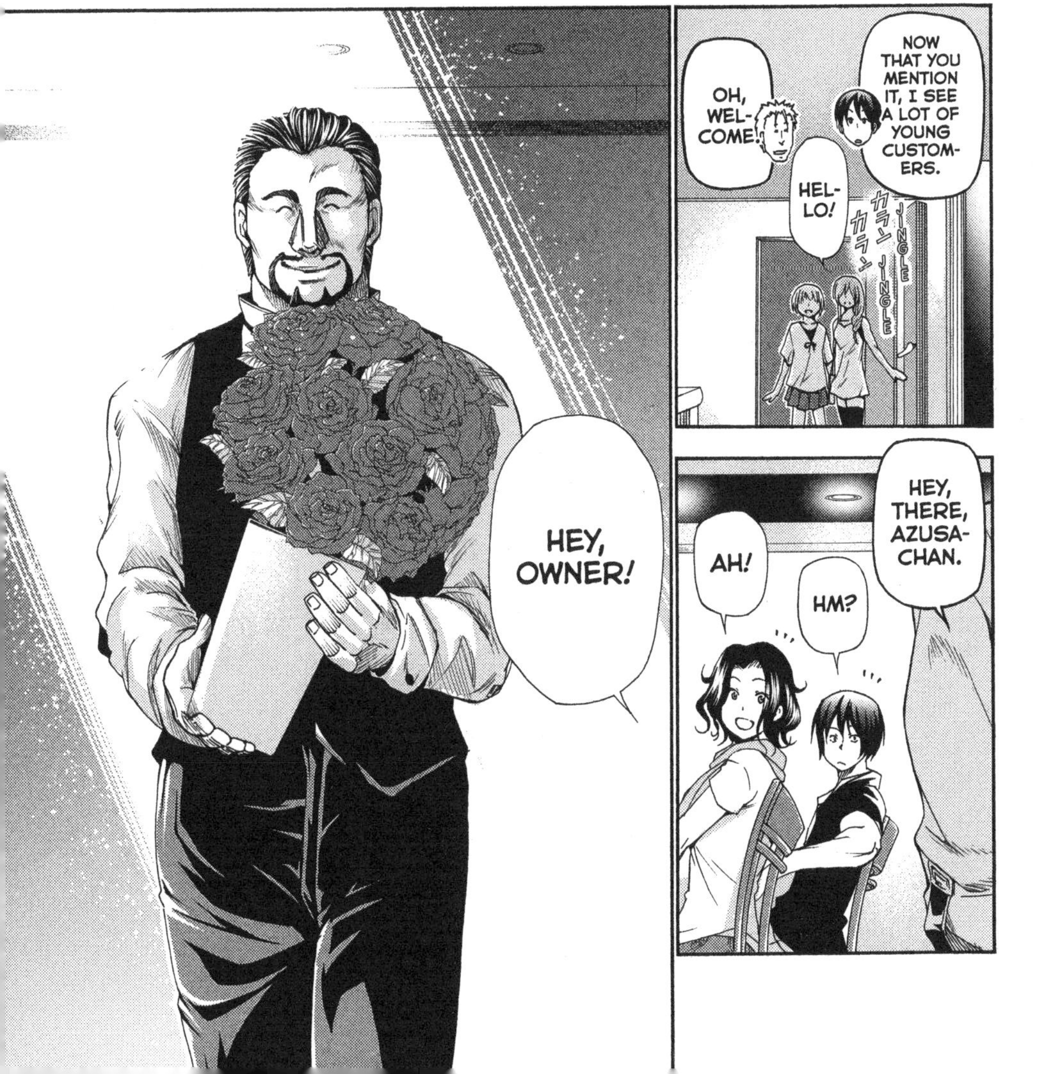
NOW THAT YOU MENTION IT, I SEE A LOT OF YOUNG CUSTOMERS.
OH, WELCOME!
JINGLE JINGLE
HELLO!
HEY, THERE, AZUSA-CHAN.
HM?
AH!
HEY, OWNER!

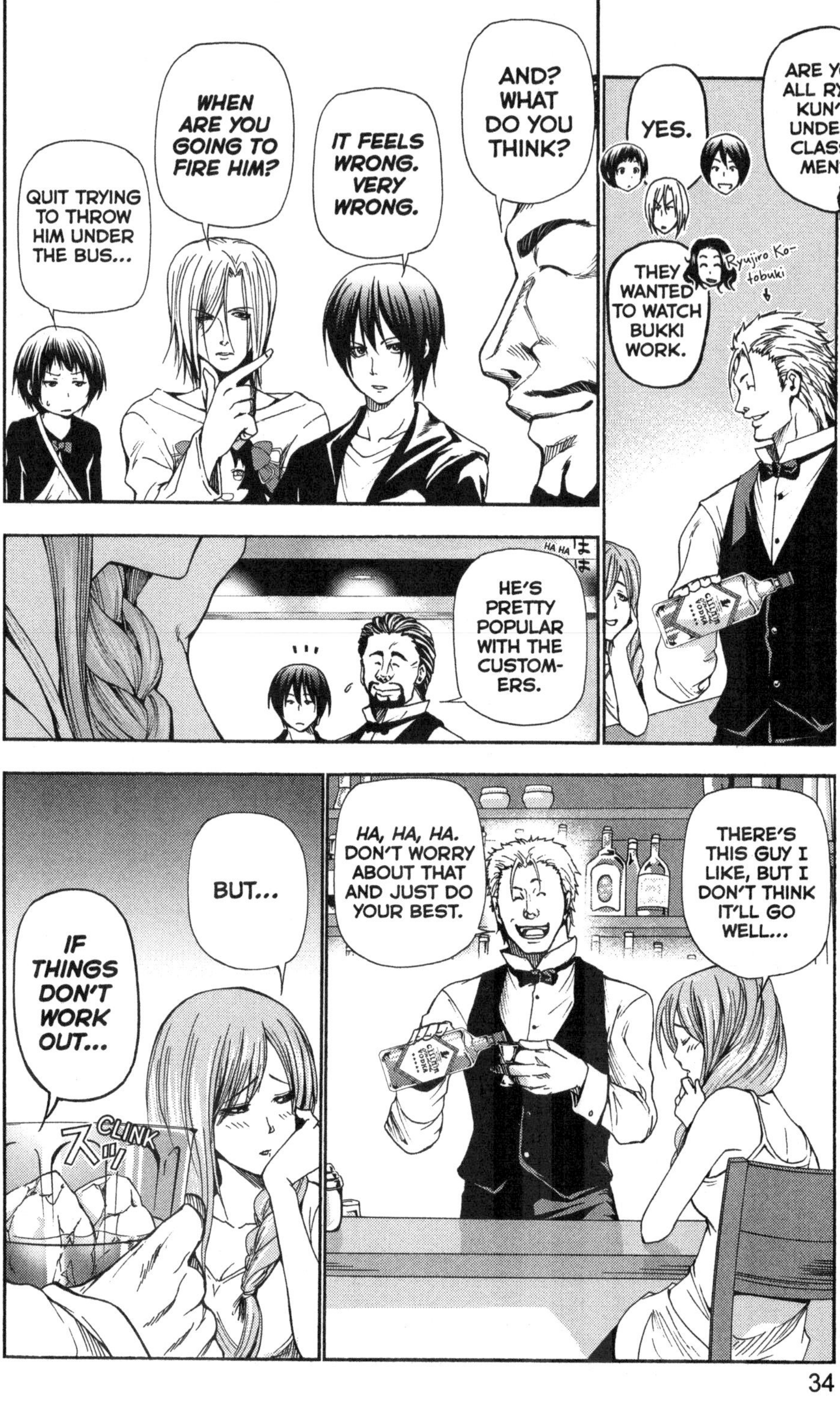
ARE YOU ALL RYU-KUN'S UNDER-CLASSMEN?
YES.
THEY WANTED TO WATCH BUKKI WORK.
Ryujiro Kotobuki
AND? WHAT DO YOU THINK?
IT FEELS WRONG. VERY WRONG.
WHEN ARE YOU GOING TO FIRE HIM?
QUIT TRYING TO THROW HIM UNDER THE BUS...
HA HA
HE'S PRETTY POPULAR WITH THE CUSTOMERS.
THERE'S THIS GUY I LIKE, BUT I DON'T THINK IT'LL GO WELL...
HA, HA, HA. DON'T WORRY ABOUT THAT AND JUST DO YOUR BEST.
BUT...
IF THINGS DON'T WORK OUT...
CLINK

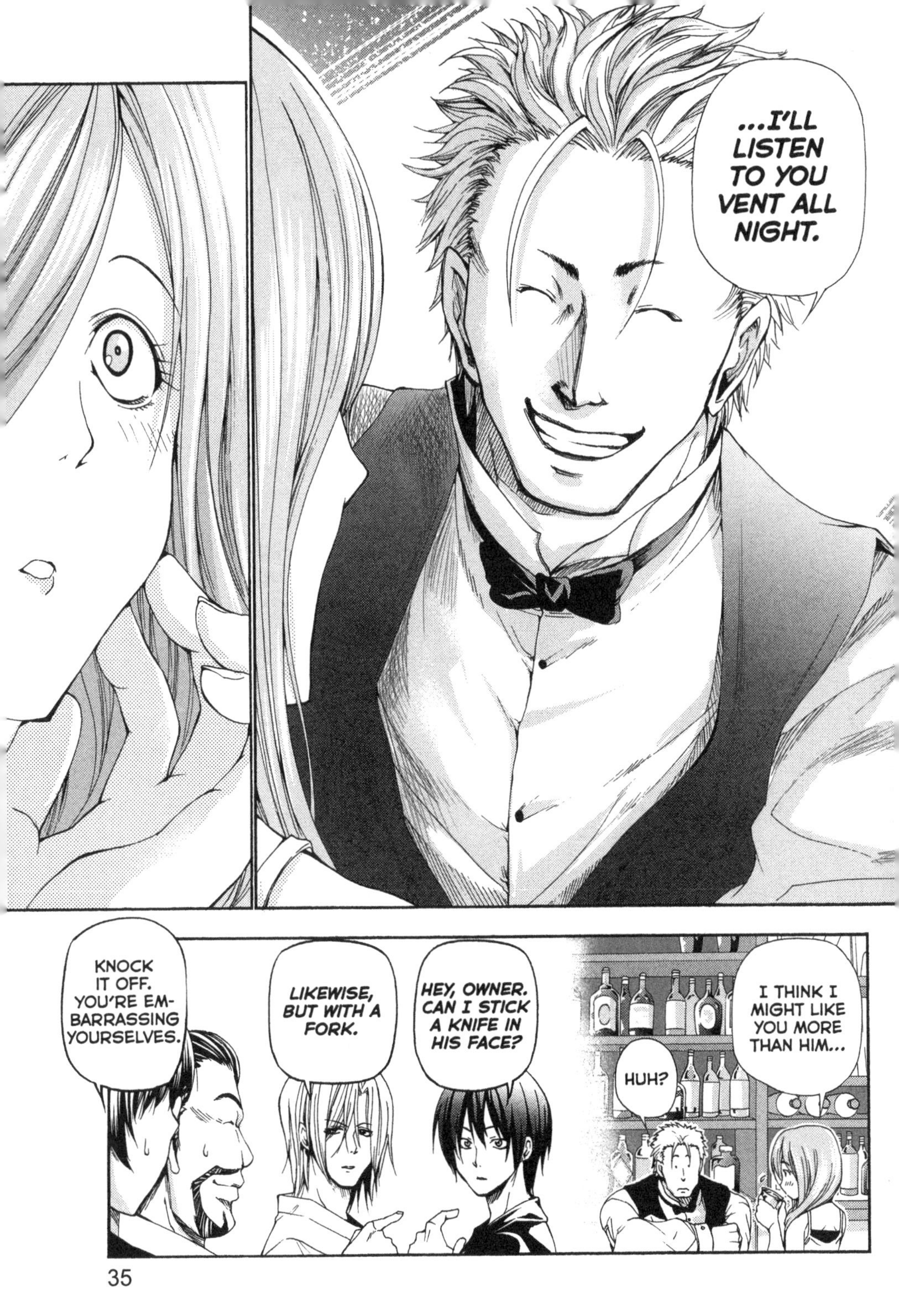
...I'LL LISTEN TO YOU VENT ALL NIGHT.
I THINK I MIGHT LIKE YOU MORE THAN HIM...
HUH?
HEY, OWNER. CAN I STICK A KNIFE IN HIS FACE?
LIKEWISE, BUT WITH A FORK.
KNOCK IT OFF. YOU'RE EM-BARRASSING YOURSELVES.

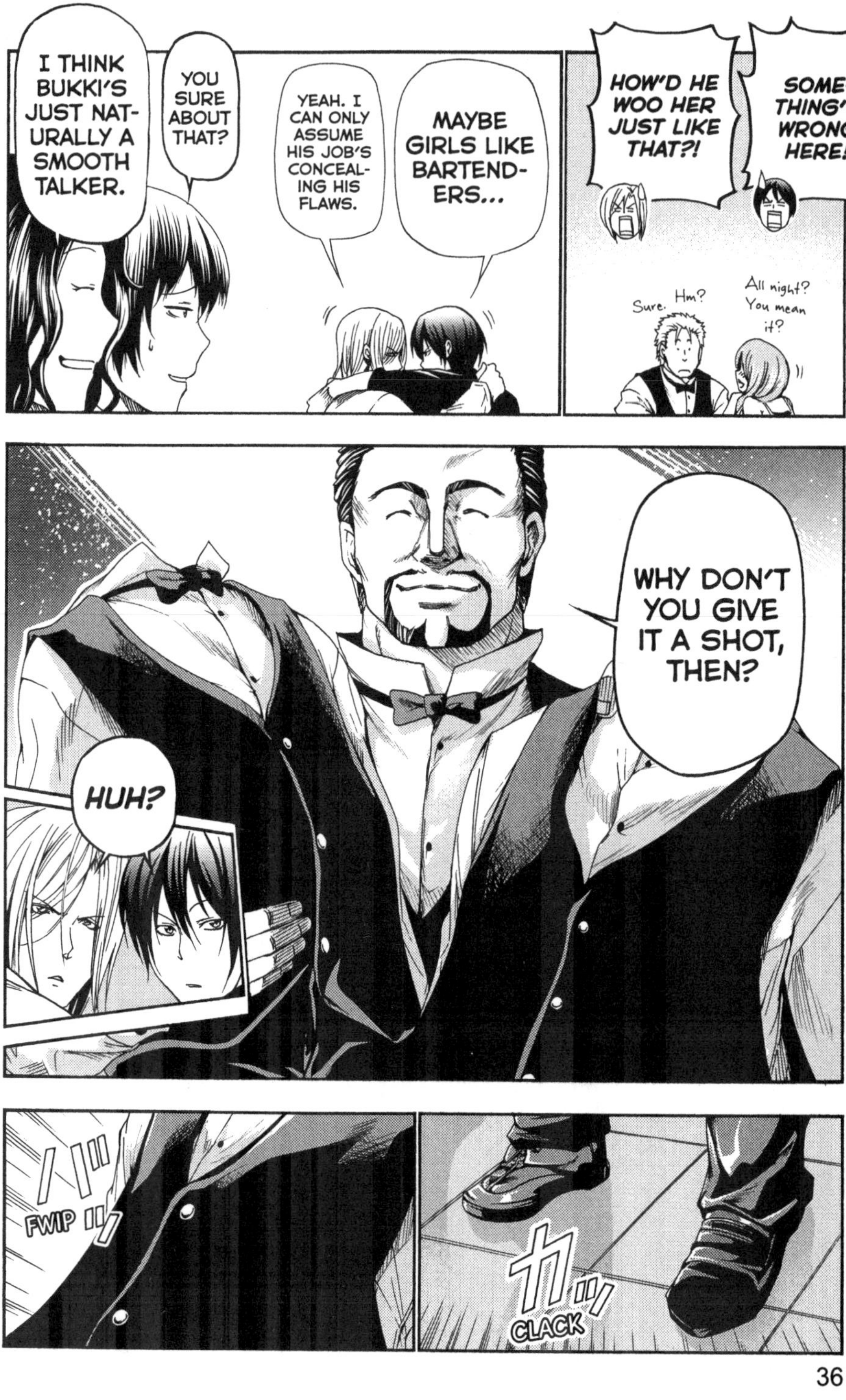
SOME-THING'S WRONG HERE!
HOW'D HE WOO HER JUST LIKE THAT?!
All night? You mean it?
Hm?
Sure.
MAYBE GIRLS LIKE BARTEND-ERS...
YEAH. I CAN ONLY ASSUME HIS JOB'S CONCEAL-ING HIS FLAWS.
YOU SURE ABOUT THAT?
I THINK BUKKI'S JUST NAT-URALLY A SMOOTH TALKER.
WHY DON'T YOU GIVE IT A SHOT, THEN?
HUH?
CLACK
FWIP

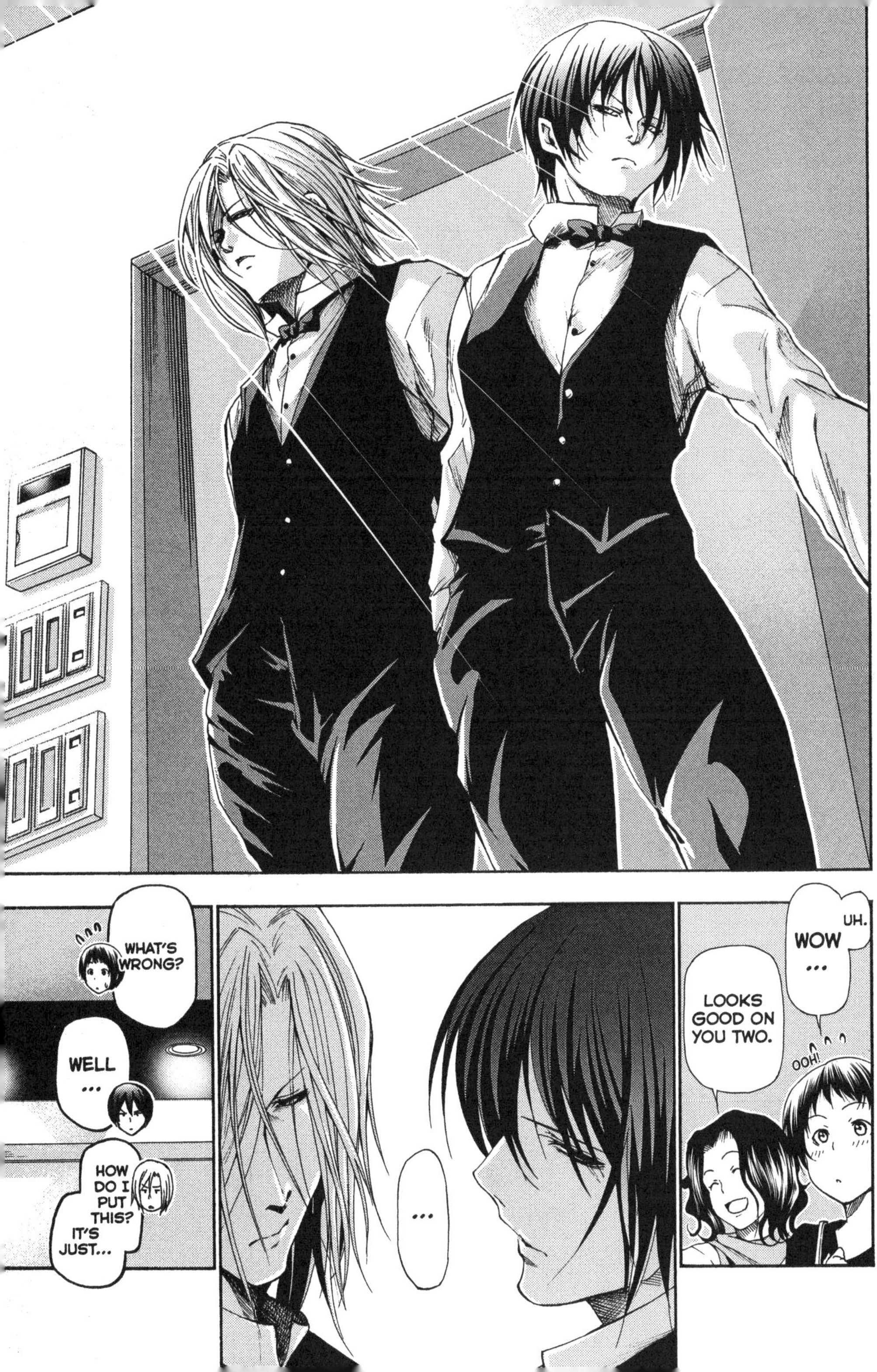
UH.
WOW ...
LOOKS GOOD ON YOU TWO.
OOH!
...
WHAT'S WRONG?
WELL ...
HOW DO I PUT THIS? IT'S JUST...

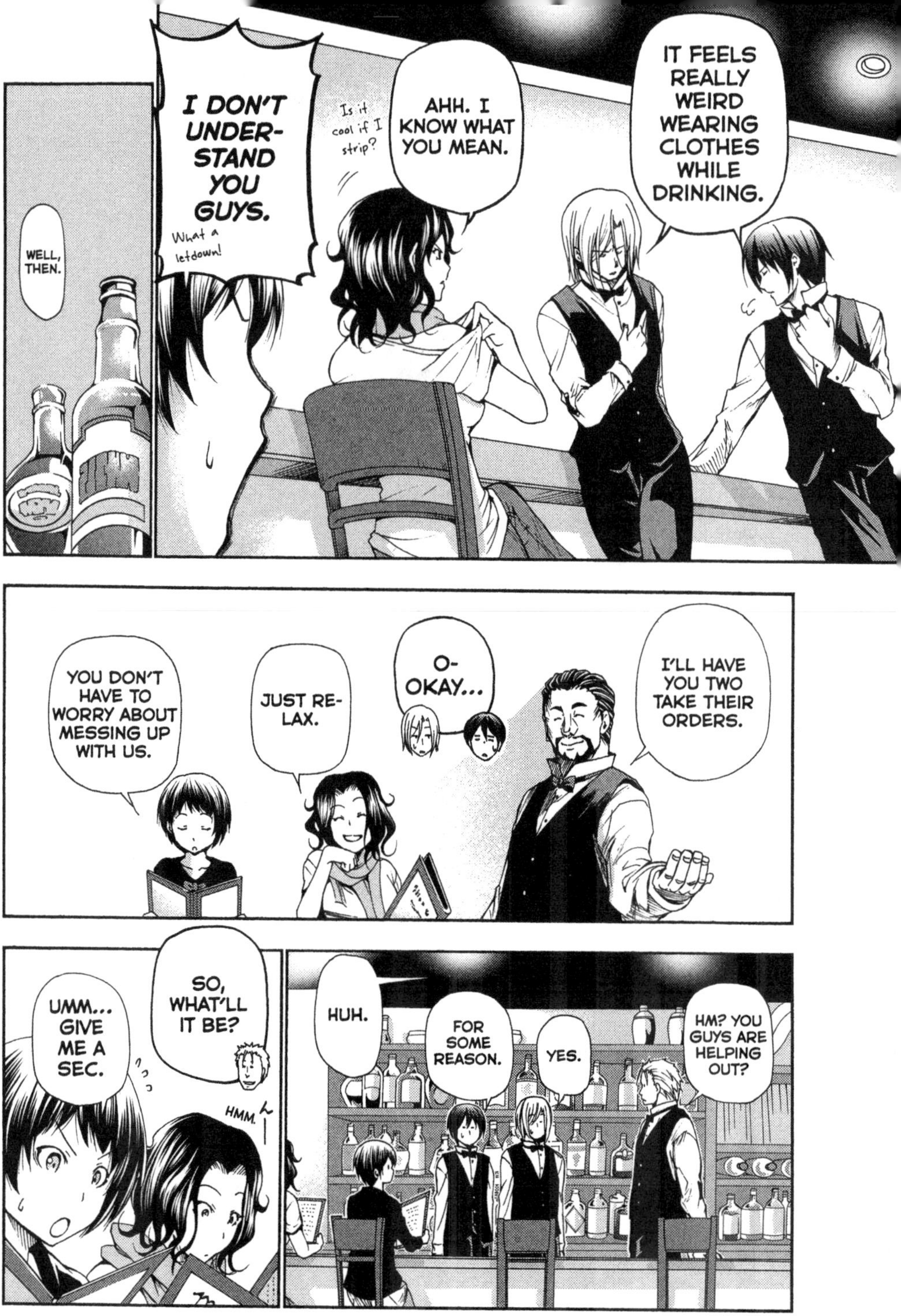
IT FEELS REALLY WEIRD WEARING CLOTHES WHILE DRINKING.
AHH. I KNOW WHAT YOU MEAN.
Is it cool if I strip?
I DON'T UNDER-STAND YOU GUYS.
What a letdown!
WELL, THEN.
I'LL HAVE YOU TWO TAKE THEIR ORDERS.
O-OKAY...
JUST RE-LAX.
YOU DON'T HAVE TO WORRY ABOUT MESSING UP WITH US.
HM? YOU GUYS ARE HELPING OUT?
YES.
FOR SOME REASON.
HUH.
SO, WHAT'LL IT BE?
UMM... GIVE ME A SEC.
HMM.

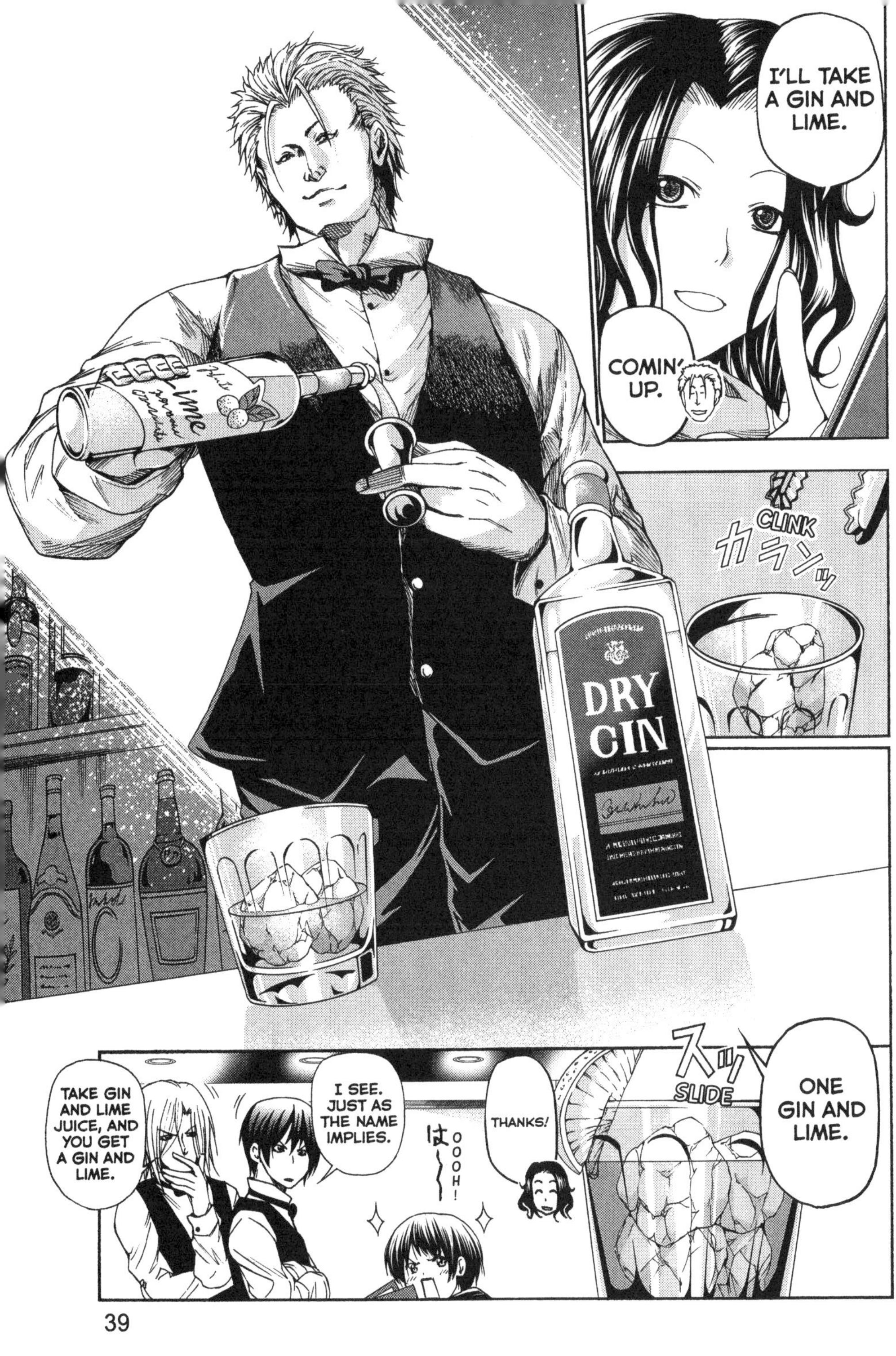
I'LL TAKE A GIN AND LIME.
COMIN' UP.
CLINK
カランッ
DRY GIN
スッ
SLIDE
ONE GIN AND LIME.
THANKS!
はー
OOOH!
I SEE. JUST AS THE NAME IMPLIES.
TAKE GIN AND LIME JUICE, AND YOU GET A GIN AND LIME.

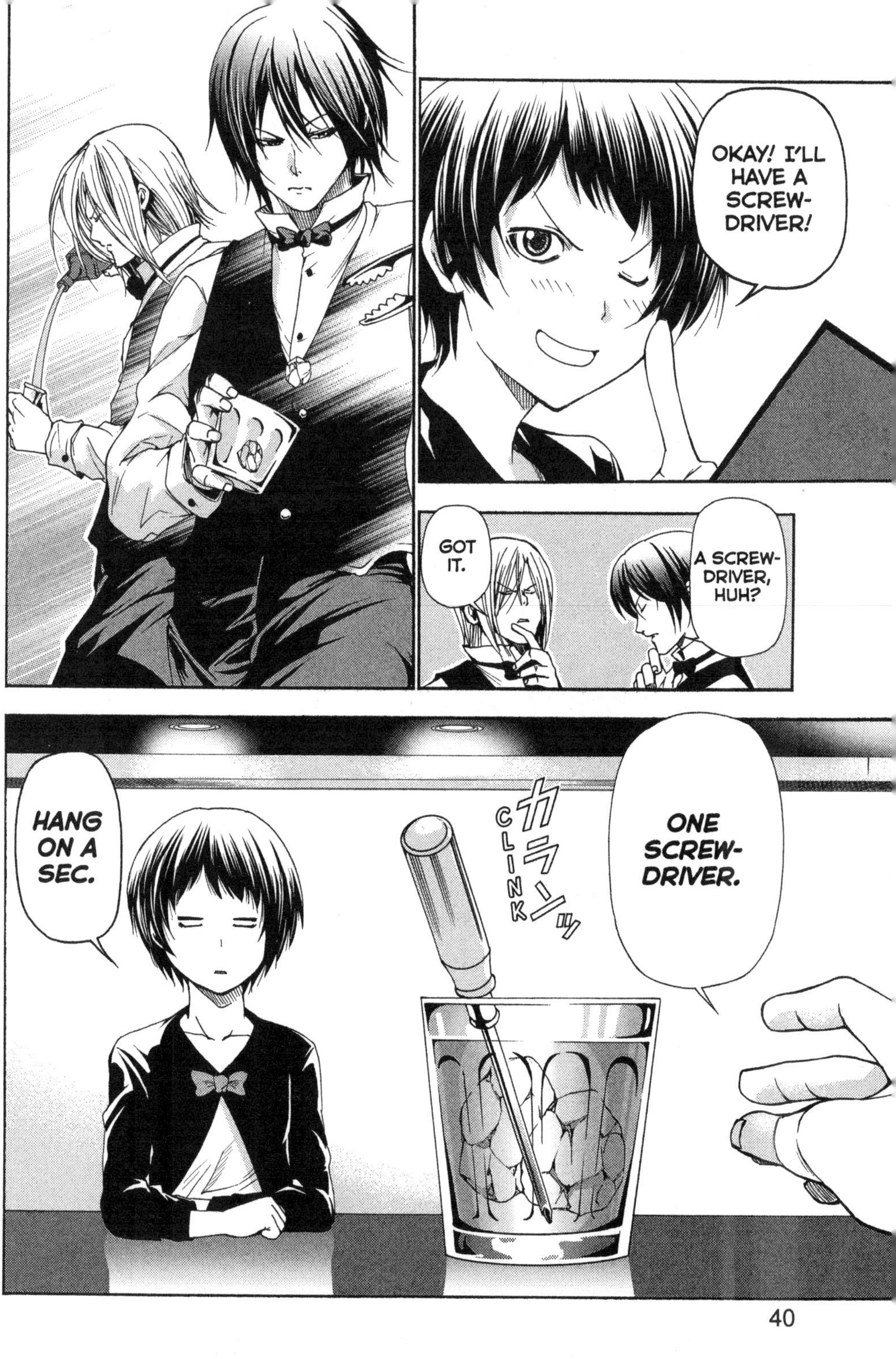
OKAY! I'LL HAVE A SCREW-DRIVER!
A SCREW-DRIVER, HUH?
GOT IT.
ONE SCREW-DRIVER.
カラーンッ
CLINK
HANG ON A SEC.

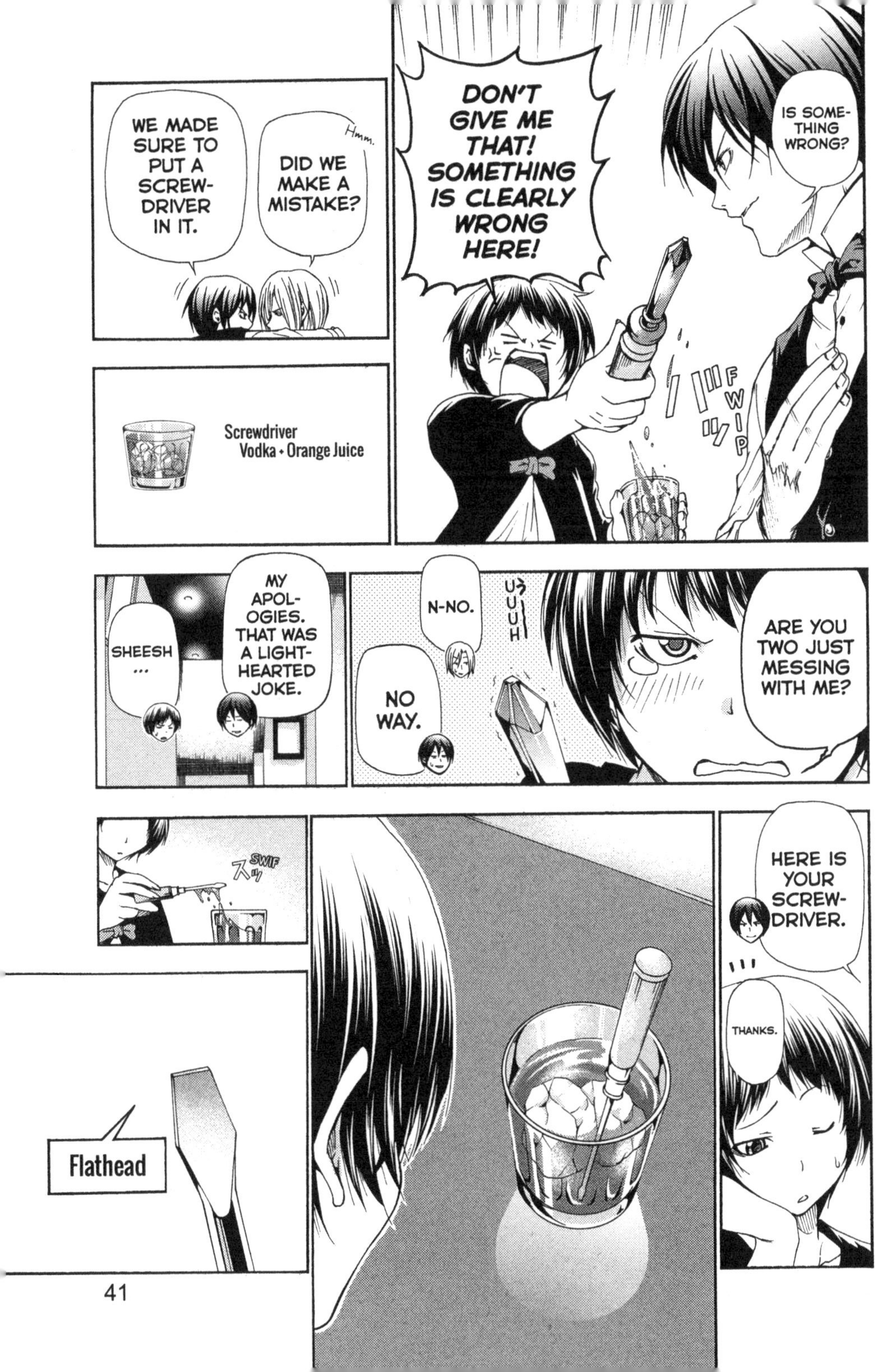

IS SOME-THING WRONG?
DON'T GIVE ME THAT! SOMETHING IS CLEARLY WRONG HERE!
FWIP
Hmm.
DID WE MAKE A MISTAKE?
WE MADE SURE TO PUT A SCREW-DRIVER IN IT.
Screwdriver
Vodka + Orange Juice
ARE YOU TWO JUST MESSING WITH ME?
UUUH
N-NO.
NO WAY.
MY APOLOGIES. THAT WAS A LIGHT-HEARTED JOKE.
SHEESH ...
HERE IS YOUR SCREW-DRIVER.
THANKS.
SWIF
Flathead

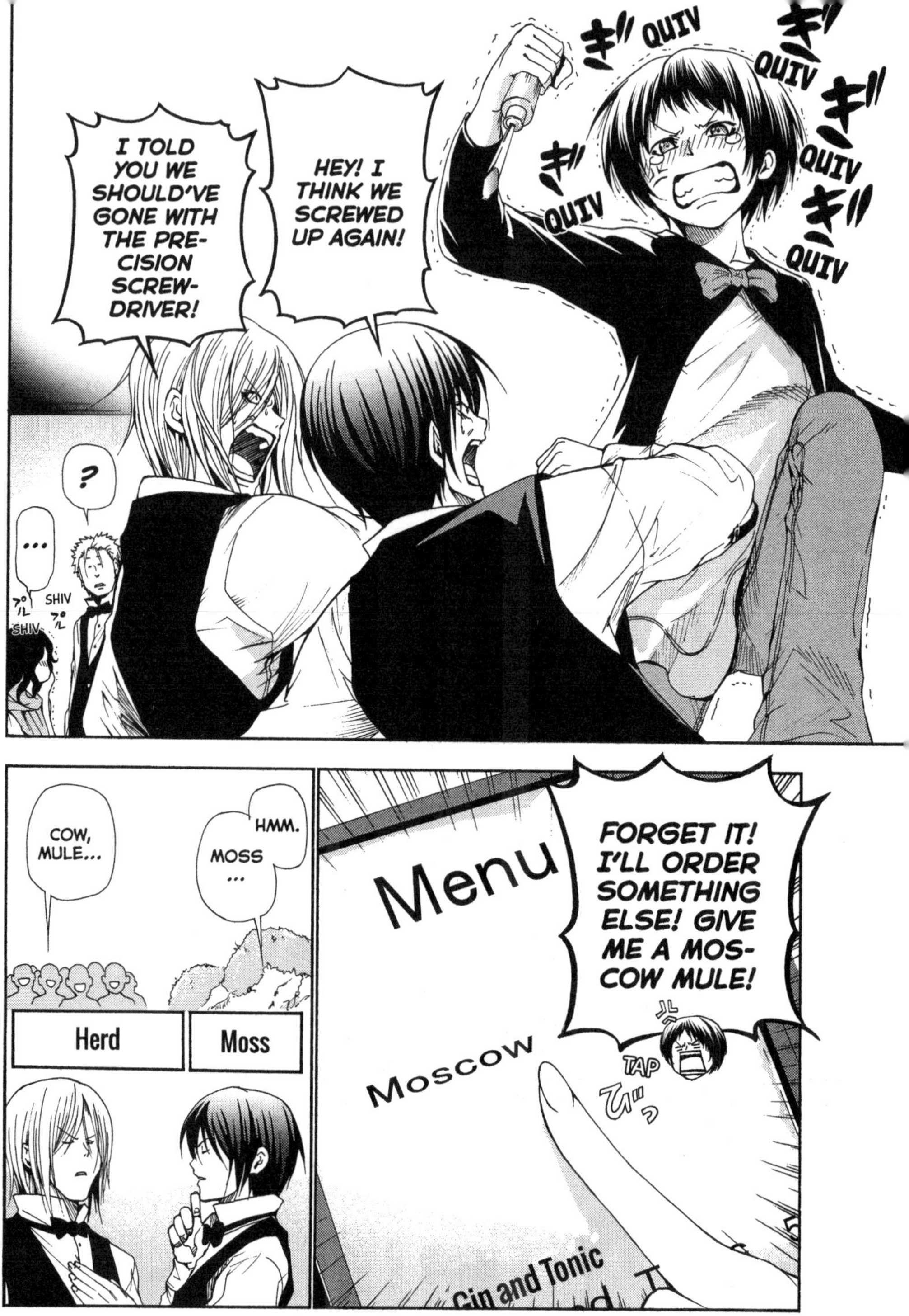

QUIV
QUIV
QUIV
QUIV
QUIV
HEY! I THINK WE SCREWED UP AGAIN!
I TOLD YOU WE SHOULD'VE GONE WITH THE PRE-CISION SCREW-DRIVER!
?
...
SHIV
SHIV
FORGET IT! I'LL ORDER SOMETHING ELSE! GIVE ME A MOS-COW MULE!
Menu
Moscow
Gin and Tonic
TAP
HMM.
MOSS ...
COW, MULE...
Herd
Moss

*Marimo: Also known as "moss balls", a species of algae that grow into large balls and form colonies.

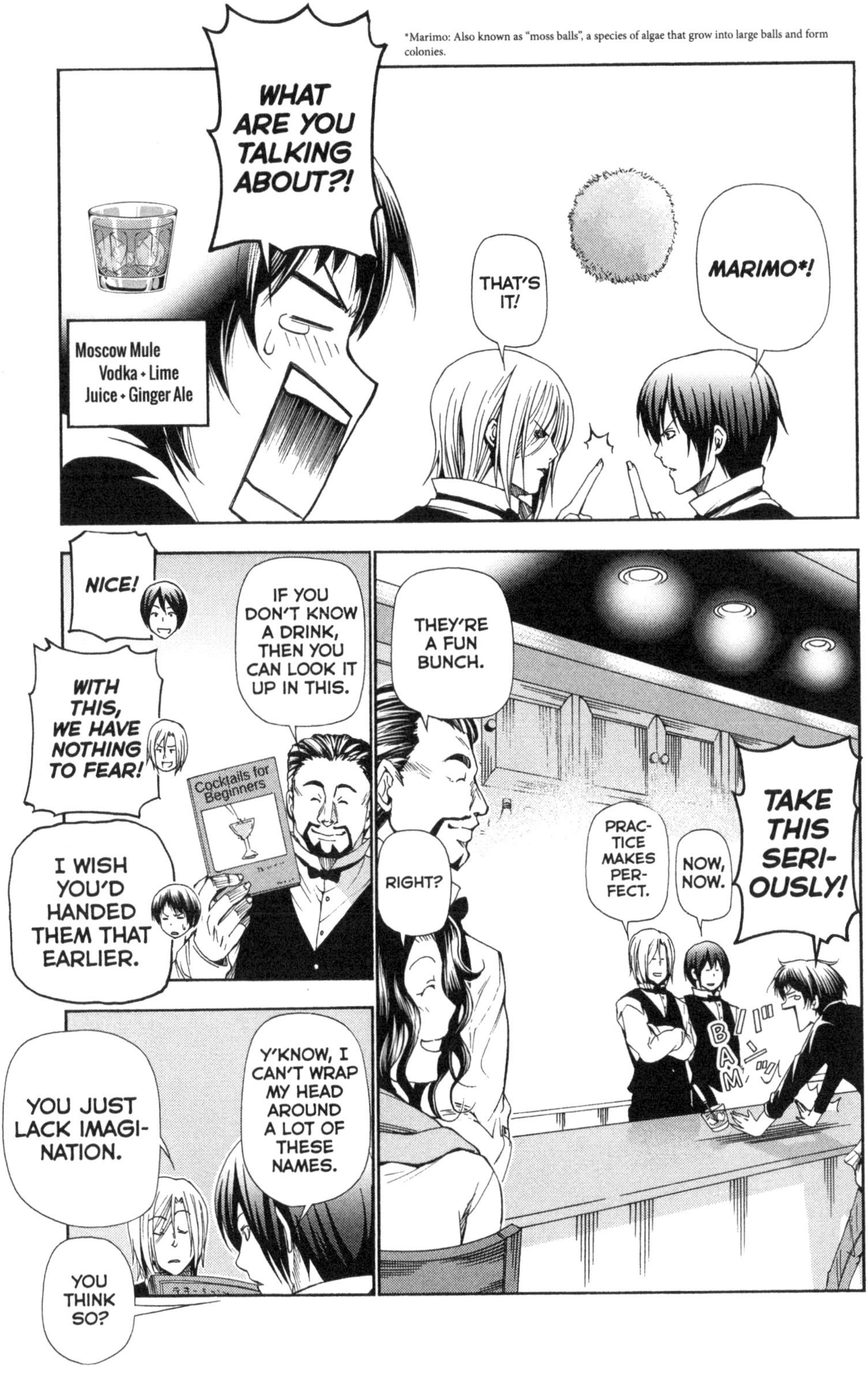

MARIMO*!
THAT'S IT!
WHAT ARE YOU TALKING ABOUT?!
Moscow Mule
Vodka + Lime Juice + Ginger Ale
TAKE THIS SERI-OUSLY!
NOW, NOW.
PRAC-TICE MAKES PER-FECT.
BAM
THEY'RE A FUN BUNCH.
RIGHT?
IF YOU DON'T KNOW A DRINK, THEN YOU CAN LOOK IT UP IN THIS.
NICE!
WITH THIS, WE HAVE NOTHING TO FEAR!
Cocktails for Beginners
I WISH YOU'D HANDED THEM THAT EARLIER.
Y'KNOW, I CAN'T WRAP MY HEAD AROUND A LOT OF THESE NAMES.
YOU JUST LACK IMAGI-NATION.
YOU THINK SO?

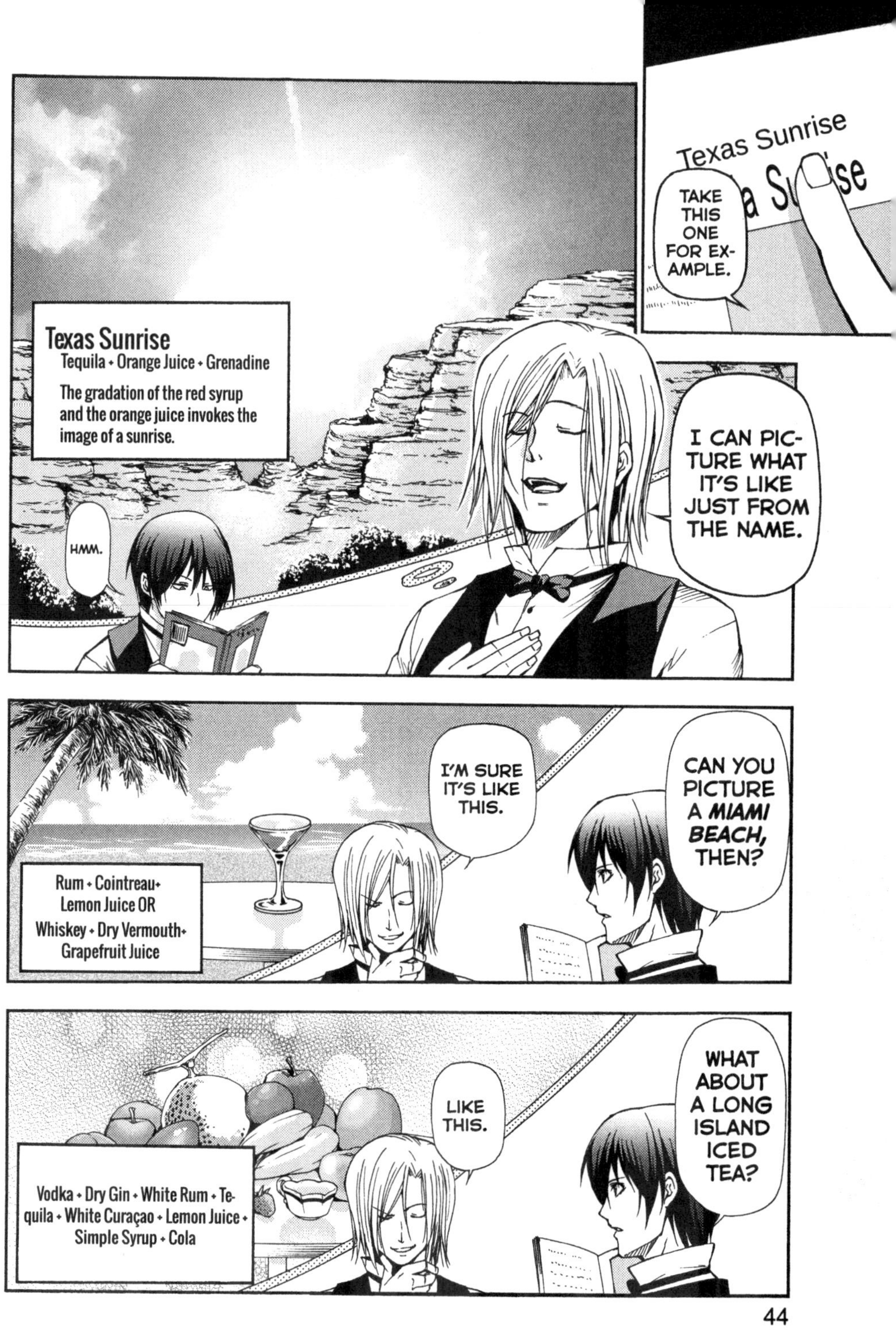
Texas Sunrise
TAKE THIS ONE FOR EX-AMPLE.
I CAN PIC-TURE WHAT IT'S LIKE JUST FROM THE NAME.
Texas Sunrise
Tequila + Orange Juice + Grenadine
The gradation of the red syrup and the orange juice invokes the image of a sunrise.
HMM.
CAN YOU PICTURE A *MIAMI BEACH,* THEN?
I'M SURE IT'S LIKE THIS.
Rum + Cointreau + Lemon Juice OR Whiskey + Dry Vermouth + Grapefruit Juice
WHAT ABOUT A LONG ISLAND ICED TEA?
LIKE THIS.
Vodka + Dry Gin + White Rum + Tequila + White Curaçao + Lemon Juice + Simple Syrup + Cola

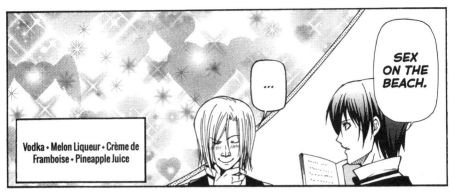

SEX ON THE BEACH.
...
Vodka + Melon Liqueur + Crème de Framboise + Pineapple Juice
CHERRY BLOSSOM.
...
I'M GONNA LOSE MY VIRGINITY!
Cherry Brandy + Brandy + Lemon Juice + Grenadine + Orange Curaçao
RAAAH
WHAT THE HELL ARE YOU MAKING ME IMAGINE?!
YOU PICTURED IT YOURSELF, DUMBASS!
RAAAH
KNOCK IT OFF! YOU'RE EMBARRASSING YOURSELVES!
CAN'T YOU TWO ACT A LITTLE CLASSIER?
OH?
WHAT DO YOU MEAN?

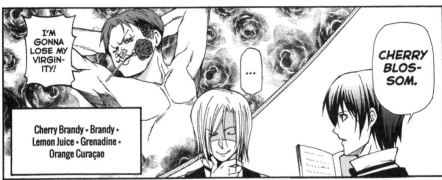

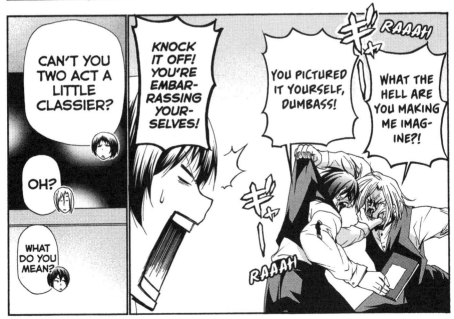

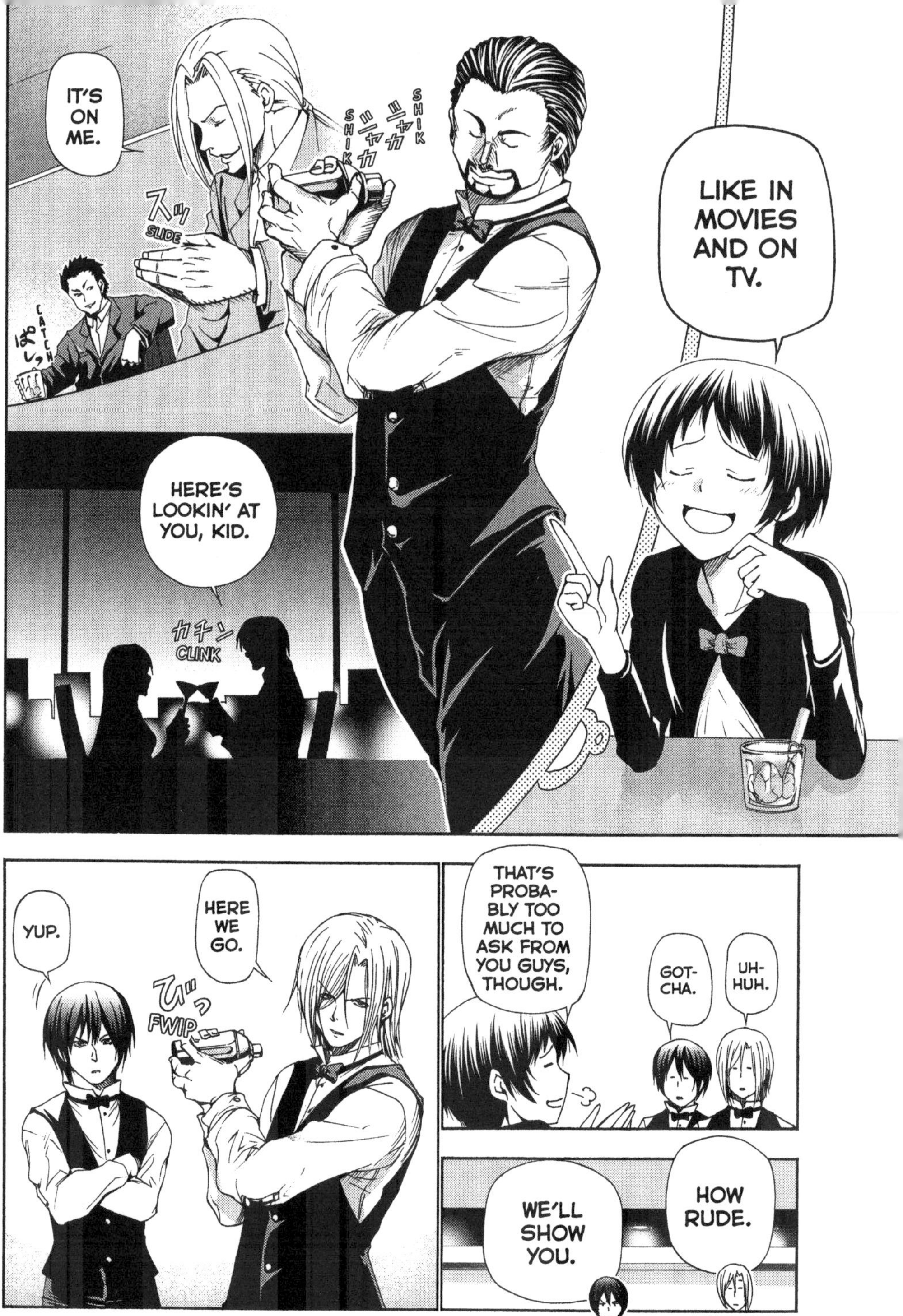
LIKE IN MOVIES AND ON TV.
SHIK
SHIK
IT'S ON ME.
SLIDE
CATCH
HERE'S LOOKIN' AT YOU, KID.
CLINK
THAT'S PROBA-BLY TOO MUCH TO ASK FROM YOU GUYS, THOUGH.
UH-HUH.
GOT-CHA.
HOW RUDE.
WE'LL SHOW YOU.
HERE WE GO.
FWIP
YUP.

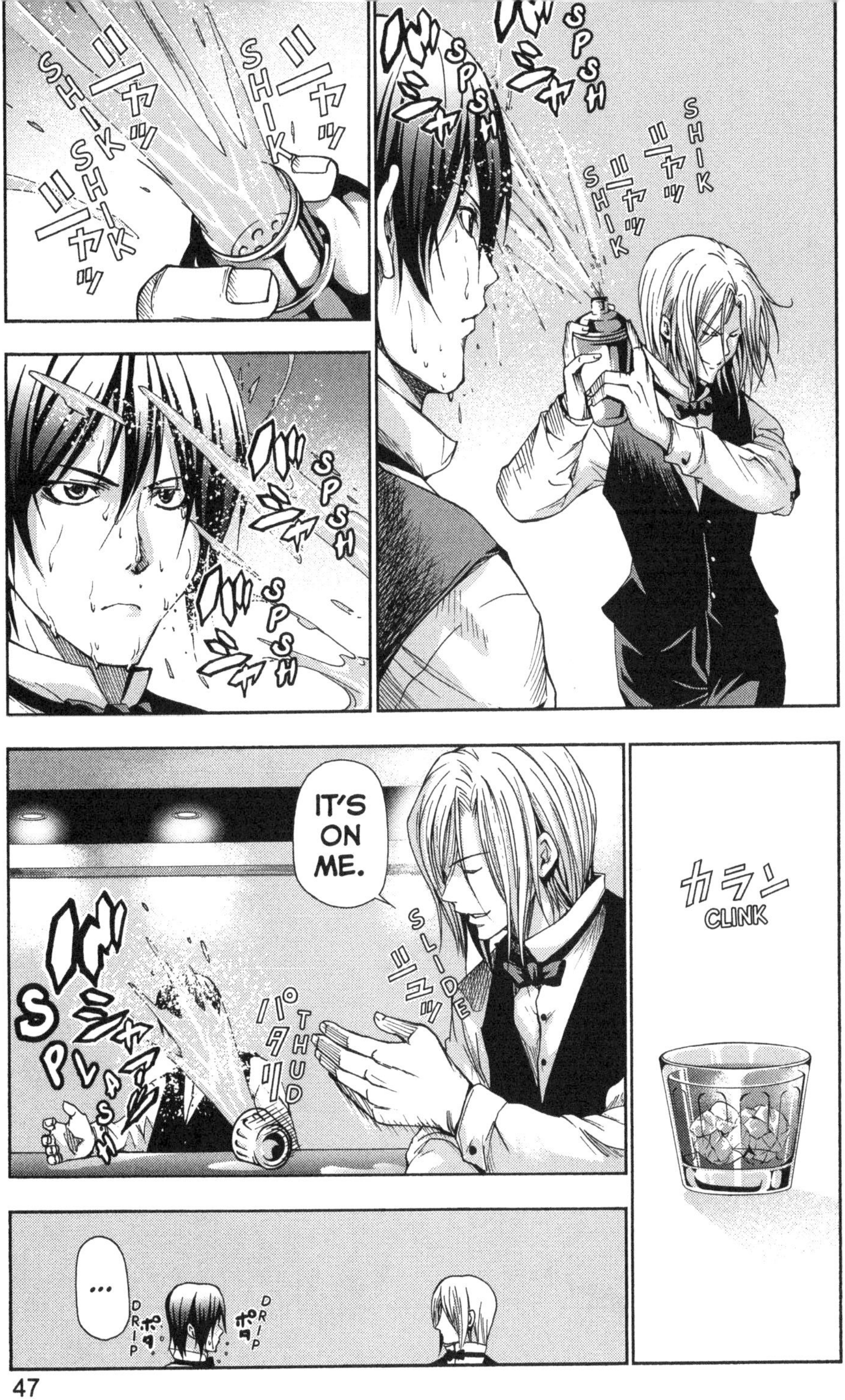
SPSH
SPSH
SHIK
SHIK
SHIK
SHIK
SPSH
SPSH
カラン
CLINK
IT'S ON ME.
SLIDE
THUD
SPLASH
...
DRIP
DRIP

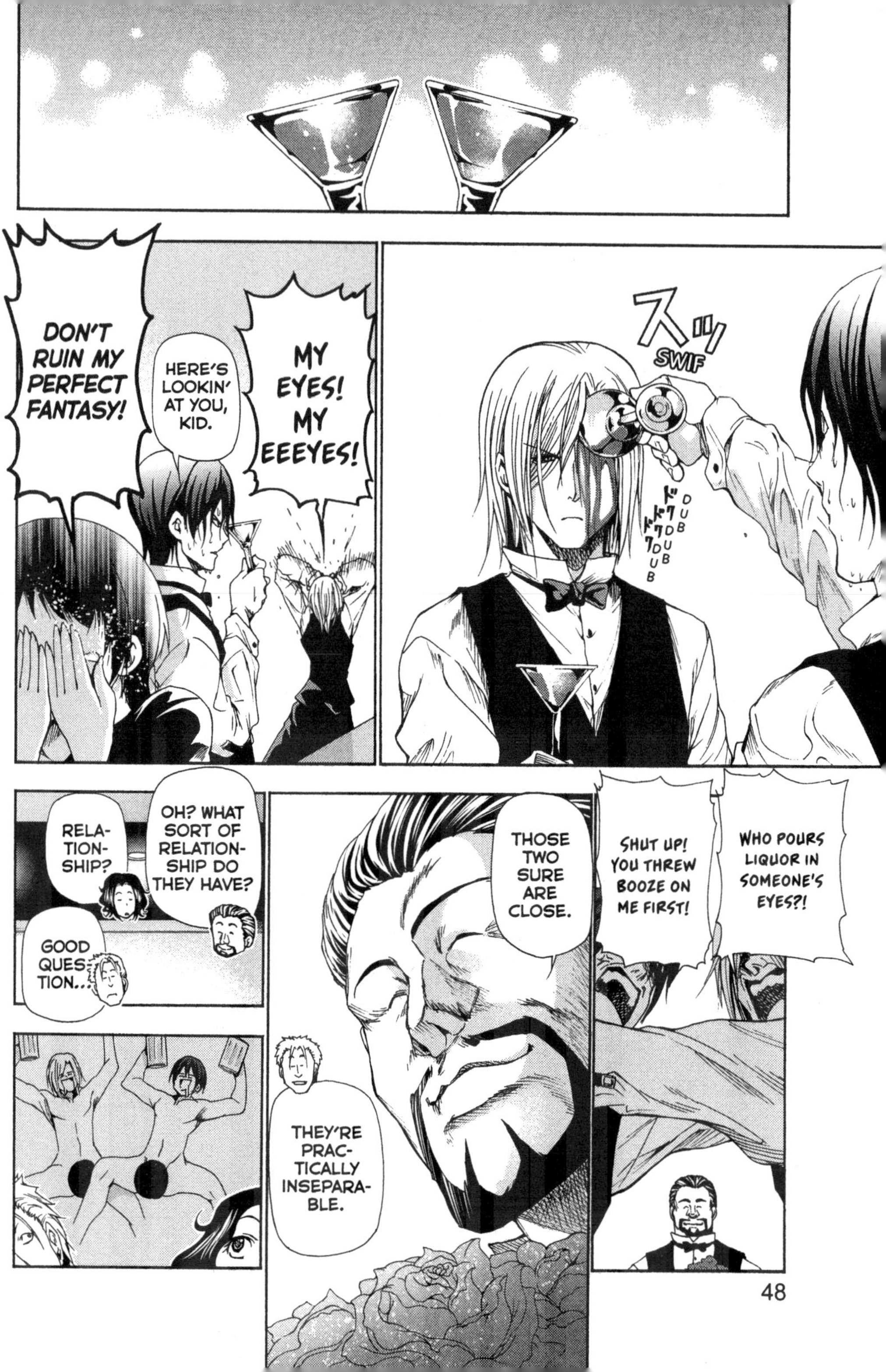
スッ
SWIF
DUB DUB DUB
MY EYES! MY EEEYES!
HERE'S LOOKIN' AT YOU, KID.
DON'T RUIN MY PERFECT FANTASY!
WHO POURS LIQUOR IN SOMEONE'S EYES?!
SHUT UP! YOU THREW BOOZE ON ME FIRST!
THOSE TWO SURE ARE CLOSE.
THEY'RE PRACTICALLY INSEPARABLE.
OH? WHAT SORT OF RELATIONSHIP DO THEY HAVE?
RELATIONSHIP?
GOOD QUESTION...

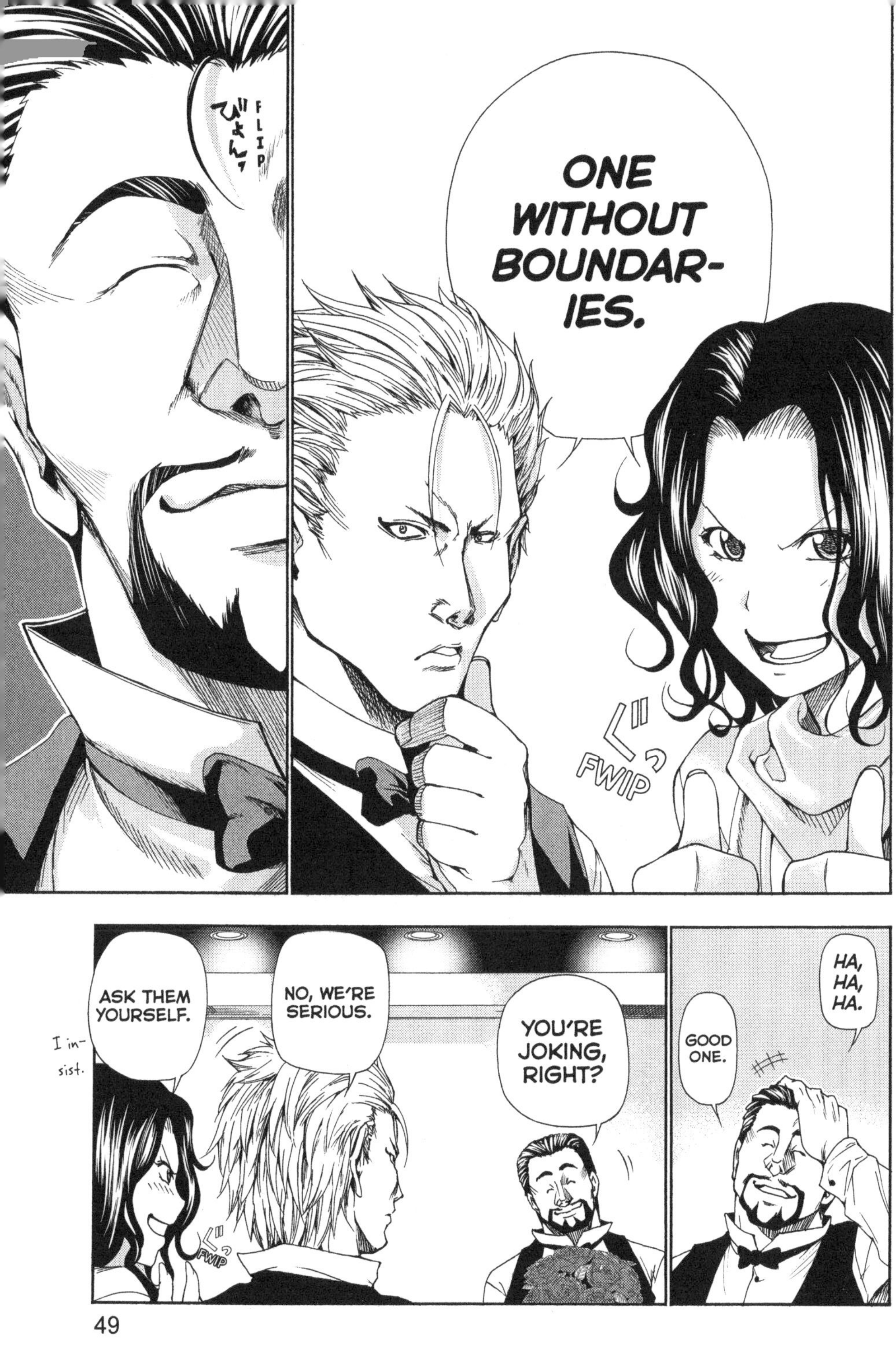
ONE WITHOUT BOUNDAR-IES.
ぐっ
FWIP
ぴょんっ
FLIP
HA, HA, HA.
GOOD ONE.
YOU'RE JOKING, RIGHT?
NO, WE'RE SERIOUS.
ASK THEM YOURSELF.
I in-sist.
ぐっ
FWIP

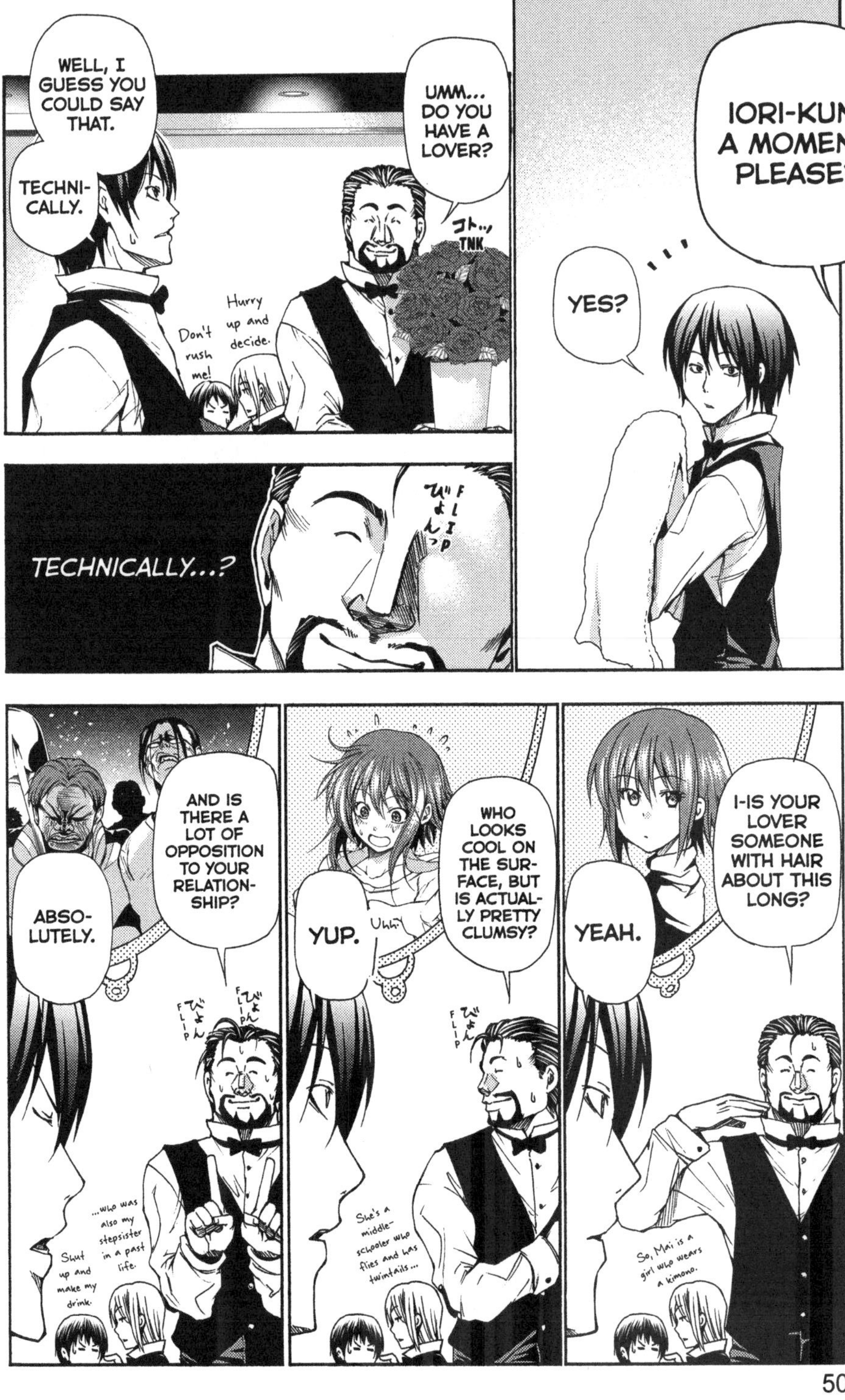

IORI-KUN. A MOMENT, PLEASE?
YES?
UMM... DO YOU HAVE A LOVER?
コトッ TNK
WELL, I GUESS YOU COULD SAY THAT.
TECHNI-CALLY.
Hurry up and decide.
Don't rush me!
びよんっ FLIP
TECHNICALLY...?
I-IS YOUR LOVER SOMEONE WITH HAIR ABOUT THIS LONG?
YEAH.
So, Mai is a girl who wears a kimono.
WHO LOOKS COOL ON THE SUR-FACE, BUT IS ACTUAL-LY PRETTY CLUMSY?
YUP.
びよん FLIP
She's a middle-schooler who flies and has twintails...
AND IS THERE A LOT OF OPPOSITION TO YOUR RELATION-SHIP?
ABSO-LUTELY.
びよん FLIP
びよん FLIP
...who was also my stepsister in a past life.
Shut up and make my drink.

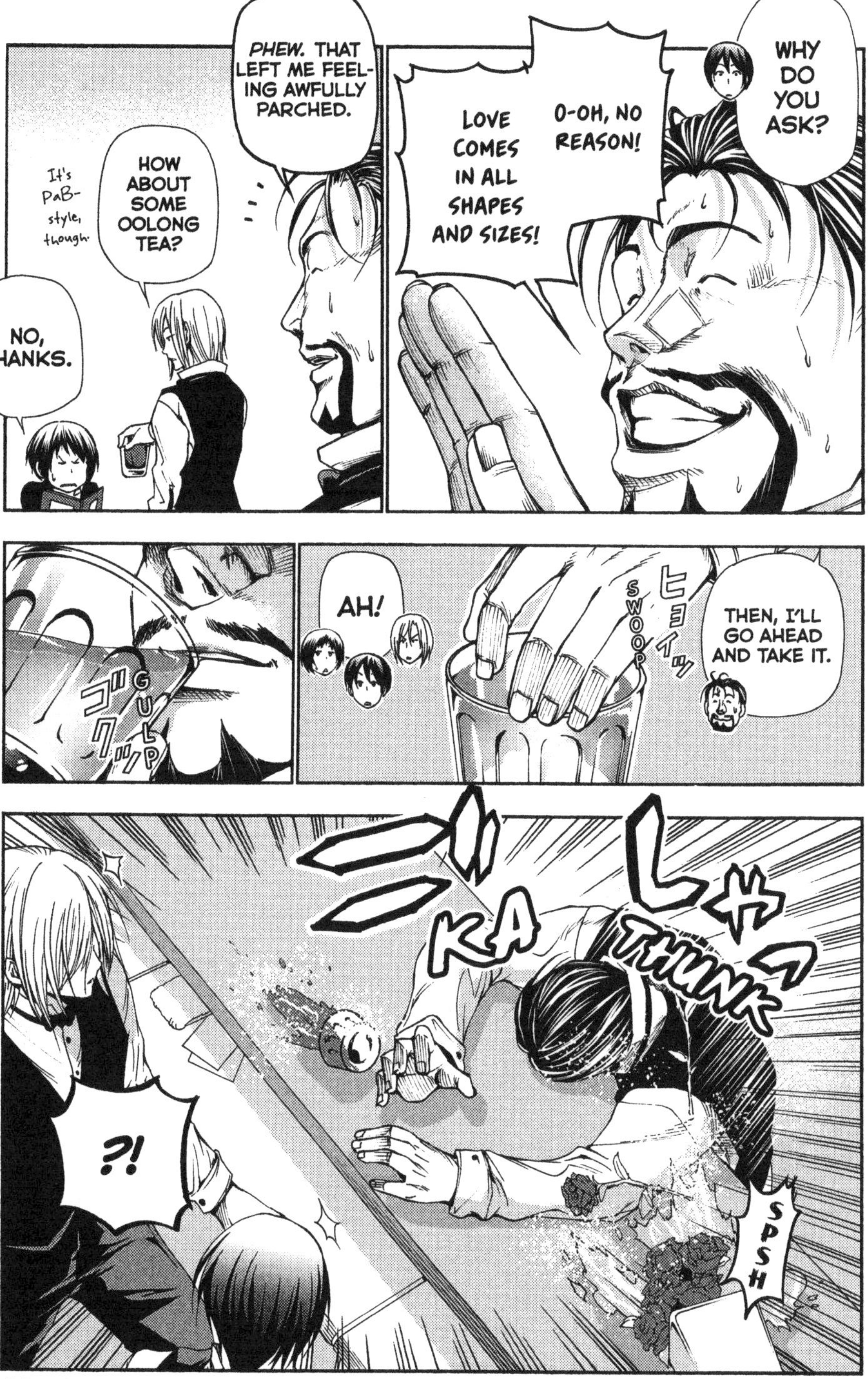
WHY DO YOU ASK?
O-OH, NO REASON!
LOVE COMES IN ALL SHAPES AND SIZES!
PHEW. THAT LEFT ME FEELING AWFULLY PARCHED.
HOW ABOUT SOME OOLONG TEA?
It's PaB-style, though.
NO, THANKS.
THEN, I'LL GO AHEAD AND TAKE IT.
ヒョイッ
SWOOP
AH!
ゴクッ
GULP
KA
THUNK
SPSH
?!

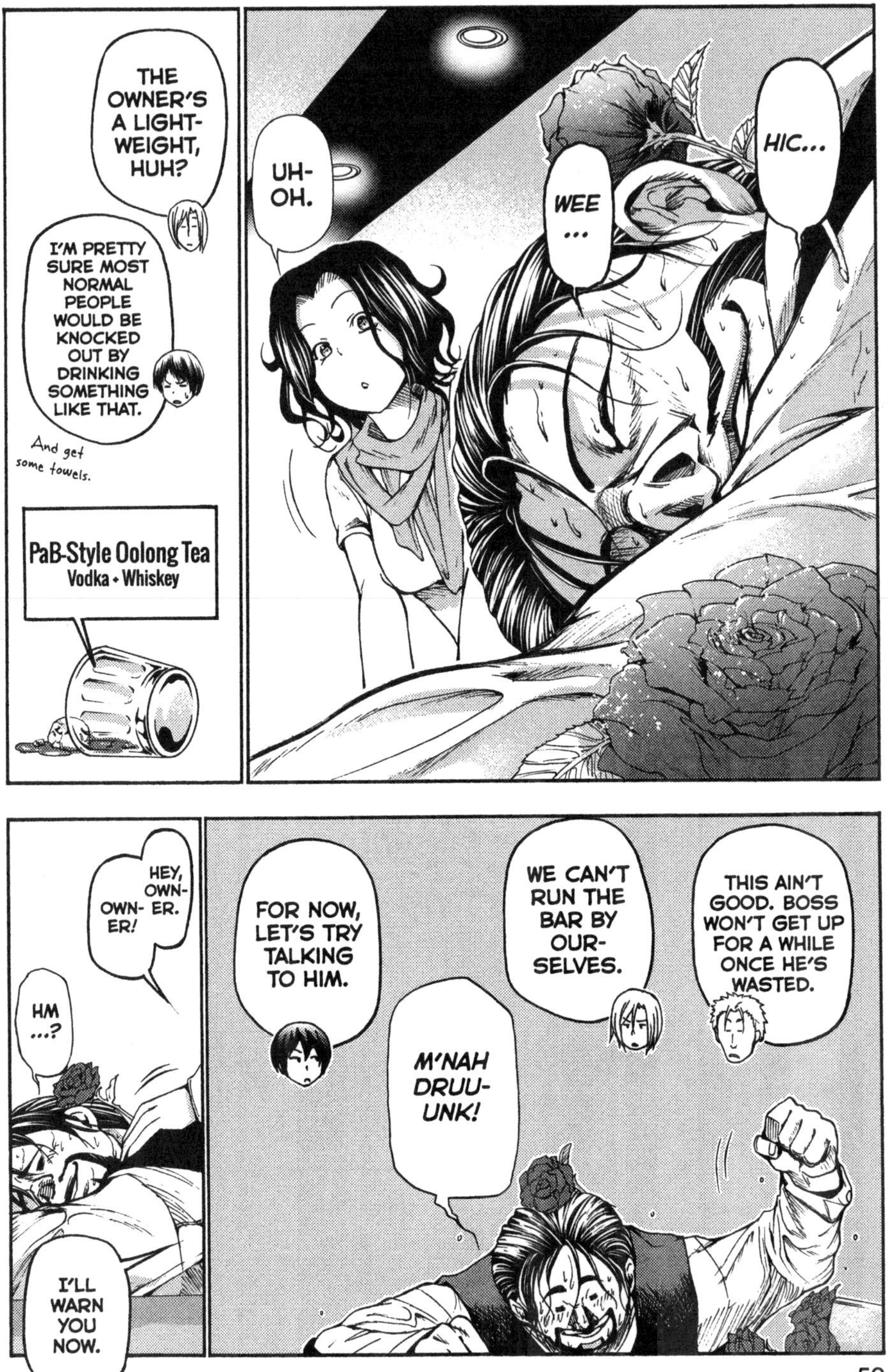
HIC...
WEE ...
UH-OH.
THE OWNER'S A LIGHTWEIGHT, HUH?
I'M PRETTY SURE MOST NORMAL PEOPLE WOULD BE KNOCKED OUT BY DRINKING SOMETHING LIKE THAT.
And get some towels.
PaB-Style Oolong Tea
Vodka + Whiskey
THIS AIN'T GOOD. BOSS WON'T GET UP FOR A WHILE ONCE HE'S WASTED.
WE CAN'T RUN THE BAR BY OURSELVES.
FOR NOW, LET'S TRY TALKING TO HIM.
M'NAH DRUU-UNK!
HEY, OWNER. OWNER!
HM ...?
I'LL WARN YOU NOW.

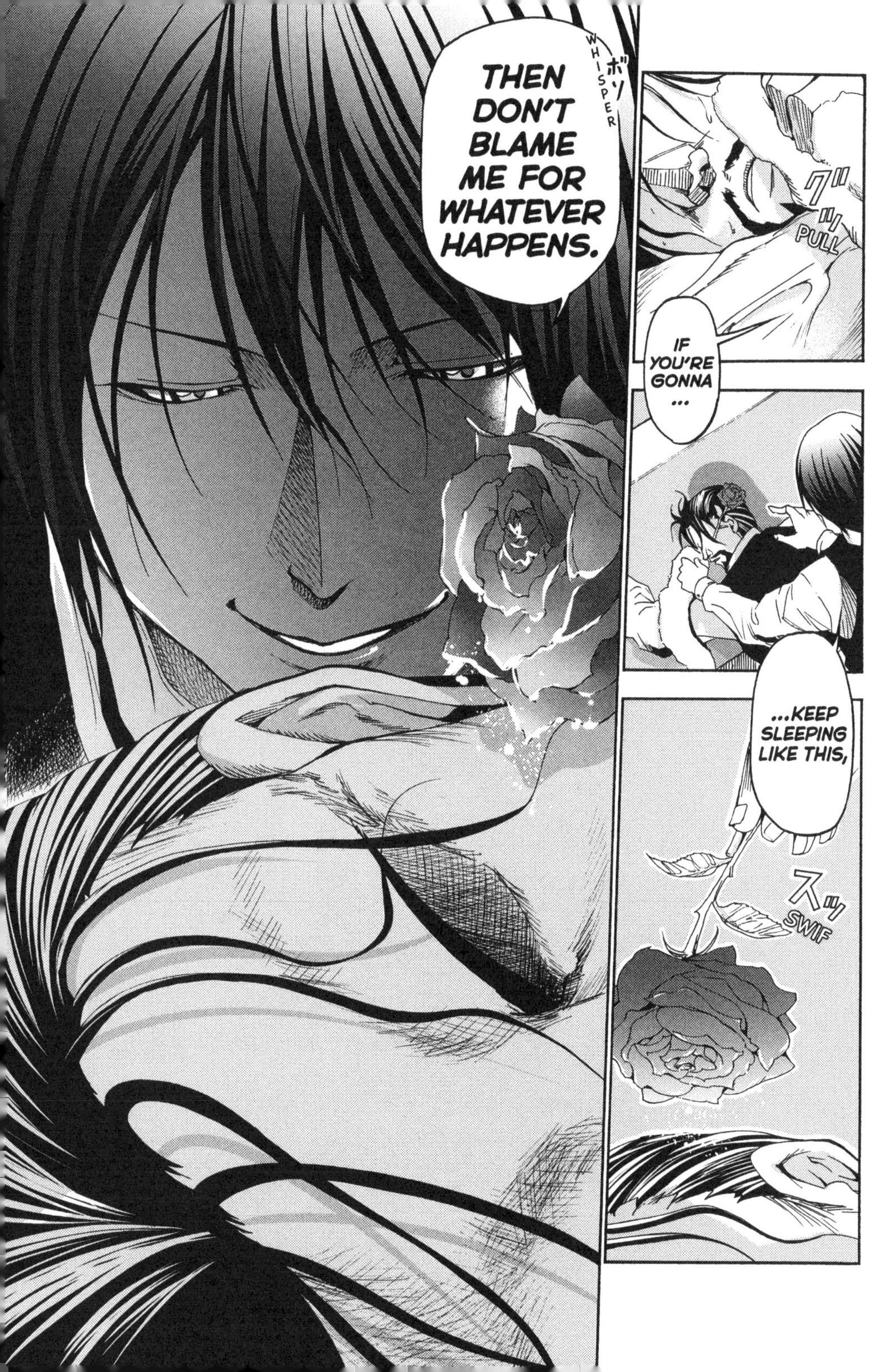
グッ
PULL
IF YOU'RE GONNA ...
...KEEP SLEEPING LIKE THIS,
スッ
SWIF
THEN DON'T BLAME ME FOR WHATEVER HAPPENS.
ボソ
WHISPER

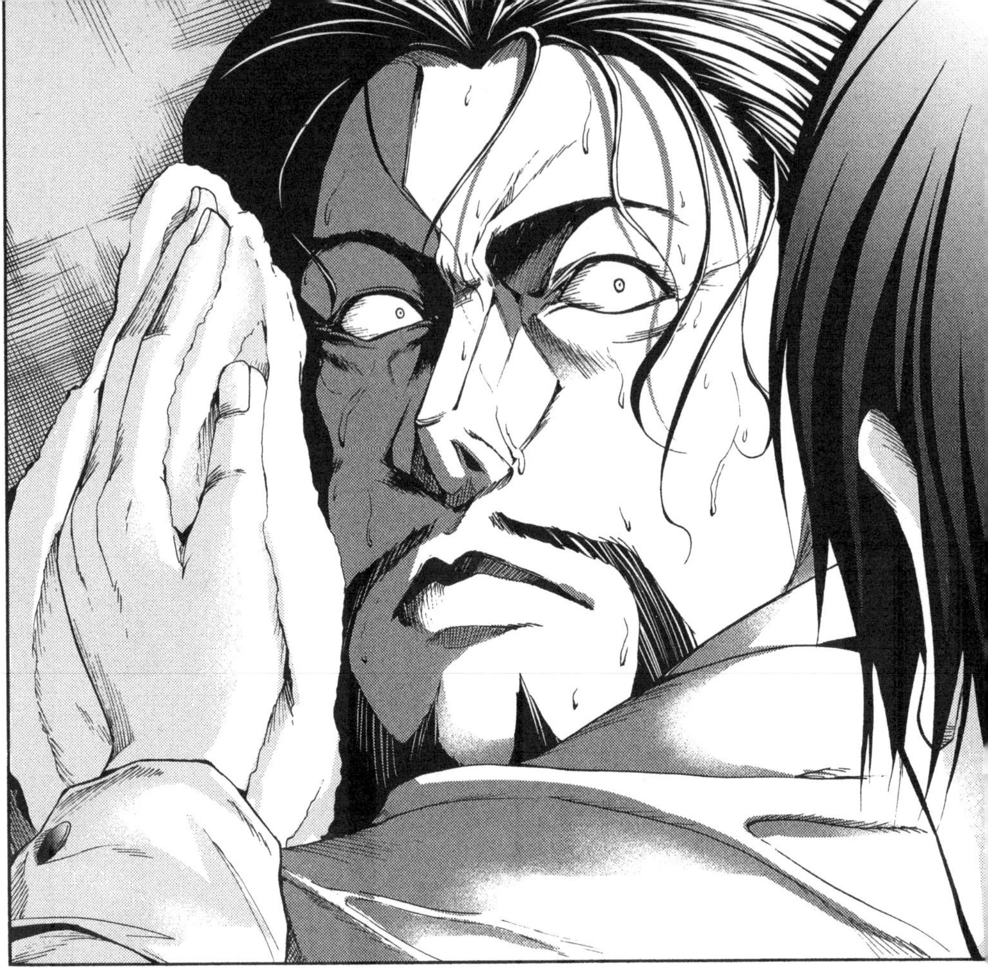

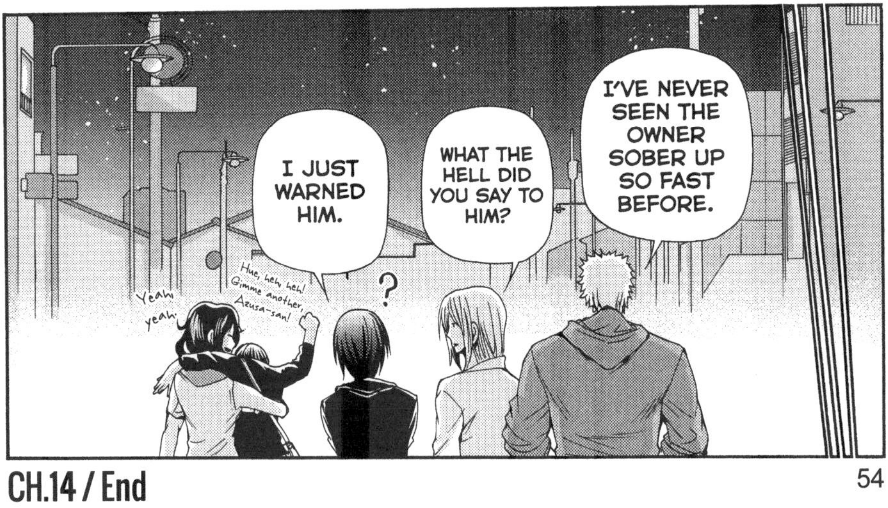
I'VE NEVER SEEN THE OWNER SOBER UP SO FAST BEFORE.
WHAT THE HELL DID YOU SAY TO HIM?
?
I JUST WARNED HIM.
Hue, heh heh! Gimme another, Azusa-san!
Yeah, yeah.

CH.14 / End

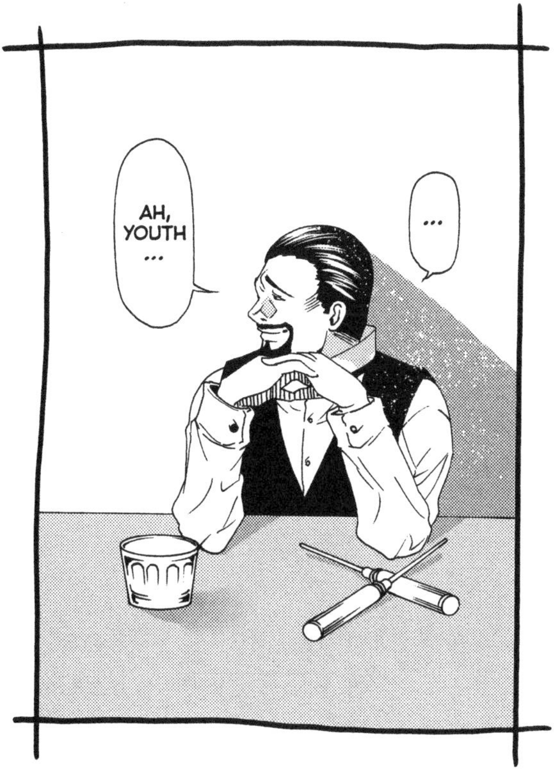
...
AH, YOUTH ...

Grand Blue Dreaming

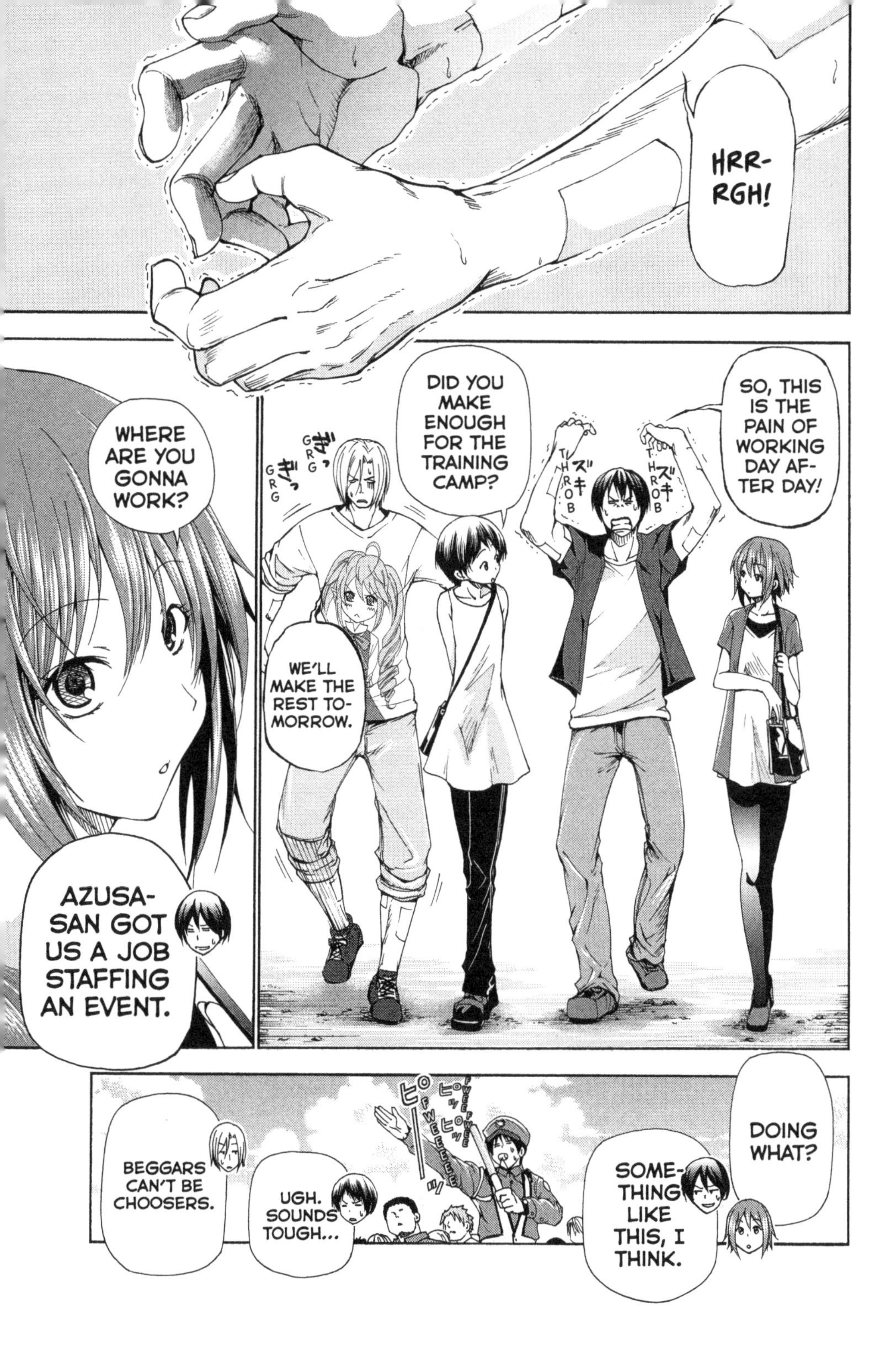
HRR-RGH!
SO, THIS IS THE PAIN OF WORKING DAY AFTER DAY!
THROB ズキ
THROB ズキ
DID YOU MAKE ENOUGH FOR THE TRAINING CAMP?
GRG ぎっ
GRG ぎっ
WE'LL MAKE THE REST TOMORROW.
WHERE ARE YOU GONNA WORK?
AZUSA-SAN GOT US A JOB STAFFING AN EVENT.
DOING WHAT?
SOMETHING LIKE THIS, I THINK.
FWEEFWEE ピッピッ
FWEEEEE ピー
UGH. SOUNDS TOUGH...
BEGGARS CAN'T BE CHOOSERS.

Ch. 15 Shopping!

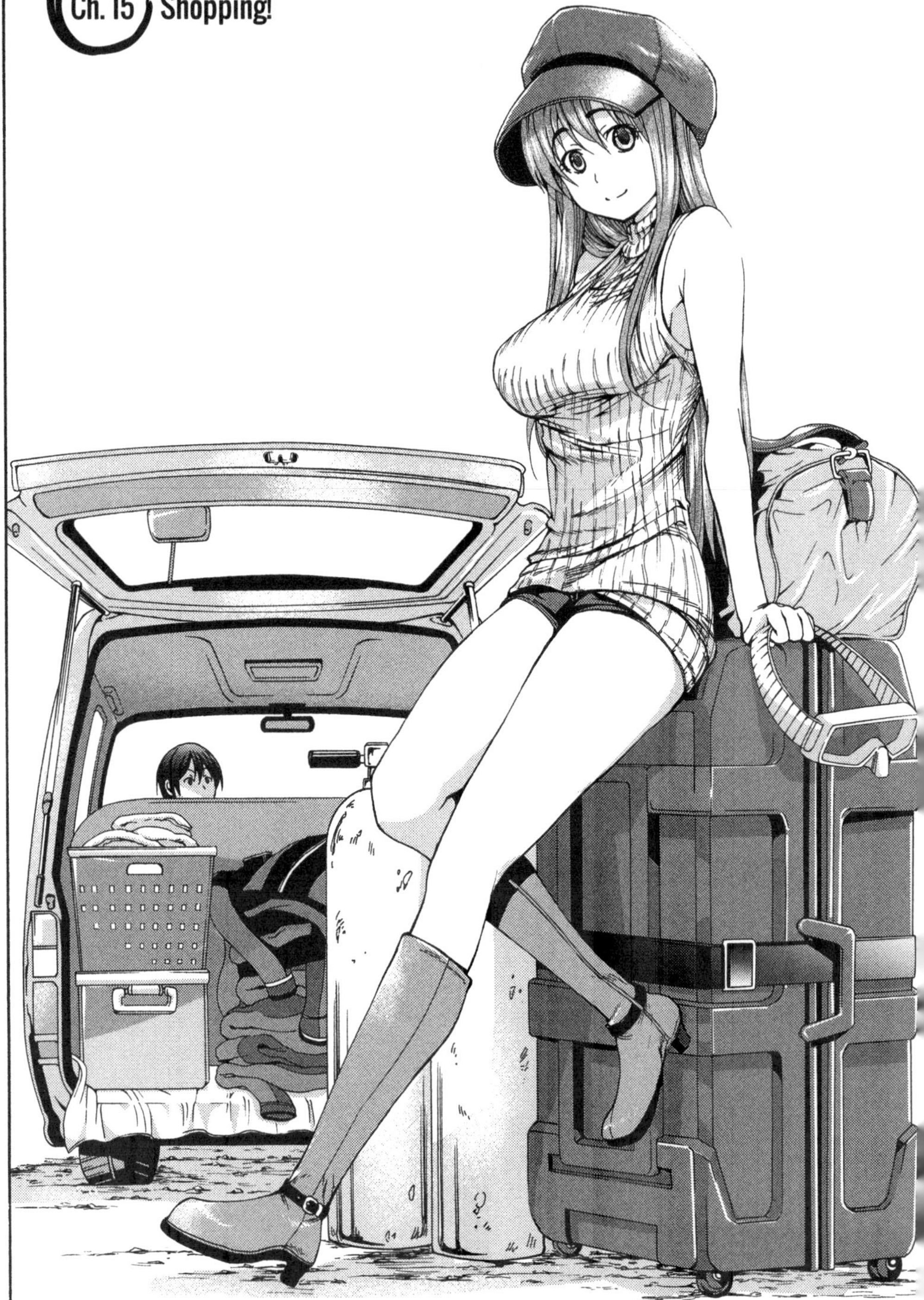

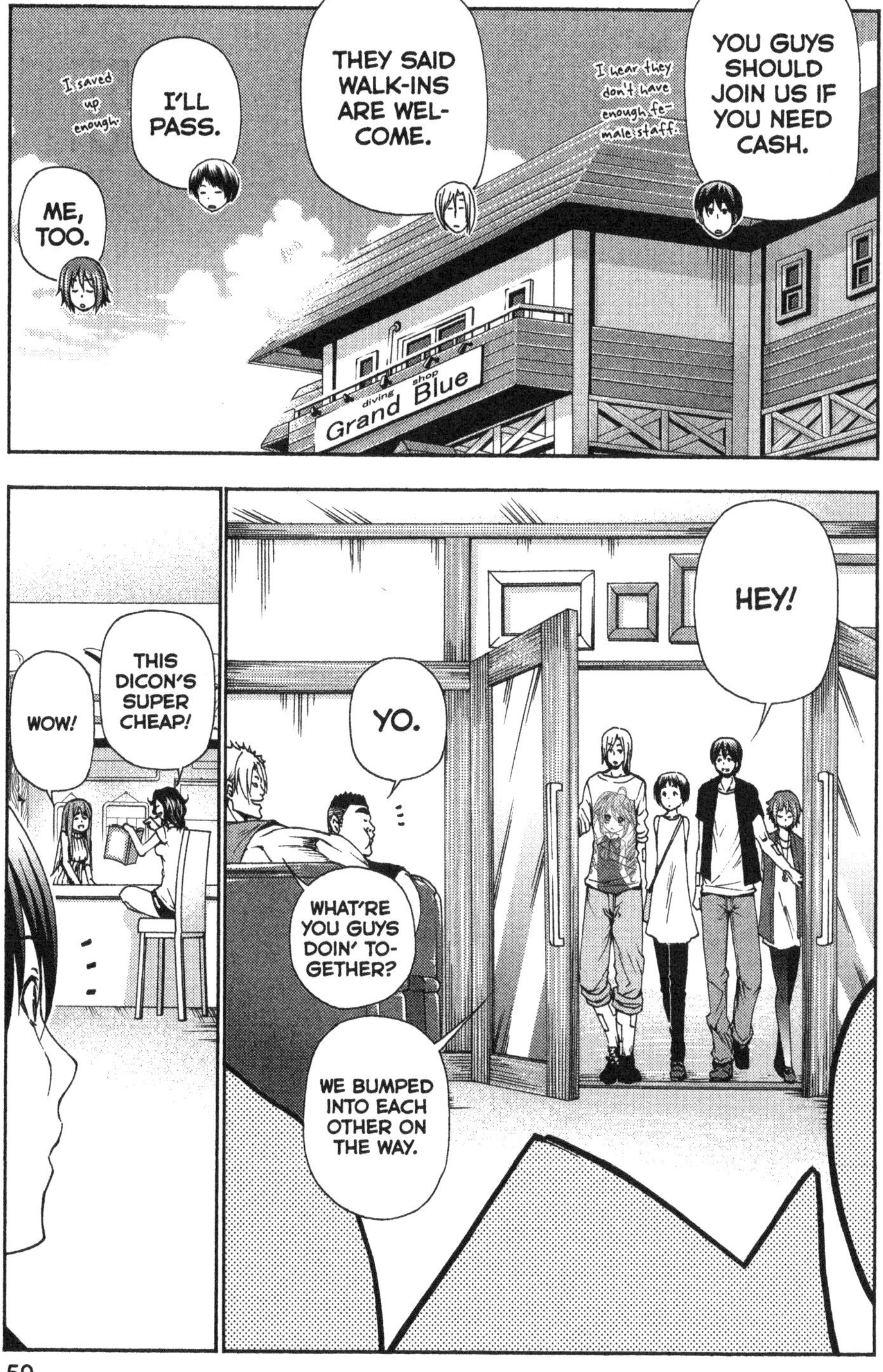

YOU GUYS SHOULD JOIN US IF YOU NEED CASH.
I hear they don't have enough female staff.
THEY SAID WALK-INS ARE WELCOME.
I'LL PASS.
I saved up enough.
ME, TOO.
diving shop Grand Blue
HEY!
YO.
...
WHAT'RE YOU GUYS DOIN' TOGETHER?
WE BUMPED INTO EACH OTHER ON THE WAY.
THIS DICON'S SUPER CHEAP!
WOW!
...

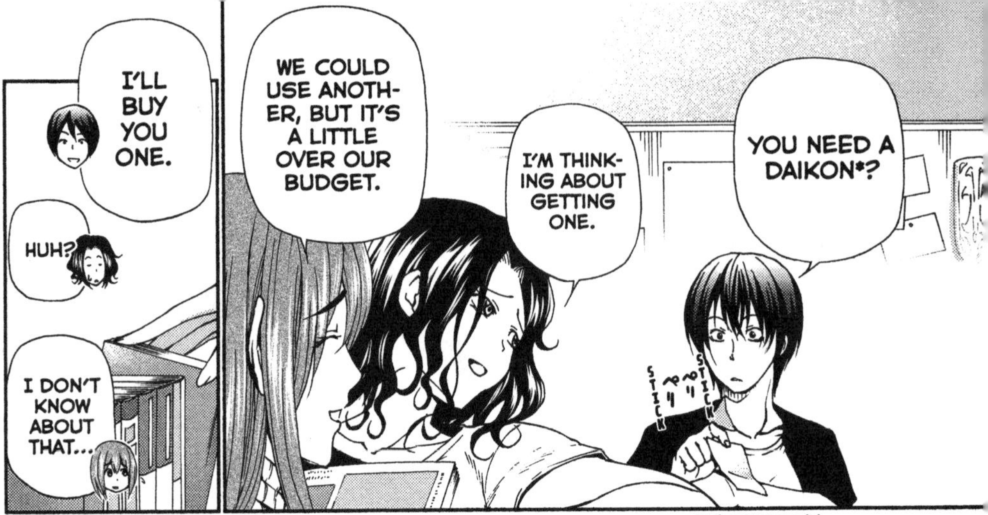
YOU NEED A DAIKON*?
STICK STICK
I'M THINKING ABOUT GETTING ONE.
WE COULD USE ANOTHER, BUT IT'S A LITTLE OVER OUR BUDGET.
I'LL BUY YOU ONE.
HUH?
I DON'T KNOW ABOUT THAT...

*Daikon: Japanese radish.

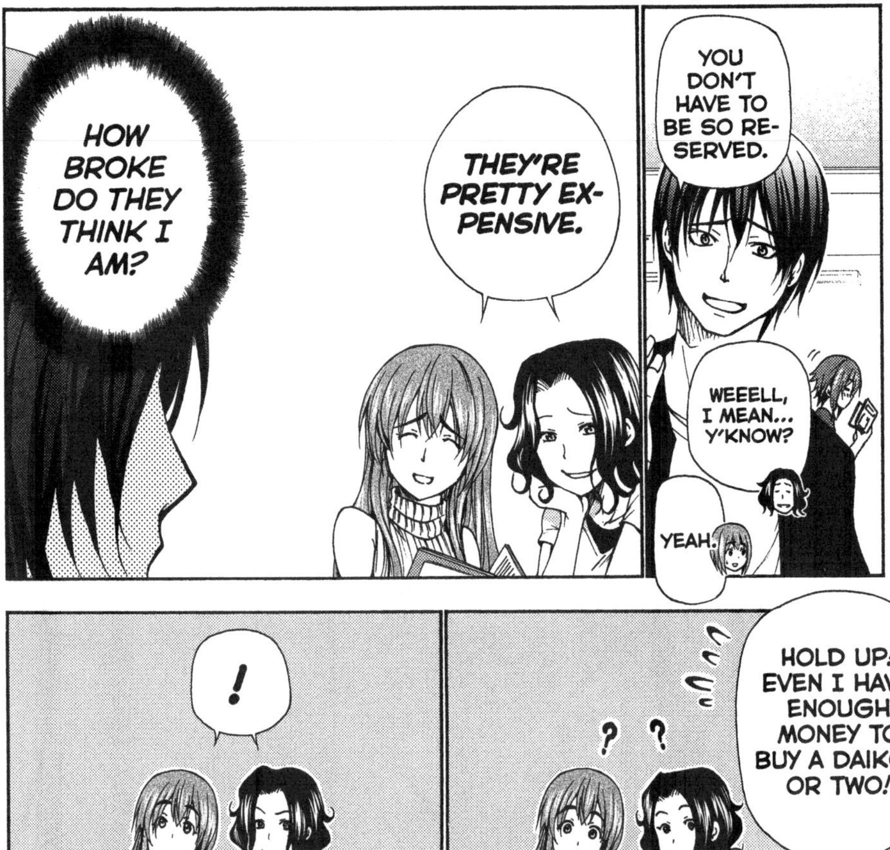
YOU DON'T HAVE TO BE SO RESERVED.
WEEELL, I MEAN... Y'KNOW?
YEAH.
THEY'RE PRETTY EXPENSIVE.
HOW BROKE DO THEY THINK I AM?
HOLD UP! EVEN I HAVE ENOUGH MONEY TO BUY A DAIKON OR TWO!
? ?
!

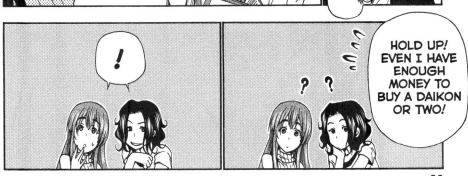

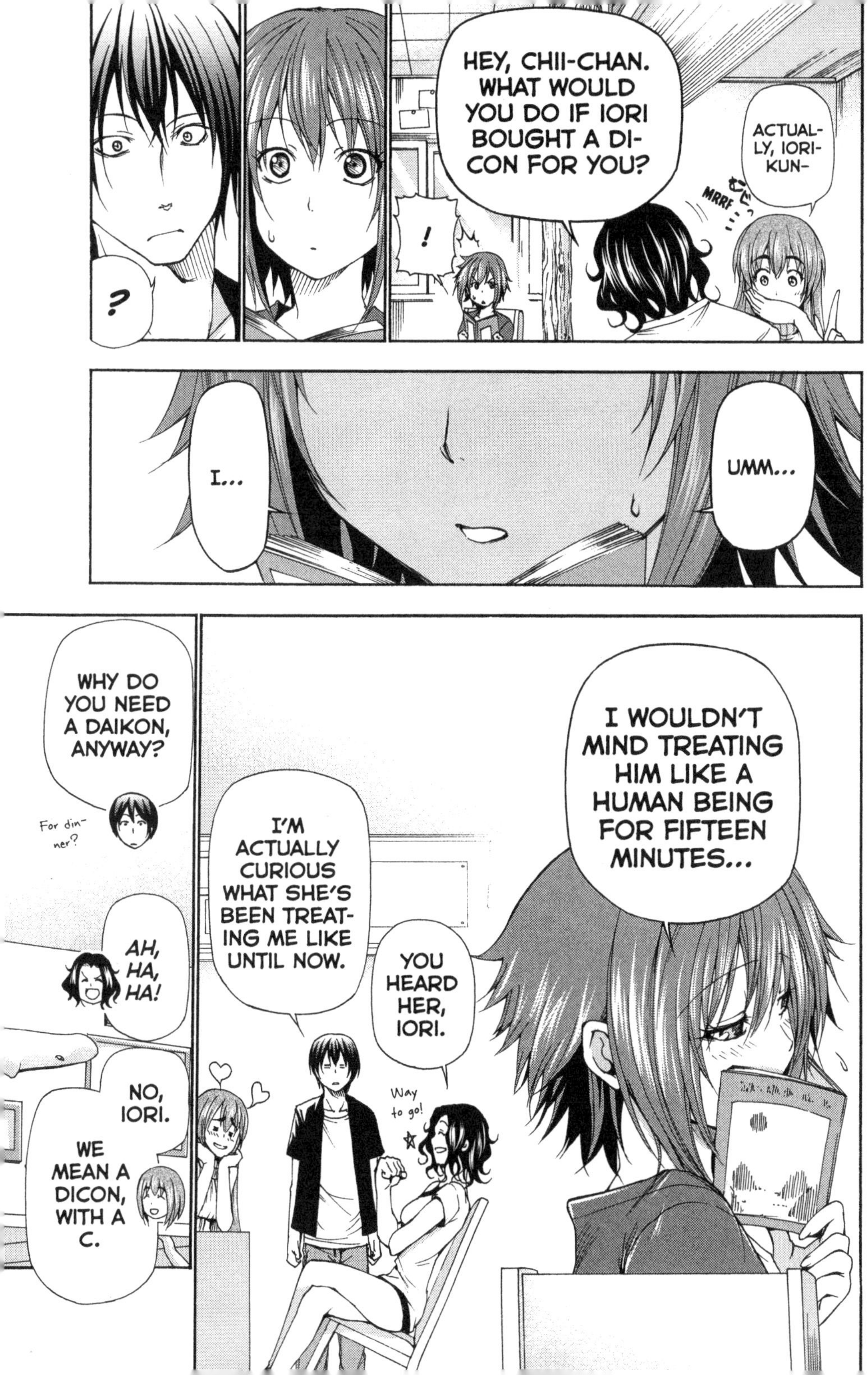
ACTUALLY, IORI-KUN-
MRRF
HEY, CHII-CHAN. WHAT WOULD YOU DO IF IORI BOUGHT A DI-CON FOR YOU?
!
?
UMM...
I...
I WOULDN'T MIND TREATING HIM LIKE A HUMAN BEING FOR FIFTEEN MINUTES...
YOU HEARD HER, IORI.
Way to go!
I'M ACTUALLY CURIOUS WHAT SHE'S BEEN TREATING ME LIKE UNTIL NOW.
WHY DO YOU NEED A DAIKON, ANYWAY?
For dinner?
AH, HA, HA!
NO, IORI.
WE MEAN A DICON, WITH A C.

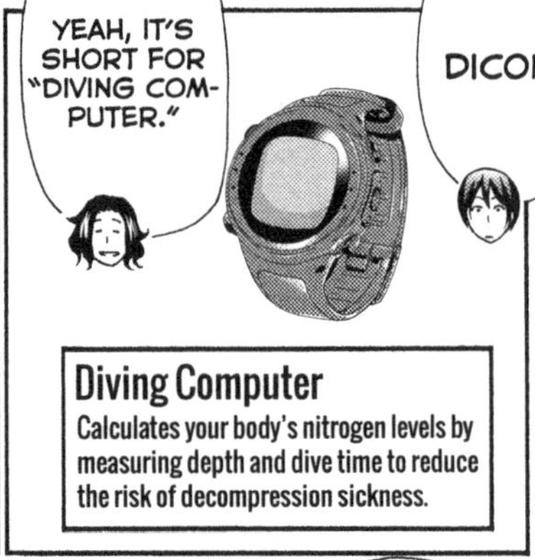
DICON?
YEAH, IT'S SHORT FOR "DIVING COM-PUTER."
Diving Computer
Calculates your body's nitrogen levels by measuring depth and dive time to reduce the risk of decompression sickness.

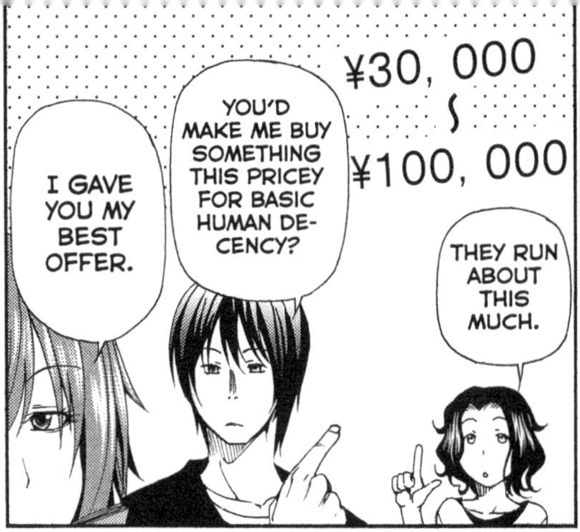
¥30, 000 ~ ¥100, 000
THEY RUN ABOUT THIS MUCH.
YOU'D MAKE ME BUY SOMETHING THIS PRICEY FOR BASIC HUMAN DE-CENCY?
I GAVE YOU MY BEST OFFER.

300 ~ 1000 dollars *

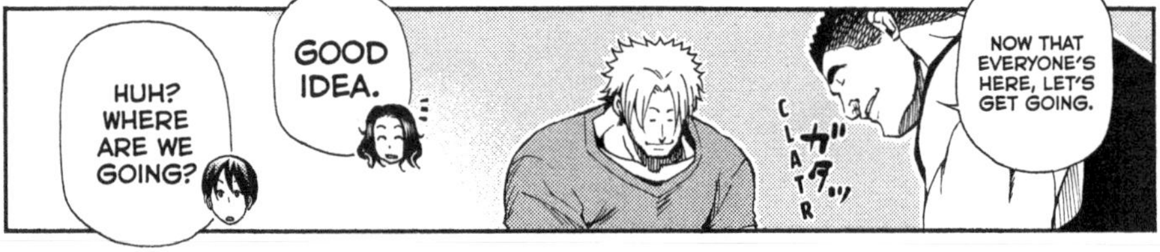
NOW THAT EVERYONE'S HERE, LET'S GET GOING.
CLATTR
GOOD IDEA.
HUH? WHERE ARE WE GOING?

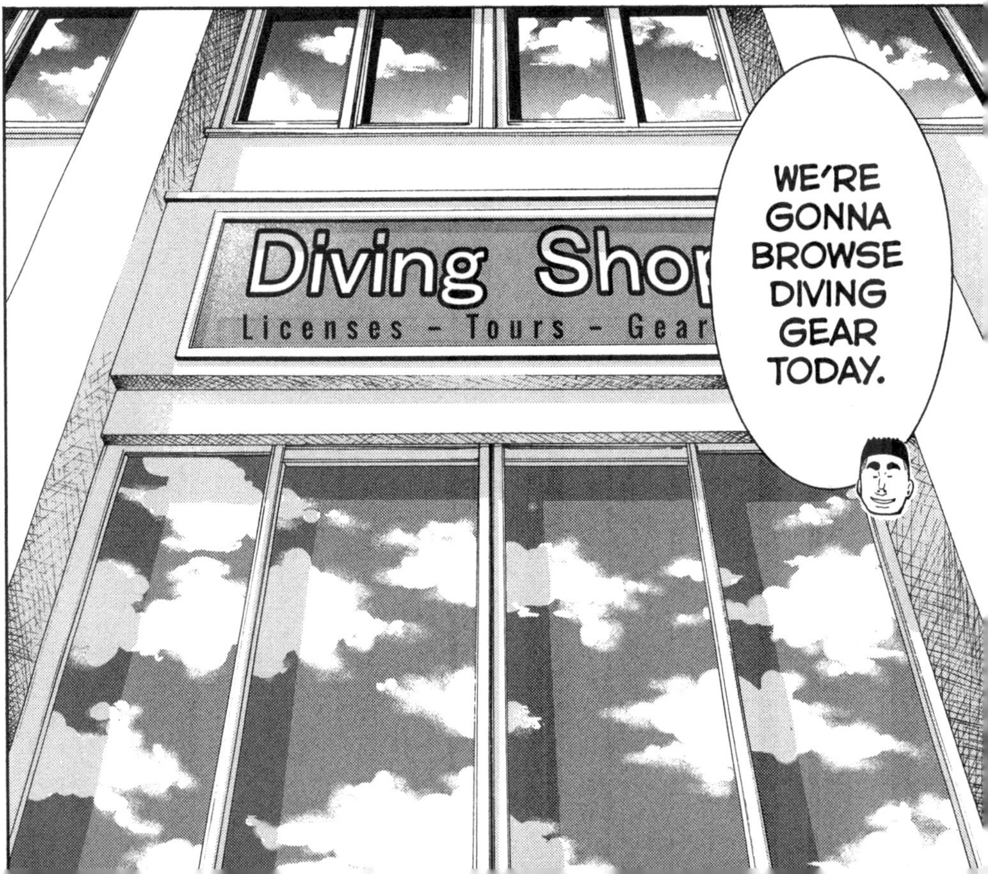
WE'RE GONNA BROWSE DIVING GEAR TODAY.
Diving Shop
Licenses - Tours - Gear

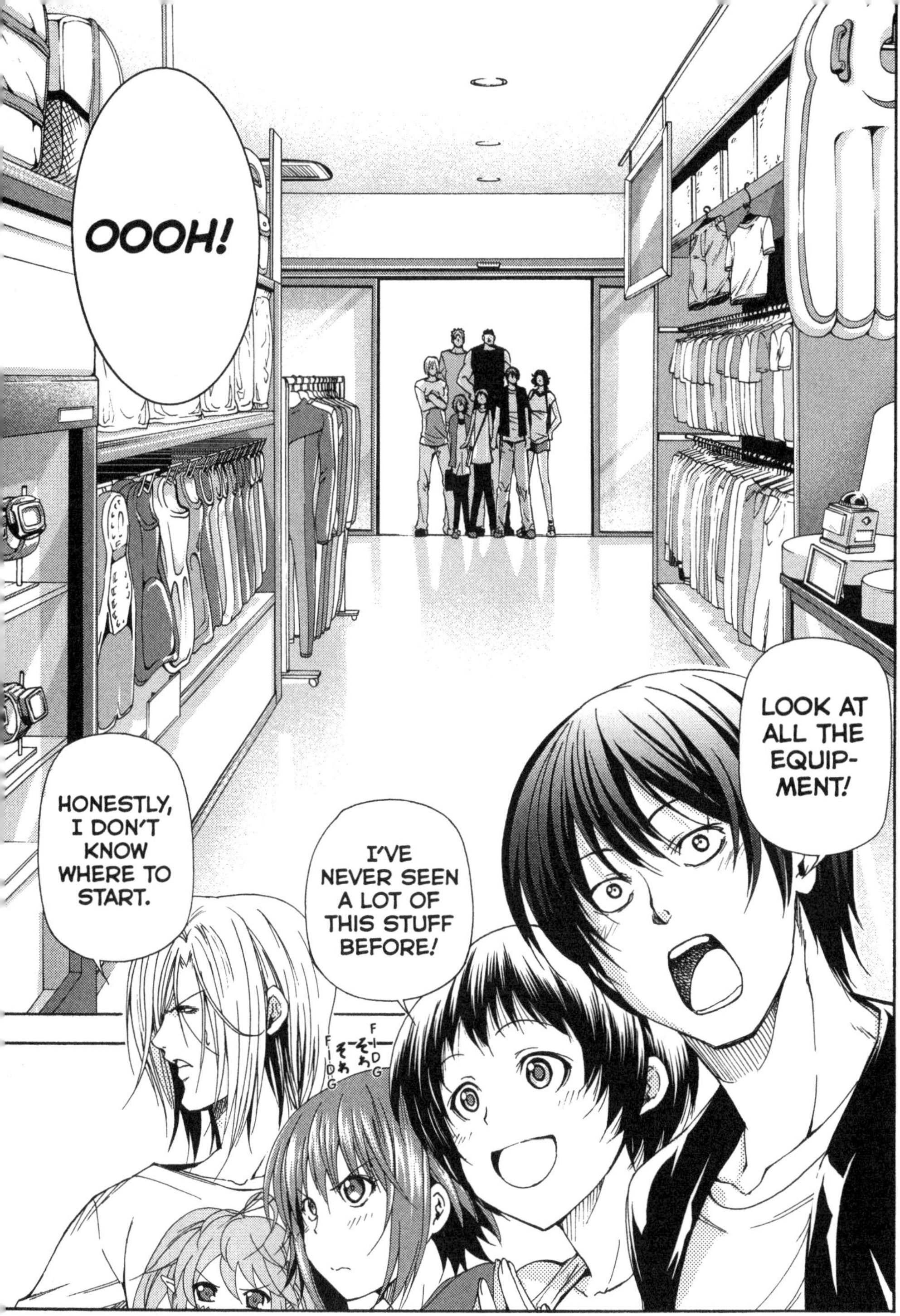
OOOH!
LOOK AT ALL THE EQUIP-MENT!
I'VE NEVER SEEN A LOT OF THIS STUFF BEFORE!
HONESTLY, I DON'T KNOW WHERE TO START.
FIDG
FIDG

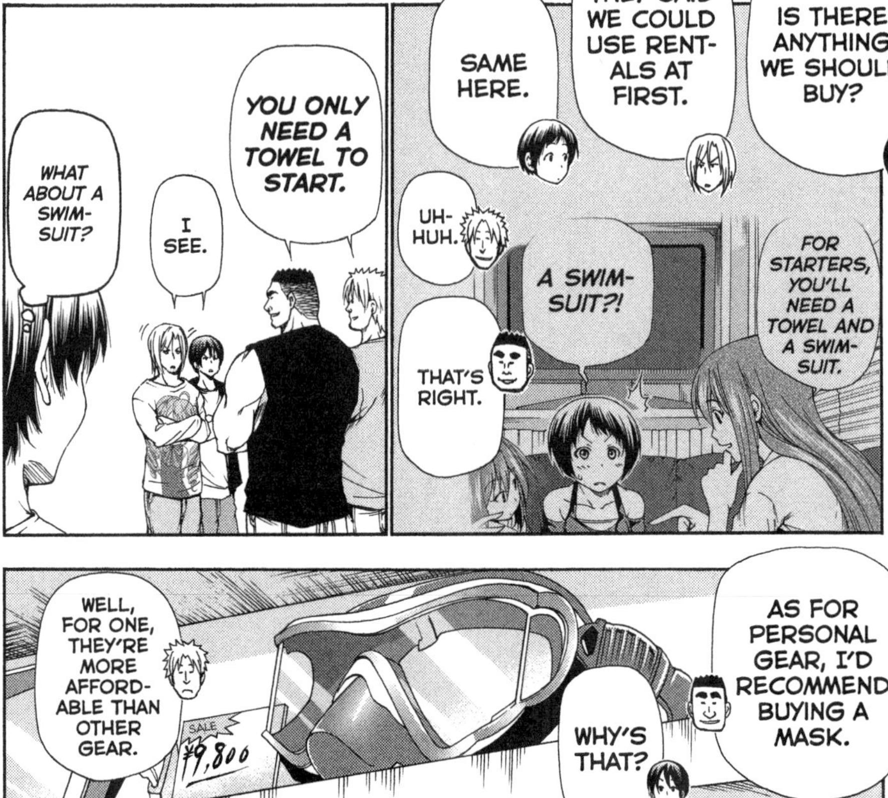
IS THERE ANYTHING WE SHOULD BUY?
THEY SAID WE COULD USE RENTALS AT FIRST.
SAME HERE.
FOR STARTERS, YOU'LL NEED A TOWEL AND A SWIMSUIT.
UH-HUH.
A SWIMSUIT?!
THAT'S RIGHT.
YOU ONLY NEED A TOWEL TO START.
I SEE.
WHAT ABOUT A SWIMSUIT?
AS FOR PERSONAL GEAR, I'D RECOMMEND BUYING A MASK.
WHY'S THAT?
WELL, FOR ONE, THEY'RE MORE AFFORDABLE THAN OTHER GEAR.
SALE
¥9,800

* 98 dollars

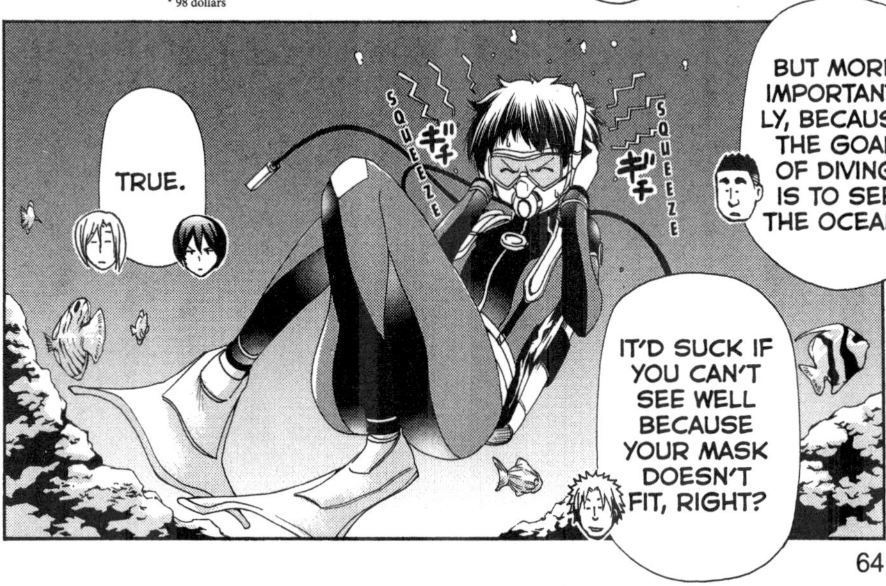
BUT MORE IMPORTANTLY, BECAUSE THE GOAL OF DIVING IS TO SEE THE OCEAN.
SQUEEZE
ギチ
SQUEEZE
ギチ
TRUE.
IT'D SUCK IF YOU CAN'T SEE WELL BECAUSE YOUR MASK DOESN'T FIT, RIGHT?

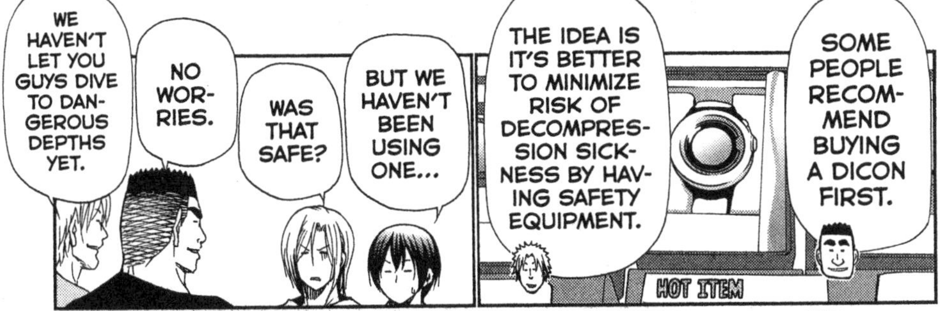
SOME PEOPLE RECOMMEND BUYING A DICON FIRST.
THE IDEA IS IT'S BETTER TO MINIMIZE RISK OF DECOMPRESSION SICKNESS BY HAVING SAFETY EQUIPMENT.
HOT ITEM
BUT WE HAVEN'T BEEN USING ONE...
WAS THAT SAFE?
NO WORRIES.
WE HAVEN'T LET YOU GUYS DIVE TO DANGEROUS DEPTHS YET.

*Decompression Sickness: A condition in which gas bubbles form in the body due to sudden depressurization, obstructing blood vessels.

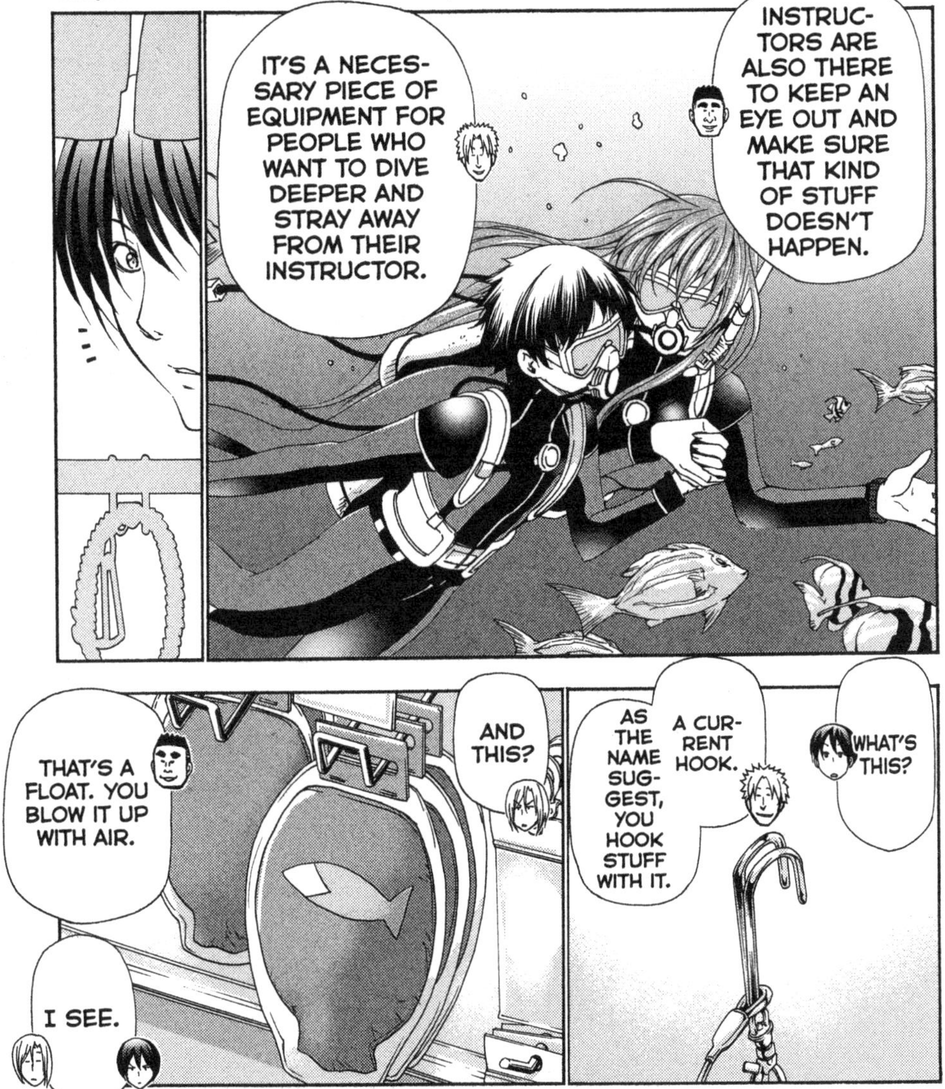
INSTRUCTORS ARE ALSO THERE TO KEEP AN EYE OUT AND MAKE SURE THAT KIND OF STUFF DOESN'T HAPPEN.
IT'S A NECESSARY PIECE OF EQUIPMENT FOR PEOPLE WHO WANT TO DIVE DEEPER AND STRAY AWAY FROM THEIR INSTRUCTOR.
WHAT'S THIS?
A CURRENT HOOK.
AS THE NAME SUGGEST, YOU HOOK STUFF WITH IT.
AND THIS?
THAT'S A FLOAT. YOU BLOW IT UP WITH AIR.
I SEE.

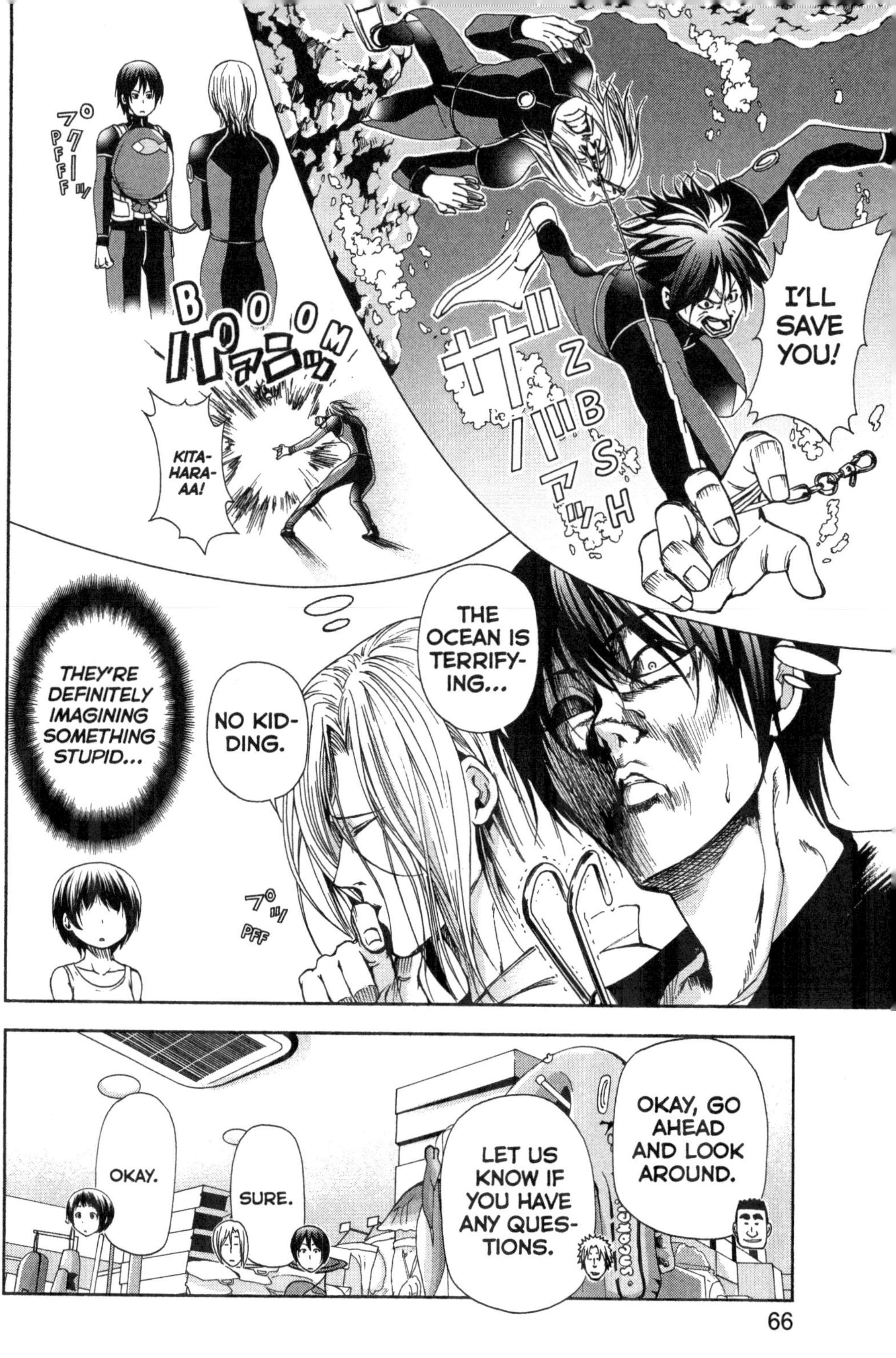
I'LL SAVE YOU!
ZBSH
PFFF
BOOM
KITA-HARA-AA!
THE OCEAN IS TERRIFY-ING...
NO KID-DING.
THEY'RE DEFINITELY IMAGINING SOMETHING STUPID...
PFF
OKAY, GO AHEAD AND LOOK AROUND.
LET US KNOW IF YOU HAVE ANY QUES-TIONS.
SURE.
OKAY.

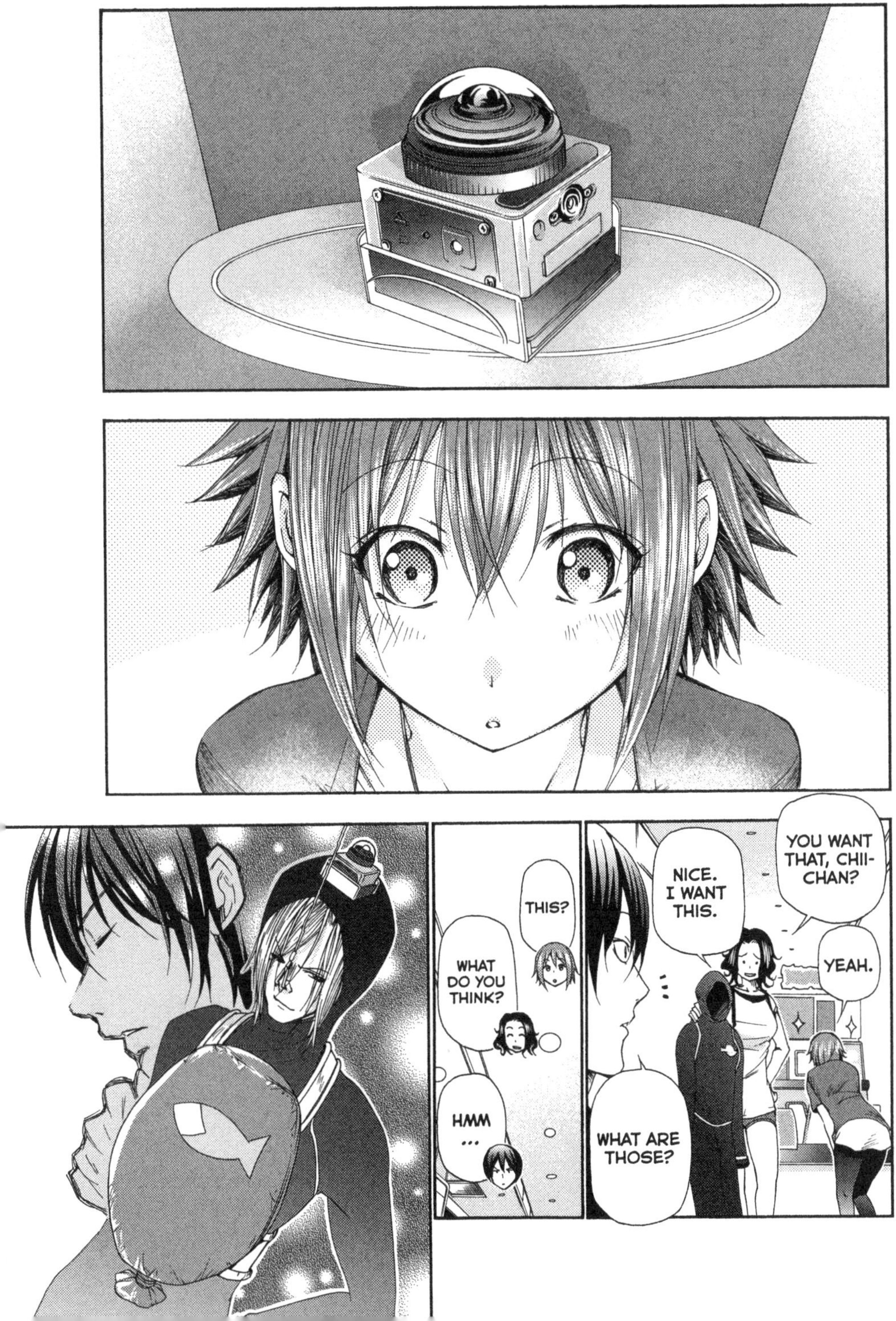
YOU WANT THAT, CHII-CHAN?
YEAH.
NICE. I WANT THIS.
...
WHAT ARE THOSE?
THIS?
WHAT DO YOU THINK?
HMM ...

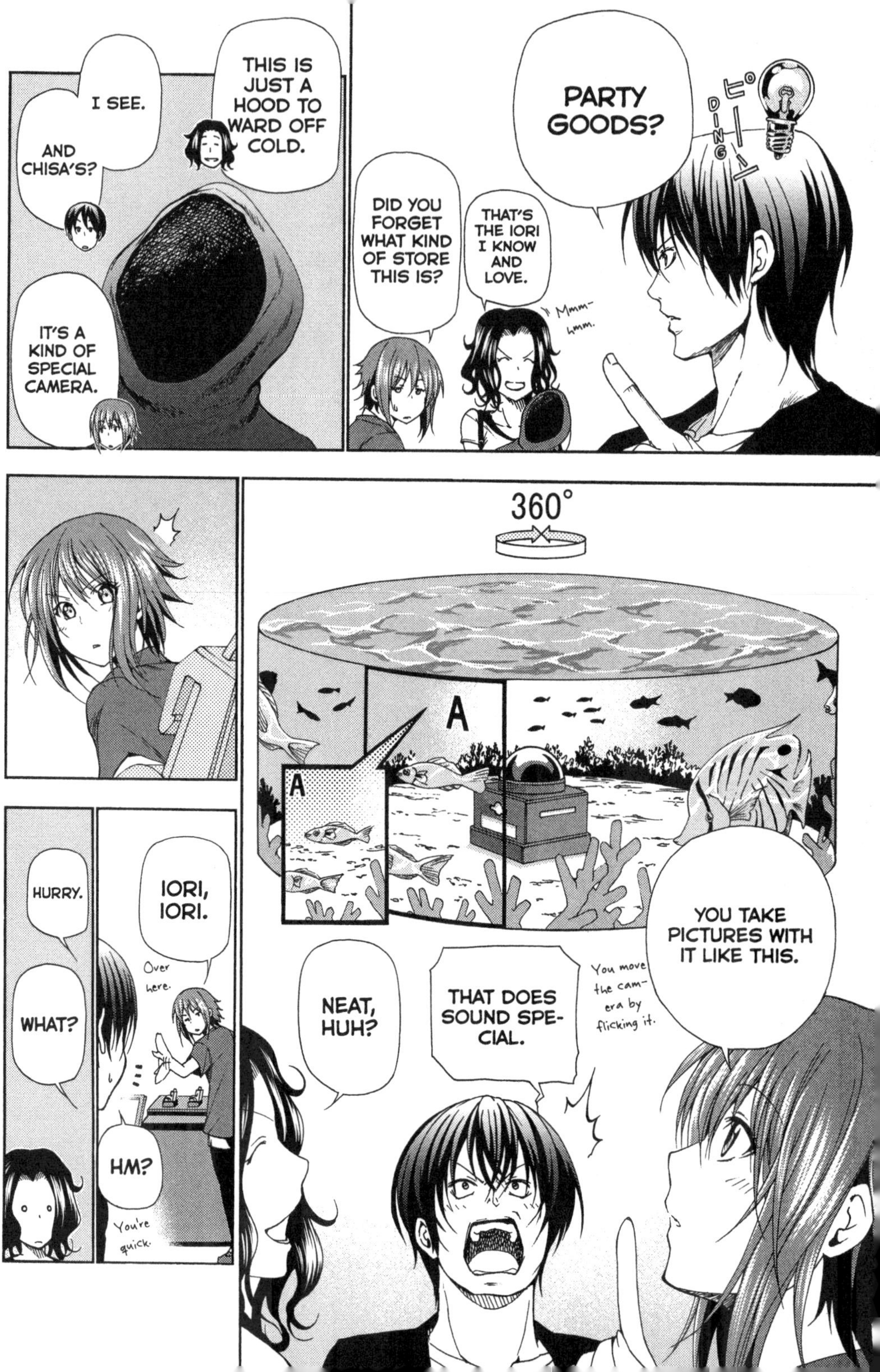
PARTY GOODS?
DING
THAT'S THE IORI I KNOW AND LOVE.
Mmm-hmm.
DID YOU FORGET WHAT KIND OF STORE THIS IS?
THIS IS JUST A HOOD TO WARD OFF COLD.
I SEE.
AND CHISA'S?
IT'S A KIND OF SPECIAL CAMERA.
360°
A
A
YOU TAKE PICTURES WITH IT LIKE THIS.
You move the camera by flicking it.
THAT DOES SOUND SPECIAL.
NEAT, HUH?
IORI, IORI.
Over here.
HM?
You're quick.
HURRY.
WHAT?

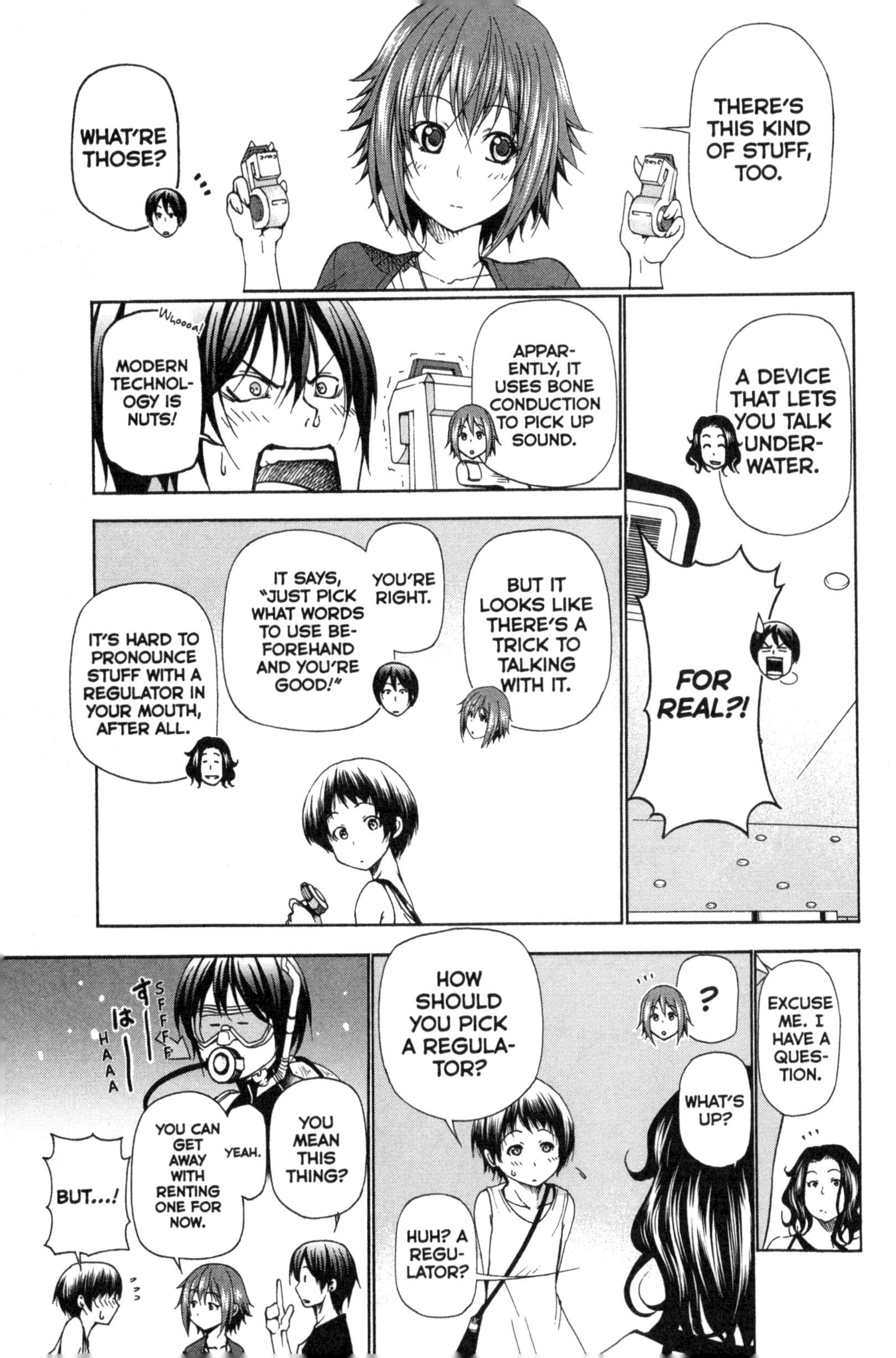
THERE'S THIS KIND OF STUFF, TOO.
WHAT'RE THOSE?
A DEVICE THAT LETS YOU TALK UNDERWATER.
FOR REAL?!
APPARENTLY, IT USES BONE CONDUCTION TO PICK UP SOUND.
Whoooa!
MODERN TECHNOLOGY IS NUTS!
BUT IT LOOKS LIKE THERE'S A TRICK TO TALKING WITH IT.
YOU'RE RIGHT.
IT SAYS, "JUST PICK WHAT WORDS TO USE BEFOREHAND AND YOU'RE GOOD!"
IT'S HARD TO PRONOUNCE STUFF WITH A REGULATOR IN YOUR MOUTH, AFTER ALL.
EXCUSE ME. I HAVE A QUESTION.
?
WHAT'S UP?
HOW SHOULD YOU PICK A REGULATOR?
HUH? A REGULATOR?
すー SFFFF
はー HAAA
YOU MEAN THIS THING?
YEAH.
YOU CAN GET AWAY WITH RENTING ONE FOR NOW.
BUT...!

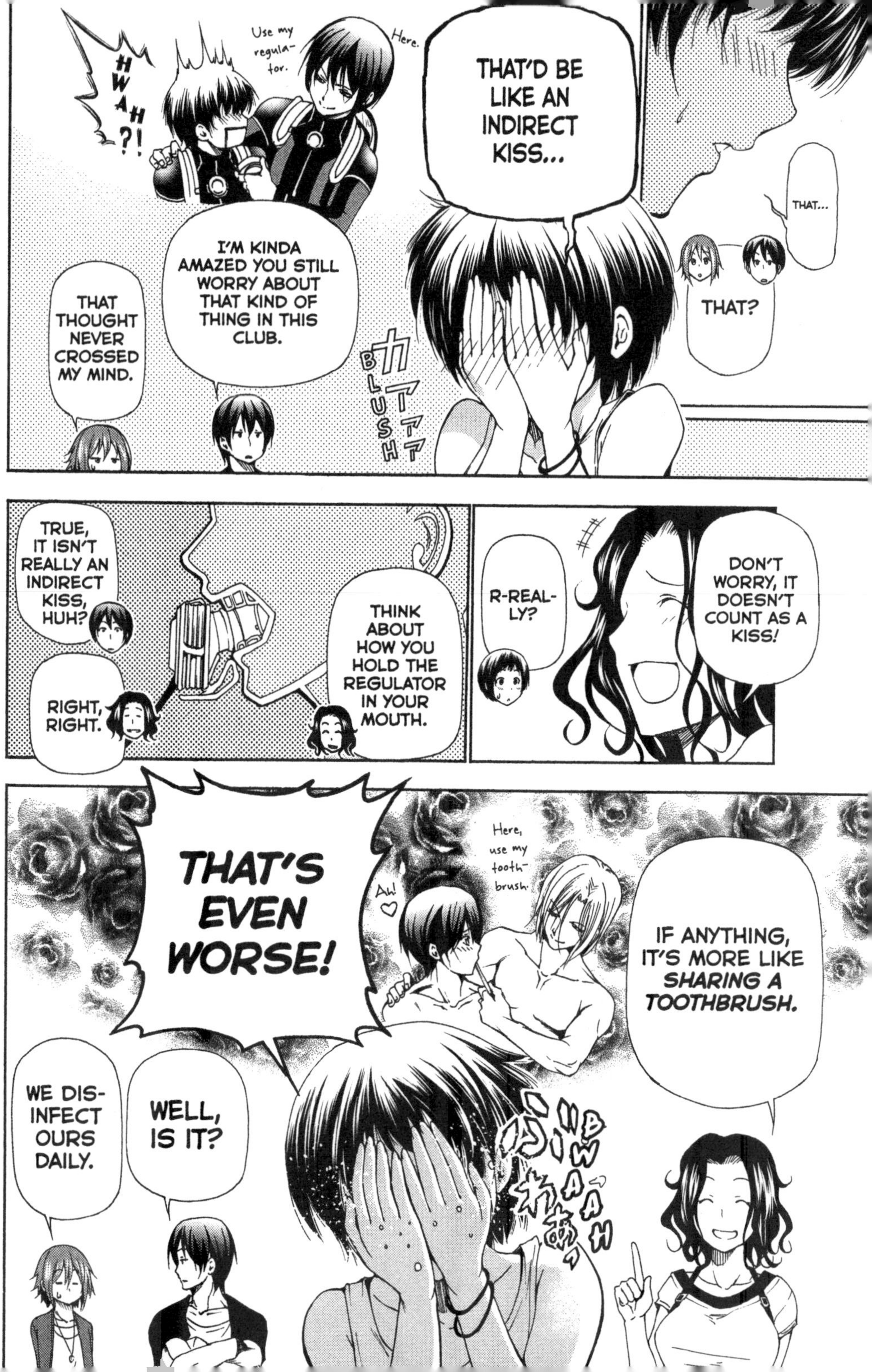
THAT...
THAT?
THAT'D BE LIKE AN INDIRECT KISS...
BLUSH
Here.
Use my regulator.
HWAH?!
I'M KINDA AMAZED YOU STILL WORRY ABOUT THAT KIND OF THING IN THIS CLUB.
THAT THOUGHT NEVER CROSSED MY MIND.
DON'T WORRY, IT DOESN'T COUNT AS A KISS!
R-REALLY?
THINK ABOUT HOW YOU HOLD THE REGULATOR IN YOUR MOUTH.
TRUE, IT ISN'T REALLY AN INDIRECT KISS, HUH?
RIGHT, RIGHT.
IF ANYTHING, IT'S MORE LIKE SHARING A TOOTHBRUSH.
Here, use my toothbrush.
Ah! ♡
THAT'S EVEN WORSE!
BWAAAH
WELL, IS IT?
WE DISINFECT OURS DAILY.

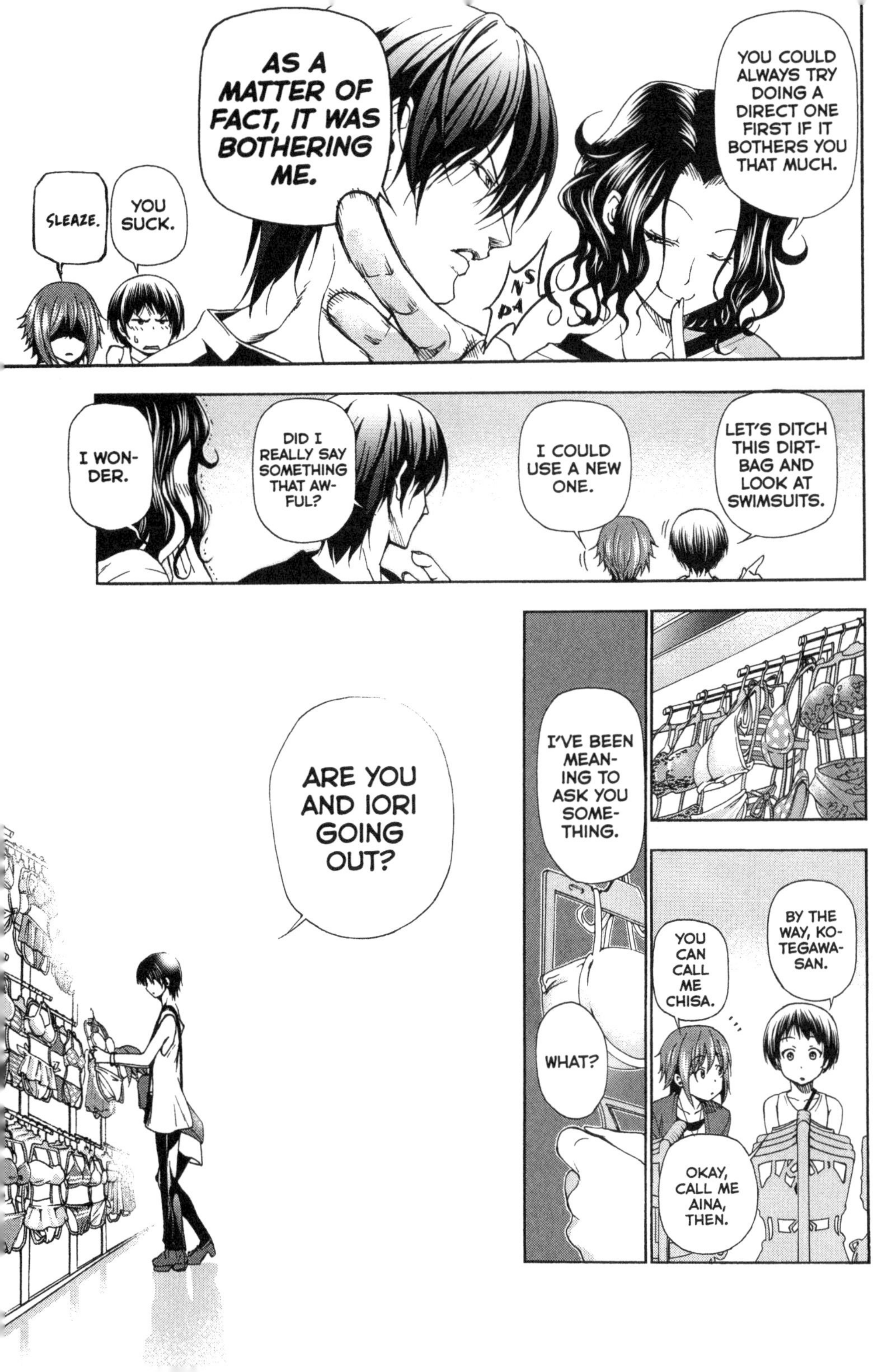
YOU COULD ALWAYS TRY DOING A DIRECT ONE FIRST IF IT BOTHERS YOU THAT MUCH.
AS A MATTER OF FACT, IT WAS BOTHERING ME.
YOU SUCK.
SLEAZE.
LET'S DITCH THIS DIRT-BAG AND LOOK AT SWIMSUITS.
I COULD USE A NEW ONE.
DID I REALLY SAY SOMETHING THAT AW-FUL?
I WON-DER.
BY THE WAY, KO-TEGAWA-SAN.
YOU CAN CALL ME CHISA.
OKAY, CALL ME AINA, THEN.
I'VE BEEN MEAN-ING TO ASK YOU SOME-THING.
WHAT?
ARE YOU AND IORI GOING OUT?

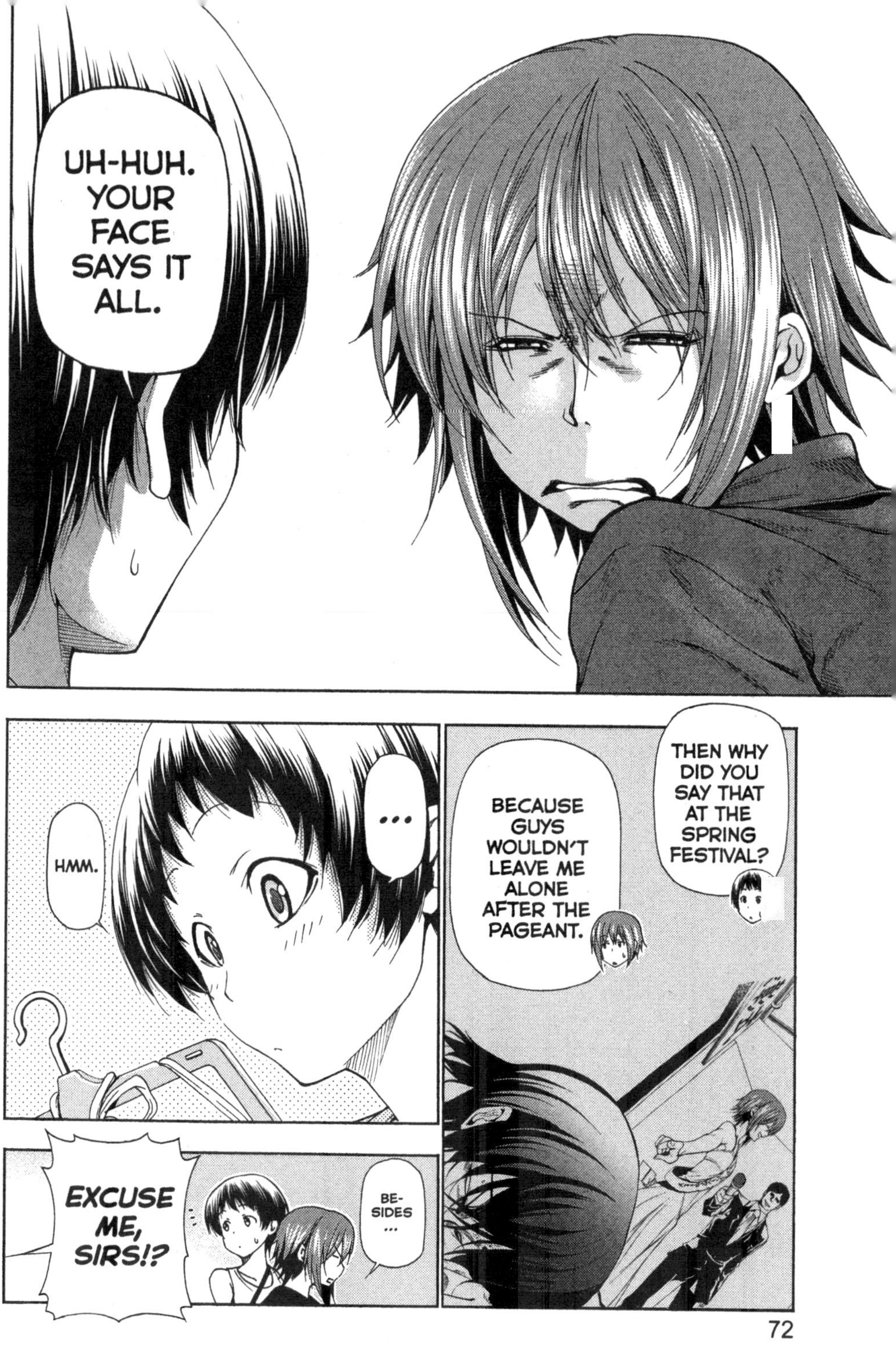
UH-HUH. YOUR FACE SAYS IT ALL.
THEN WHY DID YOU SAY THAT AT THE SPRING FESTIVAL?
BECAUSE GUYS WOULDN'T LEAVE ME ALONE AFTER THE PAGEANT.
...
HMM.
BE-SIDES ...
EXCUSE ME, SIRS!?

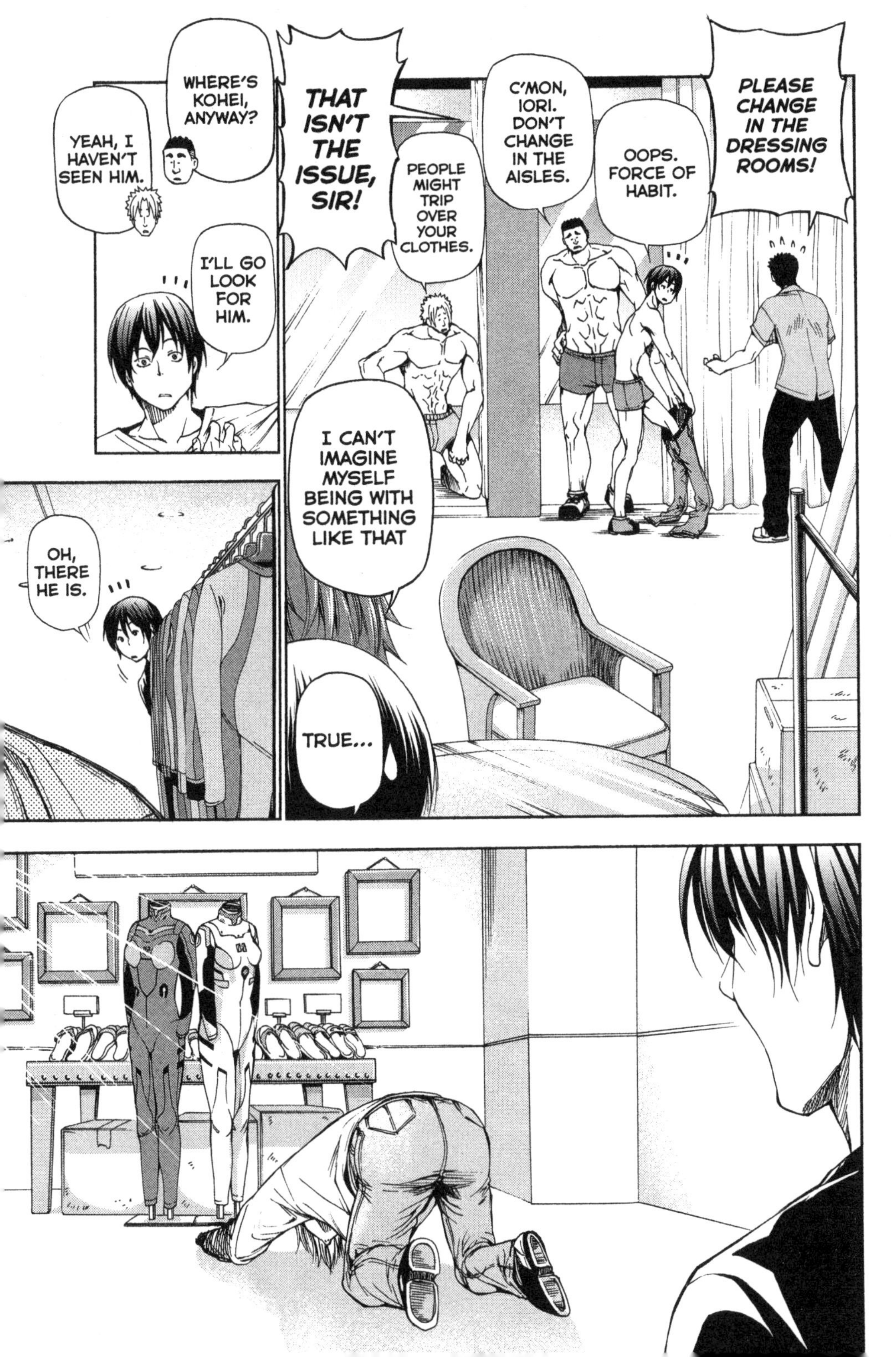
PLEASE CHANGE IN THE DRESSING ROOMS!
OOPS. FORCE OF HABIT.
C'MON, IORI. DON'T CHANGE IN THE AISLES.
PEOPLE MIGHT TRIP OVER YOUR CLOTHES.
THAT ISN'T THE ISSUE, SIR!
I CAN'T IMAGINE MYSELF BEING WITH SOMETHING LIKE THAT
TRUE...
WHERE'S KOHEI, ANYWAY?
YEAH, I HAVEN'T SEEN HIM.
I'LL GO LOOK FOR HIM.
OH, THERE HE IS.

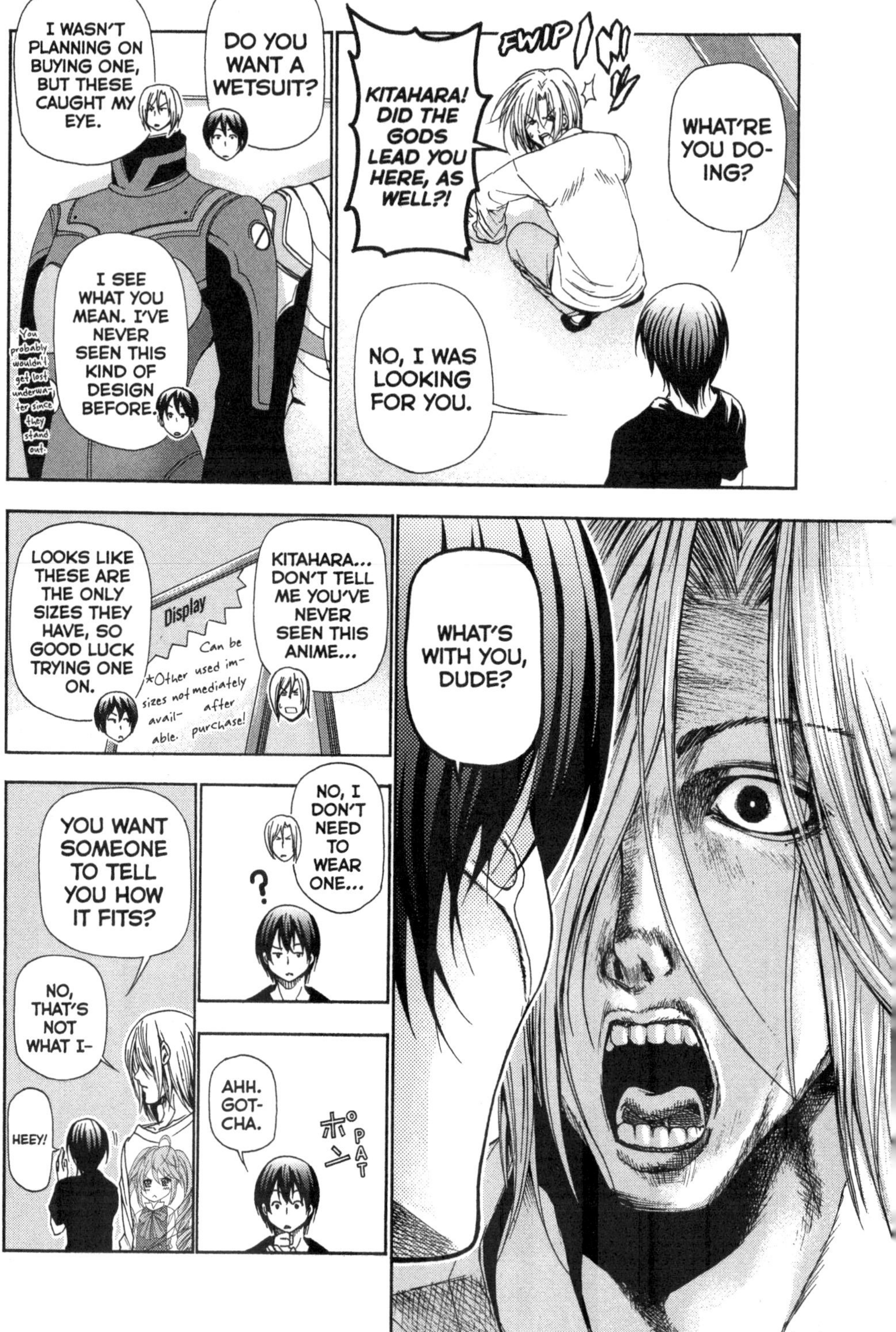
FWIP
!
KITAHARA! DID THE GODS LEAD YOU HERE, AS WELL?!
WHAT'RE YOU DO-ING?
NO, I WAS LOOKING FOR YOU.
DO YOU WANT A WETSUIT?
I WASN'T PLANNING ON BUYING ONE, BUT THESE CAUGHT MY EYE.
I SEE WHAT YOU MEAN. I'VE NEVER SEEN THIS KIND OF DESIGN BEFORE.
You probably wouldn't get lost underwa-ter since they stand out.
WHAT'S WITH YOU, DUDE?
KITAHARA... DON'T TELL ME YOU'VE NEVER SEEN THIS ANIME...
Display
LOOKS LIKE THESE ARE THE ONLY SIZES THEY HAVE, SO GOOD LUCK TRYING ONE ON.
Can be used im-mediately after purchase!
*Other sizes not avail-able.
NO, I DON'T NEED TO WEAR ONE...
?
AHH. GOT-CHA.
ポン
PAT
YOU WANT SOMEONE TO TELL YOU HOW IT FITS?
NO, THAT'S NOT WHAT I-
HEEY!

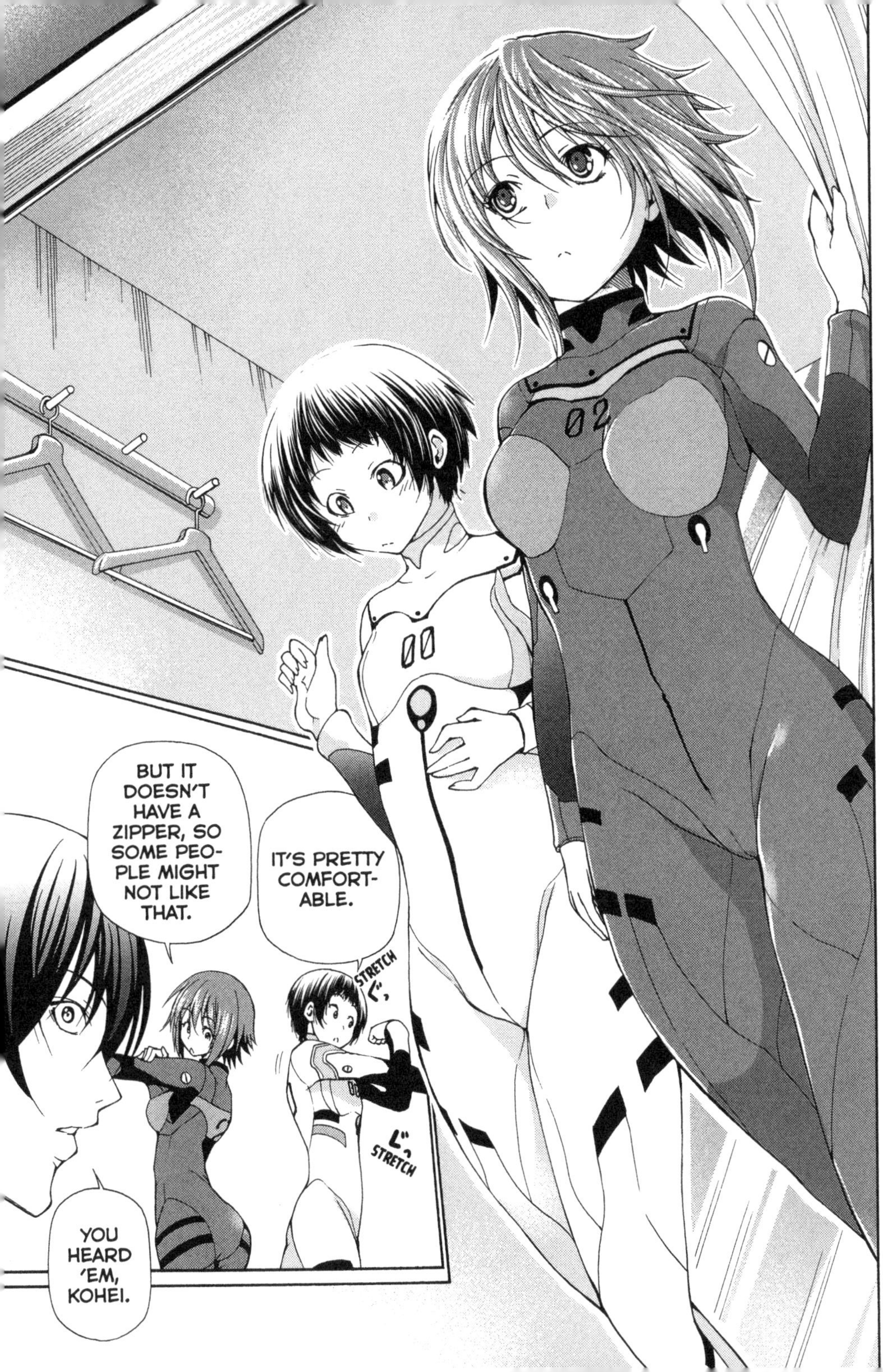
IT'S PRETTY COMFORTABLE.
BUT IT DOESN'T HAVE A ZIPPER, SO SOME PEOPLE MIGHT NOT LIKE THAT.
STRETCH
STRETCH
YOU HEARD 'EM, KOHEI.

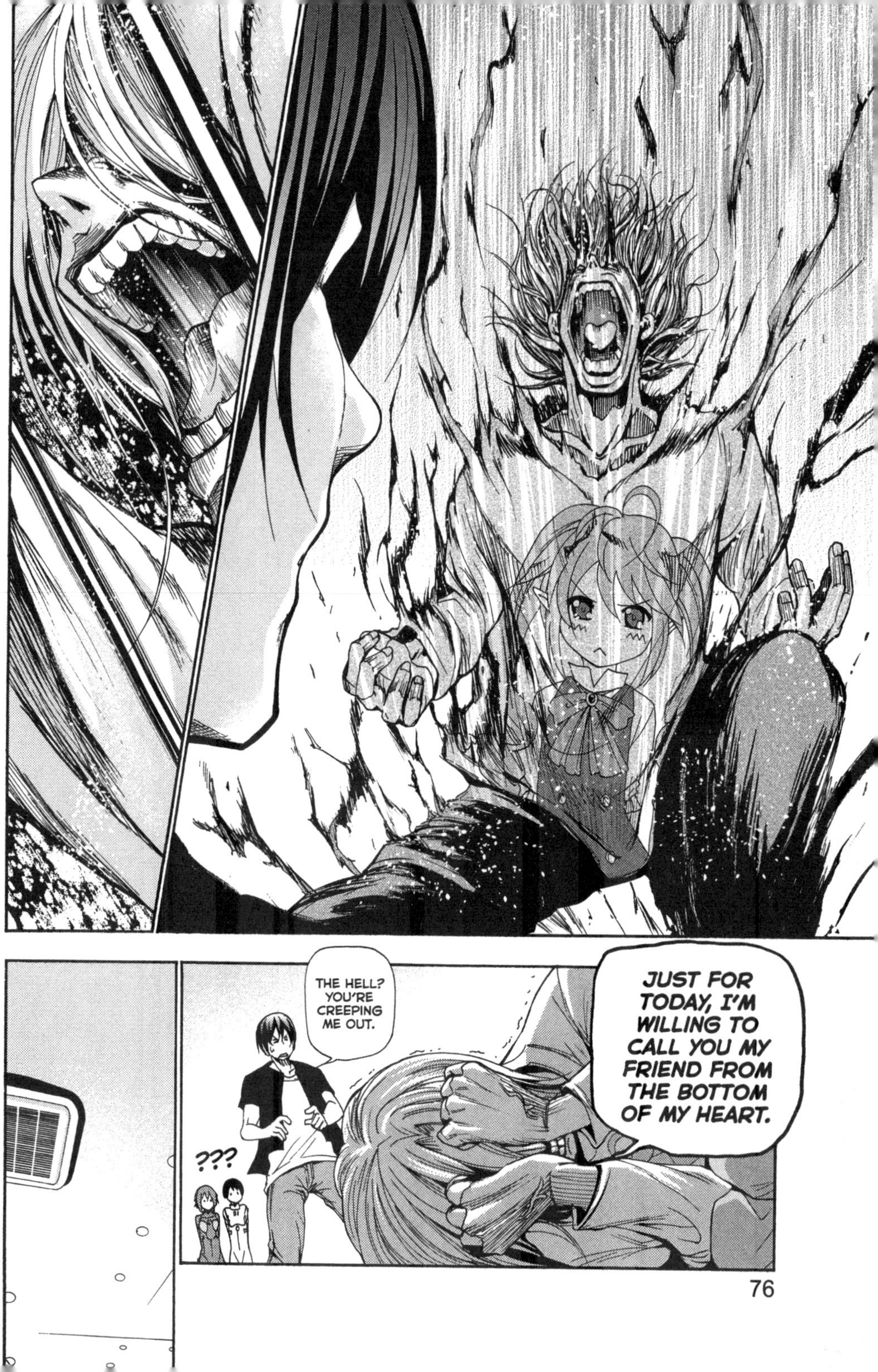
JUST FOR TODAY, I'M WILLING TO CALL YOU MY FRIEND FROM THE BOTTOM OF MY HEART.
THE HELL? YOU'RE CREEPING ME OUT.
???

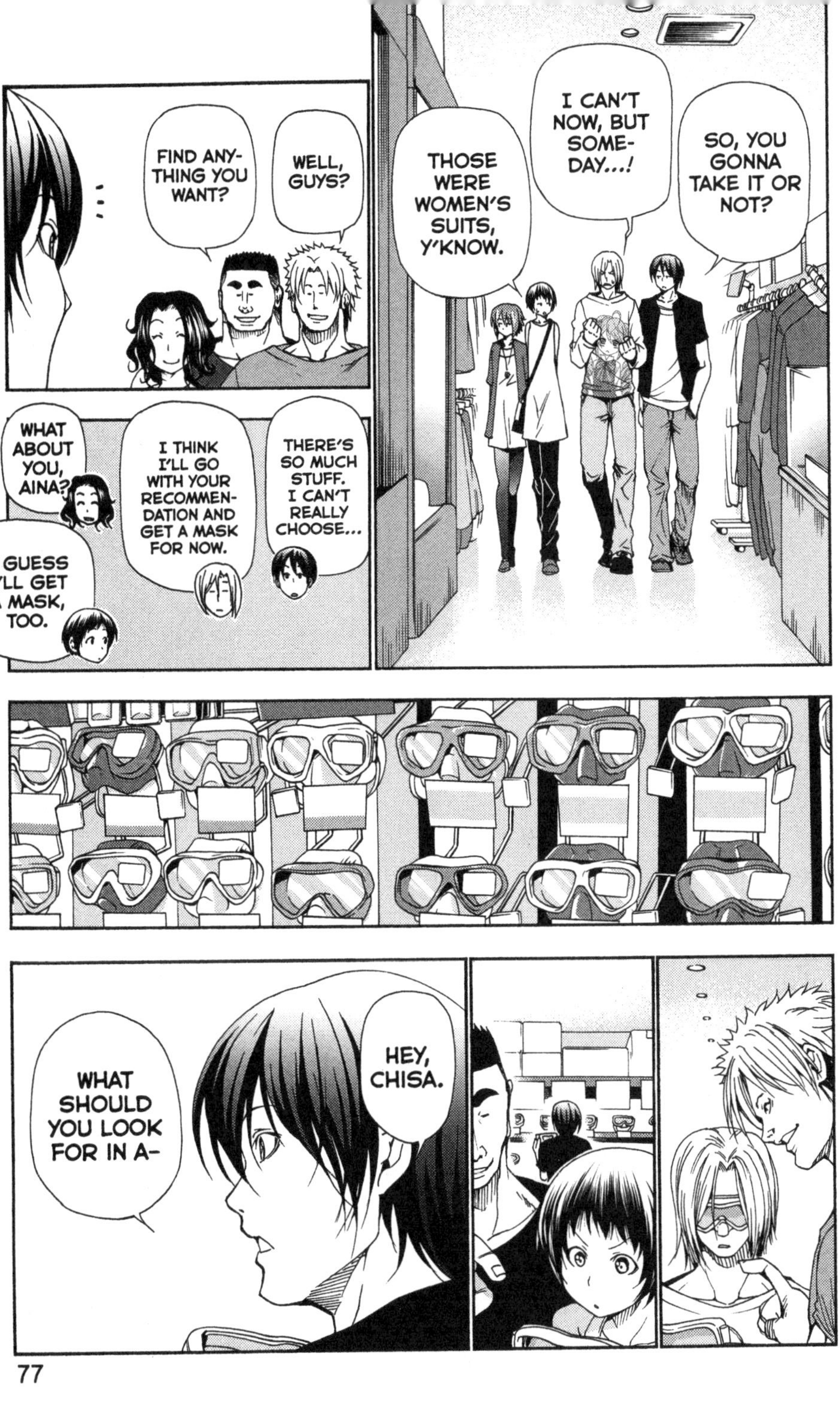
SO, YOU GONNA TAKE IT OR NOT?
I CAN'T NOW, BUT SOME-DAY...!
THOSE WERE WOMEN'S SUITS, Y'KNOW.
WELL, GUYS?
FIND ANY-THING YOU WANT?
THERE'S SO MUCH STUFF. I CAN'T REALLY CHOOSE...
I THINK I'LL GO WITH YOUR RECOMMEN-DATION AND GET A MASK FOR NOW.
WHAT ABOUT YOU, AINA?
I GUESS I'LL GET A MASK, TOO.
HEY, CHISA.
WHAT SHOULD YOU LOOK FOR IN A-

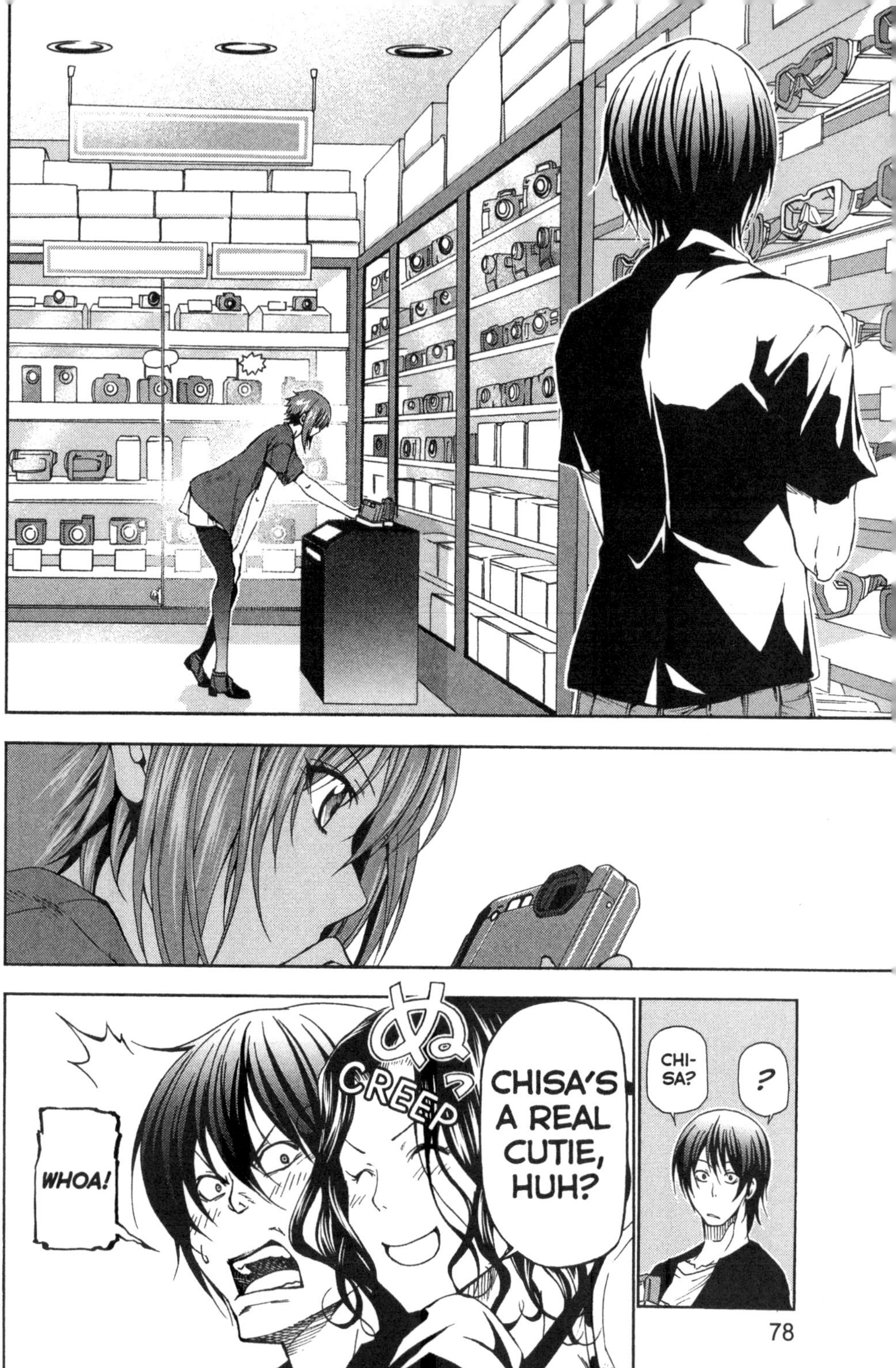
CHI-SA?
?
ぬっ
CREEP
CHISA'S A REAL CUTIE, HUH?
WHOA!

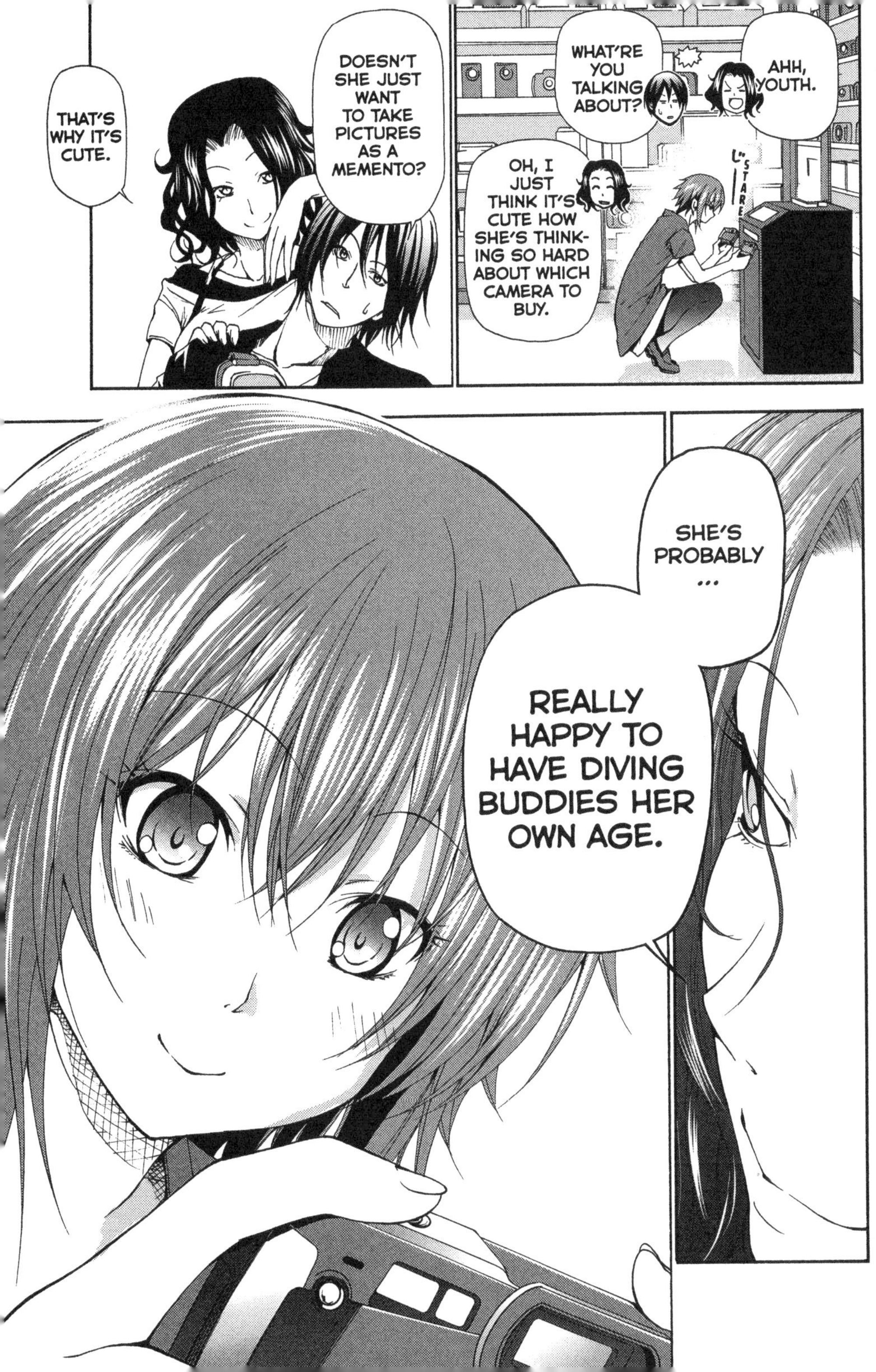
AHH, YOUTH.
WHAT'RE YOU TALKING ABOUT?
STARE
OH, I JUST THINK IT'S CUTE HOW SHE'S THINKING SO HARD ABOUT WHICH CAMERA TO BUY.
DOESN'T SHE JUST WANT TO TAKE PICTURES AS A MEMENTO?
THAT'S WHY IT'S CUTE.
SHE'S PROBABLY ...
REALLY HAPPY TO HAVE DIVING BUDDIES HER OWN AGE.

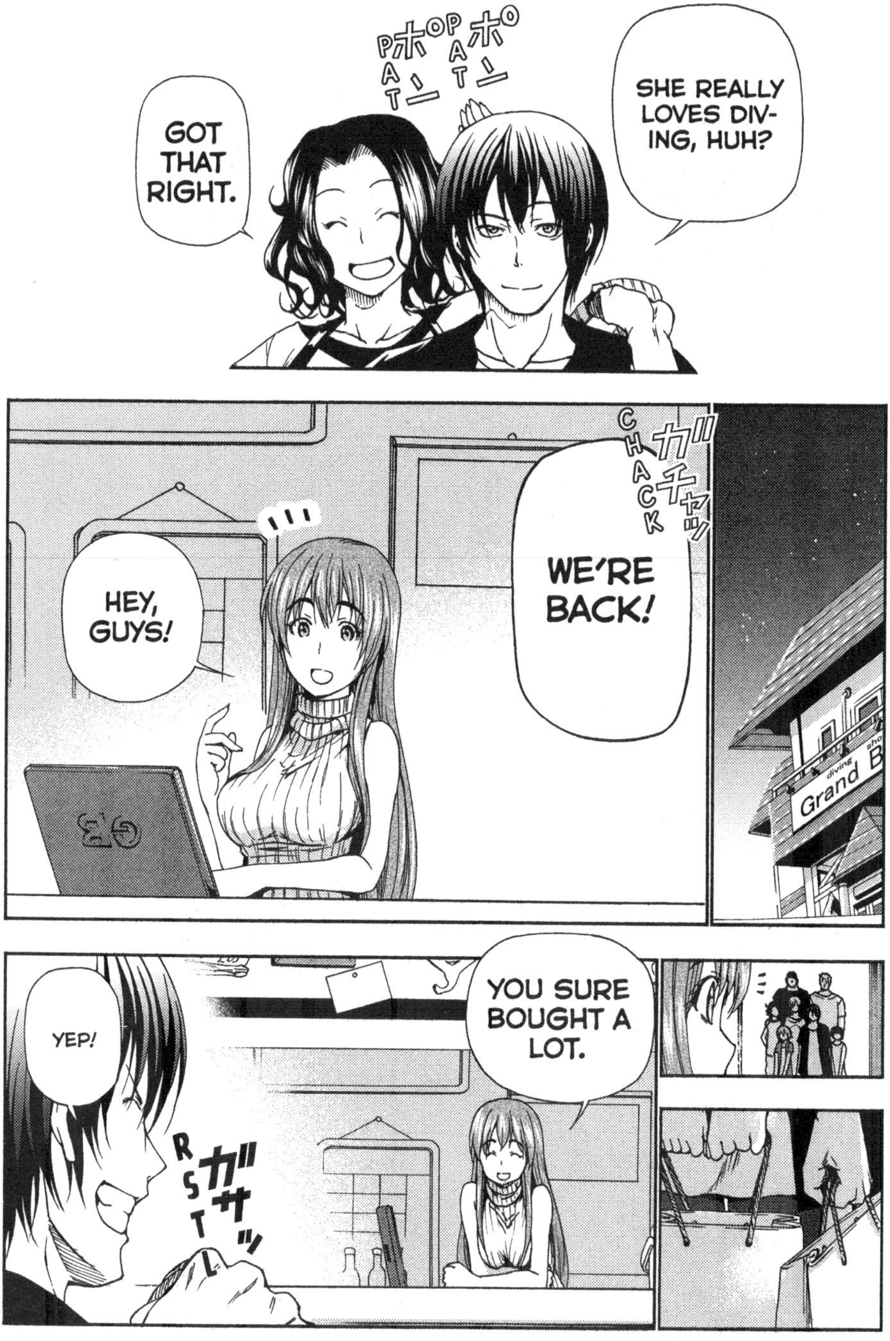
SHE REALLY LOVES DIVING, HUH?
PAT PAT
GOT THAT RIGHT.
CHACK
WE'RE BACK!
HEY, GUYS!
YOU SURE BOUGHT A LOT.
YEP!
RSTL

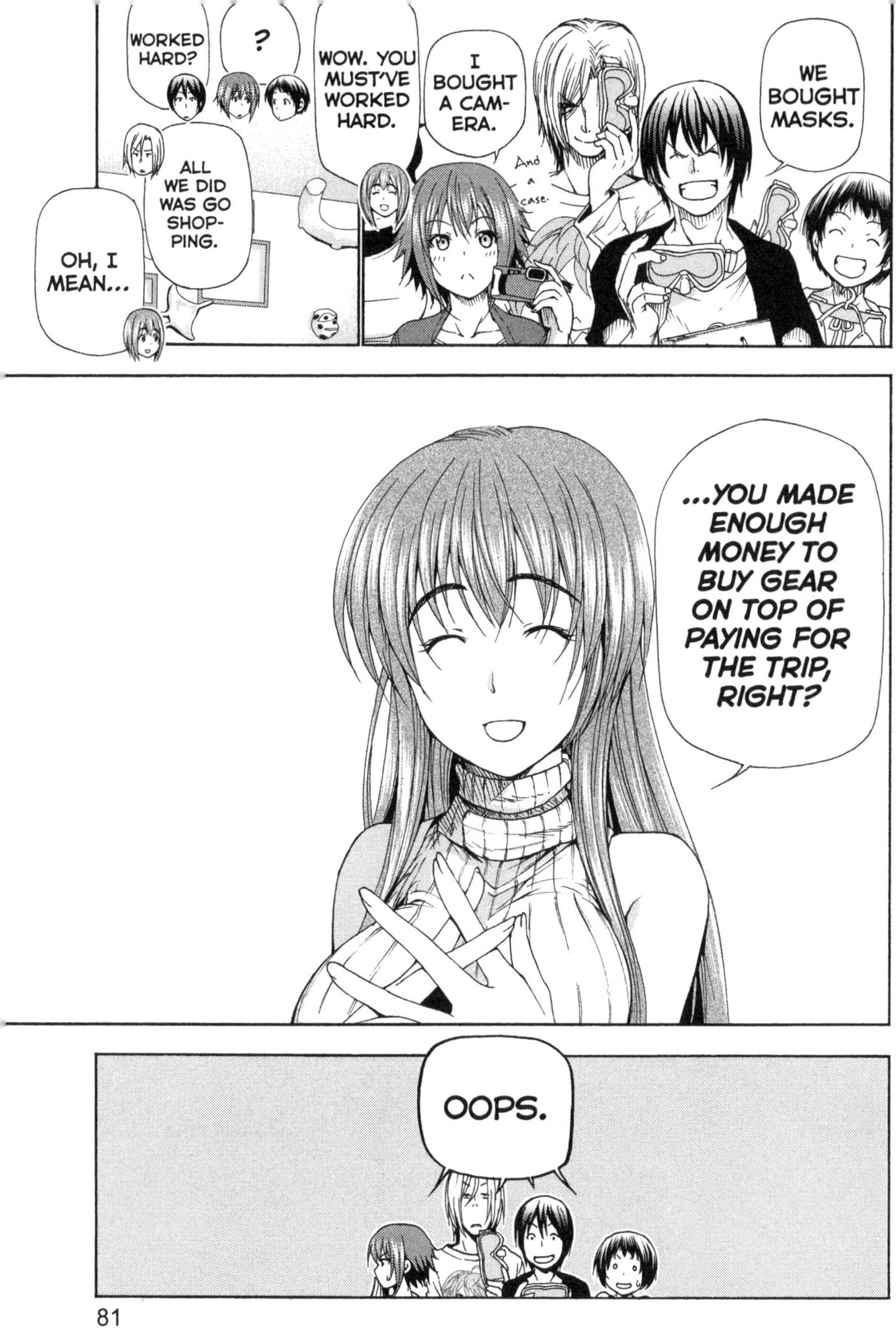
WE BOUGHT MASKS.
I BOUGHT A CAM-ERA.
And a case.
WOW. YOU MUST'VE WORKED HARD.
?
WORKED HARD?
ALL WE DID WAS GO SHOP-PING.
OH, I MEAN...
...YOU MADE ENOUGH MONEY TO BUY GEAR ON TOP OF PAYING FOR THE TRIP, RIGHT?
OOPS.

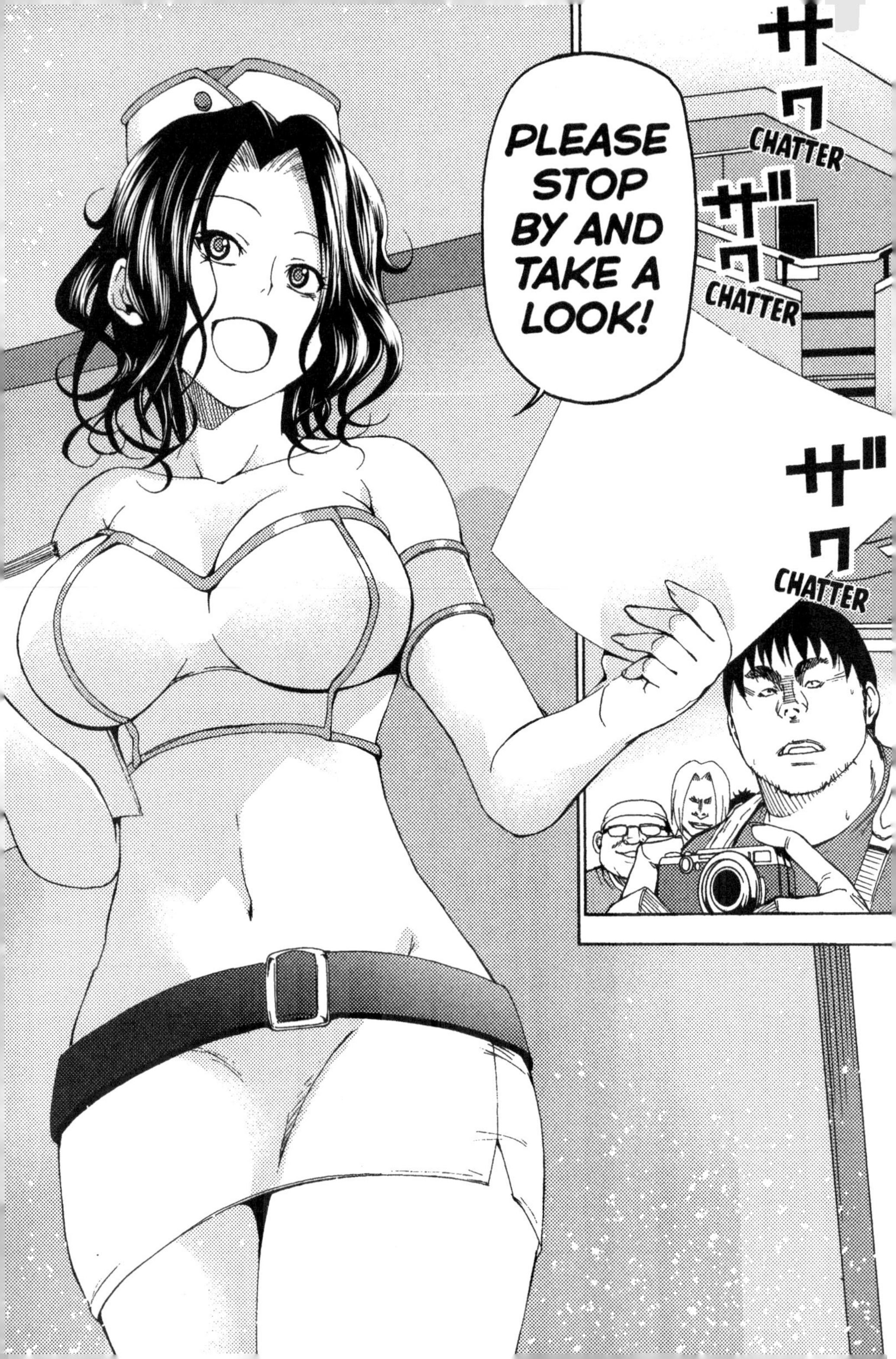
サワ
CHATTER
PLEASE STOP BY AND TAKE A LOOK!
ザワ
CHATTER
ザワ
CHATTER

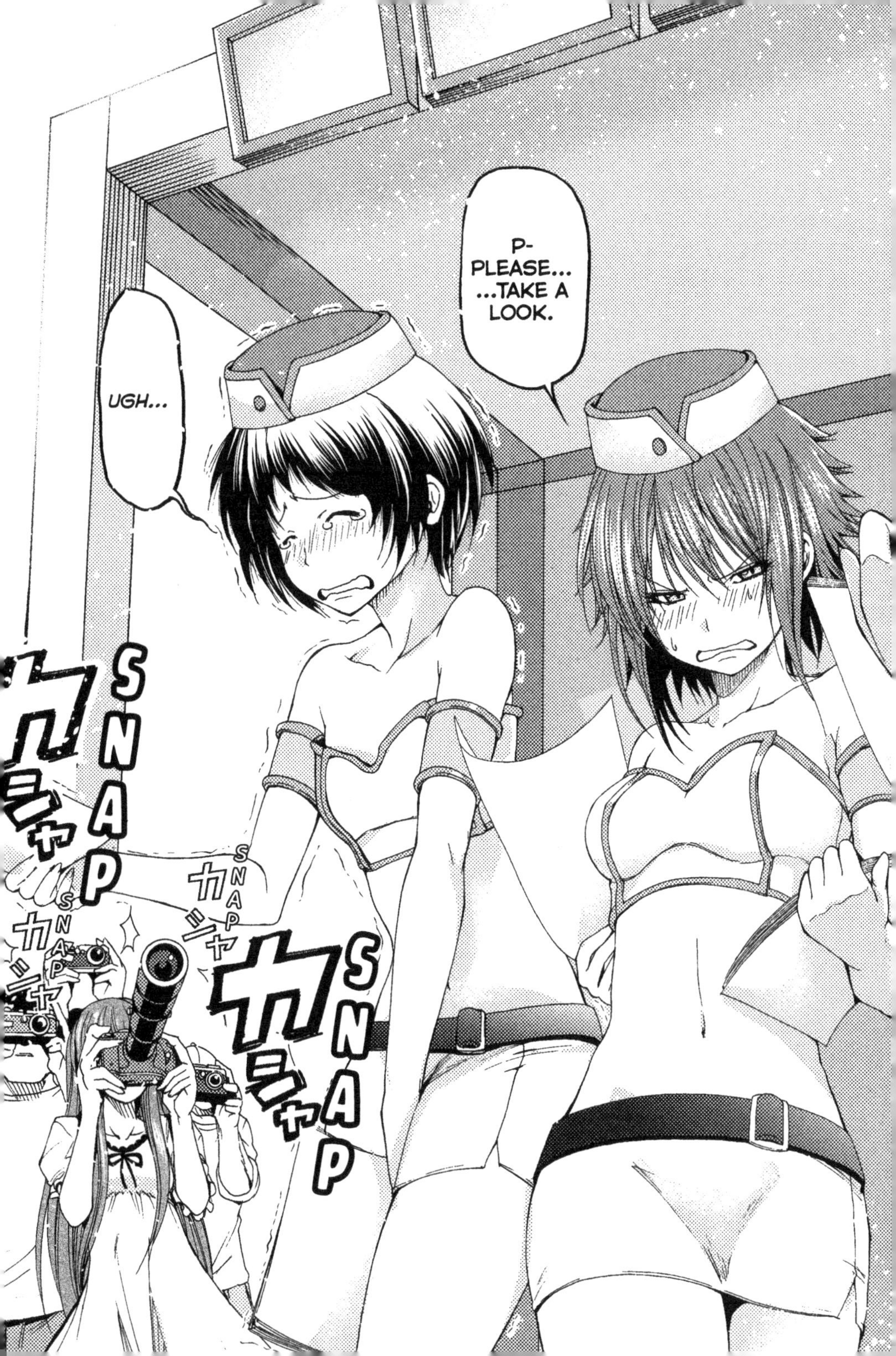
P-PLEASE... ...TAKE A LOOK.
UGH...
カシャ SNAP
カシャ SNAP
カシャ SNAP
カシャ SNAP

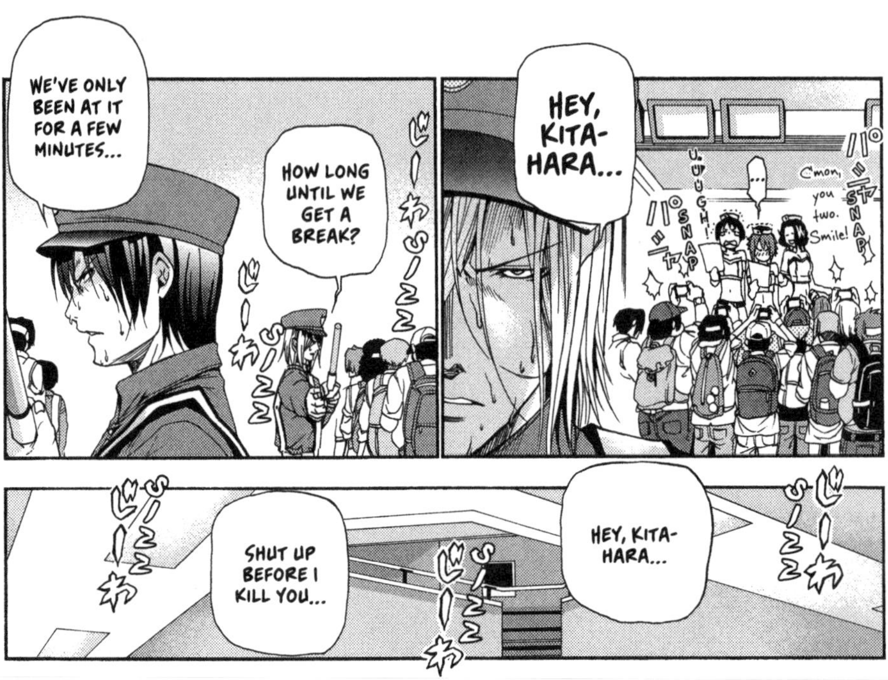
HEY, KITA-HARA...
SNAP
C'mon you two. Smile!
UUUGH!
...
SNAP
WE'VE ONLY BEEN AT IT FOR A FEW MINUTES...
SIZZZ
HOW LONG UNTIL WE GET A BREAK?
SIZZZ
SIZZZ
HEY, KITA-HARA...
SIZZZ
SHUT UP BEFORE I KILL YOU...
SIZZZ

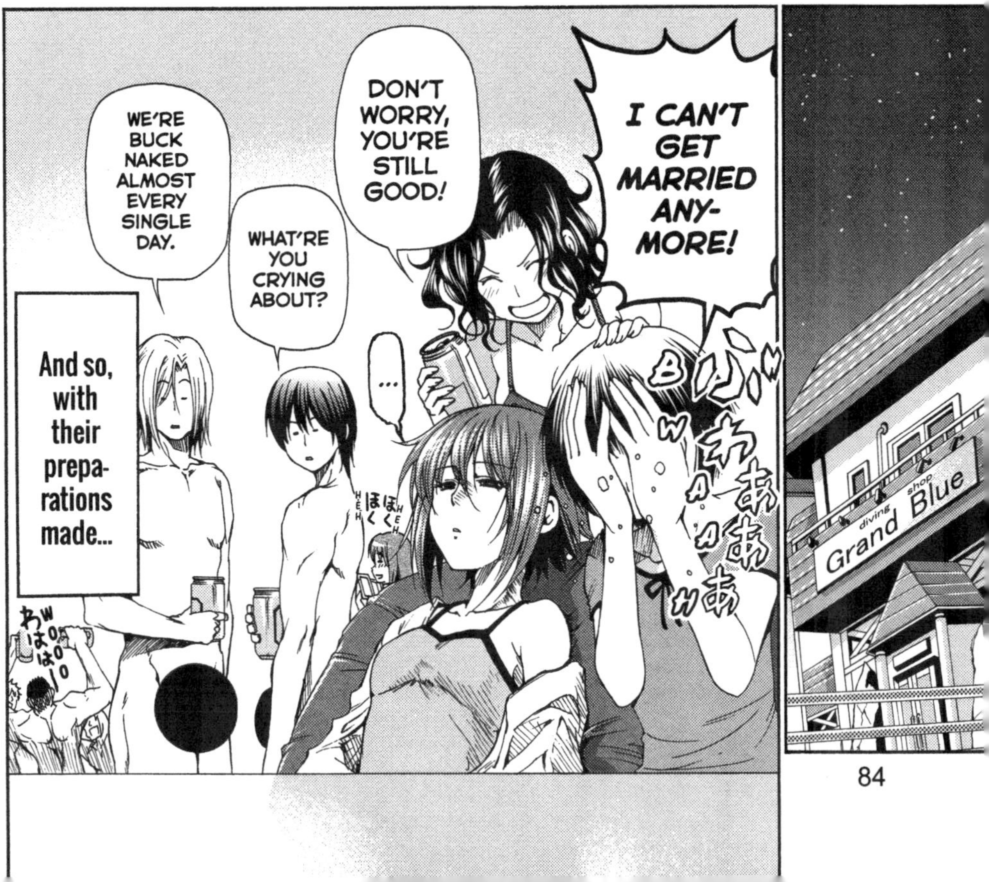
I CAN'T GET MARRIED ANY-MORE!
DON'T WORRY, YOU'RE STILL GOOD!
WHAT'RE YOU CRYING ABOUT?
WE'RE BUCK NAKED ALMOST EVERY SINGLE DAY.
...
BWAAAH
diving shop Grand Blue
HEH HEH
And so, with their prepa-rations made...
WOOOO!

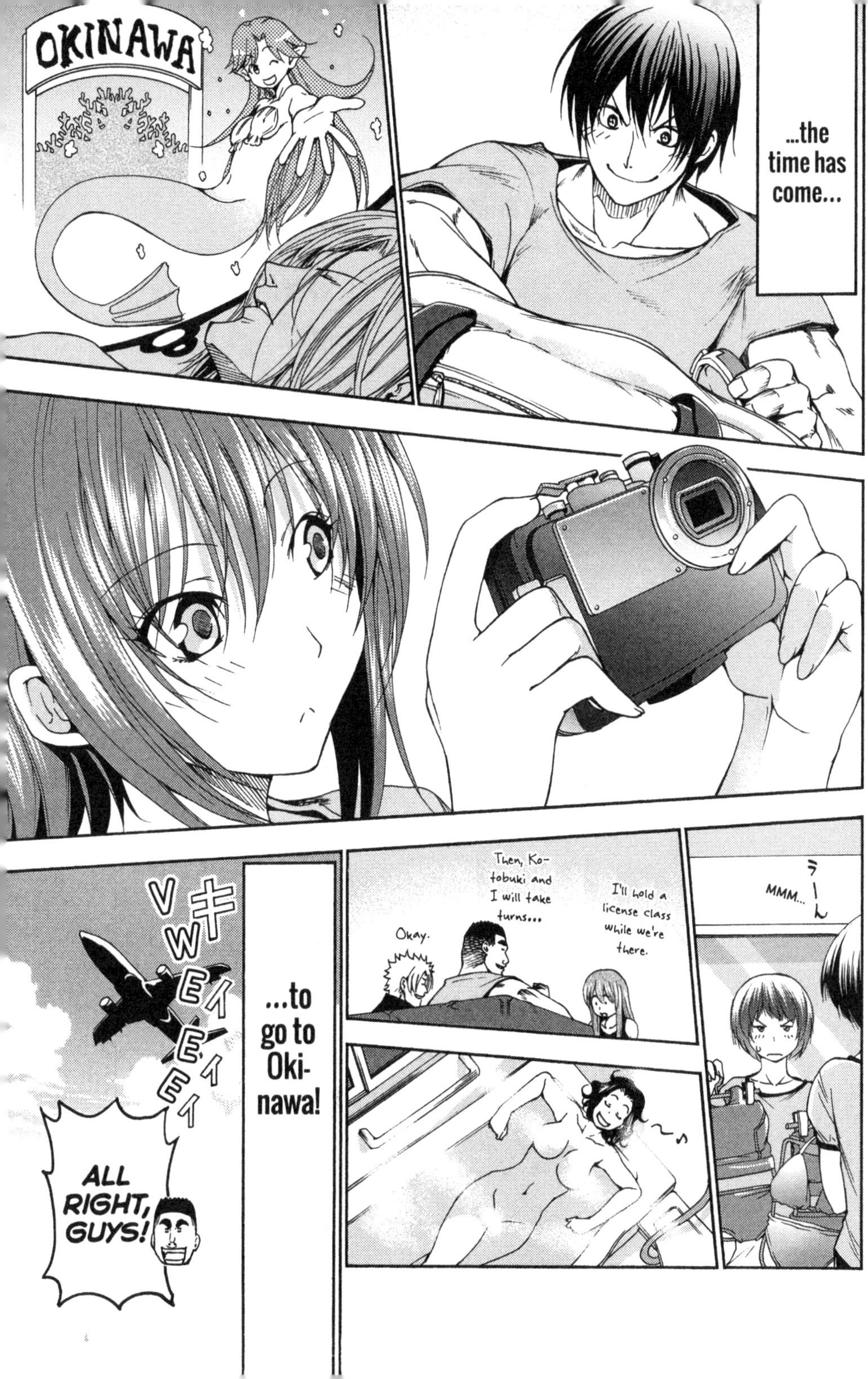
...the time has come...
OKINAWA
MMM...
う～ん
Then, Ko-tobuki and I will take turns...
I'll hold a license class while we're there.
Okay.
~♪
...to go to Oki-nawa!
VWEEE
キイイイ
ALL RIGHT, GUYS!

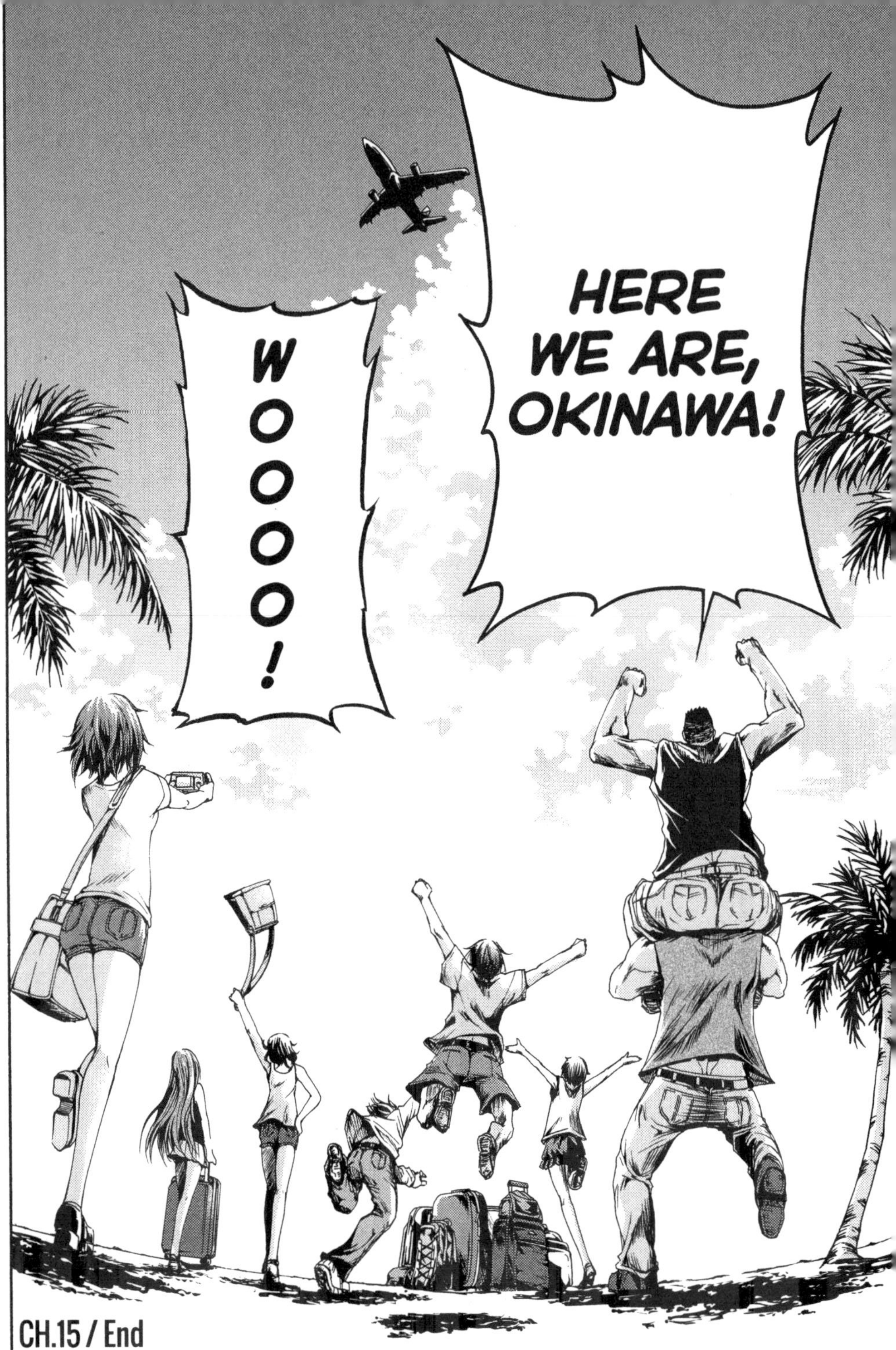
HERE WE ARE, OKINAWA!
WOOOO!

CH.15 / End

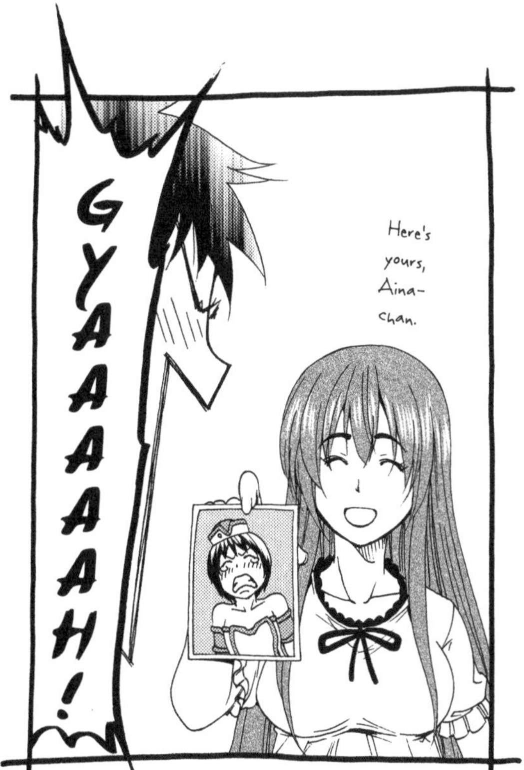
Here's yours, Aina-chan.
GYAAAAAAAH!

Grand Blue
Dreaming

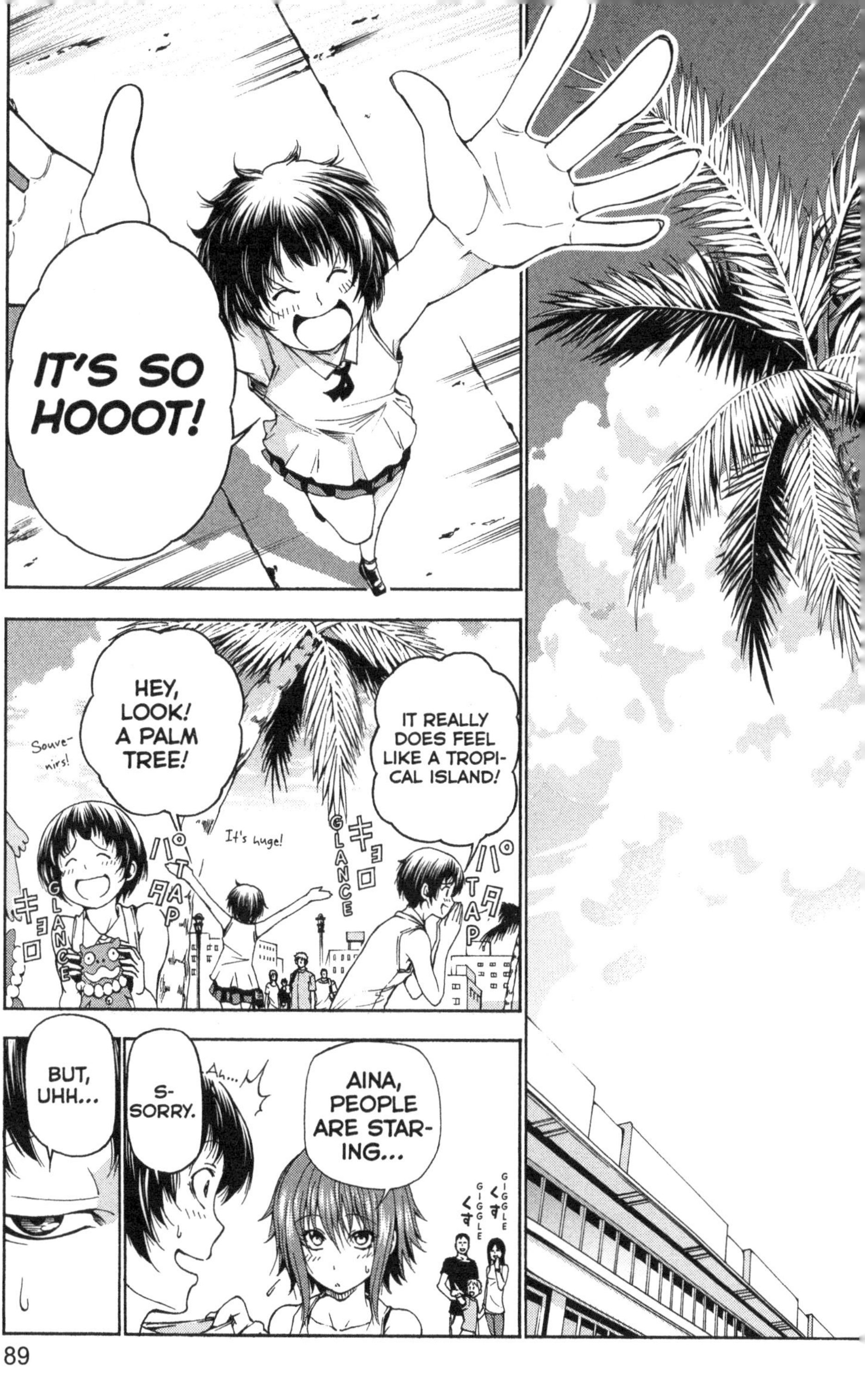
IT'S SO HOOOT!
IT REALLY DOES FEEL LIKE A TROPICAL ISLAND!
パタ TAP
キョロ GLANCE
It's huge!
HEY, LOOK! A PALM TREE!
パタ TAP
キョロ GLANCE
Souvenirs!
くす GIGGLE
くす GIGGLE
AINA, PEOPLE ARE STARING...
Ah...
S-SORRY.
BUT, UHH...

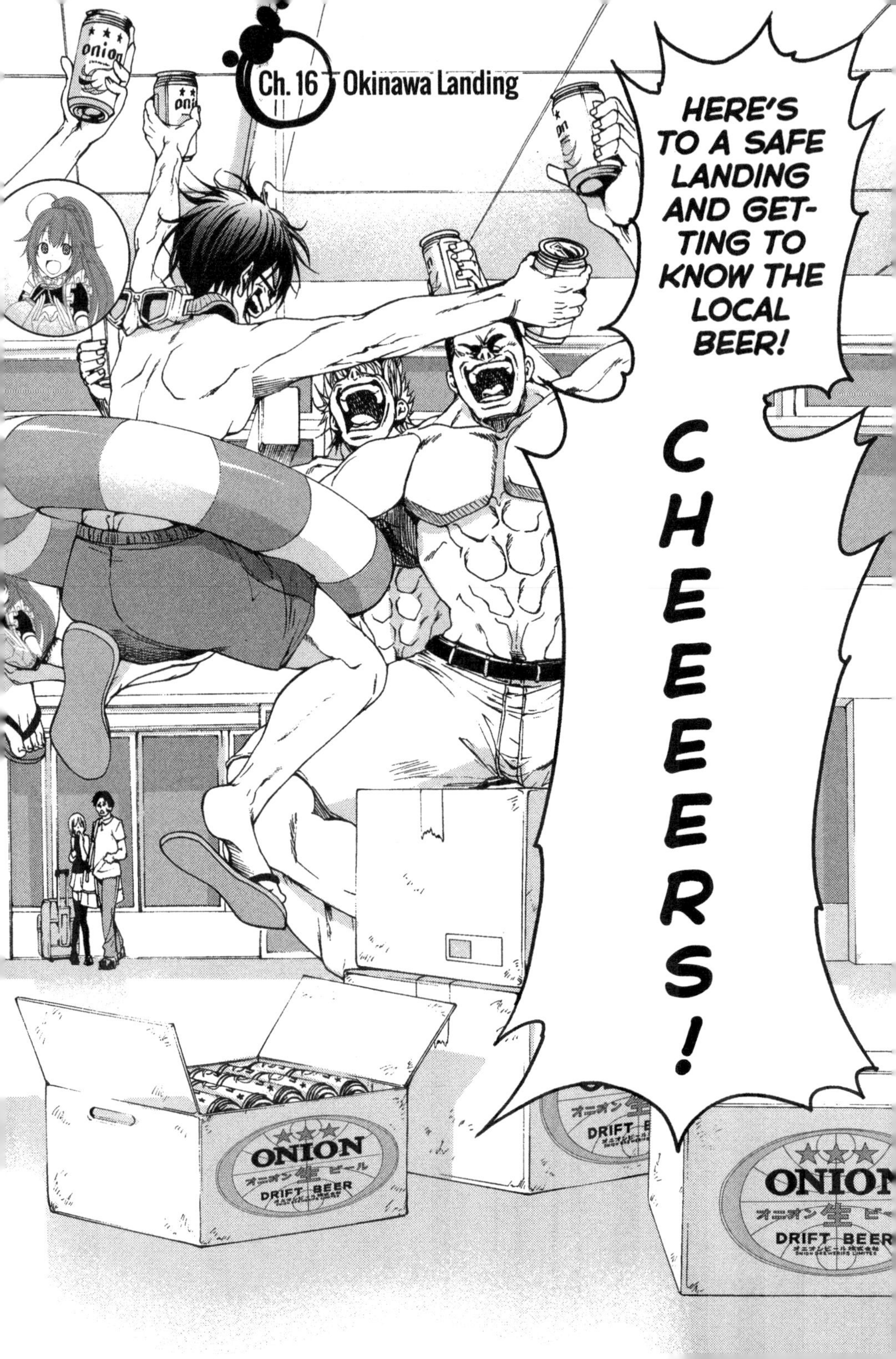
Ch. 16 Okinawa Landing
HERE'S TO A SAFE LANDING AND GETTING TO KNOW THE LOCAL BEER!
CHEEEEERS!
ONION
オニオン生ビール
DRIFT BEER
ONION
DRIFT BEER

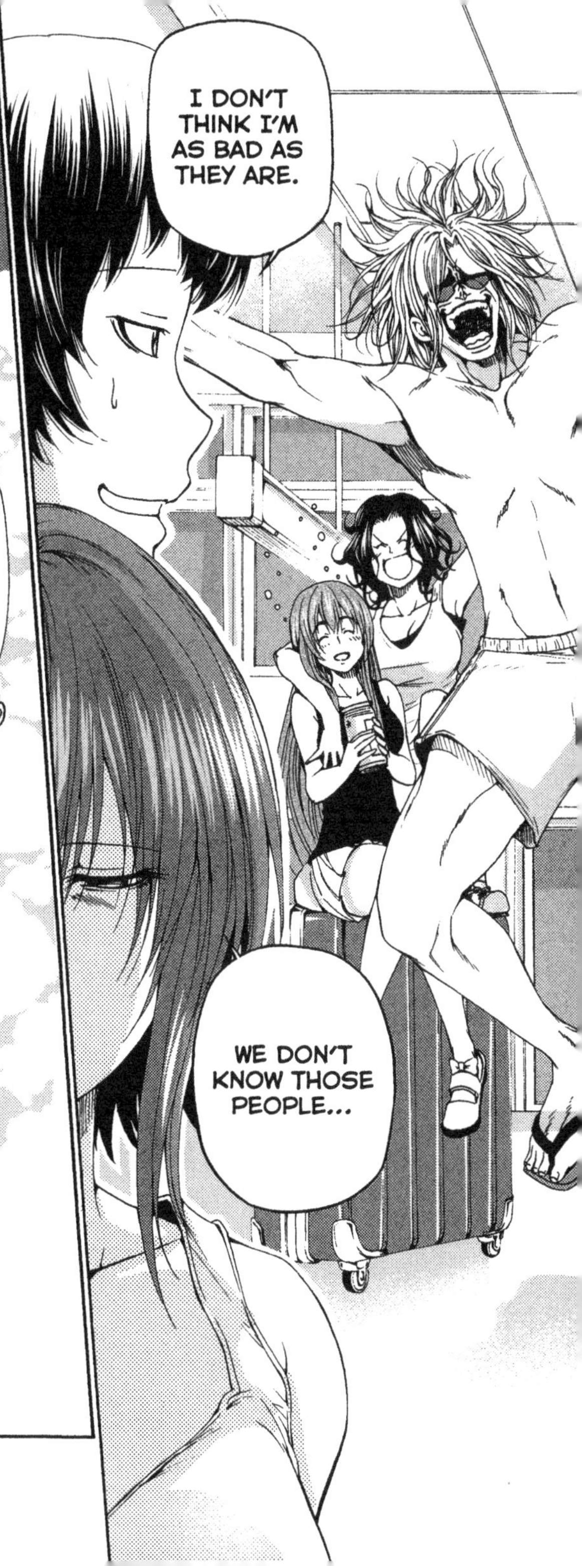
I DON'T THINK I'M AS BAD AS THEY ARE.
WE DON'T KNOW THOSE PEOPLE...

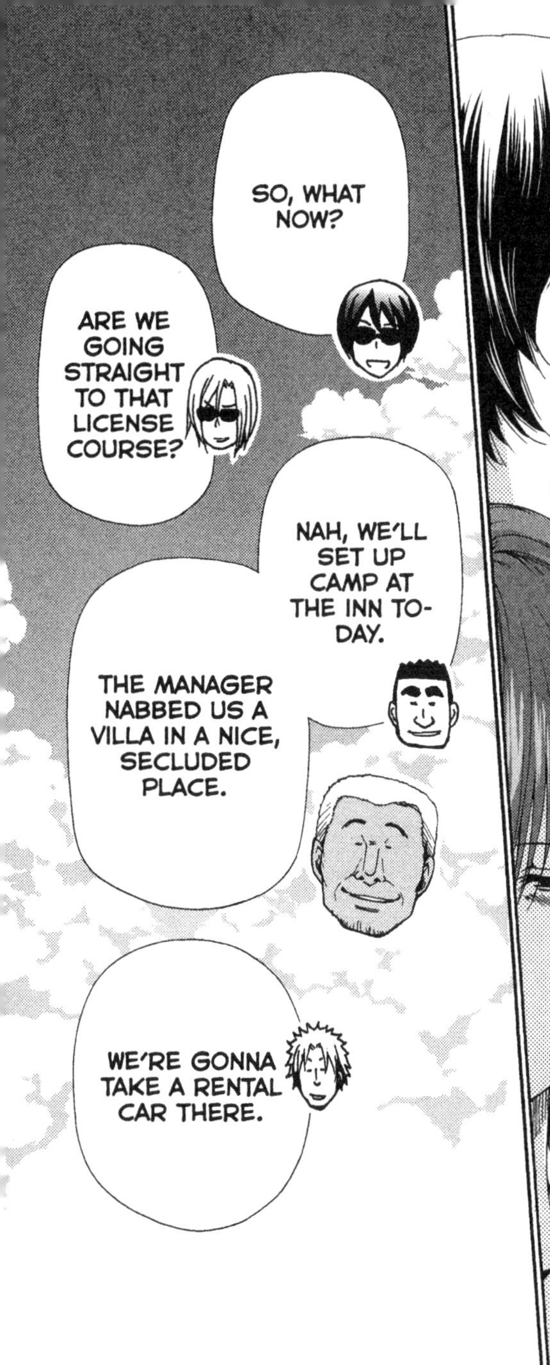
SO, WHAT NOW?
ARE WE GOING STRAIGHT TO THAT LICENSE COURSE?
NAH, WE'LL SET UP CAMP AT THE INN TO-DAY.
THE MANAGER NABBED US A VILLA IN A NICE, SECLUDED PLACE.
WE'RE GONNA TAKE A RENTAL CAR THERE.

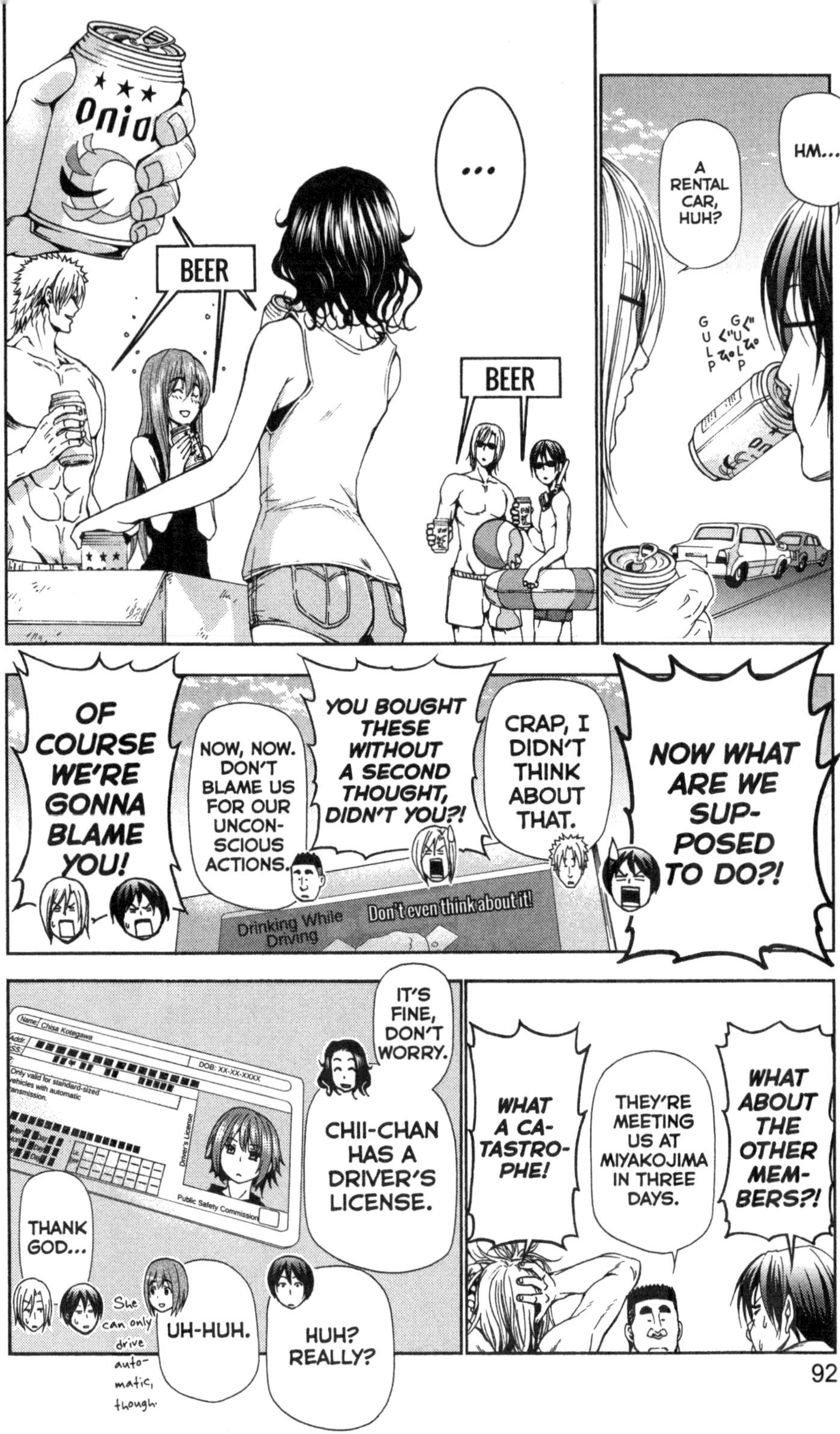
HM...
A RENTAL CAR, HUH?
GULP GULP
...
BEER
BEER
NOW WHAT ARE WE SUP-POSED TO DO?!
CRAP, I DIDN'T THINK ABOUT THAT.
YOU BOUGHT THESE WITHOUT A SECOND THOUGHT, DIDN'T YOU?!
NOW, NOW. DON'T BLAME US FOR OUR UNCON-SCIOUS ACTIONS.
OF COURSE WE'RE GONNA BLAME YOU!
Drinking While Driving
Don't even think about it!
WHAT ABOUT THE OTHER MEM-BERS?!
THEY'RE MEETING US AT MIYAKOJIMA IN THREE DAYS.
WHAT A CA-TASTRO-PHE!
IT'S FINE, DON'T WORRY.
CHII-CHAN HAS A DRIVER'S LICENSE.
Name: Chisa Kotegawa
Addr:
SS:
DOB: XX-XX-XXXX
Only valid for standard-sized vehicles with automatic transmission.
Driver's License
Public Safety Commission
HUH? REALLY?
UH-HUH.
She can only drive auto-matic, though.
THANK GOD...

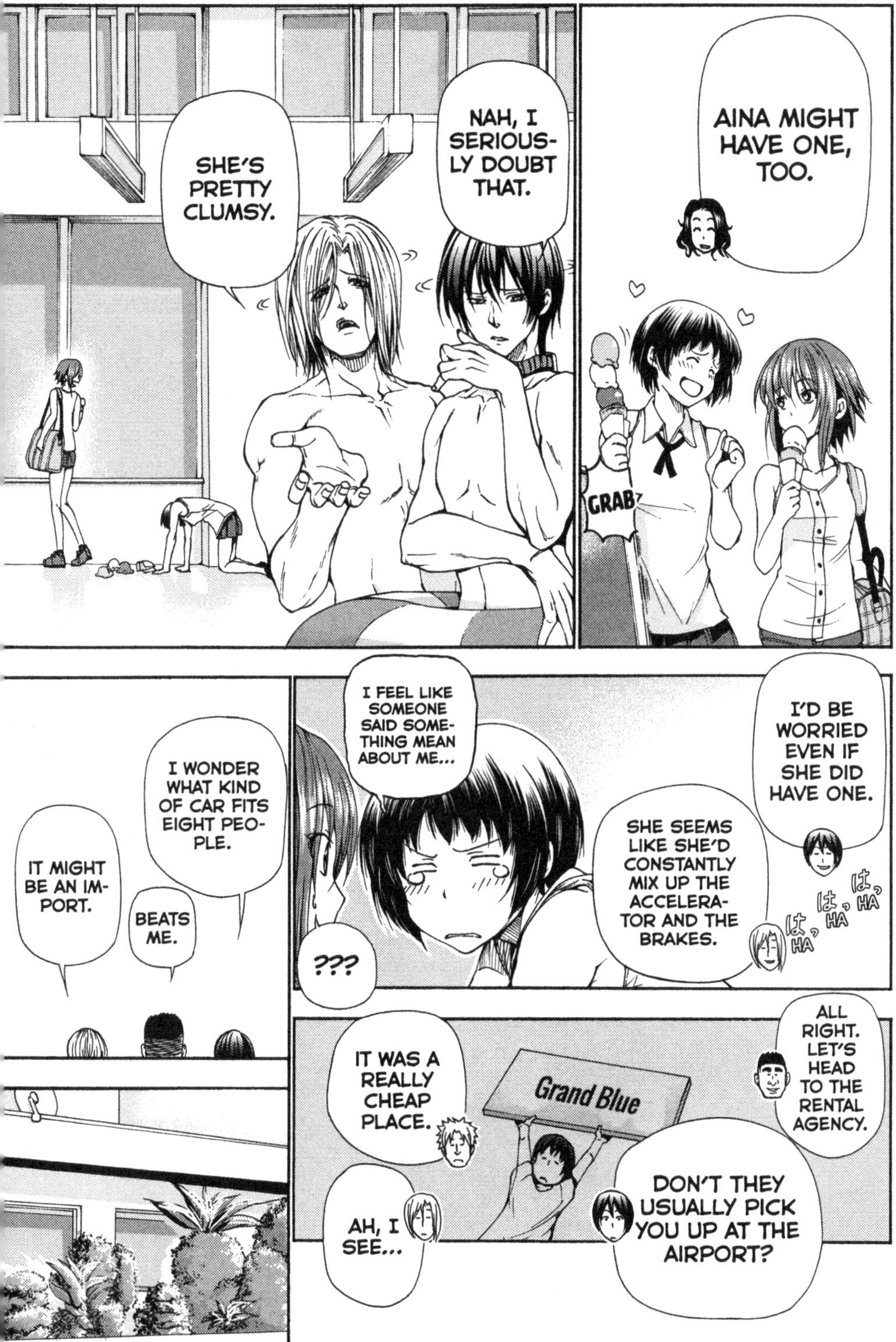
AINA MIGHT HAVE ONE, TOO.
GRAB
NAH, I SERIOUS-LY DOUBT THAT.
SHE'S PRETTY CLUMSY.
I'D BE WORRIED EVEN IF SHE DID HAVE ONE.
SHE SEEMS LIKE SHE'D CONSTANTLY MIX UP THE ACCELERA-TOR AND THE BRAKES.
HA HA HA
I FEEL LIKE SOMEONE SAID SOME-THING MEAN ABOUT ME...
???
ALL RIGHT. LET'S HEAD TO THE RENTAL AGENCY.
IT WAS A REALLY CHEAP PLACE.
Grand Blue
DON'T THEY USUALLY PICK YOU UP AT THE AIRPORT?
AH, I SEE...
I WONDER WHAT KIND OF CAR FITS EIGHT PEO-PLE.
BEATS ME.
IT MIGHT BE AN IM-PORT.

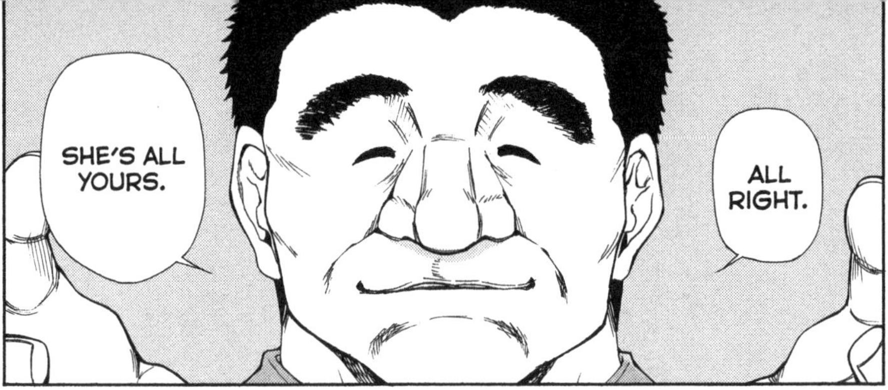
ALL RIGHT.
SHE'S ALL YOURS.
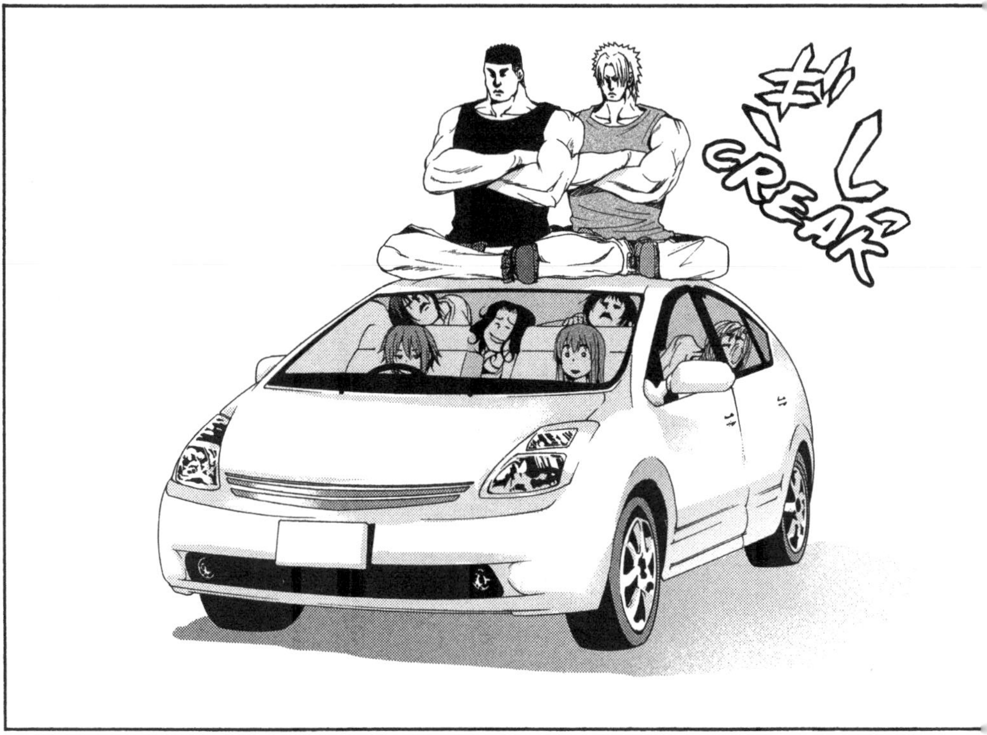
CREAK
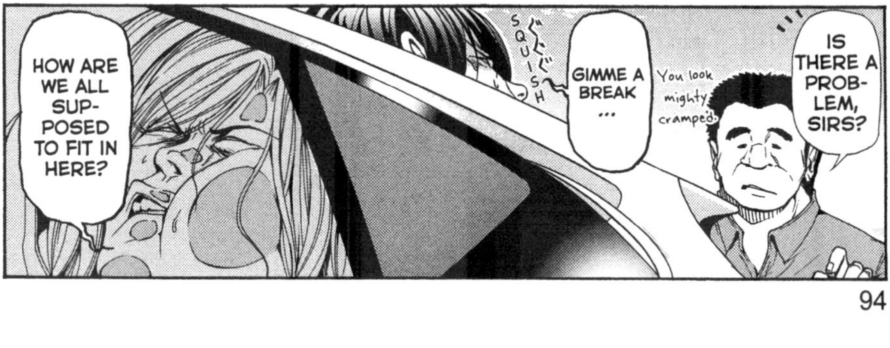
IS THERE A PROBLEM, SIRS?
You look mighty cramped.
GIMME A BREAK ...
SQUISH
HOW ARE WE ALL SUPPOSED TO FIT IN HERE?

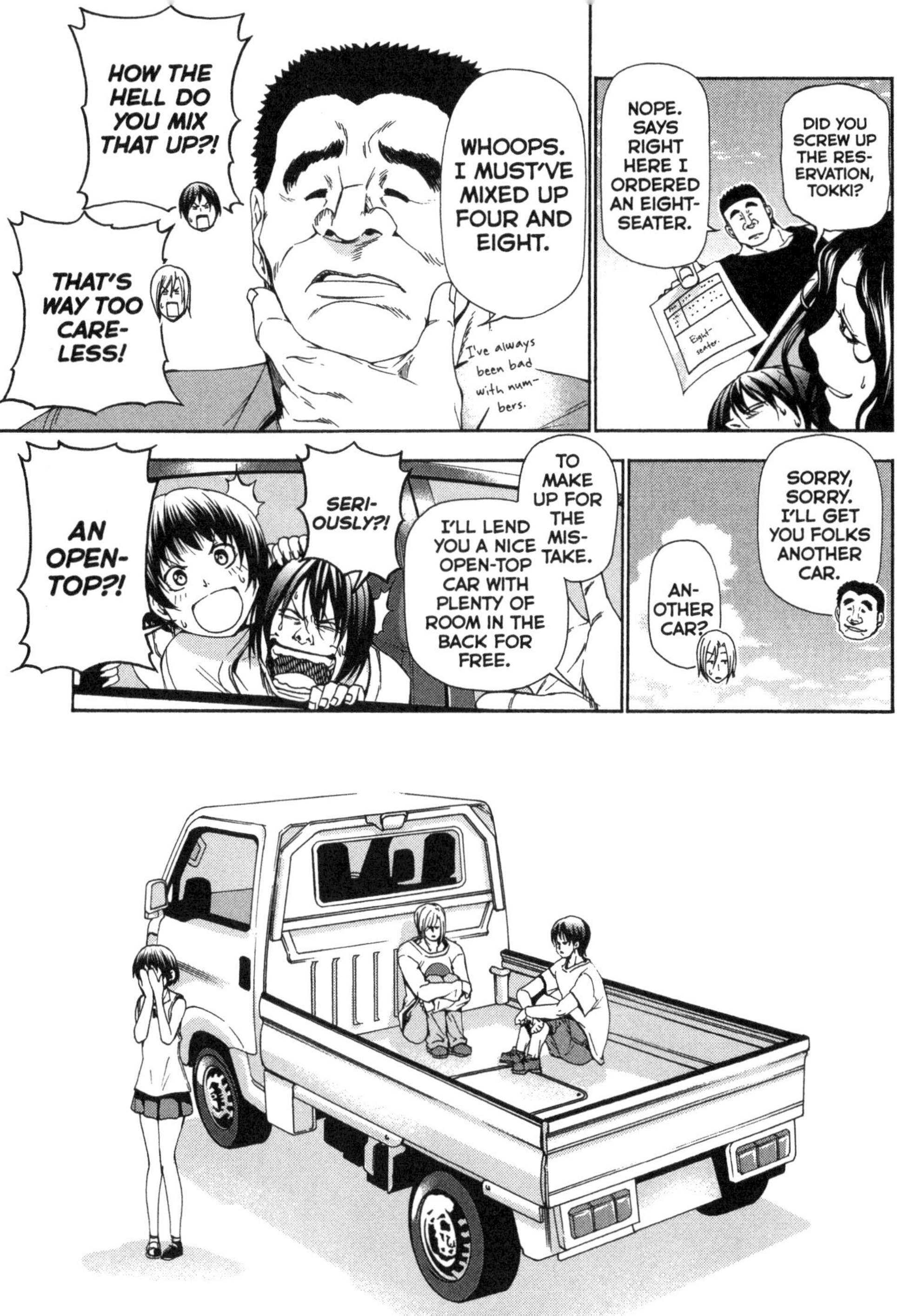
DID YOU SCREW UP THE RESERVATION, TOKKI?
NOPE. SAYS RIGHT HERE I ORDERED AN EIGHT-SEATER.
Eight-seater.
WHOOPS. I MUST'VE MIXED UP FOUR AND EIGHT.
I've always been bad with numbers.
HOW THE HELL DO YOU MIX THAT UP?!
THAT'S WAY TOO CARELESS!
SORRY, SORRY. I'LL GET YOU FOLKS ANOTHER CAR.
ANOTHER CAR?
TO MAKE UP FOR THE MISTAKE,
I'LL LEND YOU A NICE OPEN-TOP CAR WITH PLENTY OF ROOM IN THE BACK FOR FREE.
SERIOUSLY?!
AN OPEN-TOP?!

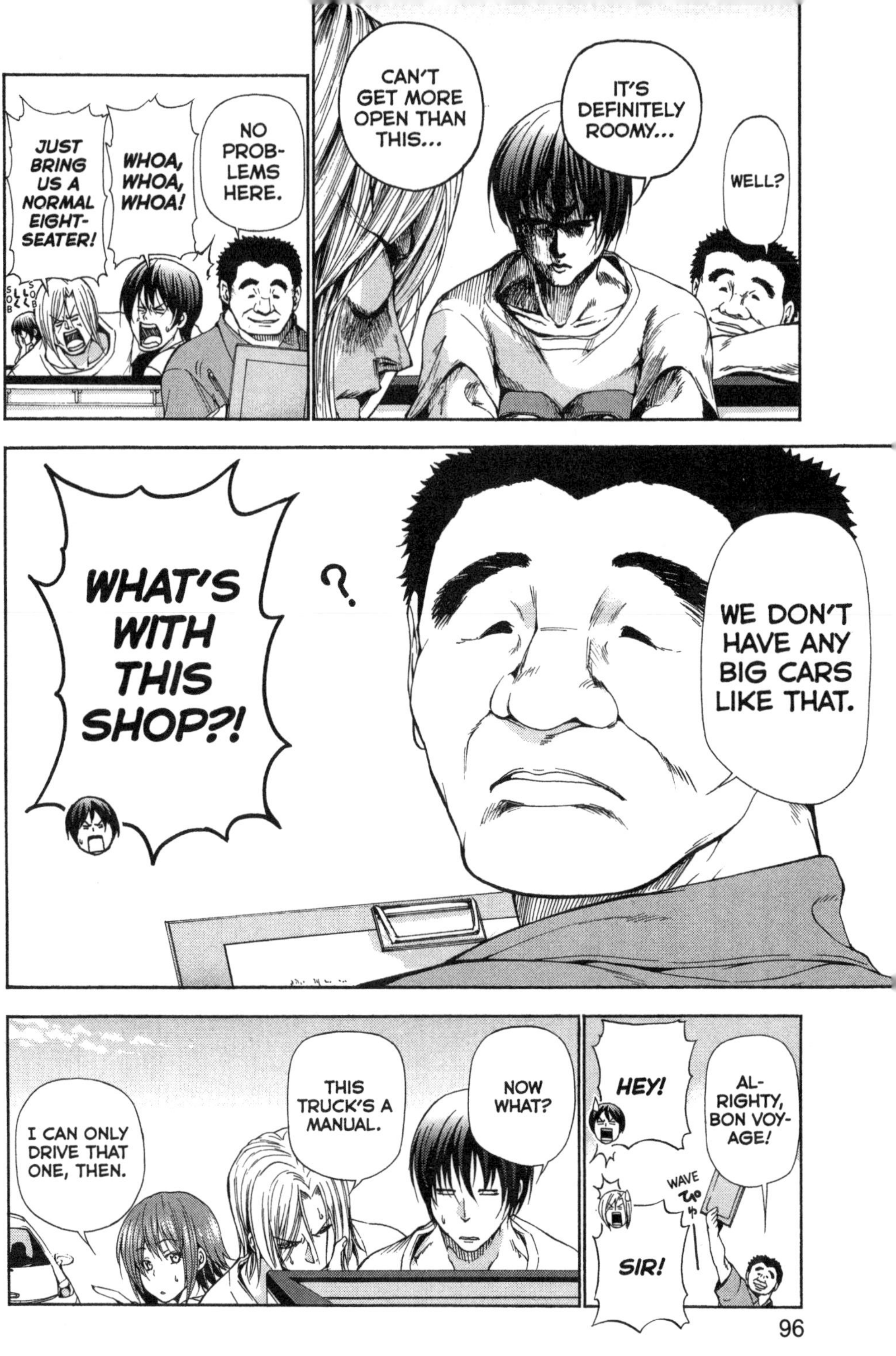

WELL?
IT'S DEFINITELY ROOMY...
CAN'T GET MORE OPEN THAN THIS...
NO PROB-LEMS HERE.
WHOA, WHOA, WHOA!
JUST BRING US A NORMAL EIGHT-SEATER!
SOB SOB
WE DON'T HAVE ANY BIG CARS LIKE THAT.
?
WHAT'S WITH THIS SHOP?!
AL-RIGHTY, BON VOY-AGE!
WAVE
HEY!
SIR!
NOW WHAT?
THIS TRUCK'S A MANUAL.
I CAN ONLY DRIVE THAT ONE, THEN.

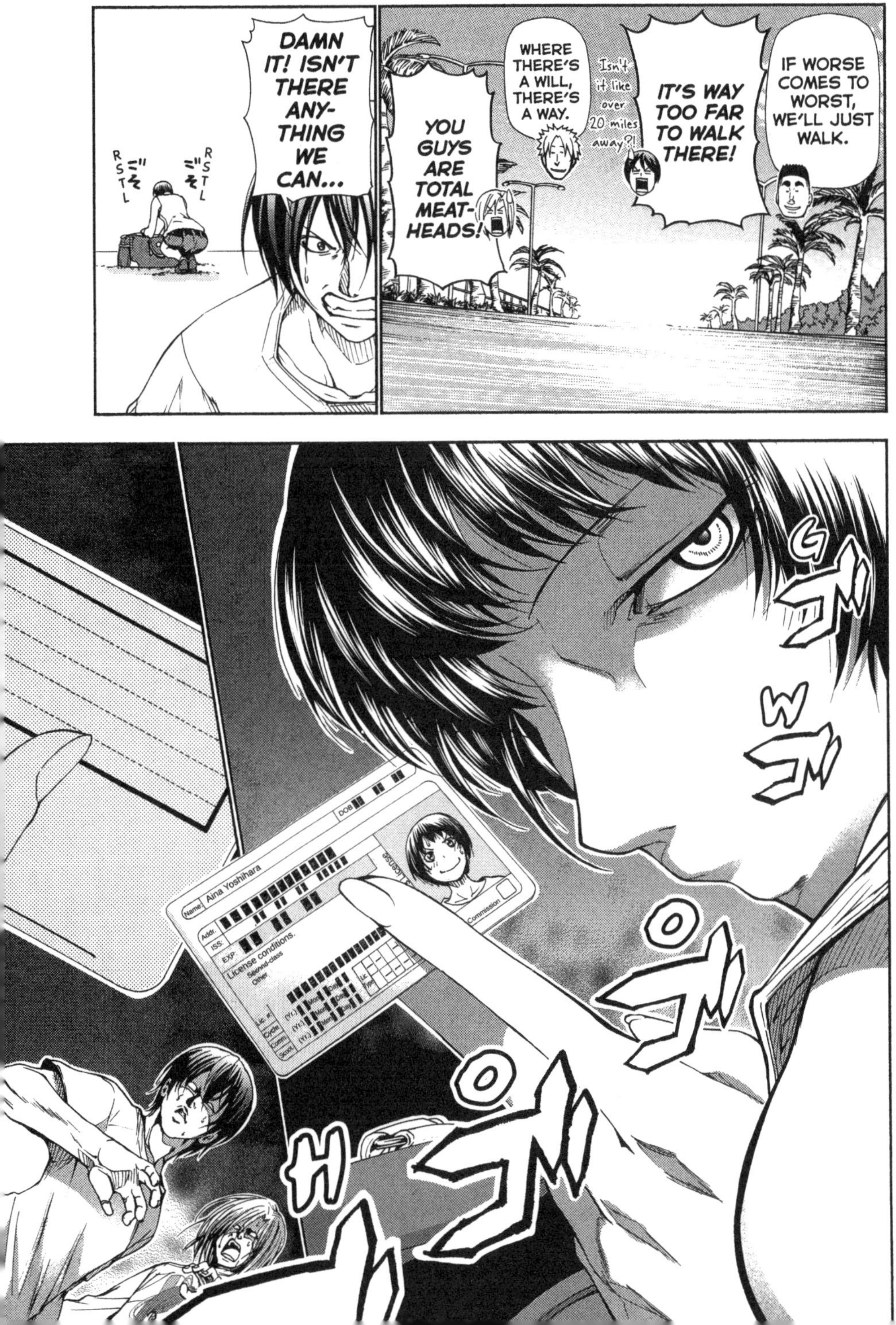
IF WORSE COMES TO WORST, WE'LL JUST WALK.
IT'S WAY TOO FAR TO WALK THERE!
Isn't it like over 20 miles away?!
WHERE THERE'S A WILL, THERE'S A WAY.
YOU GUYS ARE TOTAL MEAT-HEADS!
DAMN IT! ISN'T THERE ANY-THING WE CAN...
RSTL
RSTL
G
W
O
O
H
DOB
Name: Aina Yoshihara
Addr.
ISS.
EXP.
License conditions.
Commission

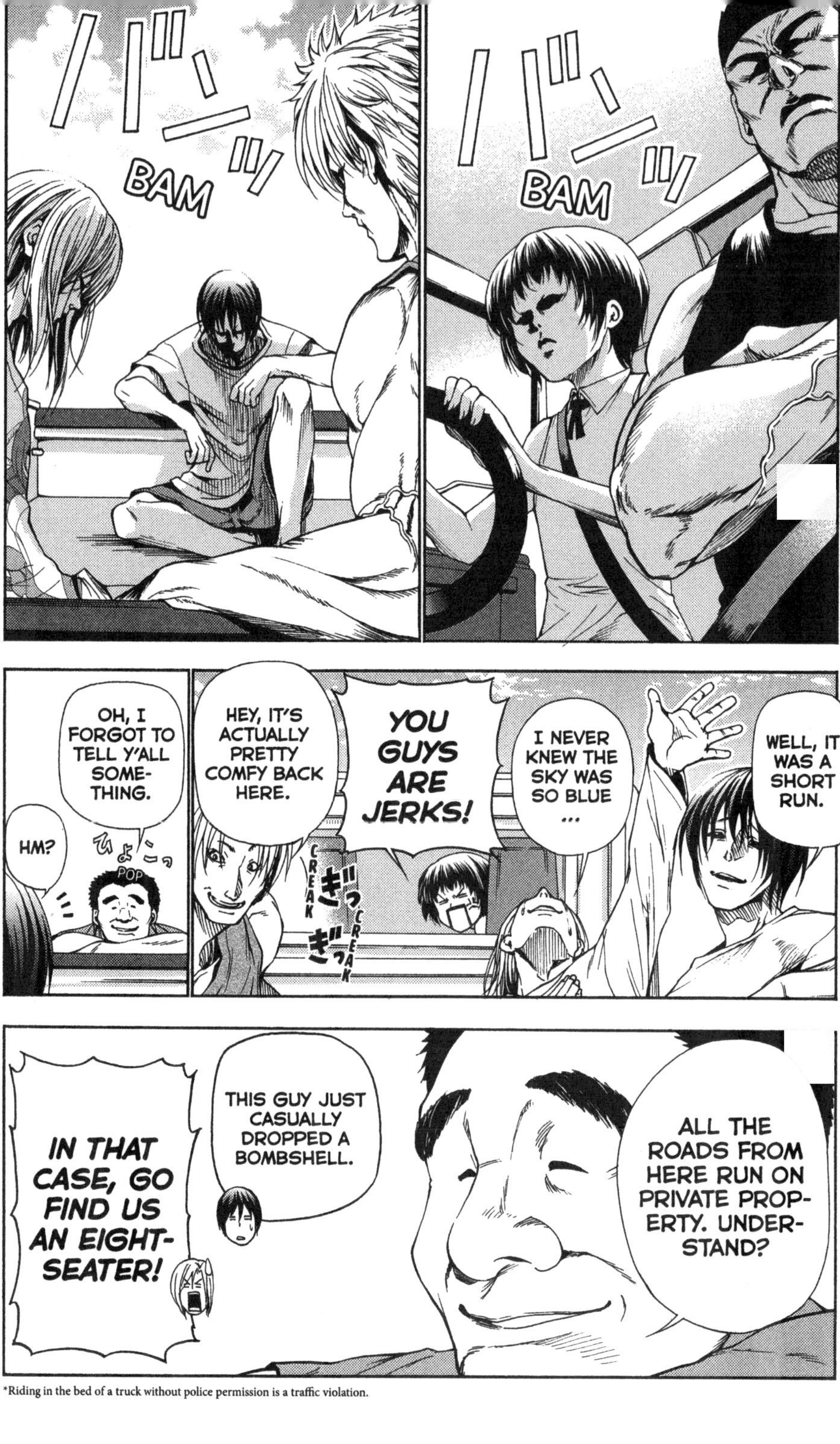
BAM
BAM
WELL, IT WAS A SHORT RUN.
I NEVER KNEW THE SKY WAS SO BLUE ...
YOU GUYS ARE JERKS!
ぎっ CREAK
ぎっ CREAK
HEY, IT'S ACTUALLY PRETTY COMFY BACK HERE.
OH, I FORGOT TO TELL Y'ALL SOME-THING.
ひょこっ POP
HM?
ALL THE ROADS FROM HERE RUN ON PRIVATE PROP-ERTY. UNDER-STAND?
THIS GUY JUST CASUALLY DROPPED A BOMBSHELL.
IN THAT CASE, GO FIND US AN EIGHT-SEATER!

*Riding in the bed of a truck without police permission is a traffic violation.

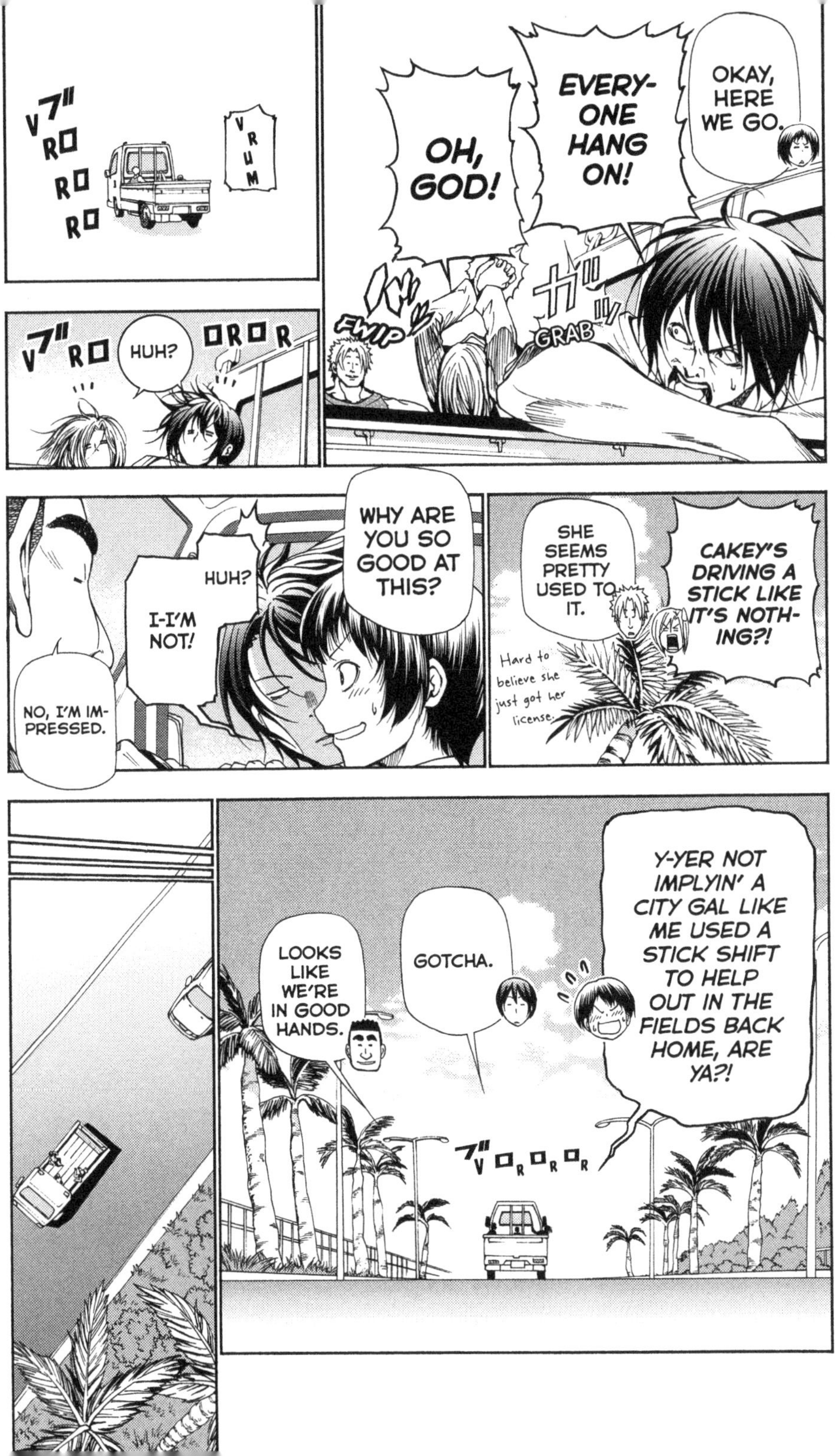
OKAY, HERE WE GO.
EVERY-ONE HANG ON!
OH, GOD!
GRAB
FWIP
VRUM
HUH?
CAKEY'S DRIVING A STICK LIKE IT'S NOTHING?!
SHE SEEMS PRETTY USED TO IT.
Hard to believe she just got her license.
WHY ARE YOU SO GOOD AT THIS?
HUH?
I-I'M NOT!
NO, I'M IMPRESSED.
Y-YER NOT IMPLYIN' A CITY GAL LIKE ME USED A STICK SHIFT TO HELP OUT IN THE FIELDS BACK HOME, ARE YA?!
GOTCHA.
LOOKS LIKE WE'RE IN GOOD HANDS.

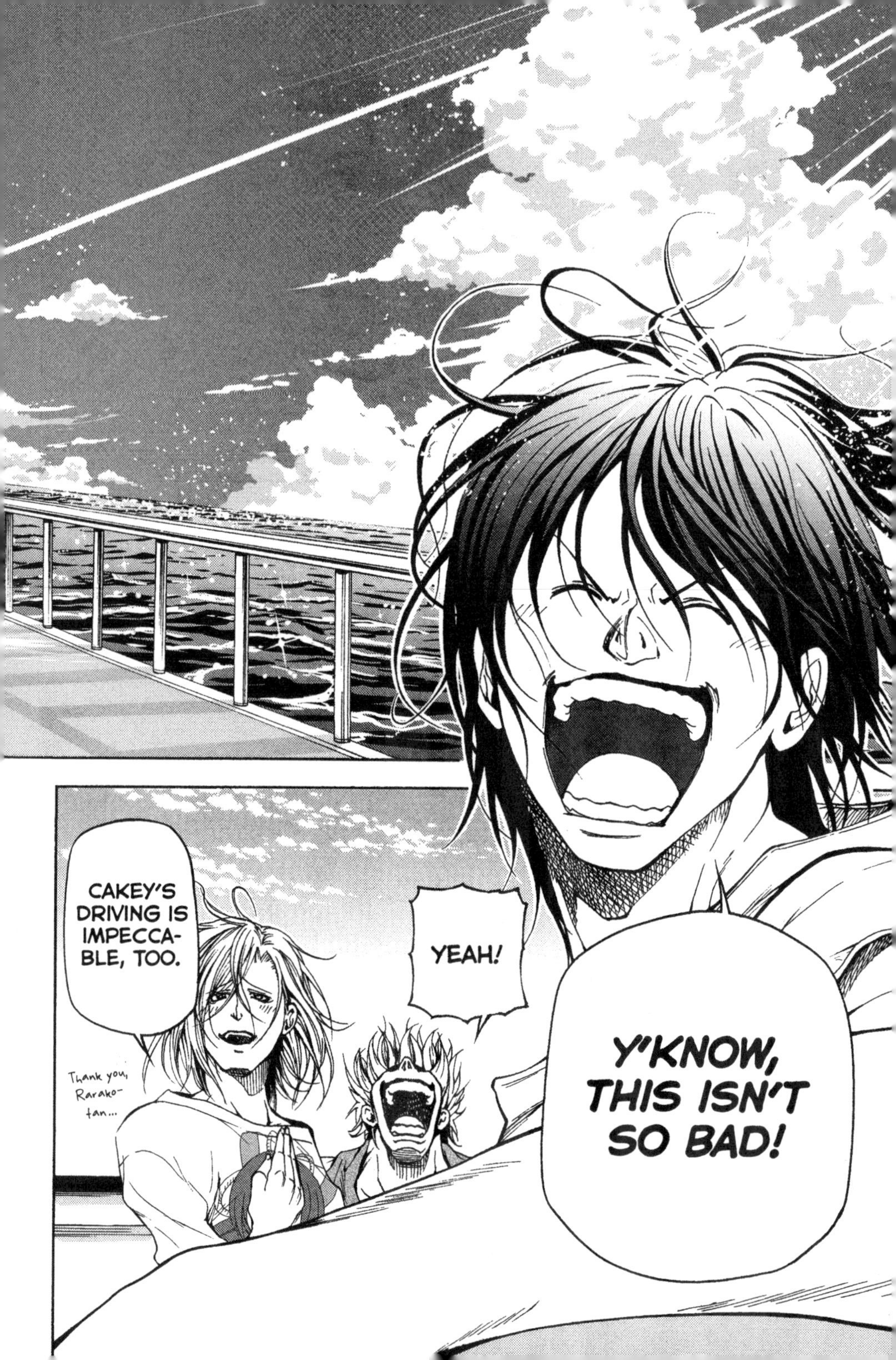
Y'KNOW, THIS ISN'T SO BAD!
YEAH!
CAKEY'S DRIVING IS IMPECCABLE, TOO.
Thank you, Rarako-tan...

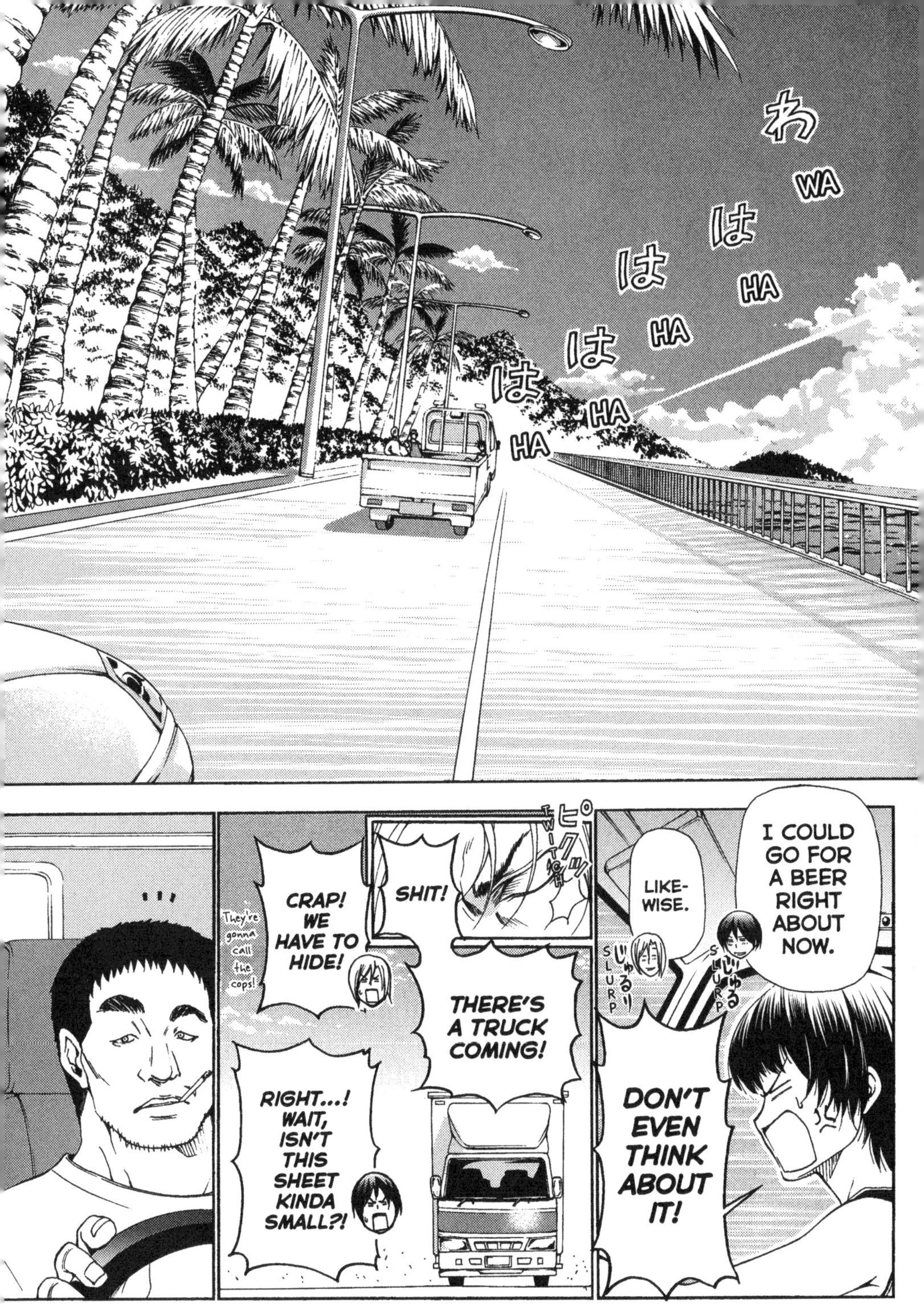
わ
WA
は
HA
は
HA
は
HA
は
HA
I COULD GO FOR A BEER RIGHT ABOUT NOW.
LIKE-WISE.
じゅるり
SLURP
じゅるり
SLURP
DON'T EVEN THINK ABOUT IT!
ピクッ
TWITCH
SHIT!
CRAP! WE HAVE TO HIDE!
They're gonna call the cops!
THERE'S A TRUCK COMING!
RIGHT...! WAIT, ISN'T THIS SHEET KINDA SMALL?!
...

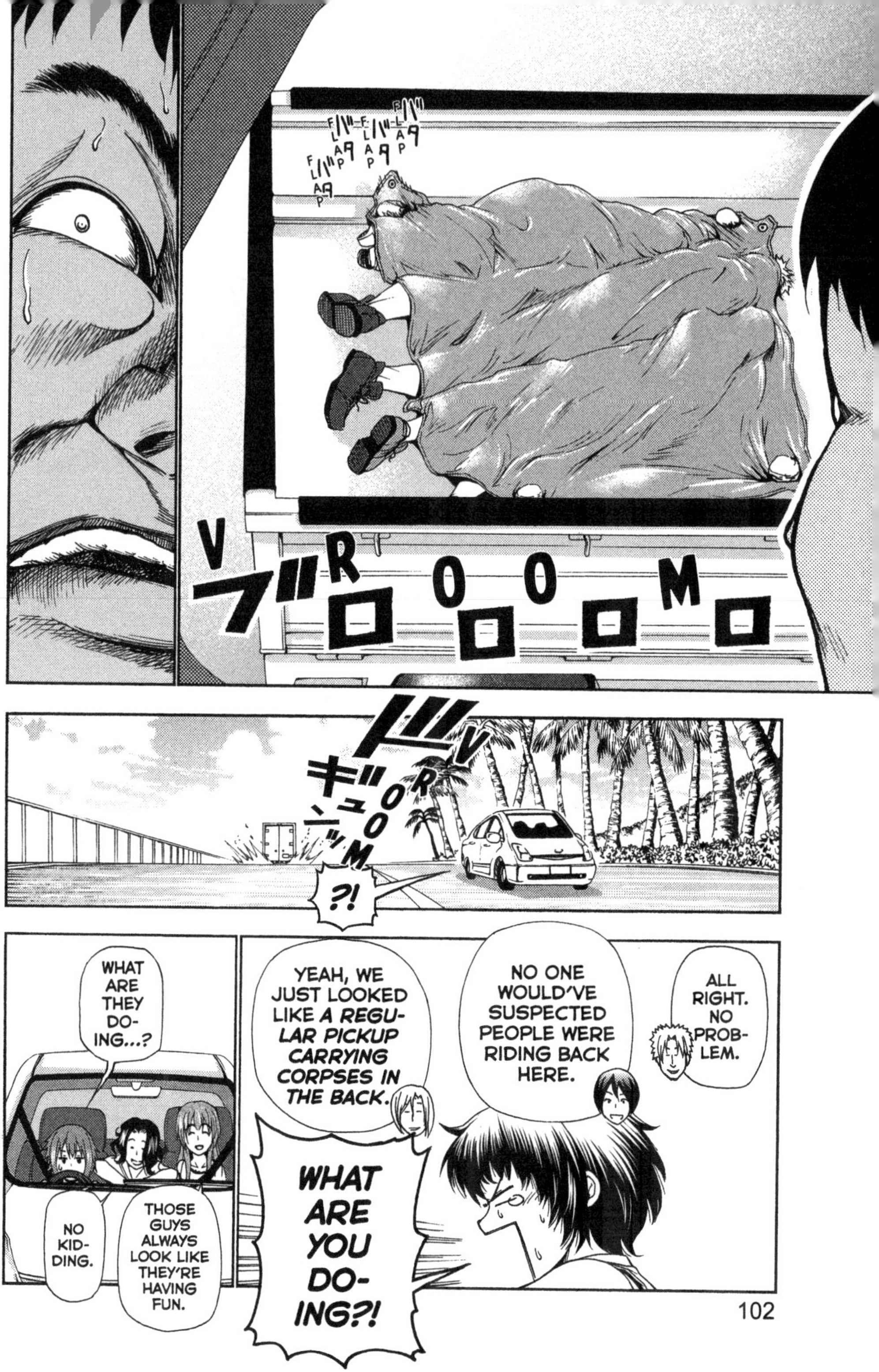
FLAP FLAP FLAP FLAP FLAP
VROOOM
VROOOM
?!
ALL RIGHT. NO PROBLEM.
NO ONE WOULD'VE SUSPECTED PEOPLE WERE RIDING BACK HERE.
YEAH, WE JUST LOOKED LIKE A *REGULAR PICKUP CARRYING CORPSES IN THE BACK.*
WHAT ARE YOU DOING?!
WHAT ARE THEY DOING...?
THOSE GUYS ALWAYS LOOK LIKE THEY'RE HAVING FUN.
NO KIDDING.

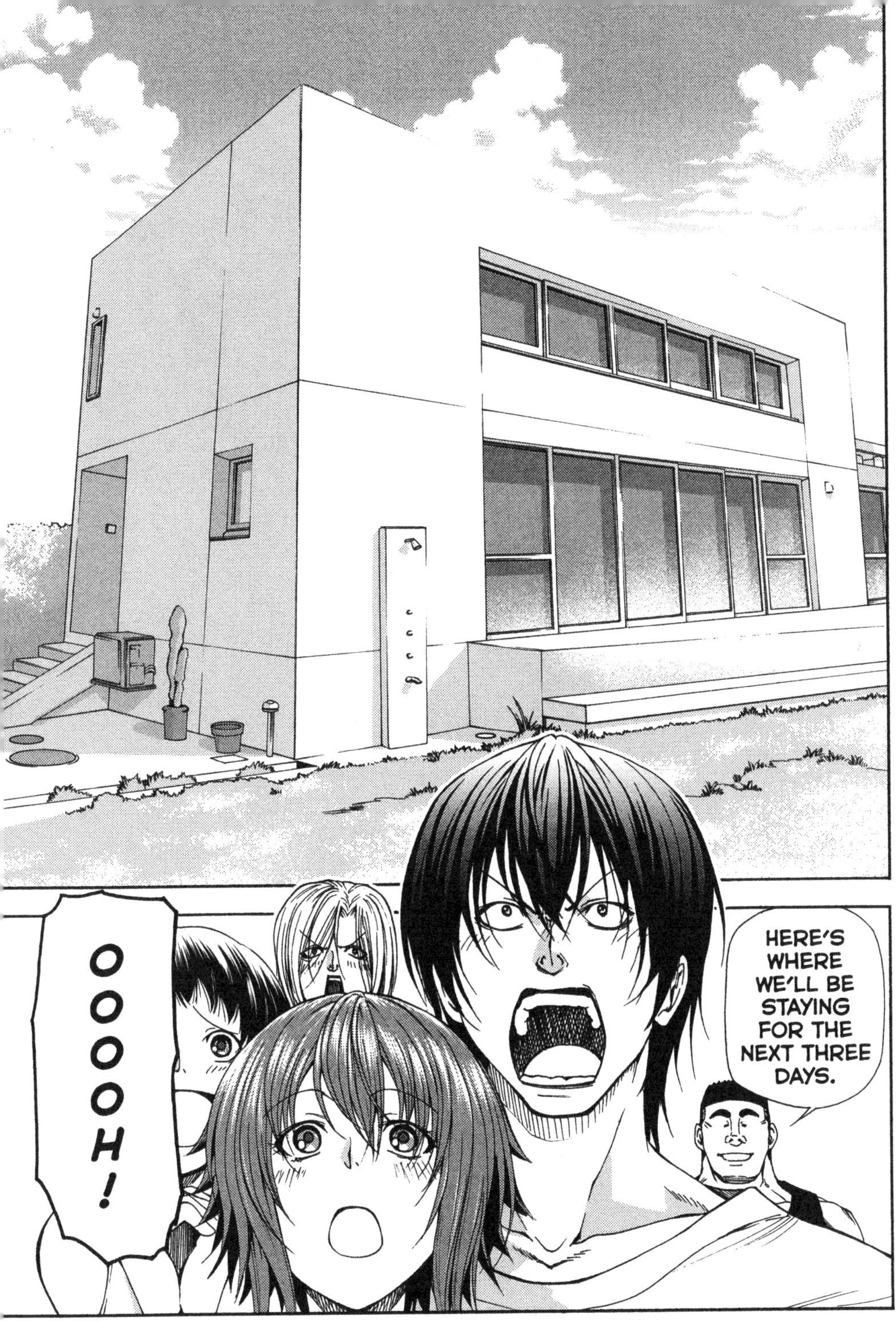
HERE'S WHERE WE'LL BE STAYING FOR THE NEXT THREE DAYS.
OOOOOH!

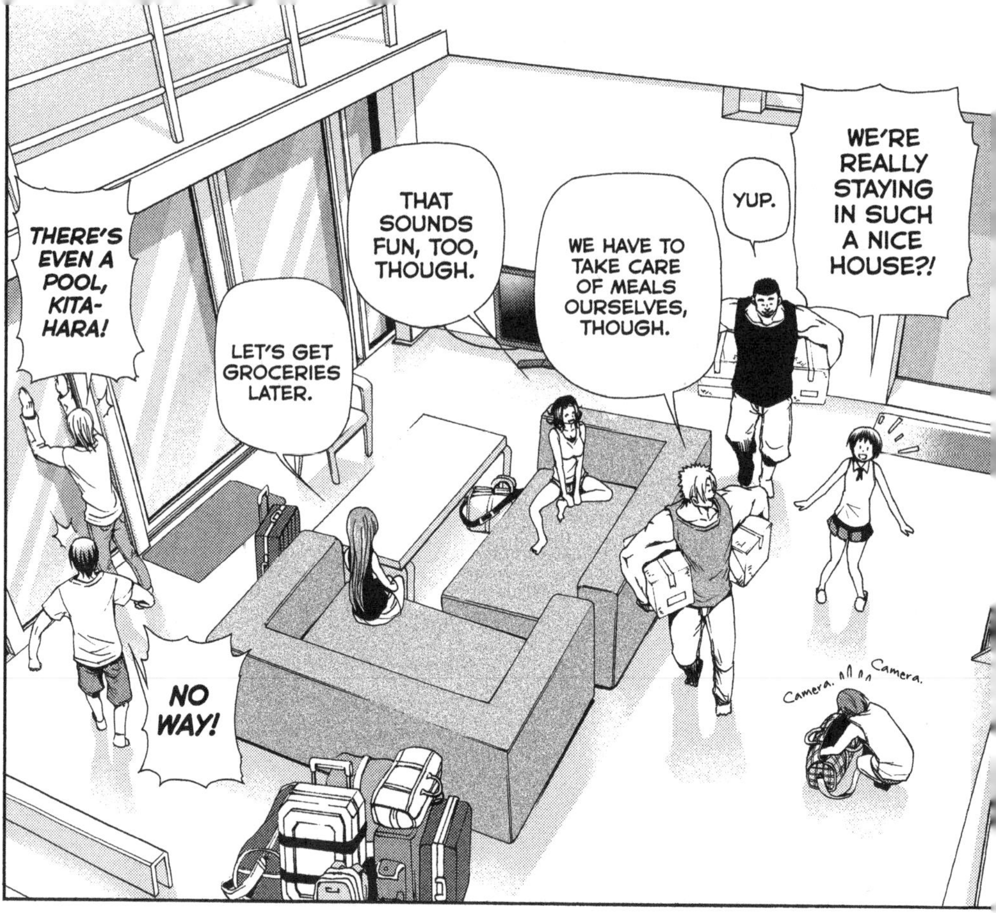
WE'RE REALLY STAYING IN SUCH A NICE HOUSE?!
YUP.
WE HAVE TO TAKE CARE OF MEALS OURSELVES, THOUGH.
THAT SOUNDS FUN, TOO, THOUGH.
LET'S GET GROCERIES LATER.
THERE'S EVEN A POOL, KITA-HARA!
Camera. Camera.
NO WAY!

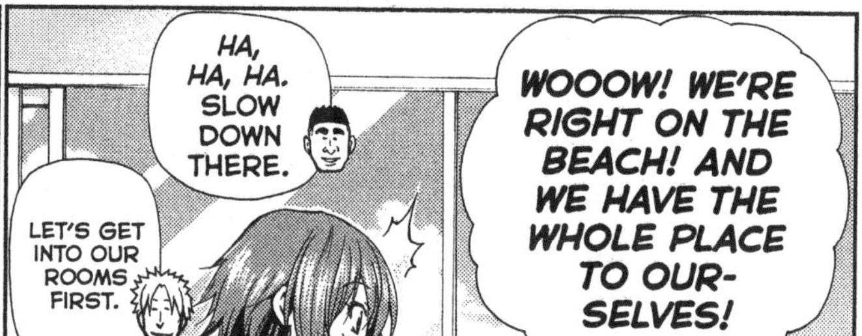
WOOOW! WE'RE RIGHT ON THE BEACH! AND WE HAVE THE WHOLE PLACE TO OUR-SELVES!
HA, HA, HA. SLOW DOWN THERE.
LET'S GET INTO OUR ROOMS FIRST.
'KAY.

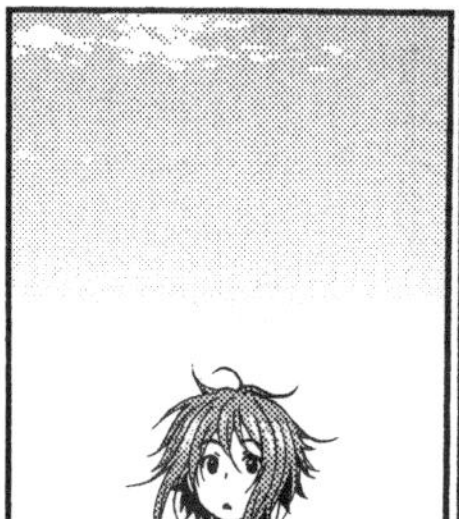

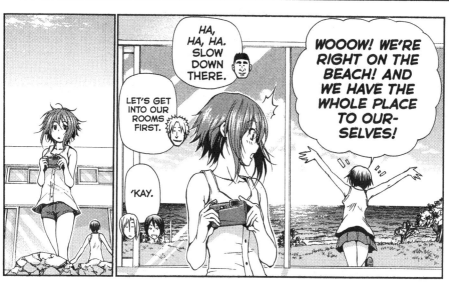

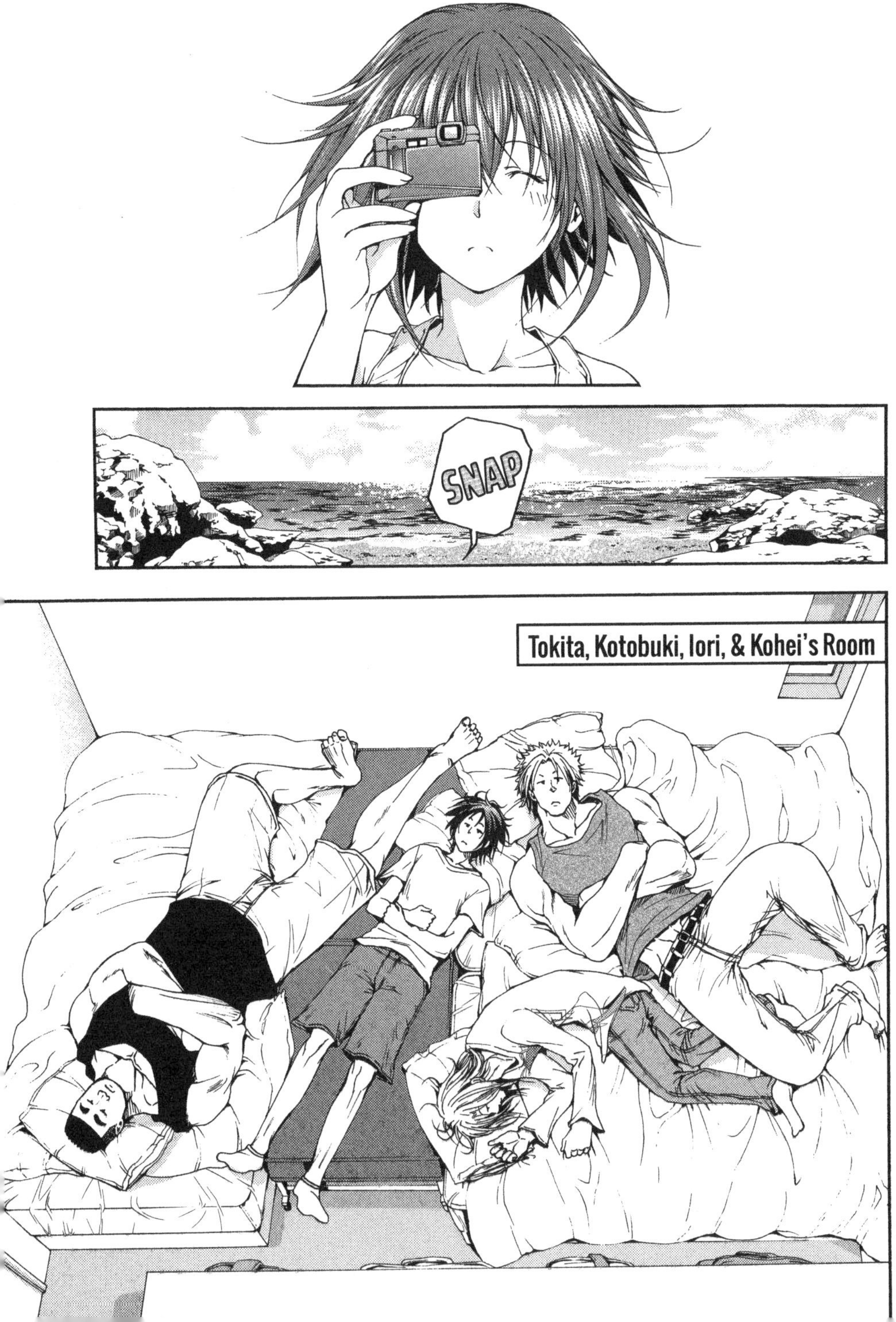
SNAP
Tokita, Kotobuki, Iori, & Kohei's Room

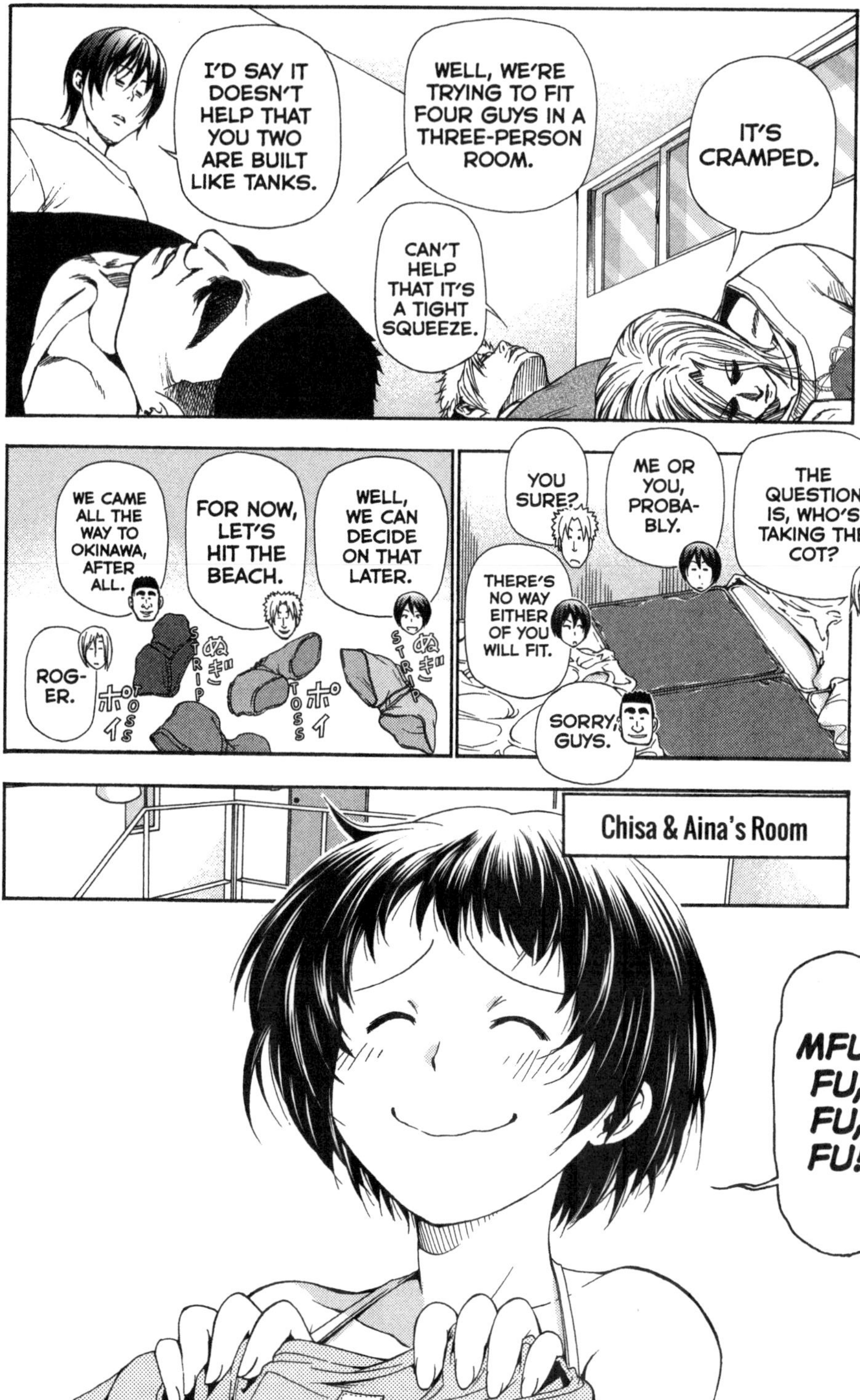
IT'S CRAMPED.
WELL, WE'RE TRYING TO FIT FOUR GUYS IN A THREE-PERSON ROOM.
CAN'T HELP THAT IT'S A TIGHT SQUEEZE.
I'D SAY IT DOESN'T HELP THAT YOU TWO ARE BUILT LIKE TANKS.
THE QUESTION IS, WHO'S TAKING THE COT?
ME OR YOU, PROBABLY.
YOU SURE?
THERE'S NO WAY EITHER OF YOU WILL FIT.
SORRY, GUYS.
WELL, WE CAN DECIDE ON THAT LATER.
ぬぎ STRIP
ポイ TOSS
FOR NOW, LET'S HIT THE BEACH.
ぬぎ STRIP
WE CAME ALL THE WAY TO OKINAWA, AFTER ALL.
ポイ TOSS
ROGER.
Chisa & Aina's Room
MFU, FU, FU, FU!

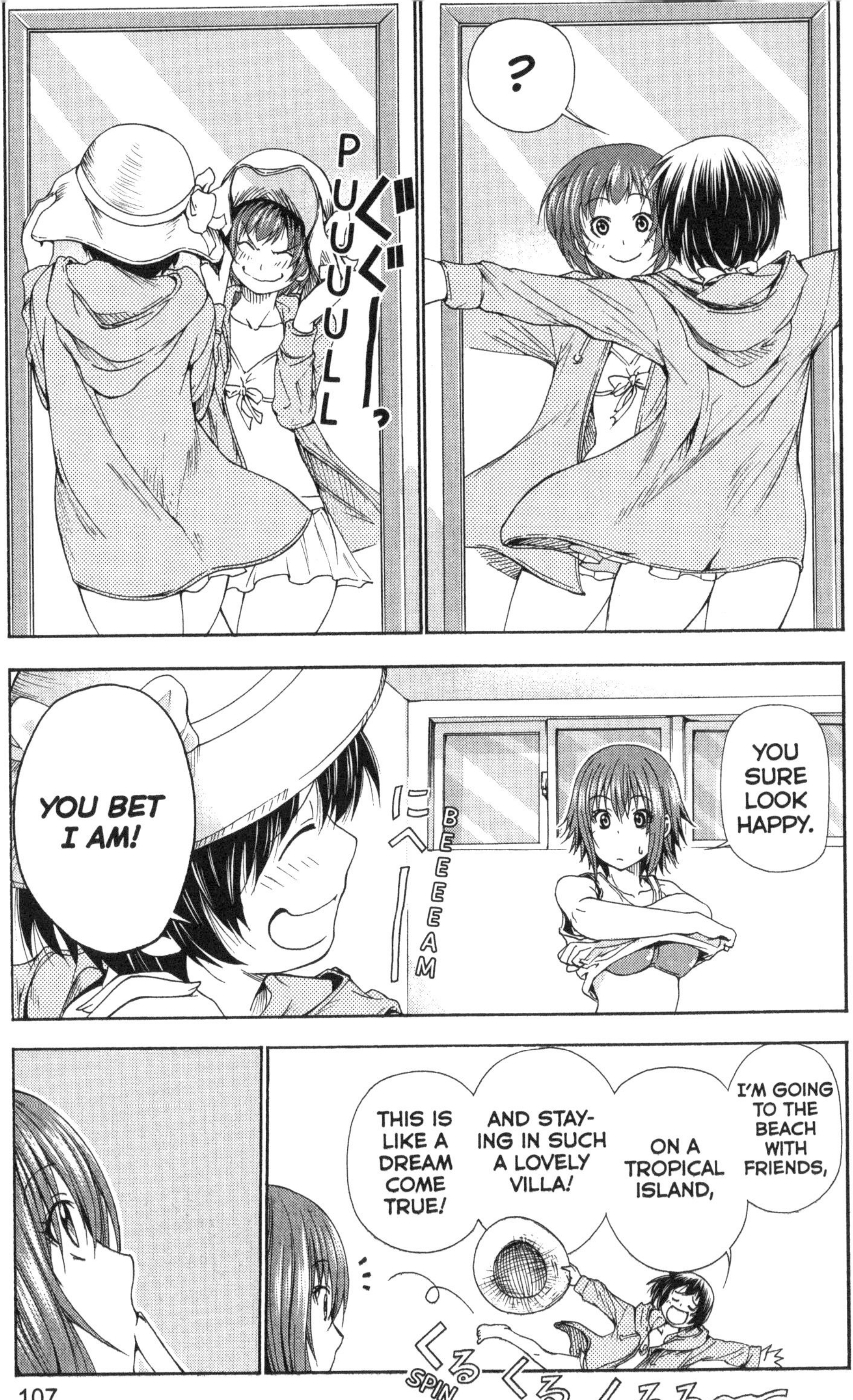
?
PUUUULL
YOU SURE LOOK HAPPY.
YOU BET I AM!
にへー
BEEEEAM
I'M GOING TO THE BEACH WITH FRIENDS,
ON A TROPICAL ISLAND,
AND STAYING IN SUCH A LOVELY VILLA!
THIS IS LIKE A DREAM COME TRUE!
くる SPIN
くる SPIN
くるる～～ SPIIIN

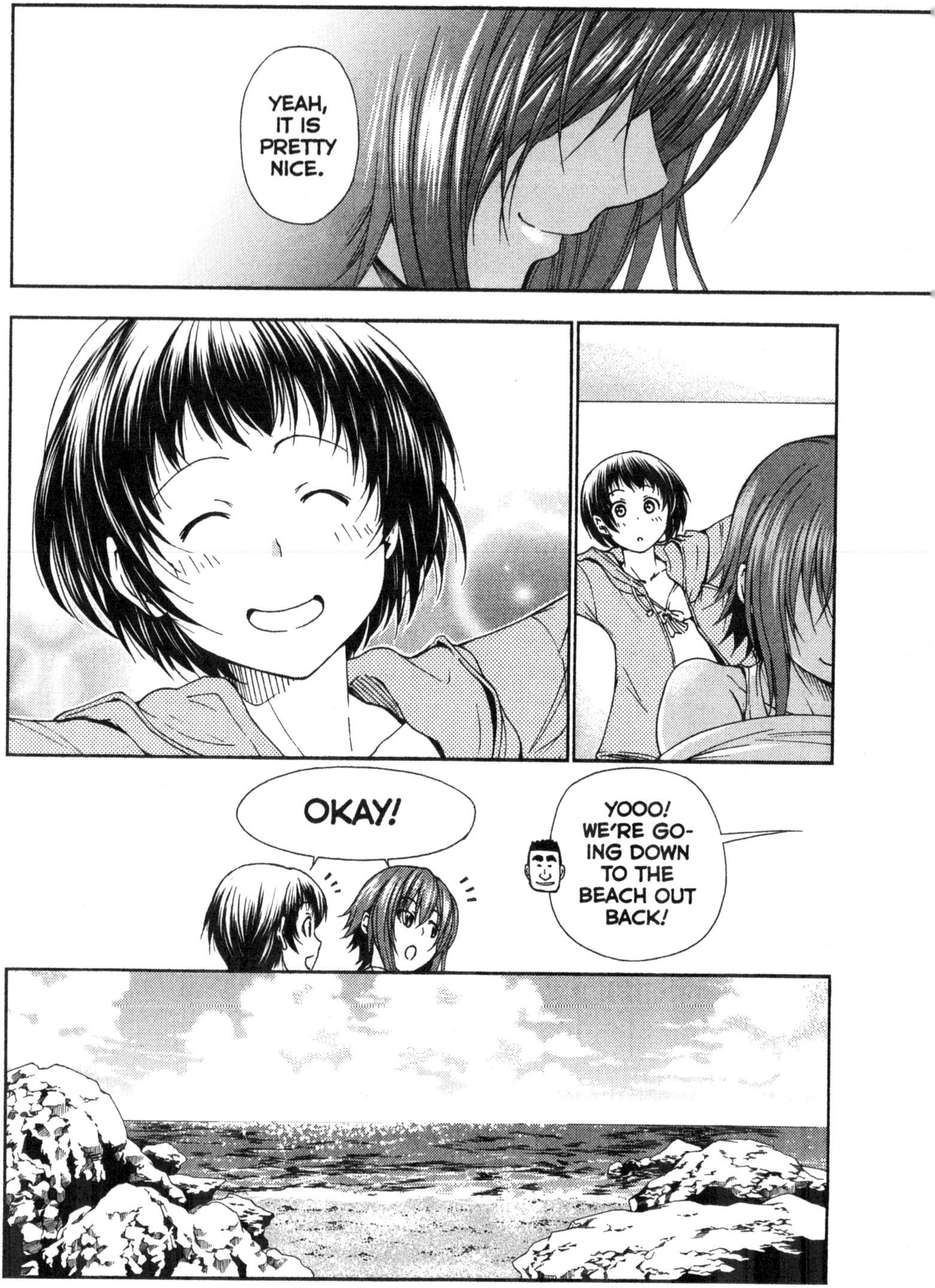
YEAH, IT IS PRETTY NICE.
YOOO! WE'RE GO-ING DOWN TO THE BEACH OUT BACK!
OKAY!

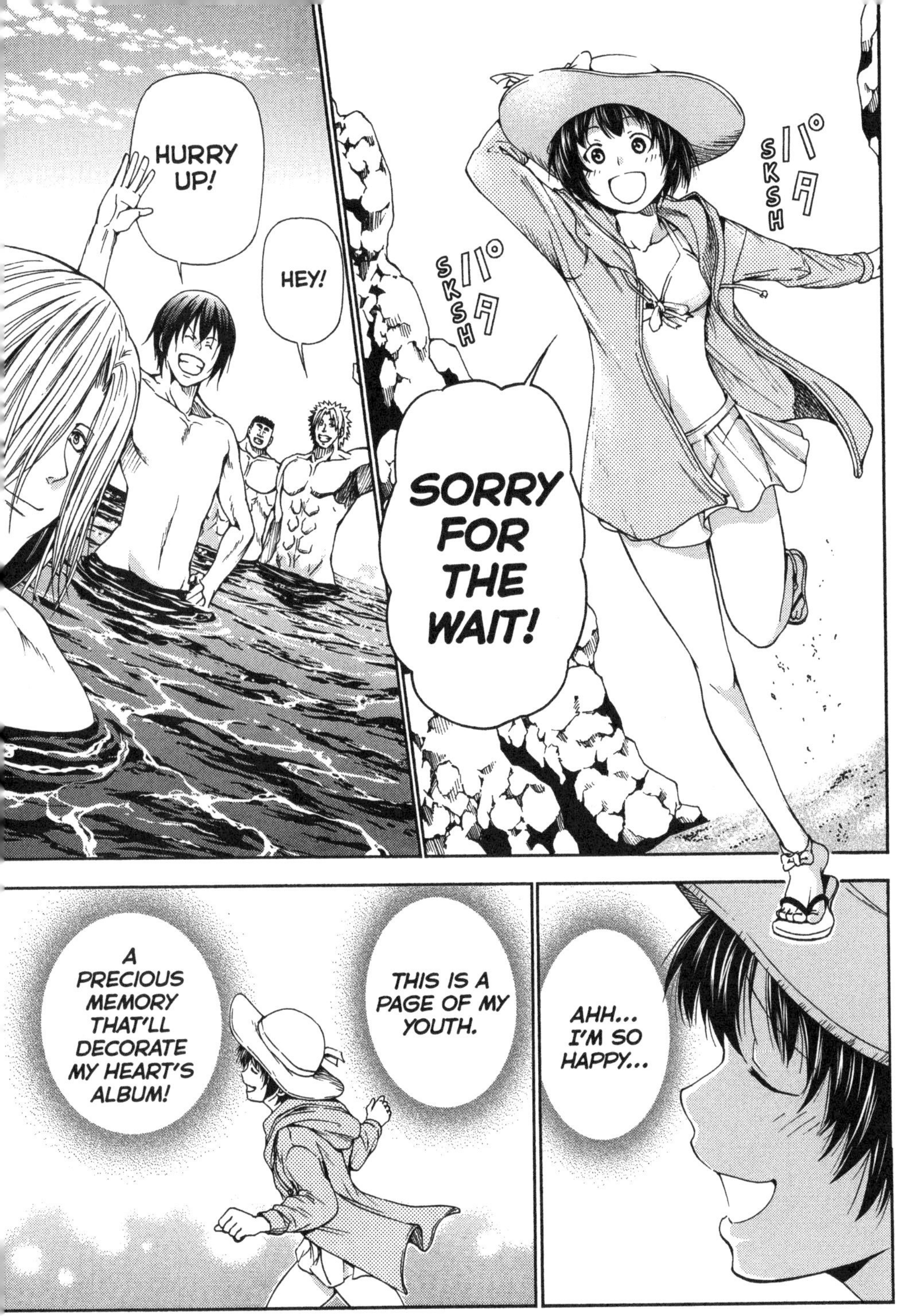
パタ
SKSH
パタ
SKSH
SORRY FOR THE WAIT!
HEY!
HURRY UP!
AHH... I'M SO HAPPY...
THIS IS A PAGE OF MY YOUTH.
A PRECIOUS MEMORY THAT'LL DECORATE MY HEART'S ALBUM!

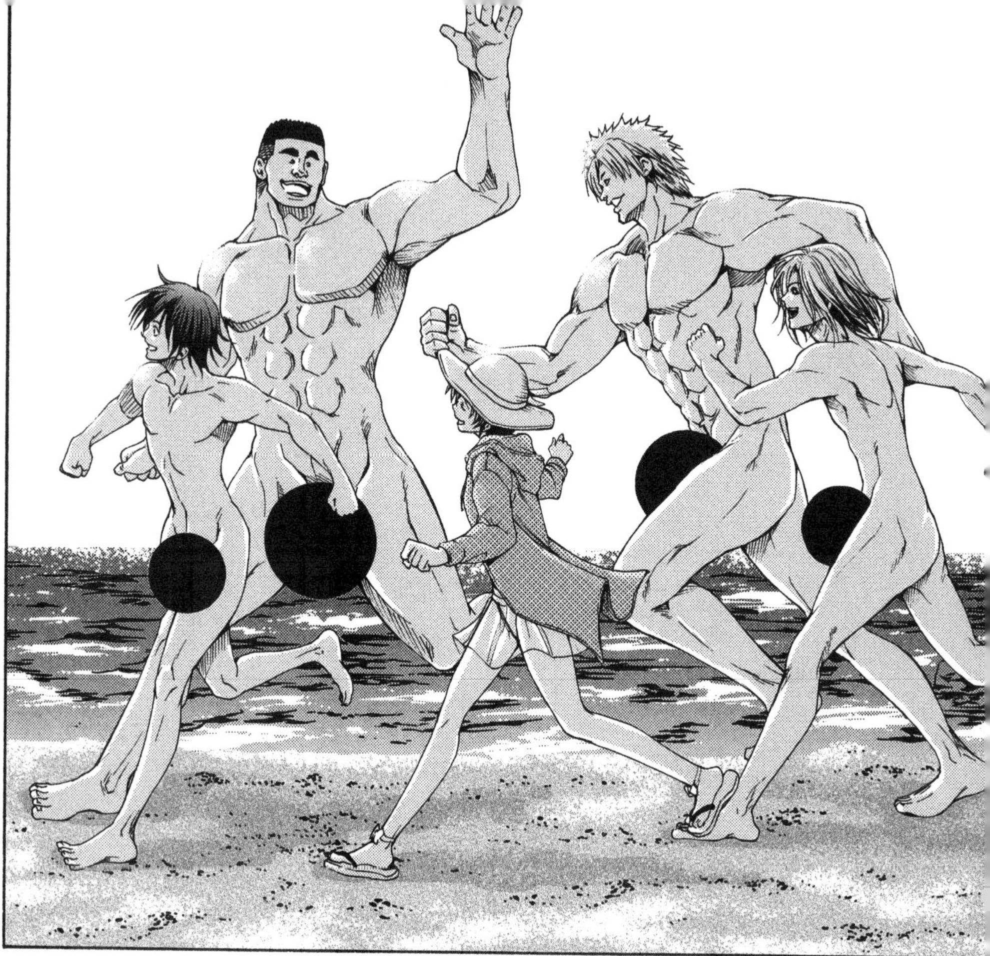

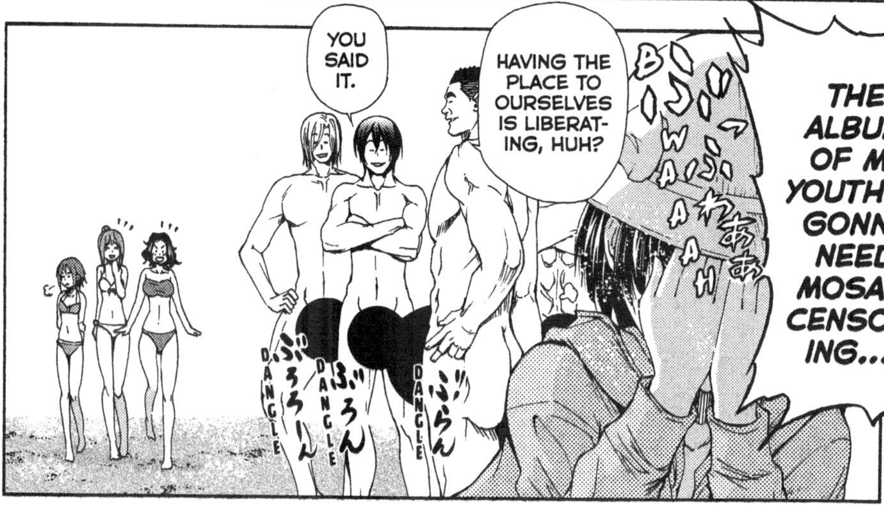
THE ALBUM OF MY YOUTH IS GONNA NEED MOSAIC CENSORING...!
BWAAAAH
HAVING THE PLACE TO OURSELVES IS LIBERATING, HUH?
YOU SAID IT.
DANGLE
ぶらん
DANGLE
ぶろん
DANGLE
ぶろろーん

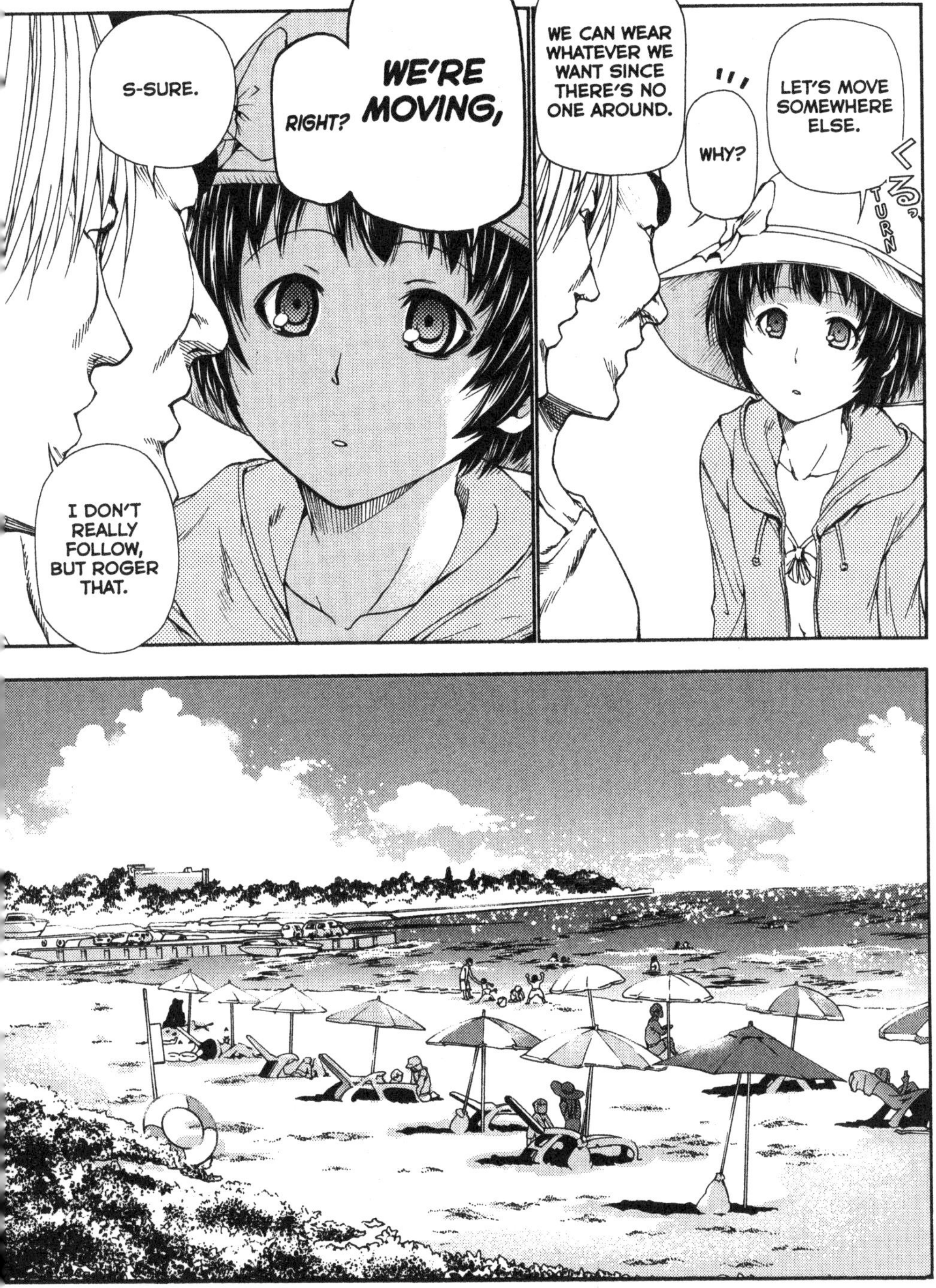
LET'S MOVE SOMEWHERE ELSE.
くるっ TURN
WHY?
WE CAN WEAR WHATEVER WE WANT SINCE THERE'S NO ONE AROUND.
WE'RE MOVING, RIGHT?
S-SURE.
I DON'T REALLY FOLLOW, BUT ROGER THAT.

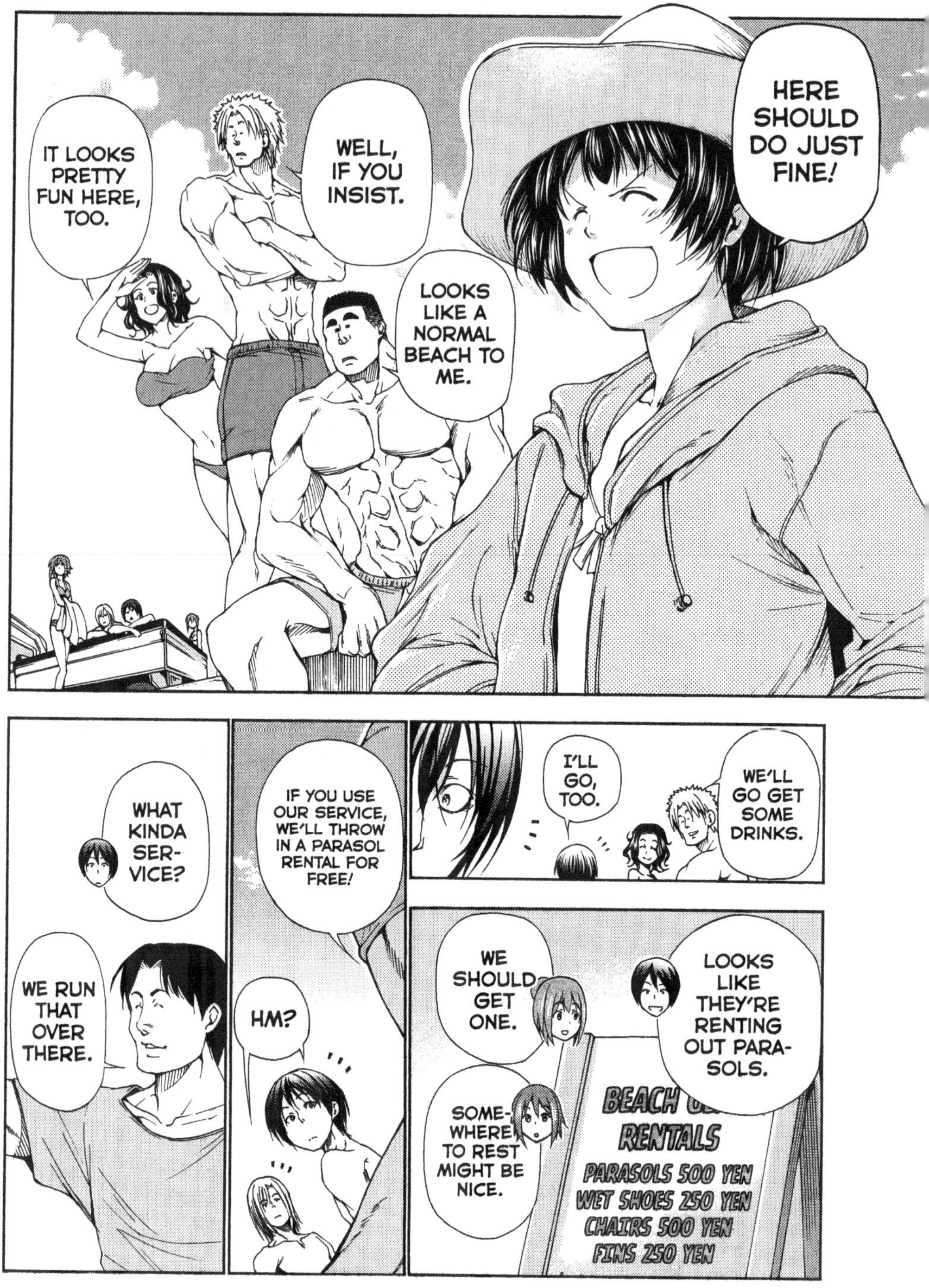
HERE SHOULD DO JUST FINE!
LOOKS LIKE A NORMAL BEACH TO ME.
WELL, IF YOU INSIST.
IT LOOKS PRETTY FUN HERE, TOO.
WE'LL GO GET SOME DRINKS.
I'LL GO, TOO.
LOOKS LIKE THEY'RE RENTING OUT PARA-SOLS.
WE SHOULD GET ONE.
SOME-WHERE TO REST MIGHT BE NICE.
BEACH
RENTALS
PARASOLS 500 YEN
WET SHOES 250 YEN
CHAIRS 500 YEN
FINS 250 YEN
IF YOU USE OUR SERVICE, WE'LL THROW IN A PARASOL RENTAL FOR FREE!
HM?
WHAT KINDA SER-VICE?
WE RUN THAT OVER THERE.

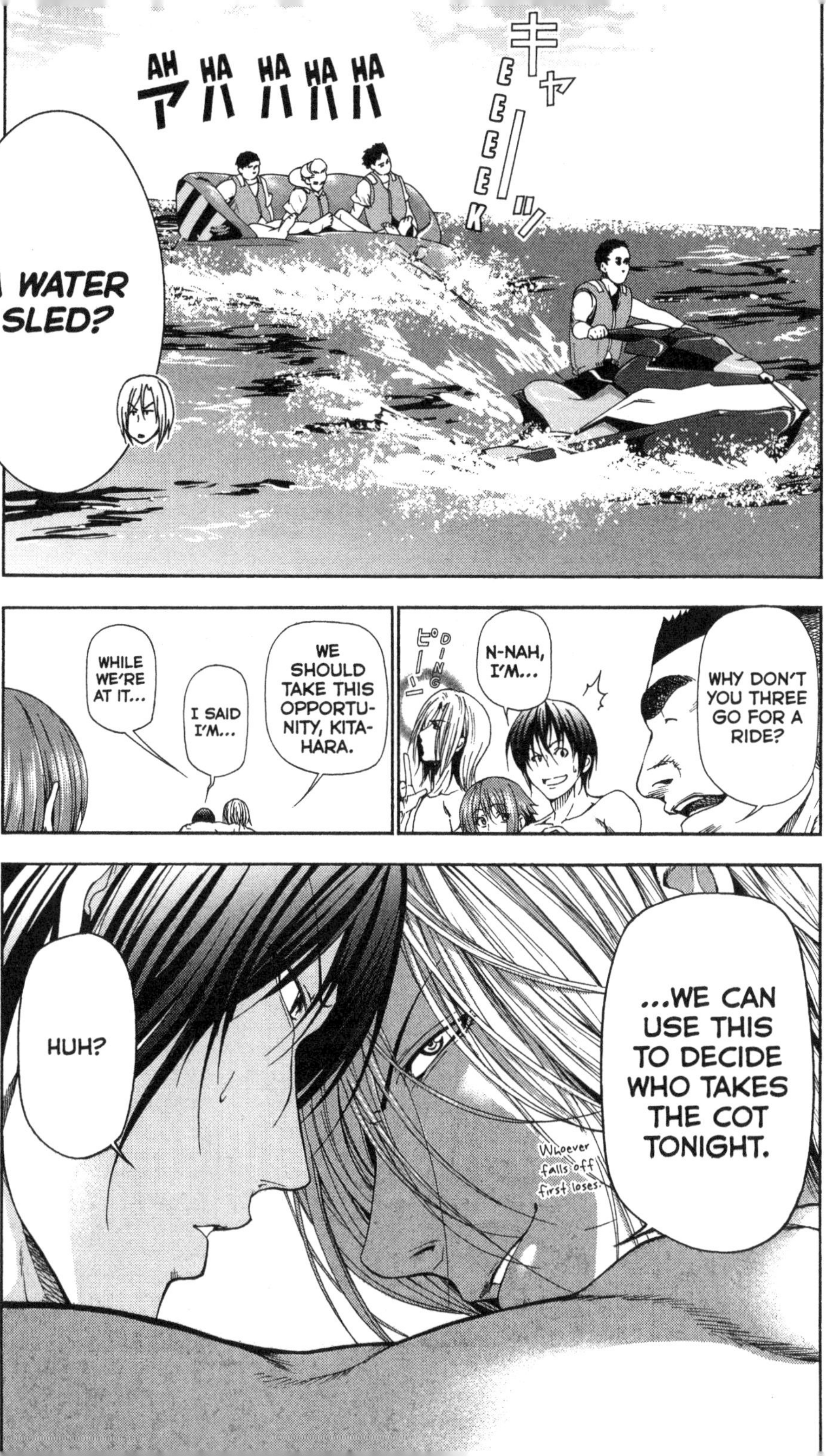
キャーッ
EEEEEK
AH HA HA HA HA
アハハハハ
A WATER SLED?
WHY DON'T YOU THREE GO FOR A RIDE?
N-NAH, I'M...
DING
ピーー
WE SHOULD TAKE THIS OPPORTUNITY, KITAHARA.
I SAID I'M...
WHILE WE'RE AT IT...
...WE CAN USE THIS TO DECIDE WHO TAKES THE COT TONIGHT.
Whoever falls off first loses.
HUH?

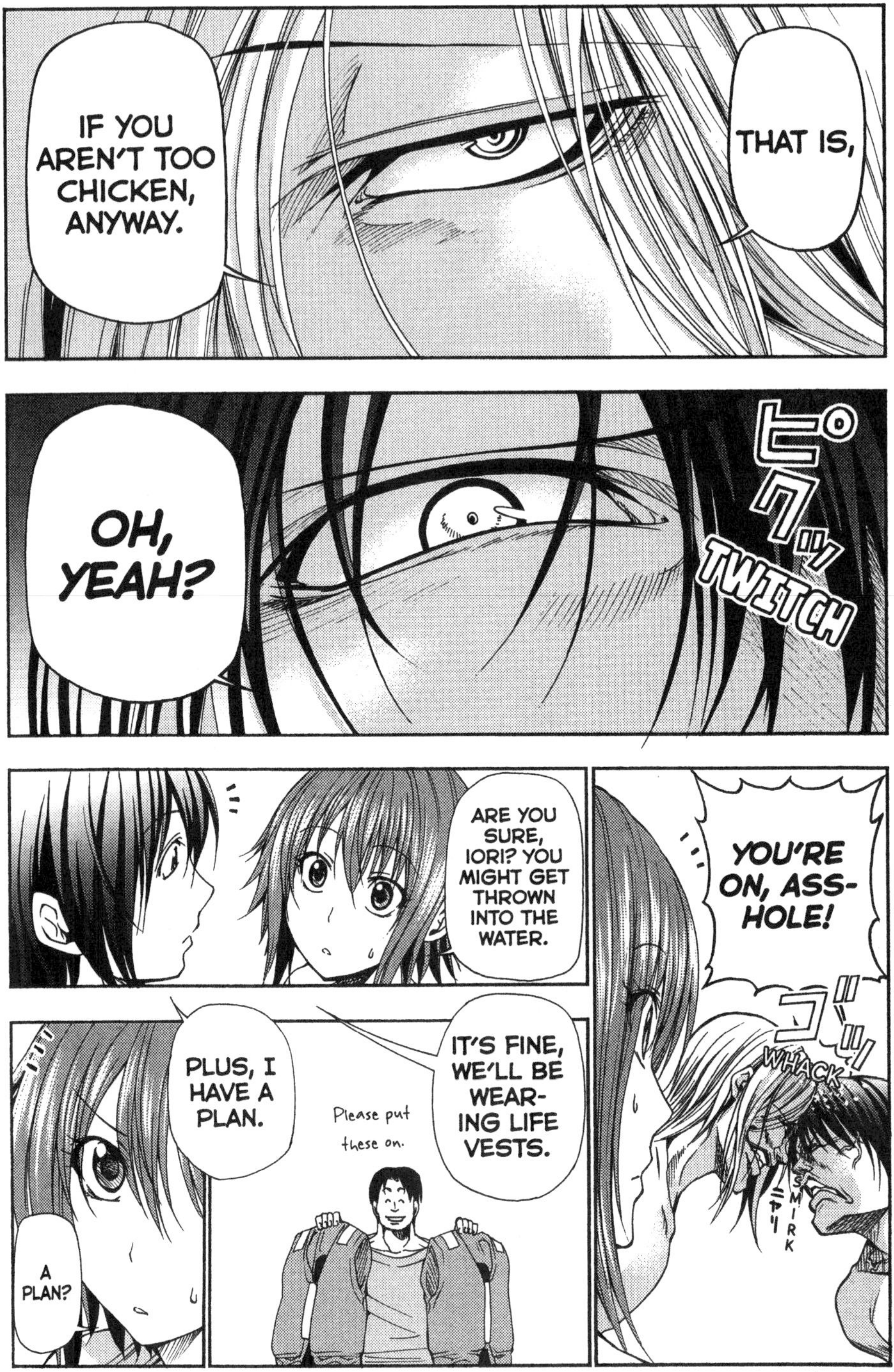
THAT IS,
IF YOU AREN'T TOO CHICKEN, ANYWAY.
ピクッ
TWITCH
OH, YEAH?
YOU'RE ON, ASS-HOLE!
ゴッ
WHACK
ニヤリ
SMIRK
ARE YOU SURE, IORI? YOU MIGHT GET THROWN INTO THE WATER.
IT'S FINE, WE'LL BE WEAR-ING LIFE VESTS.
Please put these on.
PLUS, I HAVE A PLAN.
A PLAN?

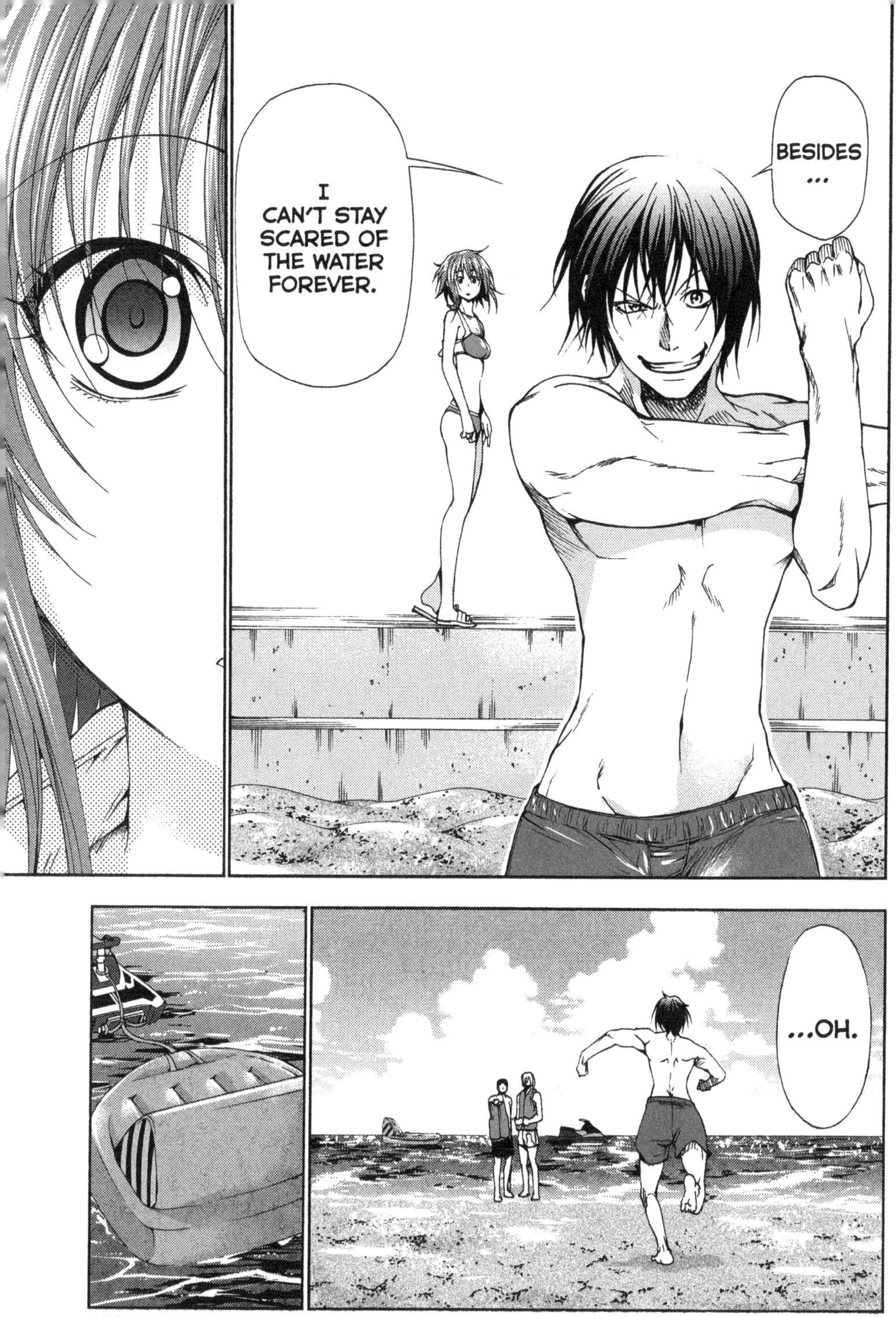
BESIDES ...
I CAN'T STAY SCARED OF THE WATER FOREVER.
...OH.

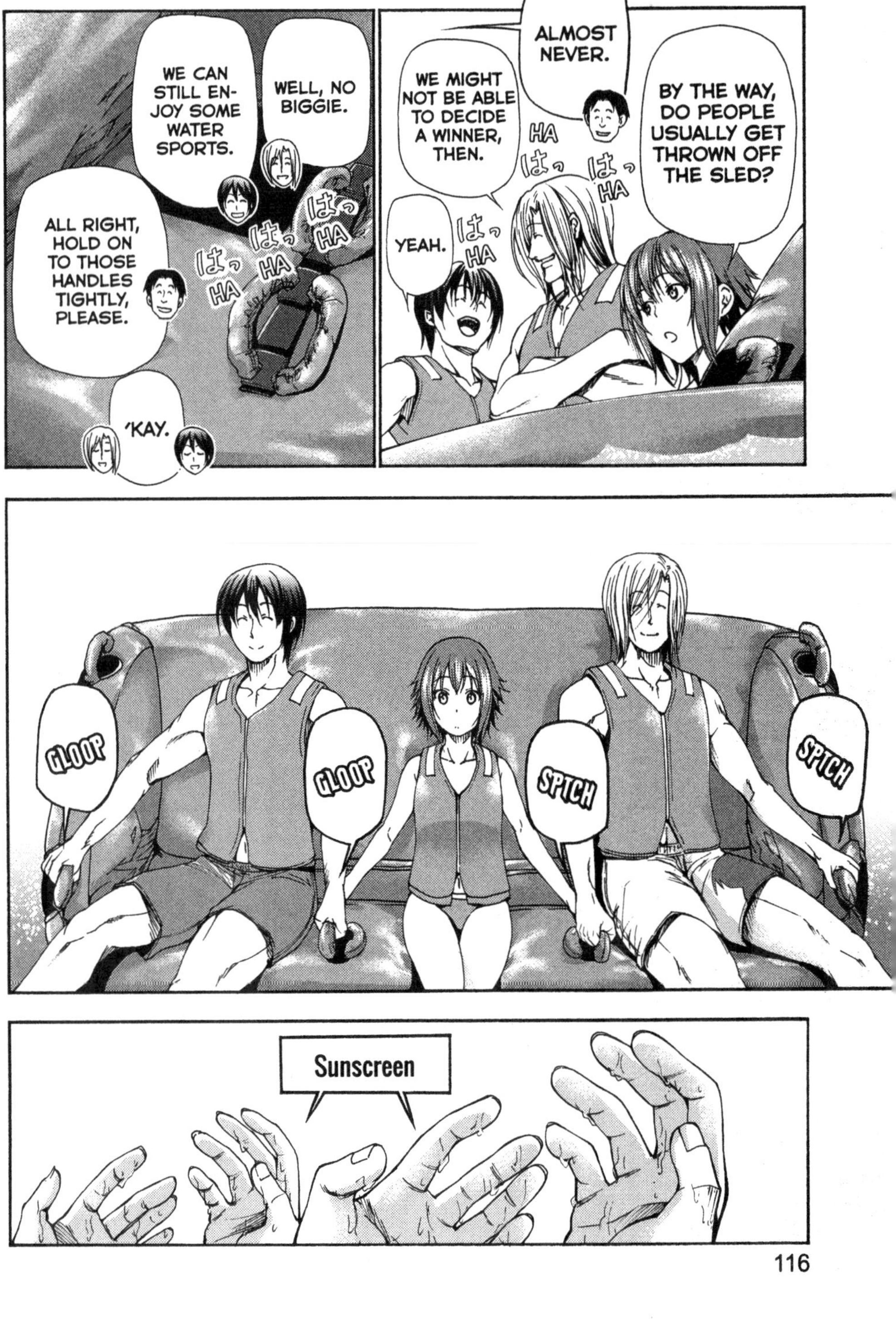
BY THE WAY, DO PEOPLE USUALLY GET THROWN OFF THE SLED?
ALMOST NEVER.
はっ HA
はっ HA
WE MIGHT NOT BE ABLE TO DECIDE A WINNER, THEN.
はっ HA
YEAH.
WELL, NO BIGGIE.
WE CAN STILL EN-JOY SOME WATER SPORTS.
はっ HA
はっ HA
はっ HA
ALL RIGHT, HOLD ON TO THOSE HANDLES TIGHTLY, PLEASE.
'KAY.
SPITCH
SPITCH
GLOOP
GLOOP
Sunscreen

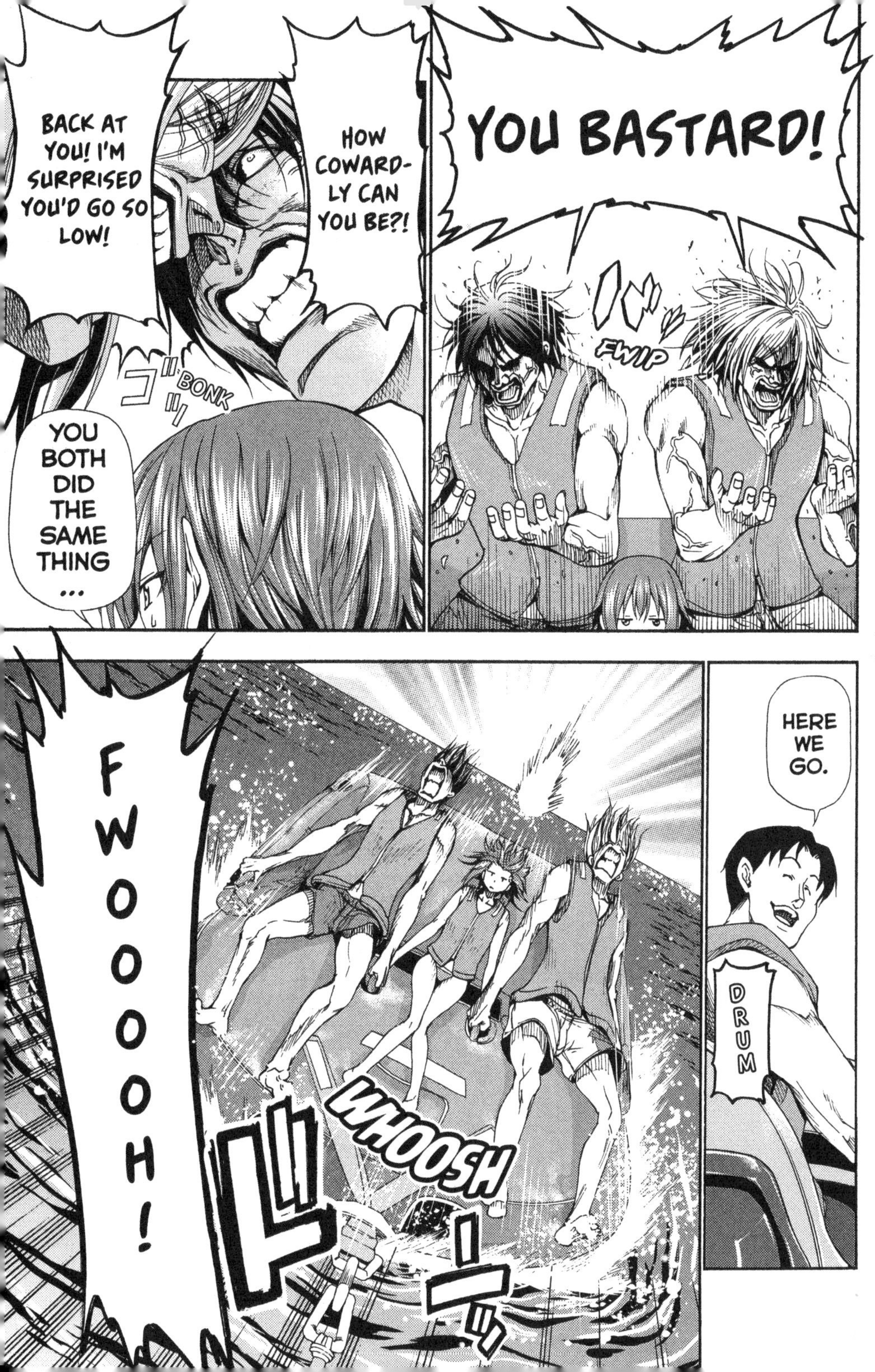
YOU BASTARD!
FWIP
HOW COWARD-LY CAN YOU BE?!
BACK AT YOU! I'M SURPRISED YOU'D GO SO LOW!
BONK
YOU BOTH DID THE SAME THING ...
HERE WE GO.
DRUM
FWOOOOOH!
WHOOSH

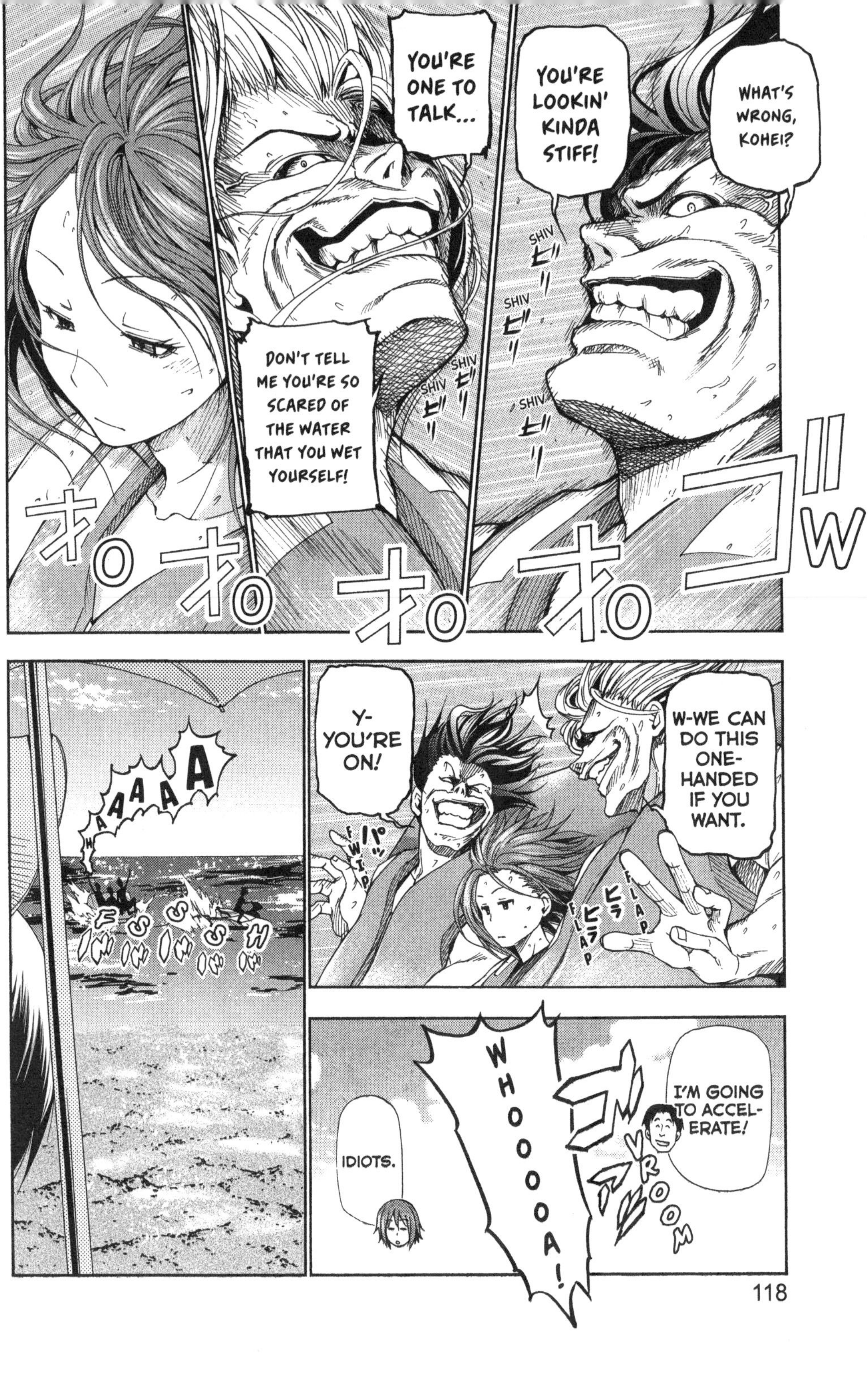
WHAT'S WRONG, KOHEI?
YOU'RE LOOKIN' KINDA STIFF!
SHIV SHIV SHIV SHIV
YOU'RE ONE TO TALK...
DON'T TELL ME YOU'RE SO SCARED OF THE WATER THAT YOU WET YOURSELF!
W O O O O
W-WE CAN DO THIS ONE-HANDED IF YOU WANT.
FLAP FLAP
Y-YOU'RE ON!
FWIP
HAAAAAA
FSSSSH
I'M GOING TO ACCEL-ERATE!
VROOM
WHOOOOOA!
IDIOTS.

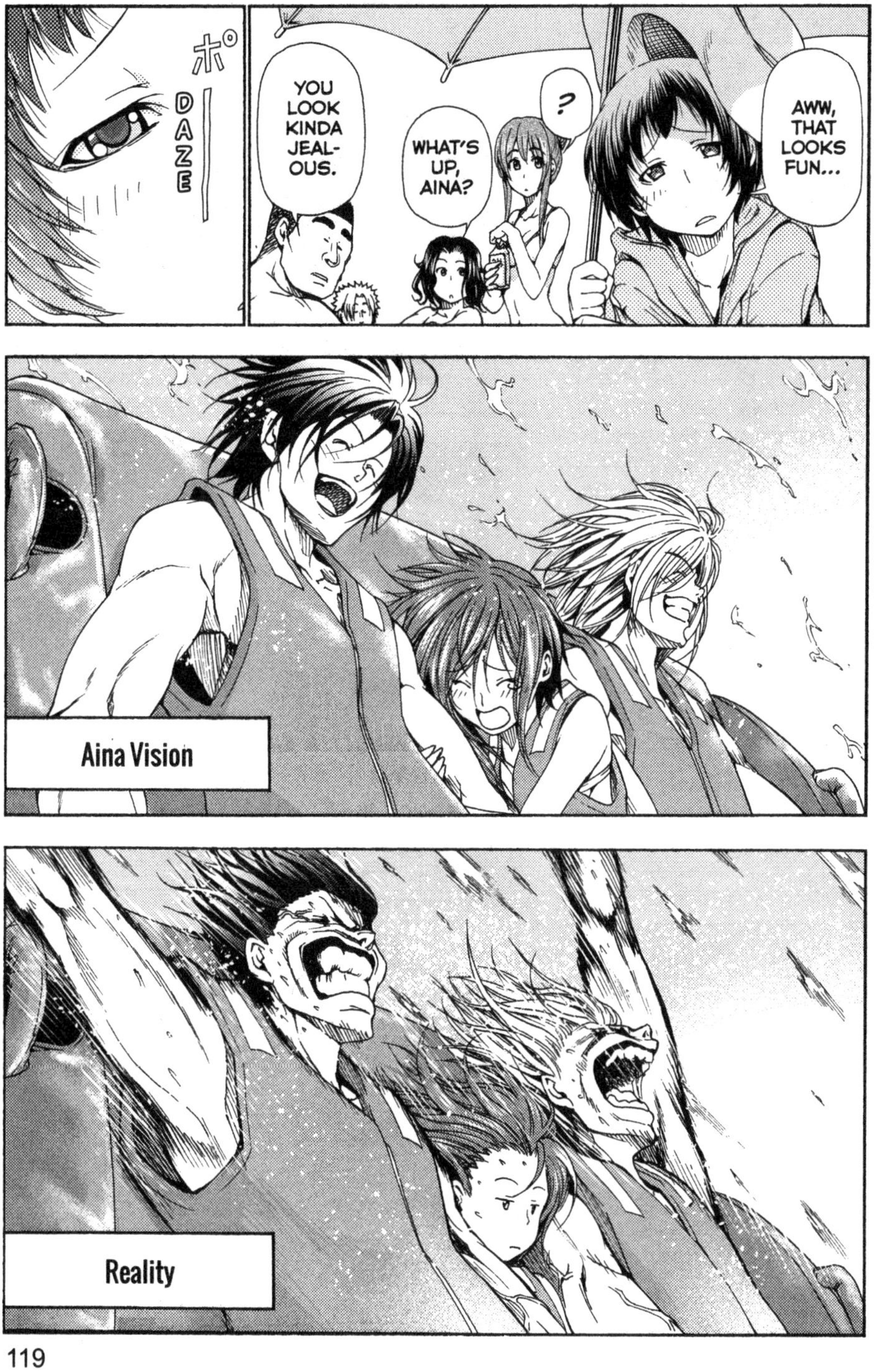
AWW, THAT LOOKS FUN...
?
WHAT'S UP, AINA?
YOU LOOK KINDA JEAL-OUS.
ポー
DAZE
Aina Vision
Reality

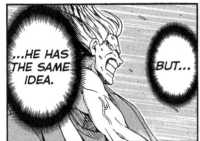

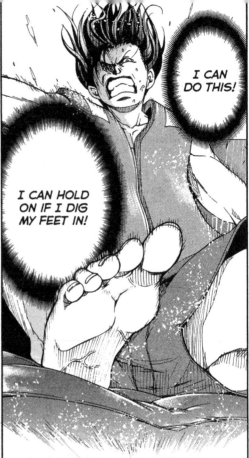

I CAN DO THIS!
I CAN HOLD ON IF I DIG MY FEET IN!
BUT...
...HE HAS THE SAME IDEA.
I HAVE TO DO SOMETHING ABOUT HIS FEET!
SUN OIL

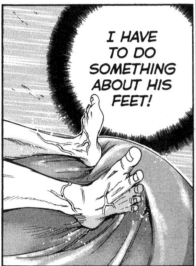

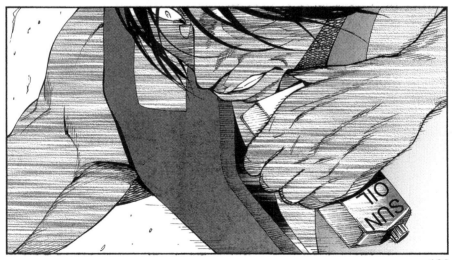

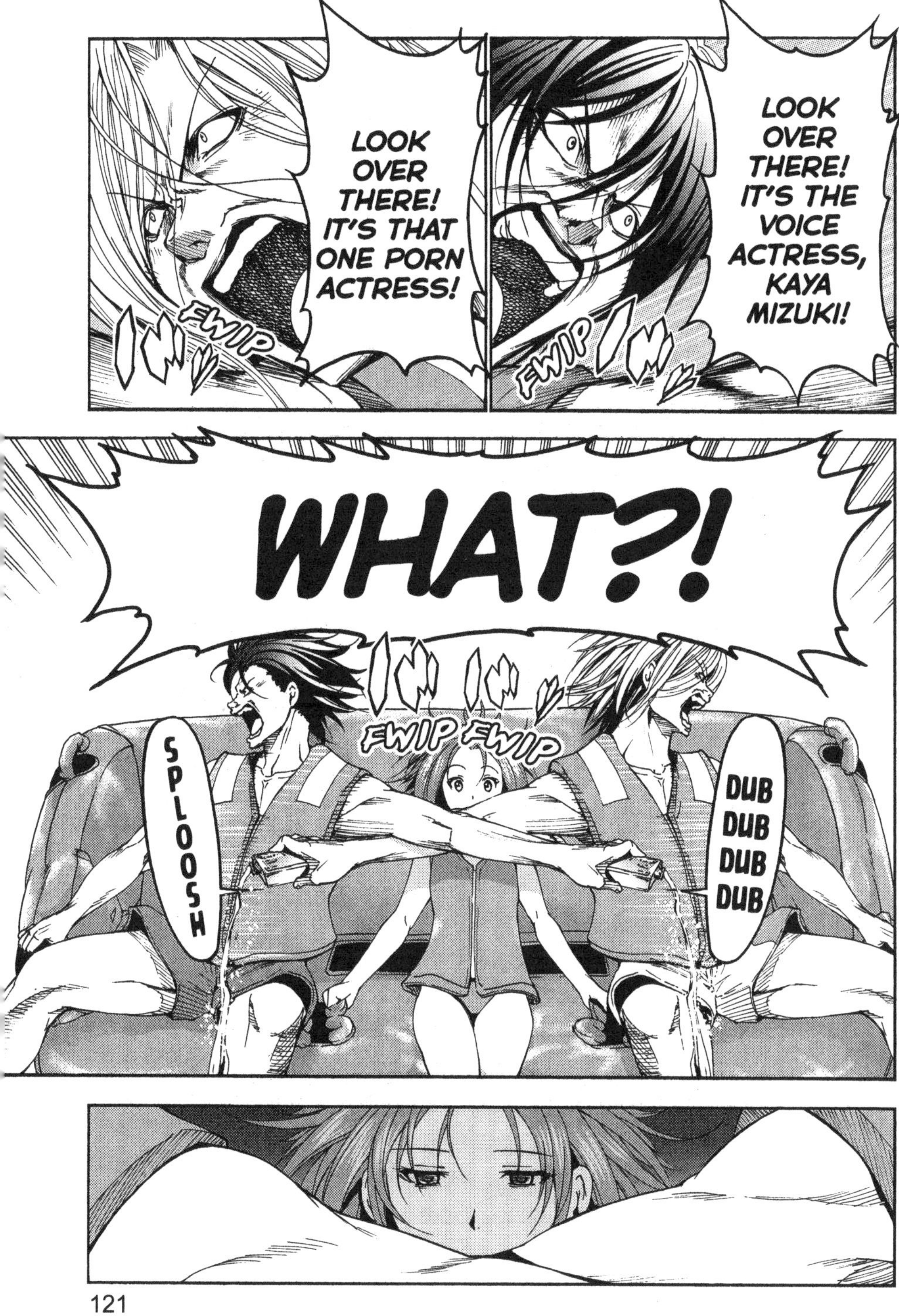
LOOK OVER THERE! IT'S THE VOICE ACTRESS, KAYA MIZUKI!
FWIP
LOOK OVER THERE! IT'S THAT ONE PORN ACTRESS!
FWIP
WHAT?!
FWIP FWIP
DUB DUB DUB DUB
SPLOOSH

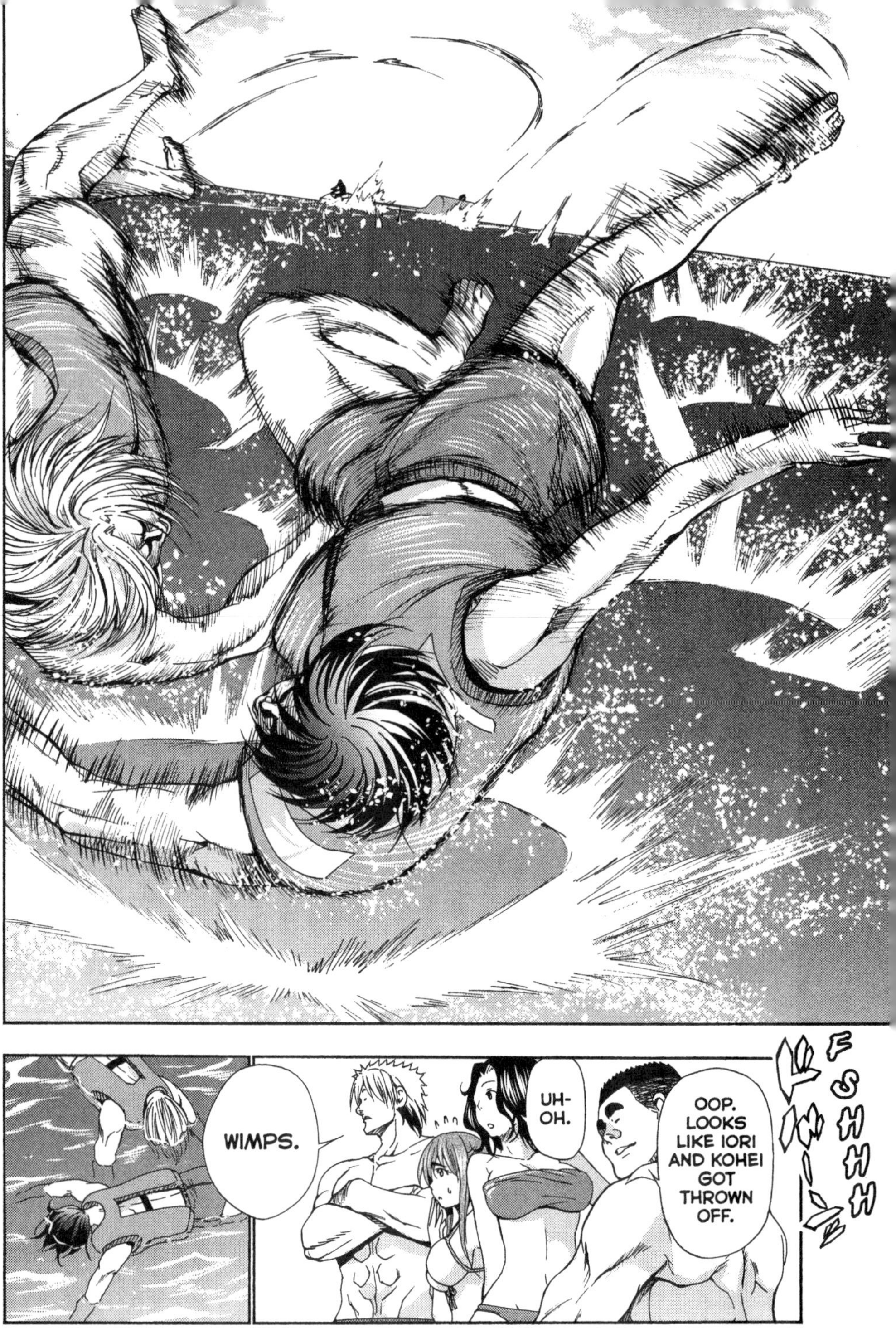
FSHHH
OOP. LOOKS LIKE IORI AND KOHEI GOT THROWN OFF.
UH-OH.
WIMPS.

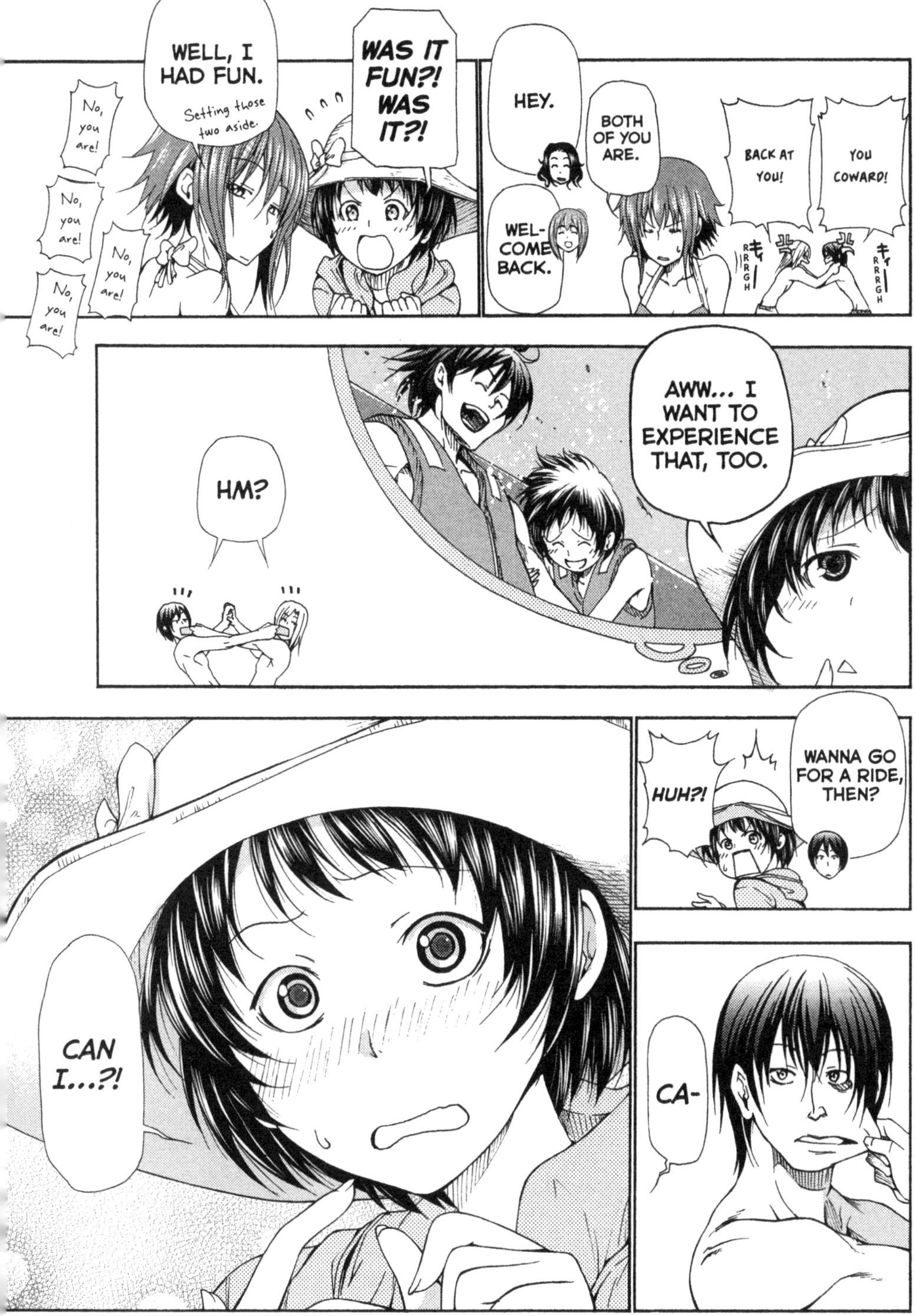

YOU COWARD!
キィ
RRRGH
BACK AT YOU!
キィ
RRRGH
BOTH OF YOU ARE.
HEY.
WEL-COME BACK.
WAS IT FUN?! WAS IT?!
WELL, I HAD FUN.
Setting those two aside.
No, you are!
No, you are!
No, you are!
No, you are!
AWW... I WANT TO EXPERIENCE THAT, TOO.
HM?
WANNA GO FOR A RIDE, THEN?
HUH?!
CA-
CAN I...?!

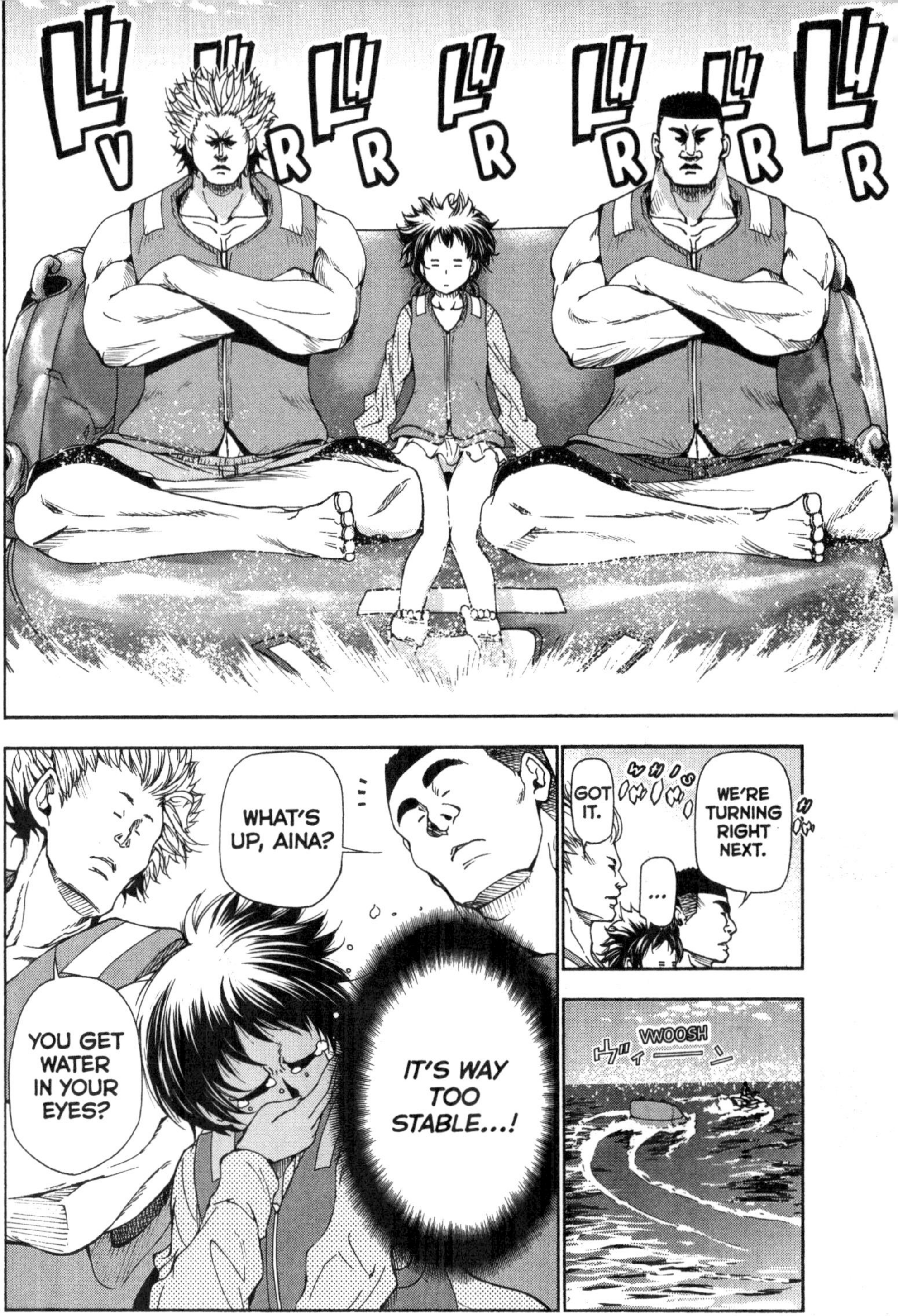
V R R R R R R
WE'RE TURNING RIGHT NEXT.
GOT IT.
...
VWOOSH
WHAT'S UP, AINA?
IT'S WAY TOO STABLE...!
YOU GET WATER IN YOUR EYES?

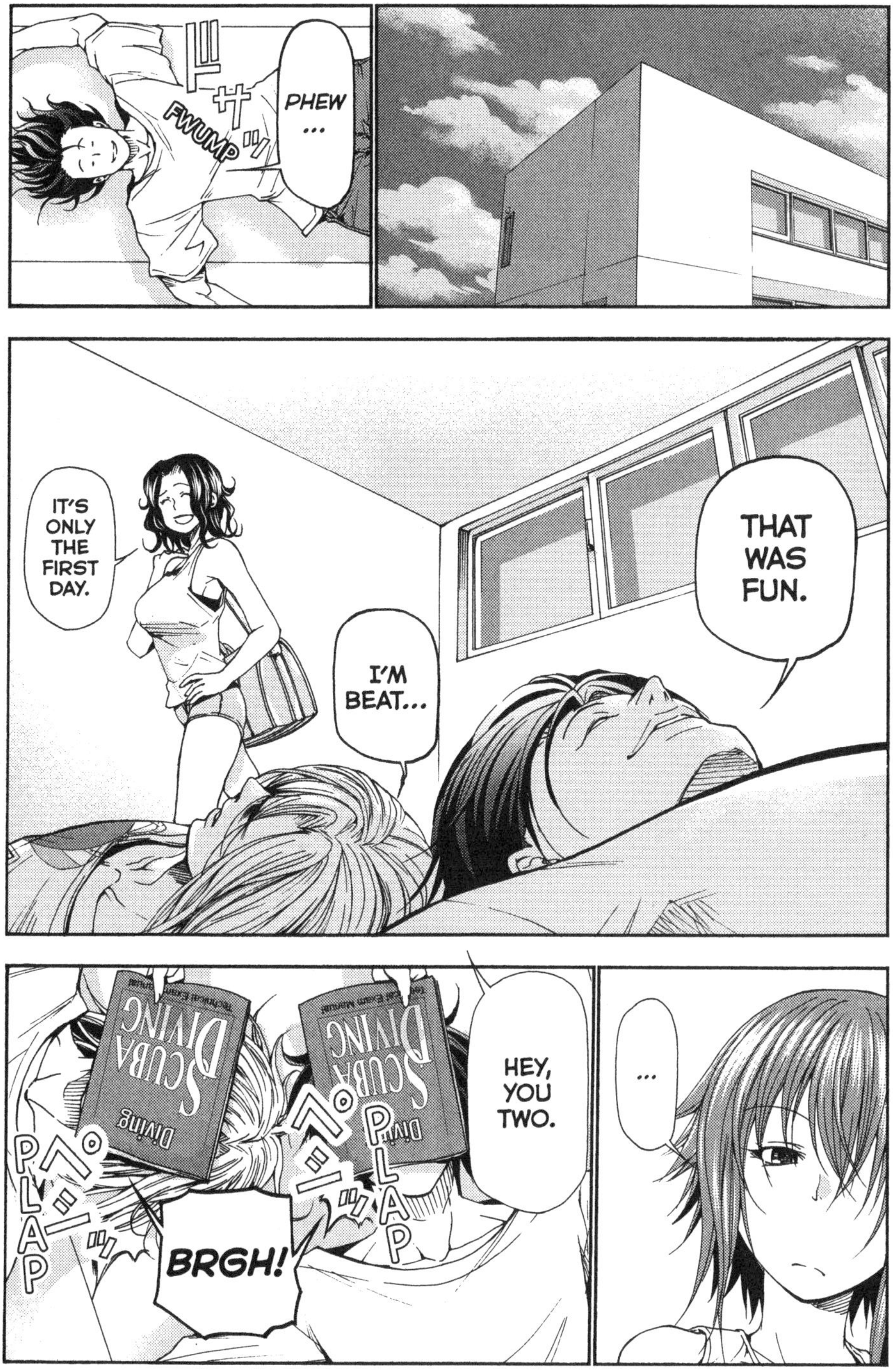
PHEW ...
FWUMP
THAT WAS FUN.
I'M BEAT...
IT'S ONLY THE FIRST DAY.
...
HEY, YOU TWO.
PLAP
PLAP
BRGH!

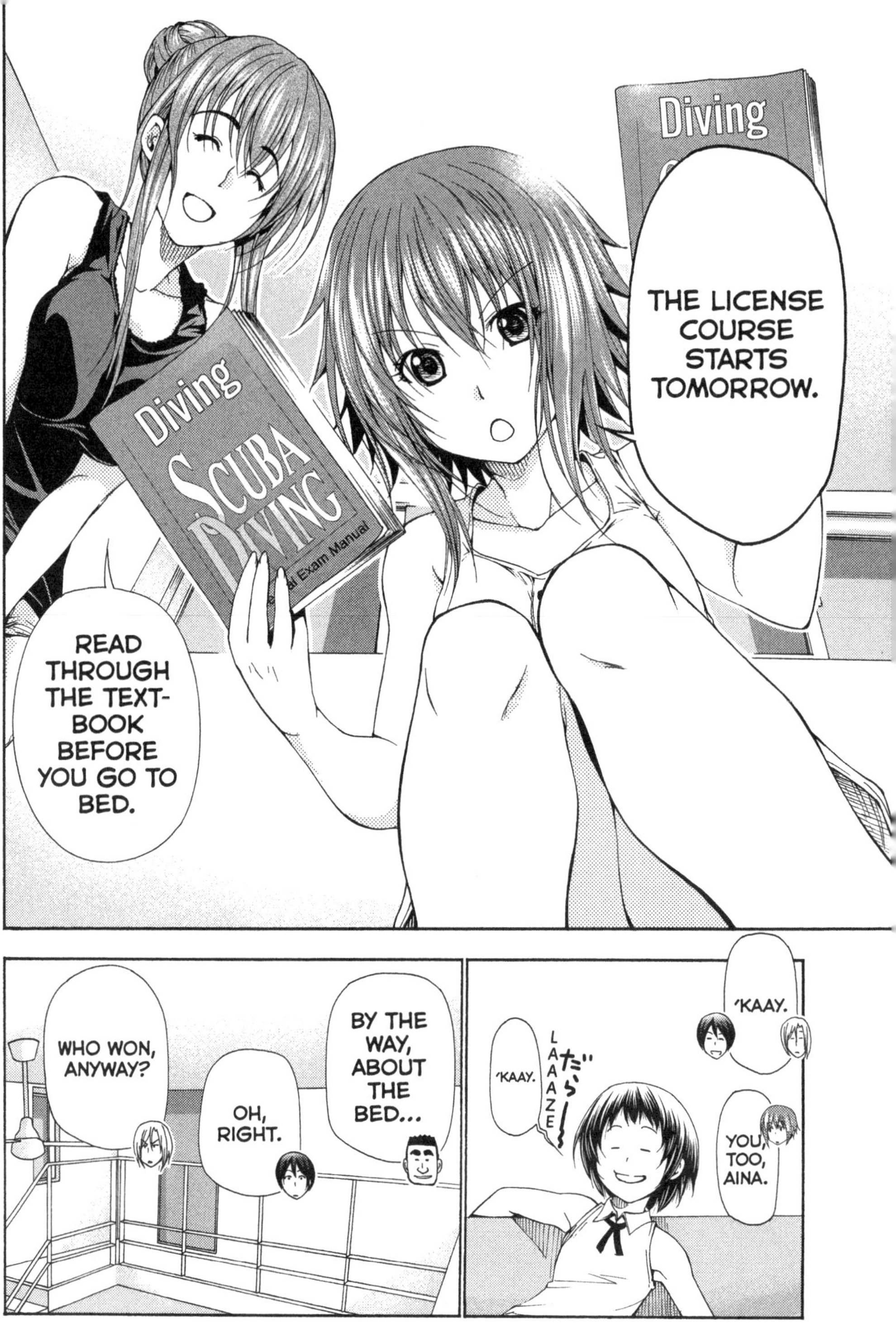
Diving
THE LICENSE COURSE STARTS TOMORROW.
Diving
SCUBA DIVING
READ THROUGH THE TEXT-BOOK BEFORE YOU GO TO BED.
'KAAY.
YOU, TOO, AINA.
'KAAY.
LAAAAZE
だら～
BY THE WAY, ABOUT THE BED...
OH, RIGHT.
WHO WON, ANYWAY?

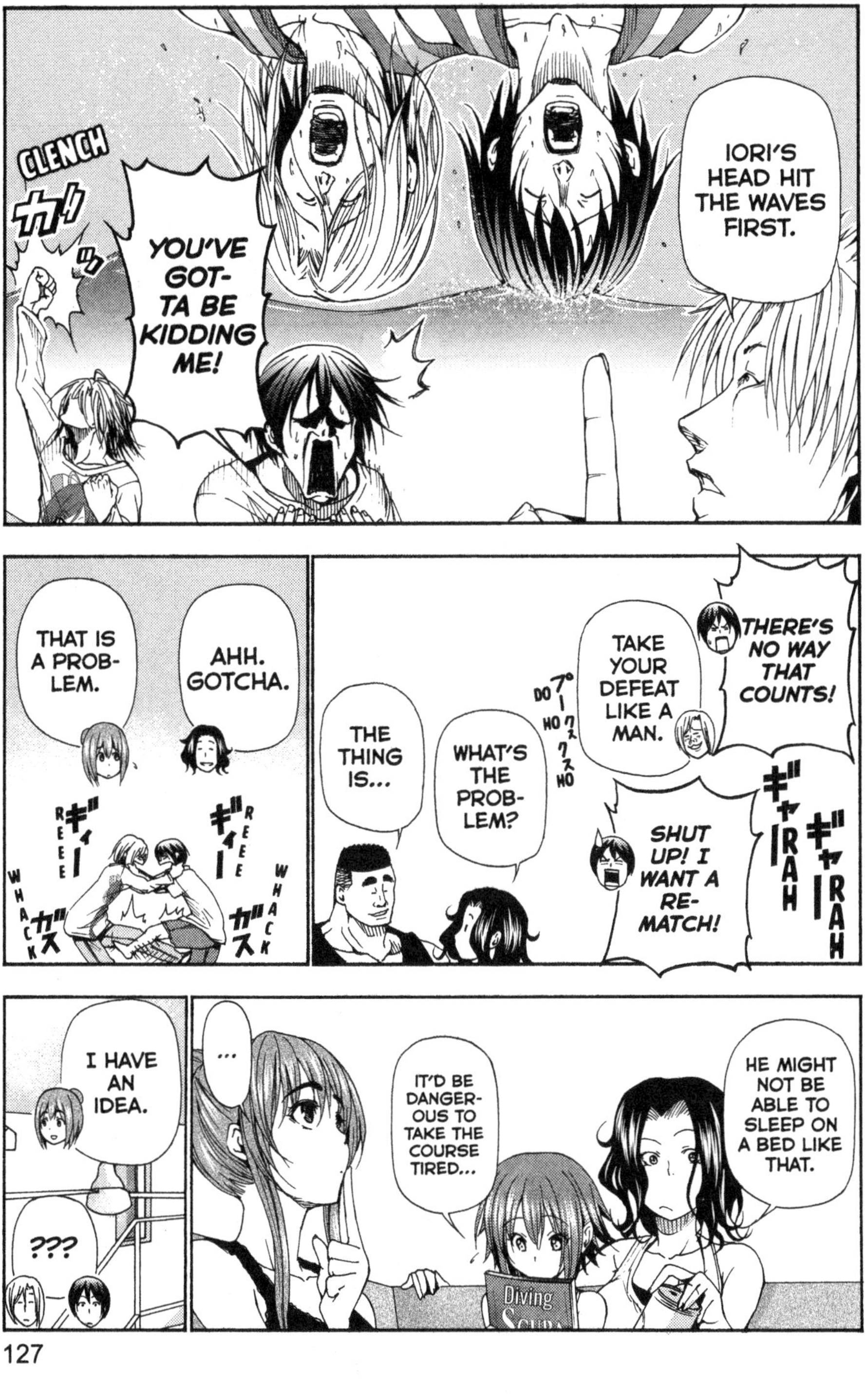
IORI'S HEAD HIT THE WAVES FIRST.
CLENCH
カタッ
YOU'VE GOTTA BE KIDDING ME!
THERE'S NO WAY THAT COUNTS!
TAKE YOUR DEFEAT LIKE A MAN.
DO プー HO クス クス HO
ギャー RAH ギャー RAH
SHUT UP! I WANT A RE-MATCH!
WHAT'S THE PROBLEM?
THE THING IS...
AHH. GOTCHA.
THAT IS A PROBLEM.
ギィー REEE ギィー REEE
ガス WHACK ガス WHACK
HE MIGHT NOT BE ABLE TO SLEEP ON A BED LIKE THAT.
IT'D BE DANGEROUS TO TAKE THE COURSE TIRED...
...
Diving
I HAVE AN IDEA.
???

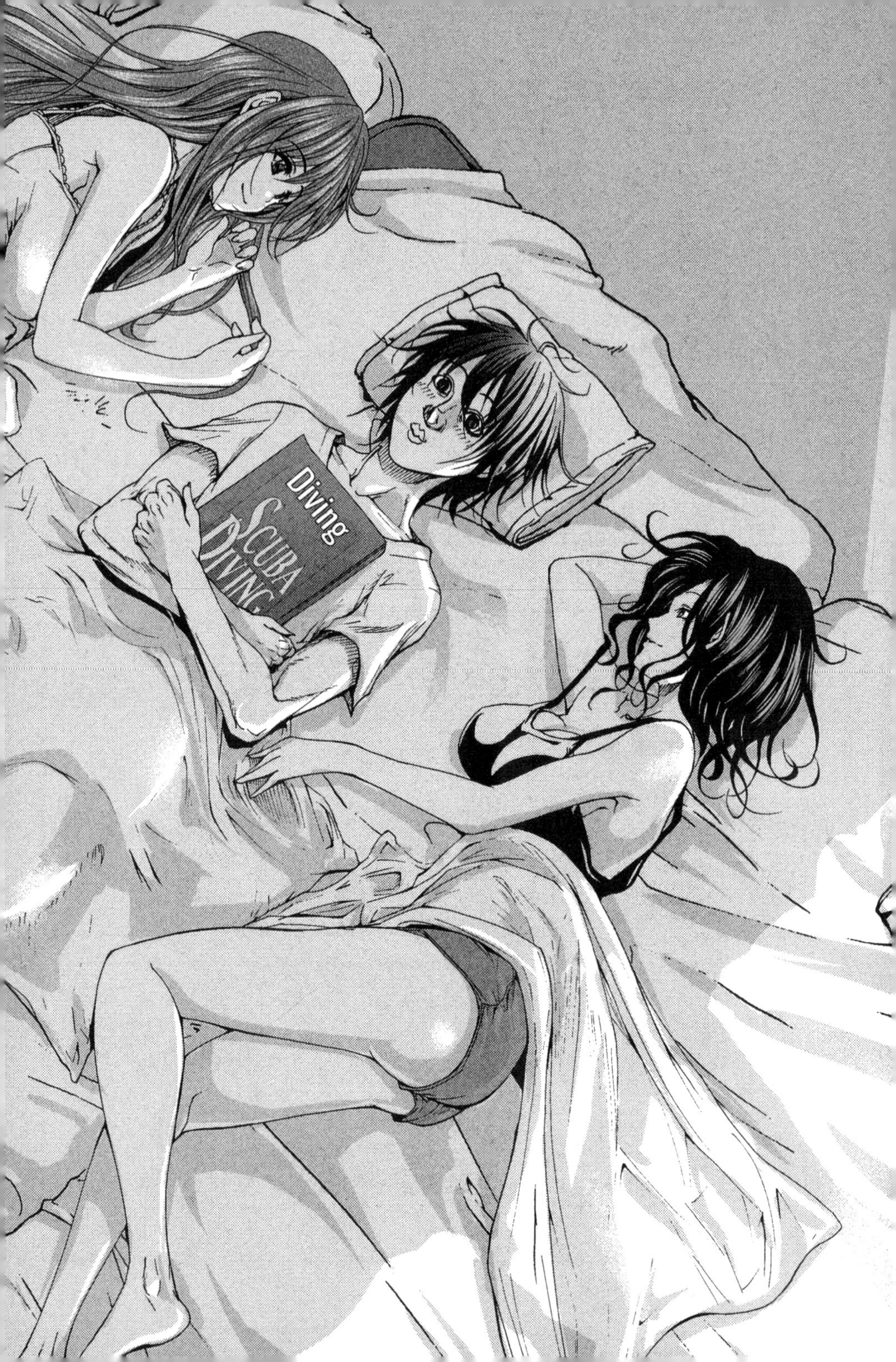
Diving
SCUBA

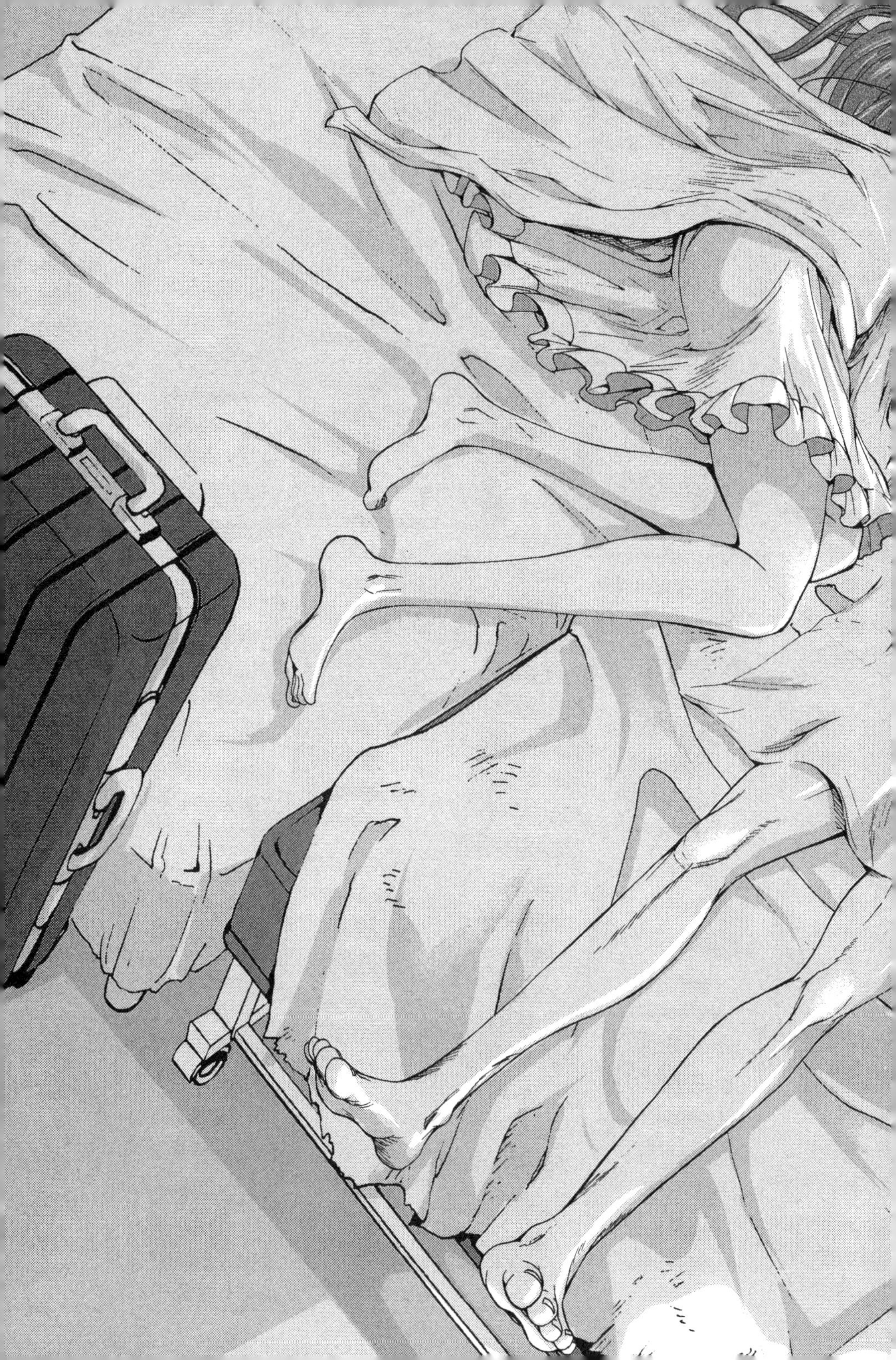

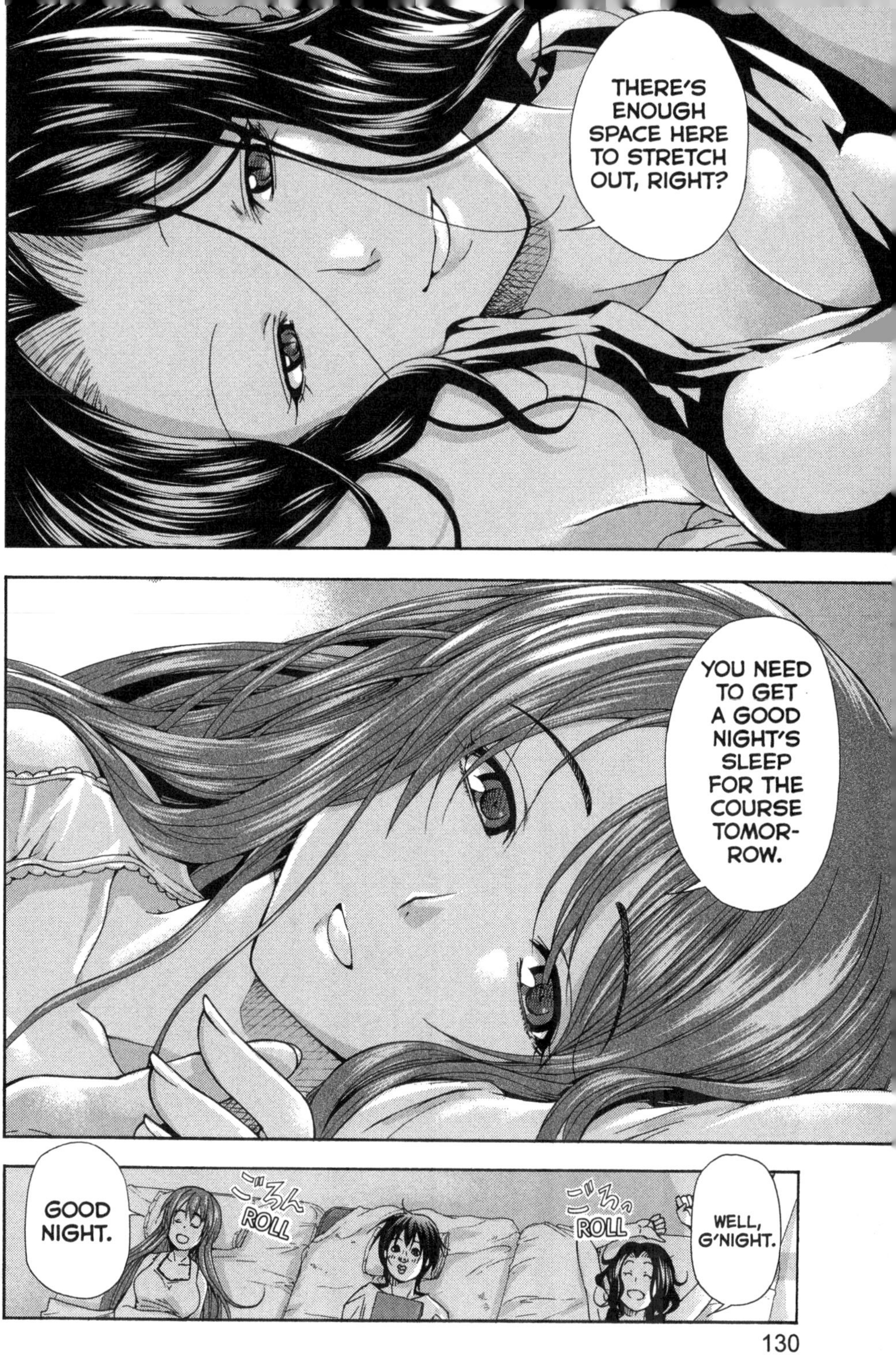
THERE'S ENOUGH SPACE HERE TO STRETCH OUT, RIGHT?
YOU NEED TO GET A GOOD NIGHT'S SLEEP FOR THE COURSE TOMOR-ROW.
WELL, G'NIGHT.
ごろっ ROLL
ごろん ROLL
GOOD NIGHT.

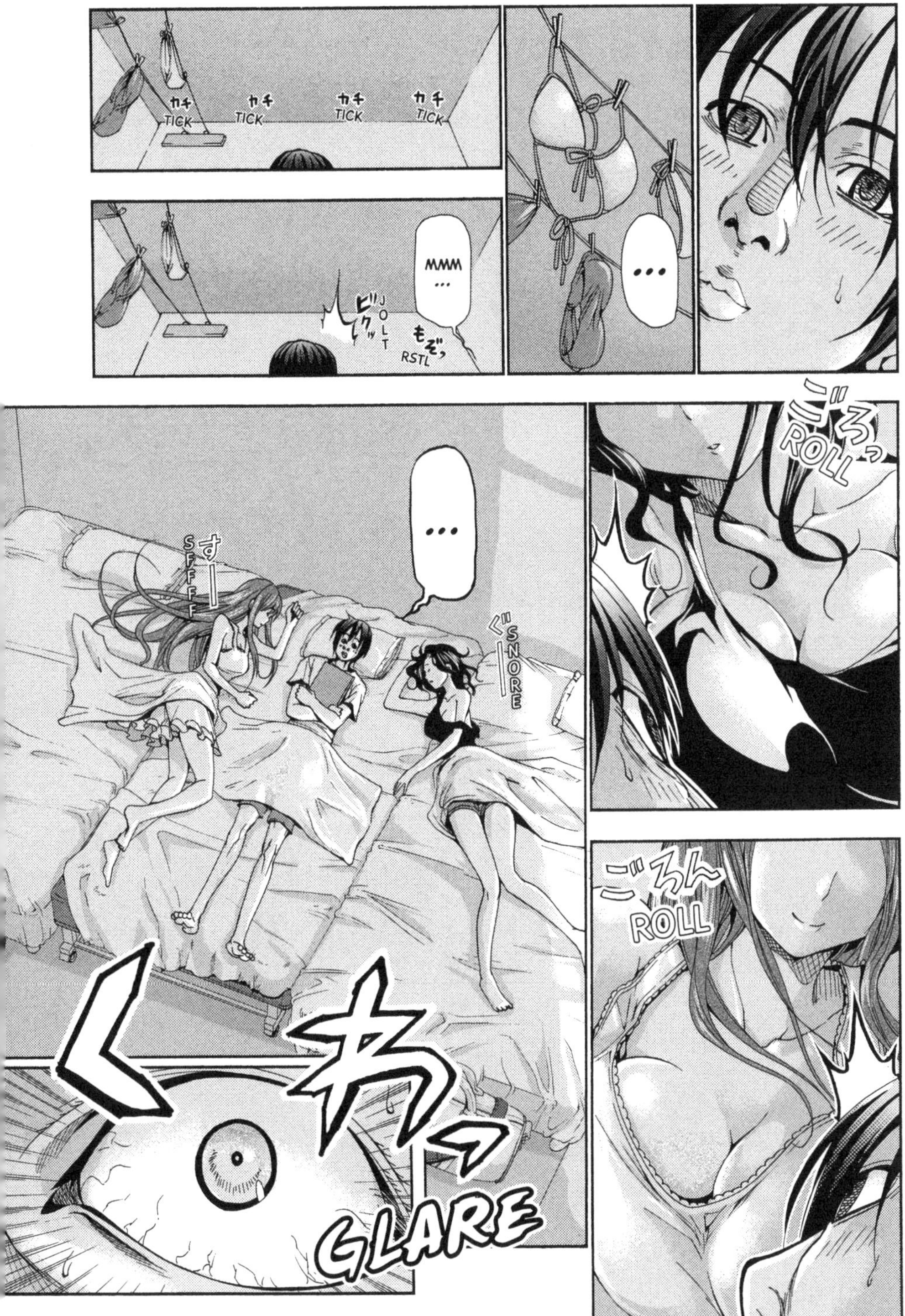
...
カチ
TICK
カチ
TICK
カチ
TICK
カチ
TICK
MMM ...
ビクッ
JOLT
もぞ
RSTL
ごろっ
ROLL
ごろん
ROLL
ぐー
SNORE
...
すー
SFFFF
くわっ
GLARE

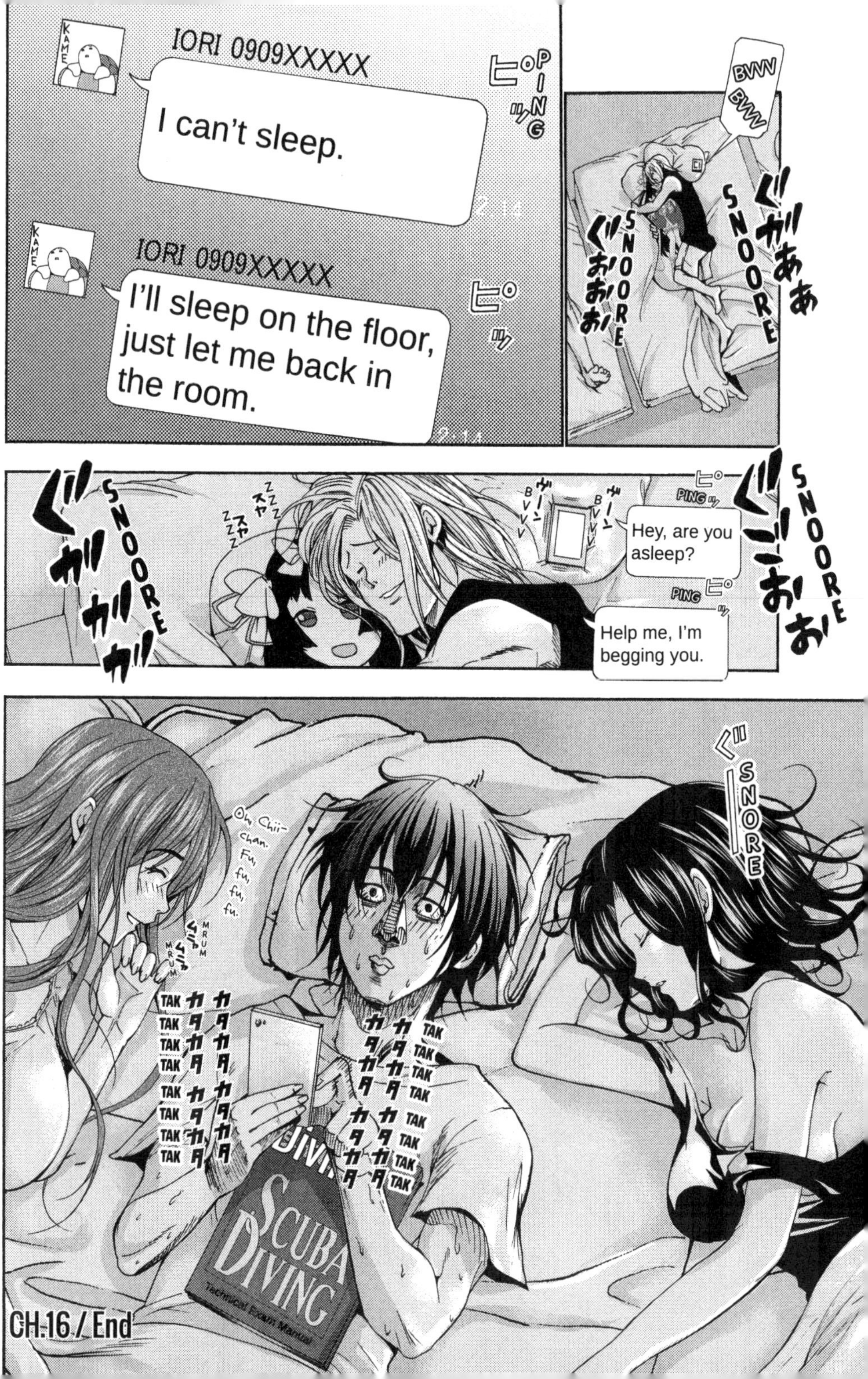
BVVV BVVV
ぐがああ SNOORE
ぐおおお SNOORE
ピッ PING
IORI 0909XXXXX
I can't sleep.
2:14
IORI 0909XXXXX
I'll sleep on the floor, just let me back in the room.
ピッ
2:14
ぐごおお SNOORE
ピッ PING
Hey, are you asleep?
ピッ PING
Help me, I'm begging you.
ヴーン BVVV
ヴーン BVVV
スヤ ZZZ
スヤ ZZZ
ぐがががが SNOORE
ぐー SNORE
カタカタ TAK TAK
Oh, Chii-chan. Fu, fu, fu, fu.
ムニャ MRUM
SCUBA DIVING
Technical Exam Manual
CH.16 / End

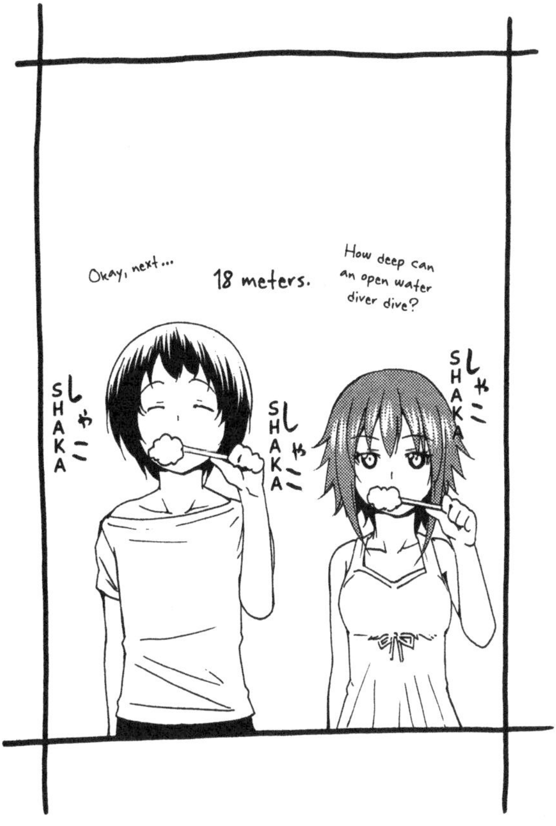
How deep can an open water diver dive?
SHAKA
18 meters.
SHAKA
Okay, next...
SHAKA

Grand Blue Dreaming

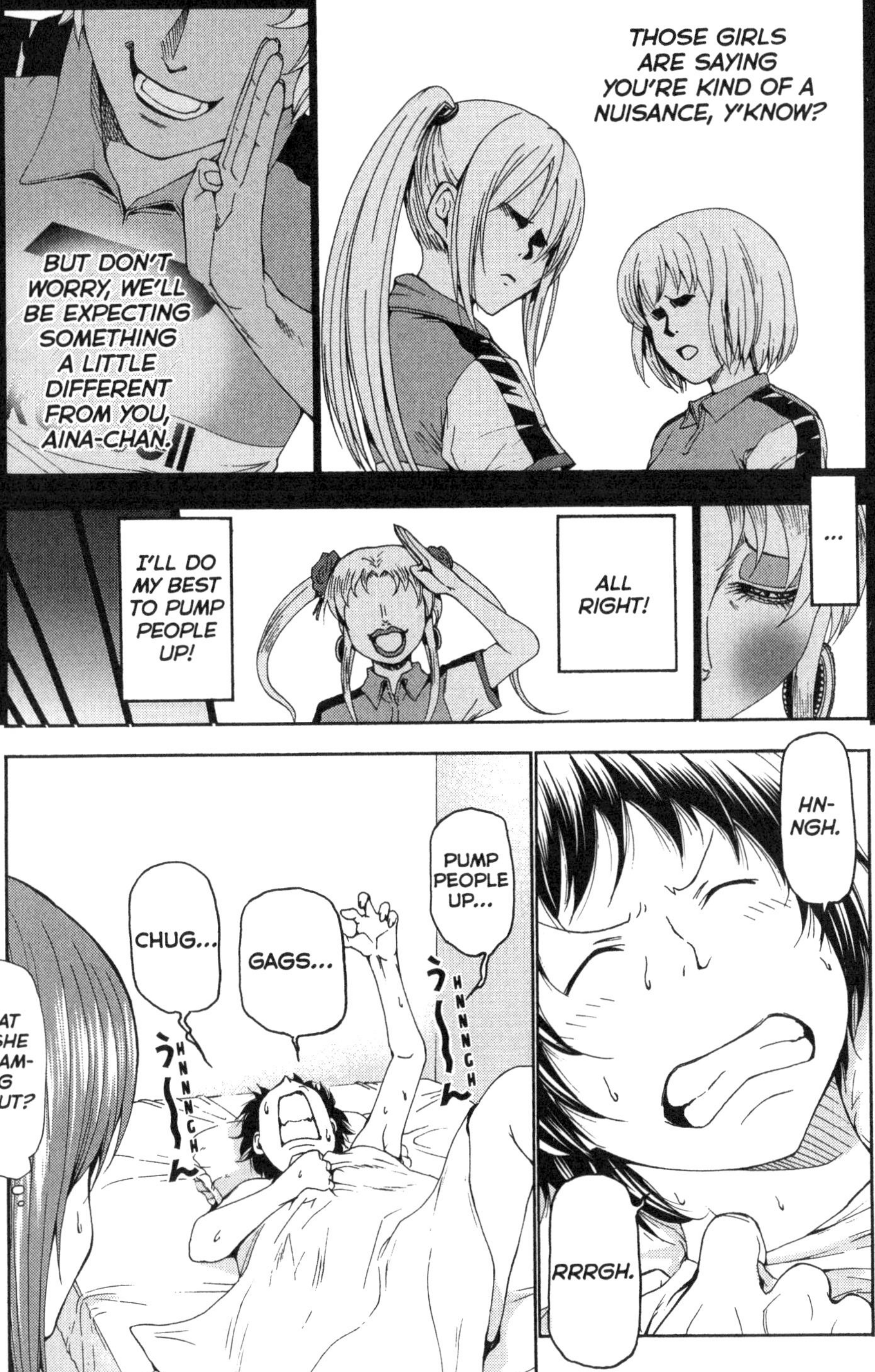
THOSE GIRLS ARE SAYING YOU'RE KIND OF A NUISANCE, Y'KNOW?
BUT DON'T WORRY, WE'LL BE EXPECTING SOMETHING A LITTLE DIFFERENT FROM YOU, AINA-CHAN.
...
ALL RIGHT!
I'LL DO MY BEST TO PUMP PEOPLE UP!
HN-NGH.
RRRGH.
PUMP PEOPLE UP...
うーん HNNNGH
GAGS...
CHUG...
うーん HNNNGH
WHAT IS SHE DREAMING ABOUT?

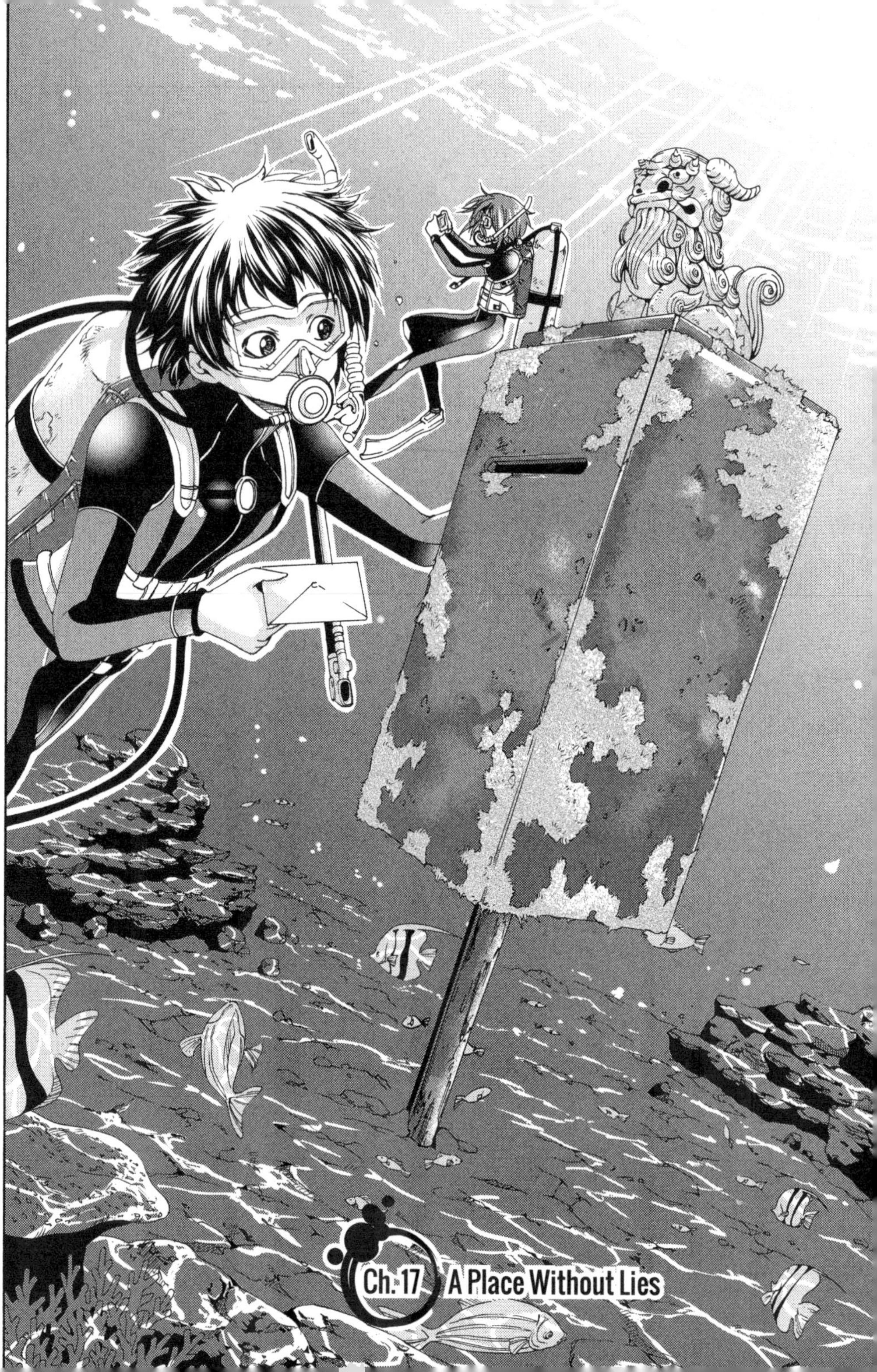
Ch. 17 A Place Without Lies

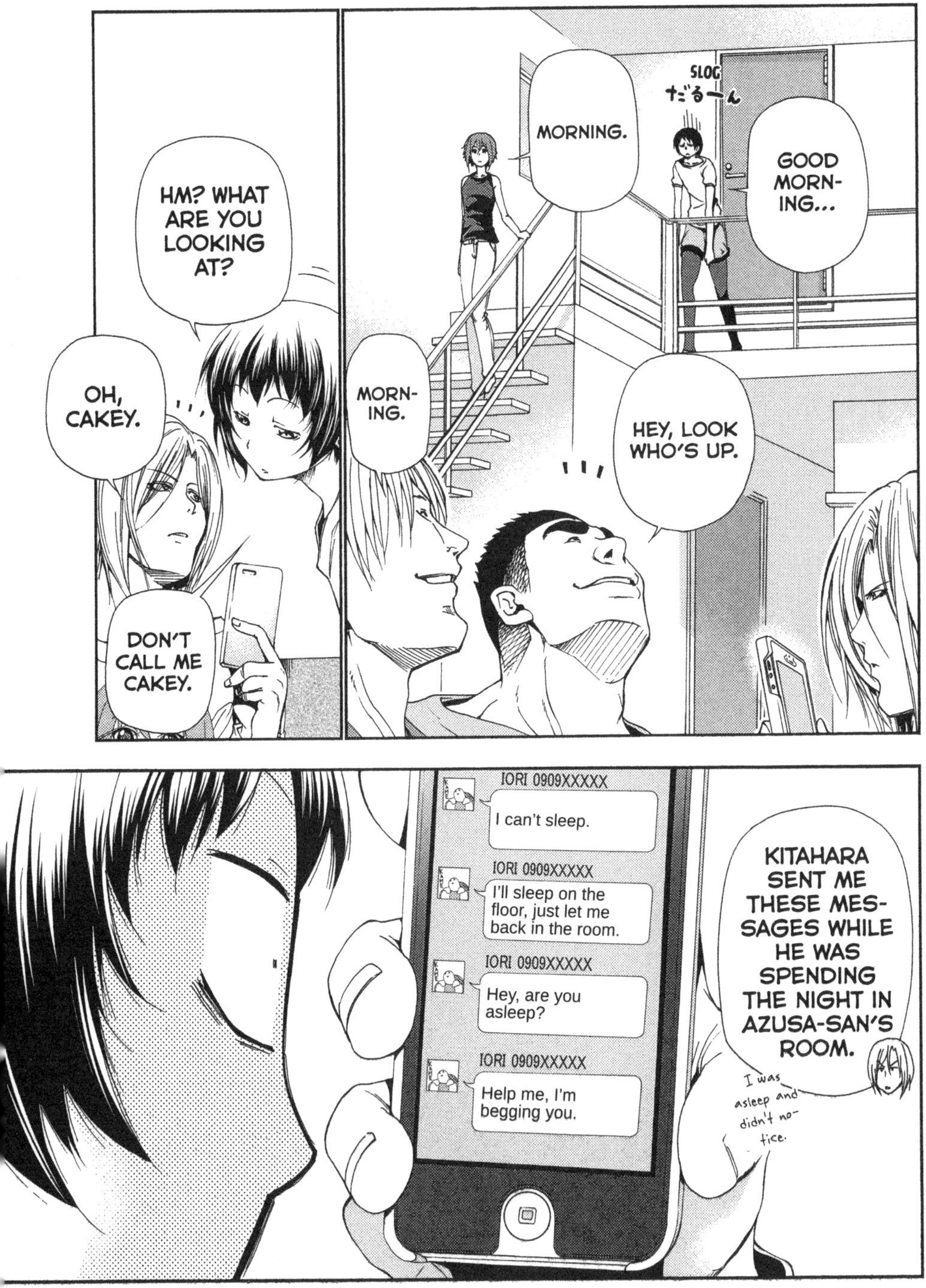
GOOD MORN-ING...
SLOG
だるーん
MORNING.
HEY, LOOK WHO'S UP.
MORN-ING.
HM? WHAT ARE YOU LOOKING AT?
OH, CAKEY.
DON'T CALL ME CAKEY.
KITAHARA SENT ME THESE MES-SAGES WHILE HE WAS SPENDING THE NIGHT IN AZUSA-SAN'S ROOM.
IORI 0909XXXXX
I can't sleep.
IORI 0909XXXXX
I'll sleep on the floor, just let me back in the room.
IORI 0909XXXXX
Hey, are you asleep?
IORI 0909XXXXX
Help me, I'm begging you.
I was asleep and didn't no-tice.

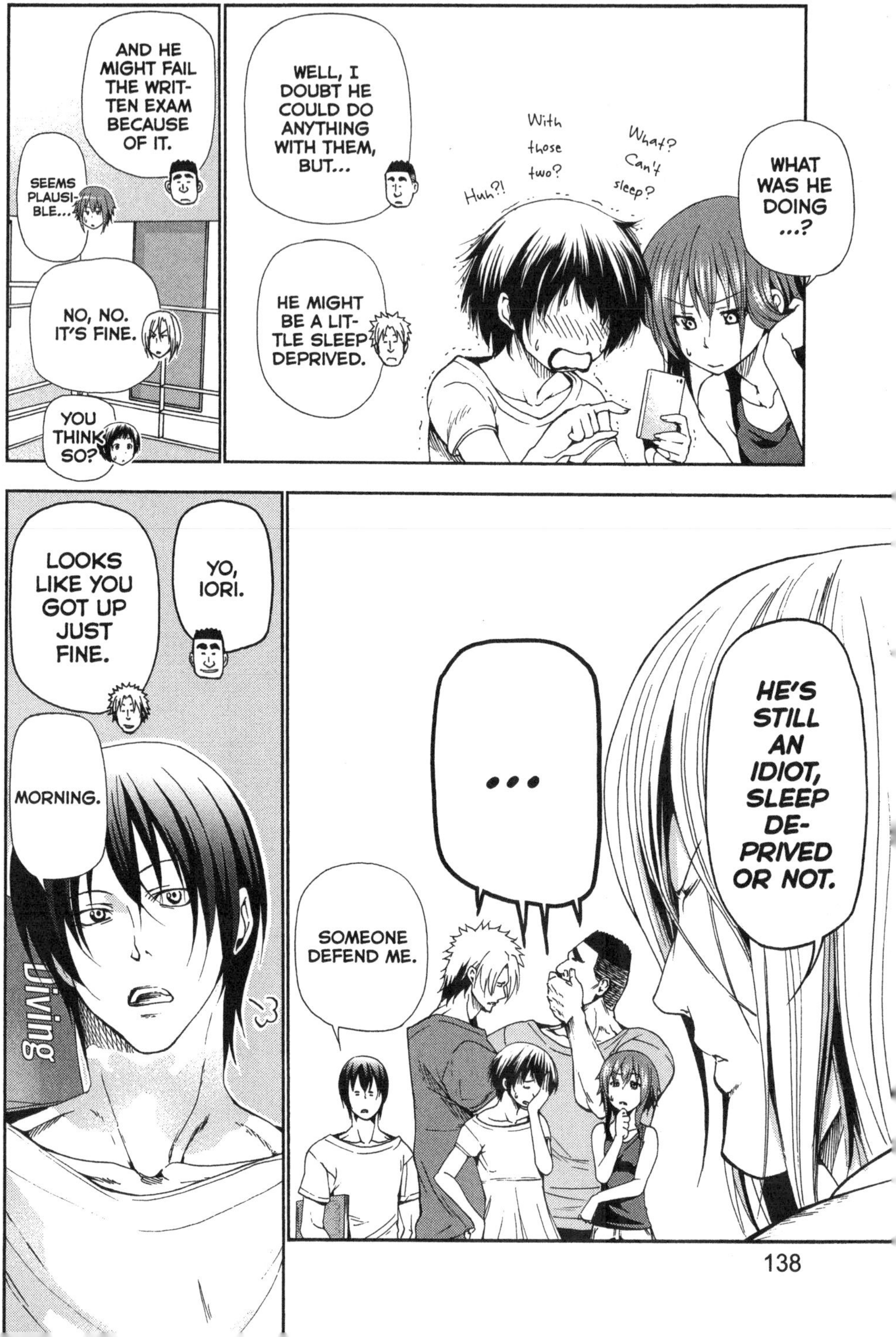
WHAT WAS HE DOING ...?
What? Can't sleep?
With those two?
Huh?!
WELL, I DOUBT HE COULD DO ANYTHING WITH THEM, BUT...
HE MIGHT BE A LITTLE SLEEP DEPRIVED.
AND HE MIGHT FAIL THE WRITTEN EXAM BECAUSE OF IT.
SEEMS PLAUSIBLE...
NO, NO. IT'S FINE.
YOU THINK SO?
HE'S STILL AN IDIOT, SLEEP DEPRIVED OR NOT.
...
SOMEONE DEFEND ME.
YO, IORI.
LOOKS LIKE YOU GOT UP JUST FINE.
MORNING.
Diving

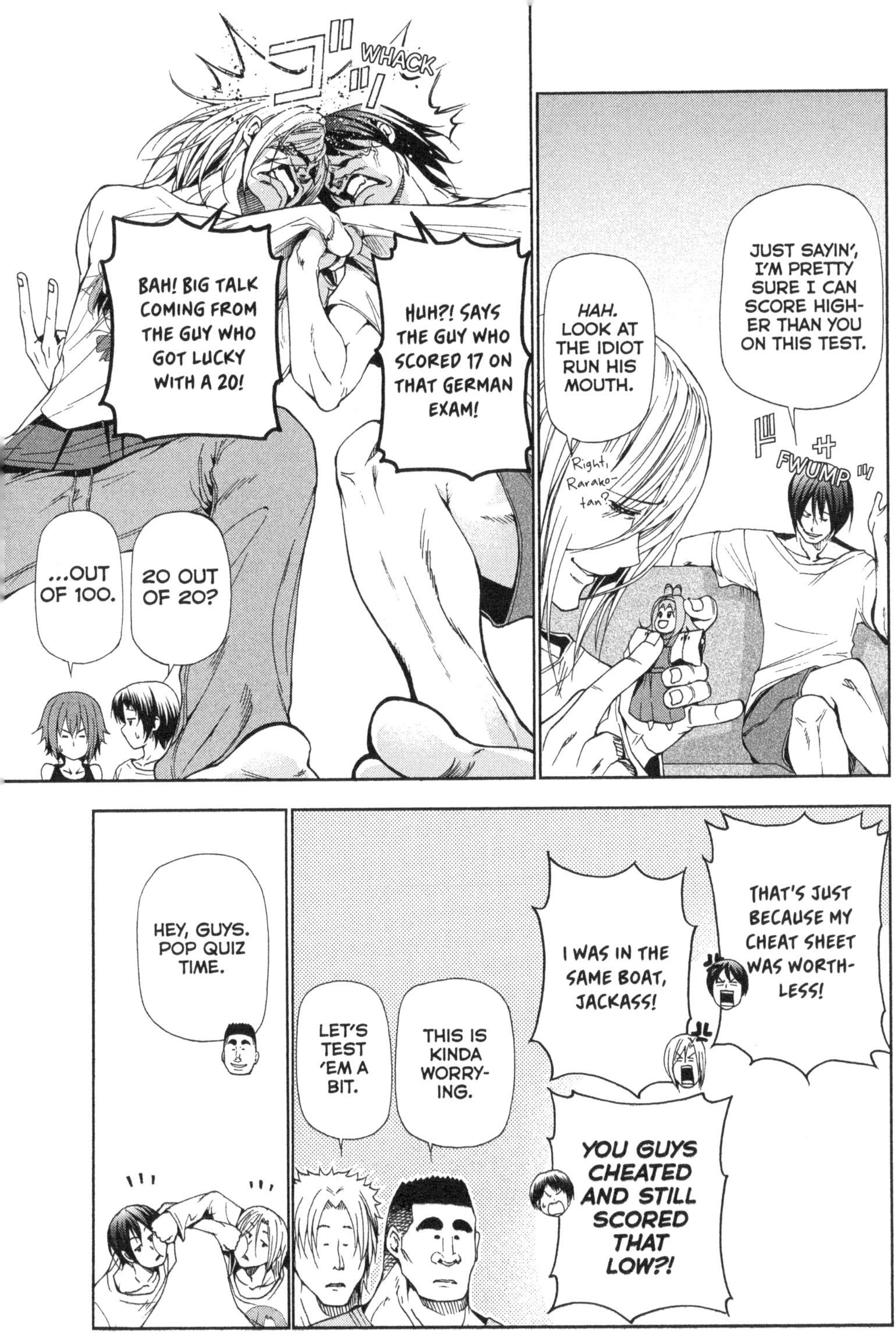
JUST SAYIN', I'M PRETTY SURE I CAN SCORE HIGH-ER THAN YOU ON THIS TEST.
FWUMP
HAH. LOOK AT THE IDIOT RUN HIS MOUTH.
Right, Rarako-tan?
WHACK
HUH?! SAYS THE GUY WHO SCORED 17 ON THAT GERMAN EXAM!
BAH! BIG TALK COMING FROM THE GUY WHO GOT LUCKY WITH A 20!
20 OUT OF 20?
...OUT OF 100.
THAT'S JUST BECAUSE MY CHEAT SHEET WAS WORTH-LESS!
I WAS IN THE SAME BOAT, JACKASS!
YOU GUYS CHEATED AND STILL SCORED THAT LOW?!
THIS IS KINDA WORRY-ING.
LET'S TEST 'EM A BIT.
HEY, GUYS. POP QUIZ TIME.

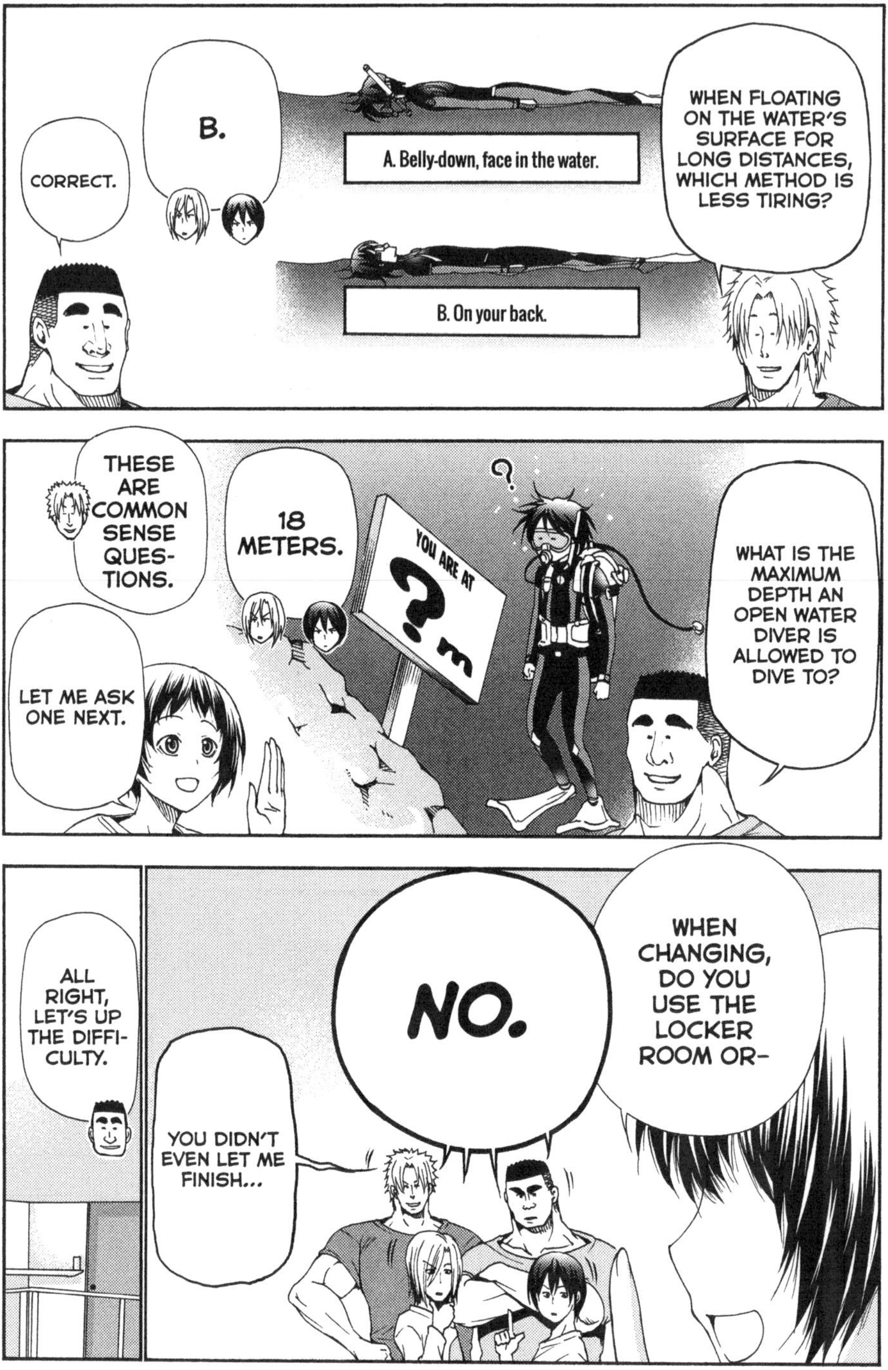
WHEN FLOATING ON THE WATER'S SURFACE FOR LONG DISTANCES, WHICH METHOD IS LESS TIRING?
A. Belly-down, face in the water.
B. On your back.
B.
CORRECT.
WHAT IS THE MAXIMUM DEPTH AN OPEN WATER DIVER IS ALLOWED TO DIVE TO?
YOU ARE AT ? m
18 METERS.
THESE ARE COMMON SENSE QUES- TIONS.
LET ME ASK ONE NEXT.
WHEN CHANGING, DO YOU USE THE LOCKER ROOM OR-
NO.
YOU DIDN'T EVEN LET ME FINISH...
ALL RIGHT, LET'S UP THE DIFFI- CULTY.

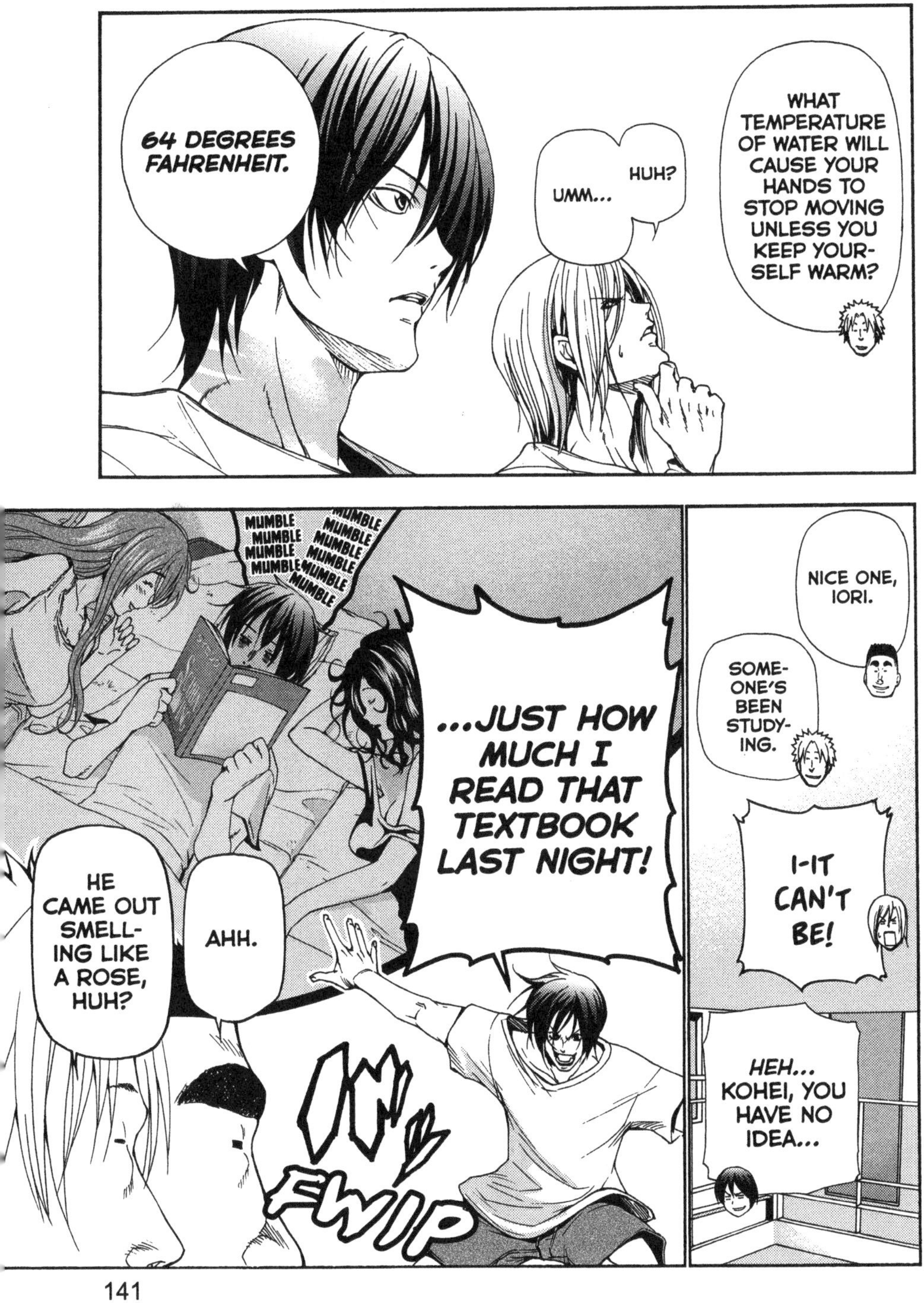
WHAT TEMPERATURE OF WATER WILL CAUSE YOUR HANDS TO STOP MOVING UNLESS YOU KEEP YOURSELF WARM?
HUH? UMM...
64 DEGREES FAHRENHEIT.
NICE ONE, IORI.
SOMEONE'S BEEN STUDYING.
I-IT CAN'T BE!
HEH... KOHEI, YOU HAVE NO IDEA...
...JUST HOW MUCH I READ THAT TEXTBOOK LAST NIGHT!
MUMBLE MUMBLE MUMBLE MUMBLE MUMBLE MUMBLE MUMBLE MUMBLE MUMBLE MUMBLE
AHH.
HE CAME OUT SMELLING LIKE A ROSE, HUH?
FWIP

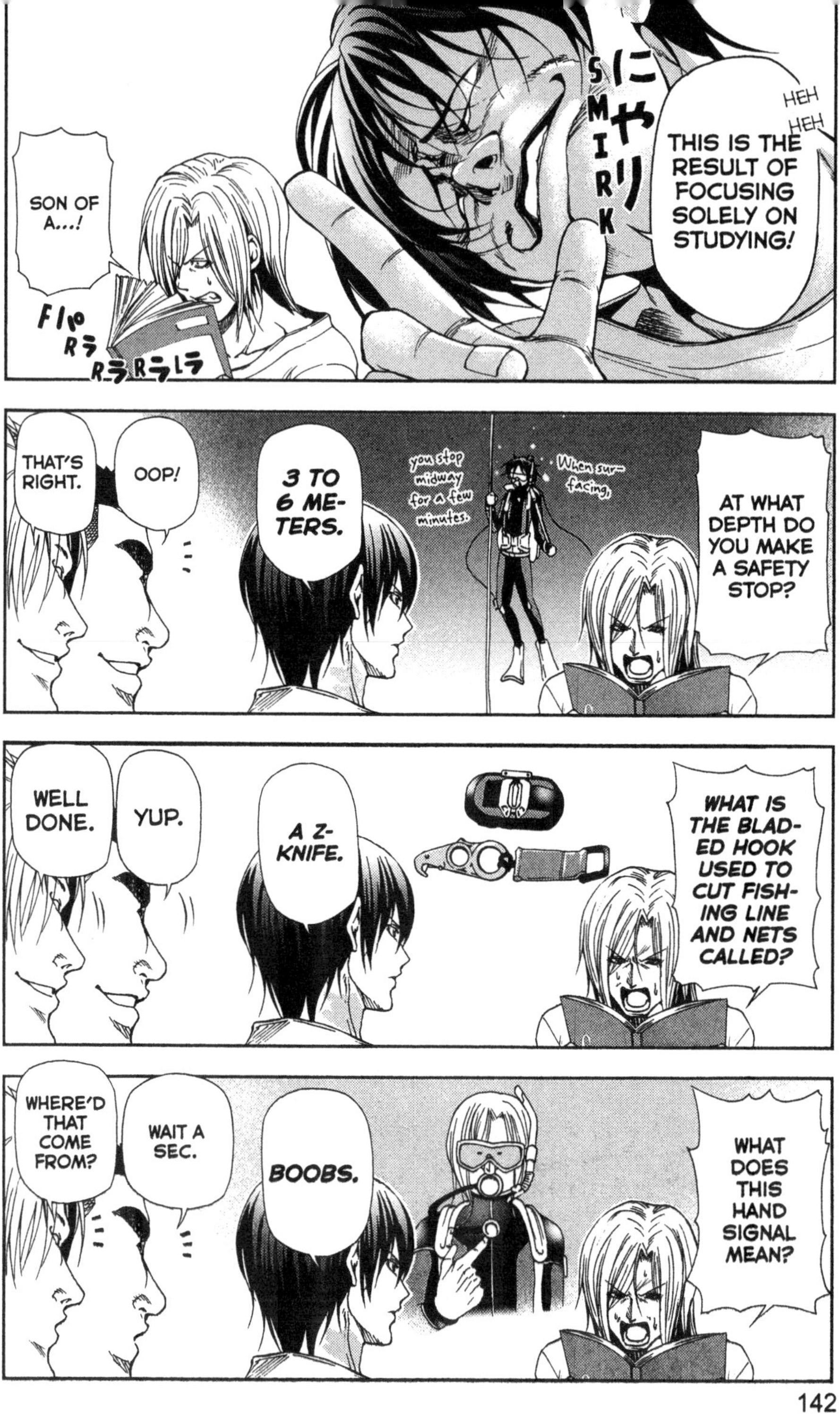
HEH HEH
SMIRK
にやり
THIS IS THE RESULT OF FOCUSING SOLELY ON STUDYING!
SON OF A...!
FIRRRL
AT WHAT DEPTH DO YOU MAKE A SAFETY STOP?
When surfacing, you stop midway for a few minutes.
3 TO 6 METERS.
OOP!
THAT'S RIGHT.
WHAT IS THE BLADED HOOK USED TO CUT FISHING LINE AND NETS CALLED?
A Z-KNIFE.
YUP.
WELL DONE.
WHAT DOES THIS HAND SIGNAL MEAN?
BOOBS.
WAIT A SEC.
WHERE'D THAT COME FROM?

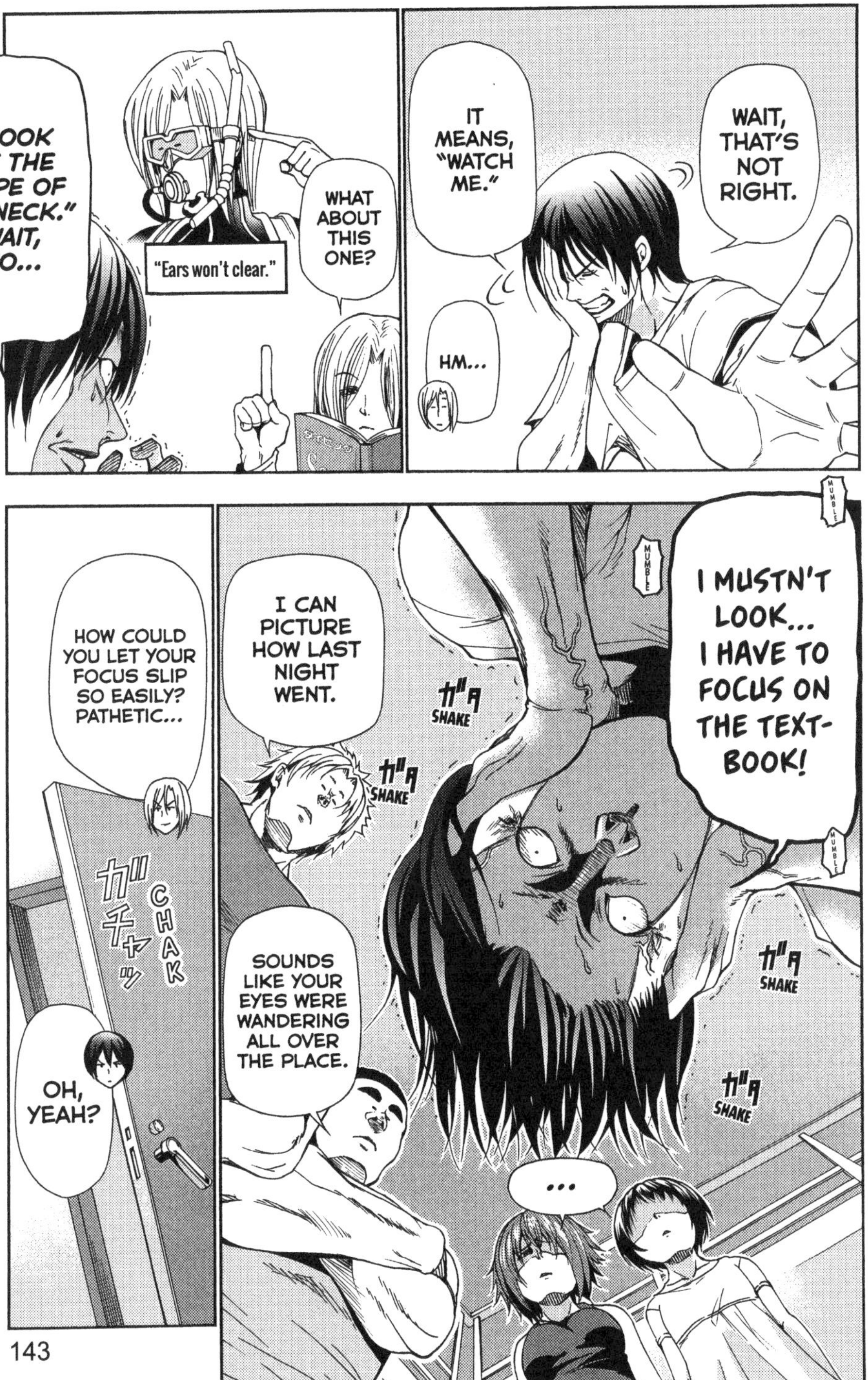
WAIT, THAT'S NOT RIGHT.
IT MEANS, "WATCH ME."
HM...
WHAT ABOUT THIS ONE?
"Ears won't clear."
"LOOK AT THE NAPE OF MY NECK." WAIT, NO...
MUMBLE
MUMBLE
I MUSTN'T LOOK... I HAVE TO FOCUS ON THE TEXT-BOOK!
MUMBLE
I CAN PICTURE HOW LAST NIGHT WENT.
ガタ SHAKE
ガタ SHAKE
ガタ SHAKE
ガタ SHAKE
SOUNDS LIKE YOUR EYES WERE WANDERING ALL OVER THE PLACE.
...
HOW COULD YOU LET YOUR FOCUS SLIP SO EASILY? PATHETIC...
ガチャッ CHAK
OH, YEAH?

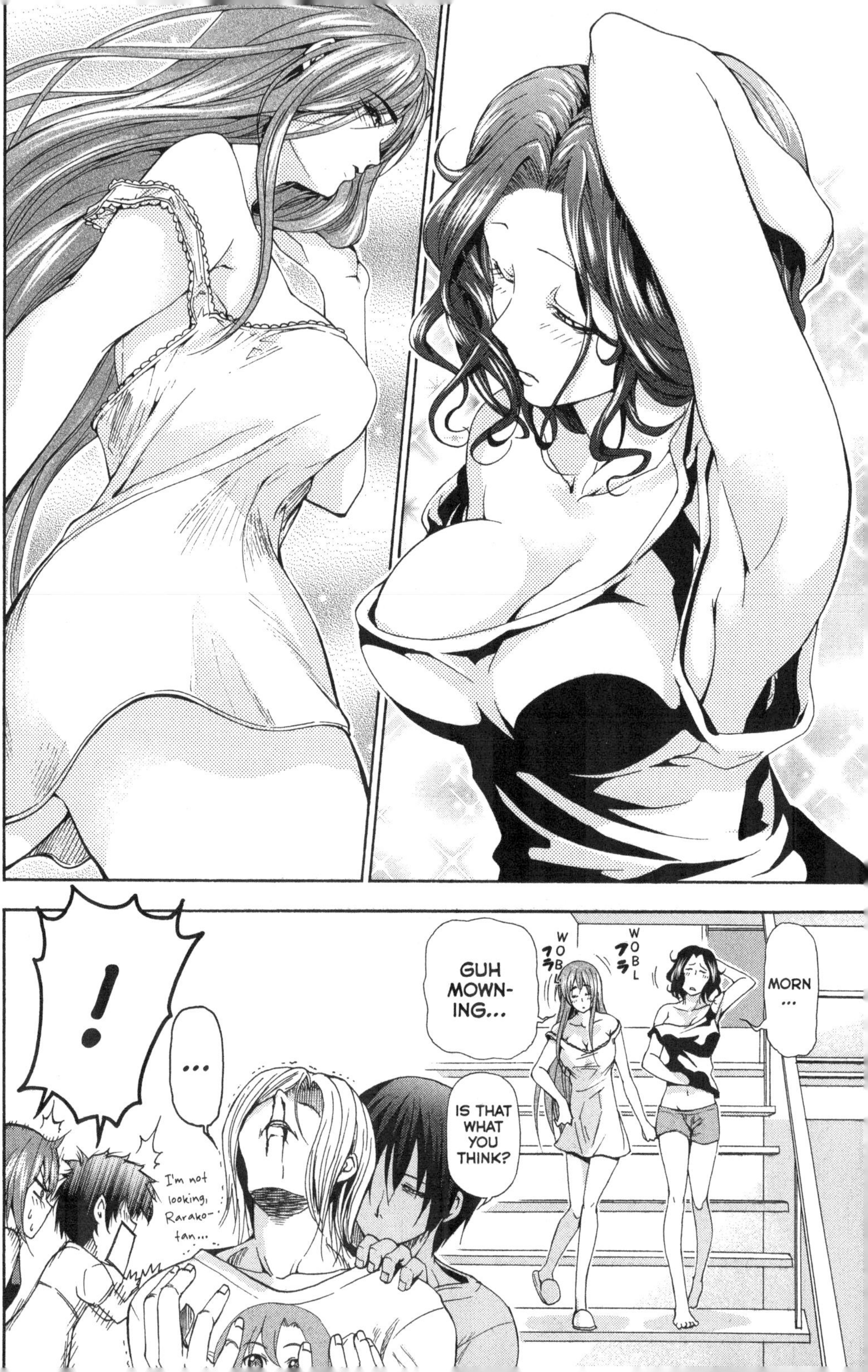
MORN...
フラ WOBL
フラ WOBL
GUH MOWN-ING...
IS THAT WHAT YOU THINK?
...
!
I'm not looking, Rarako-tan...

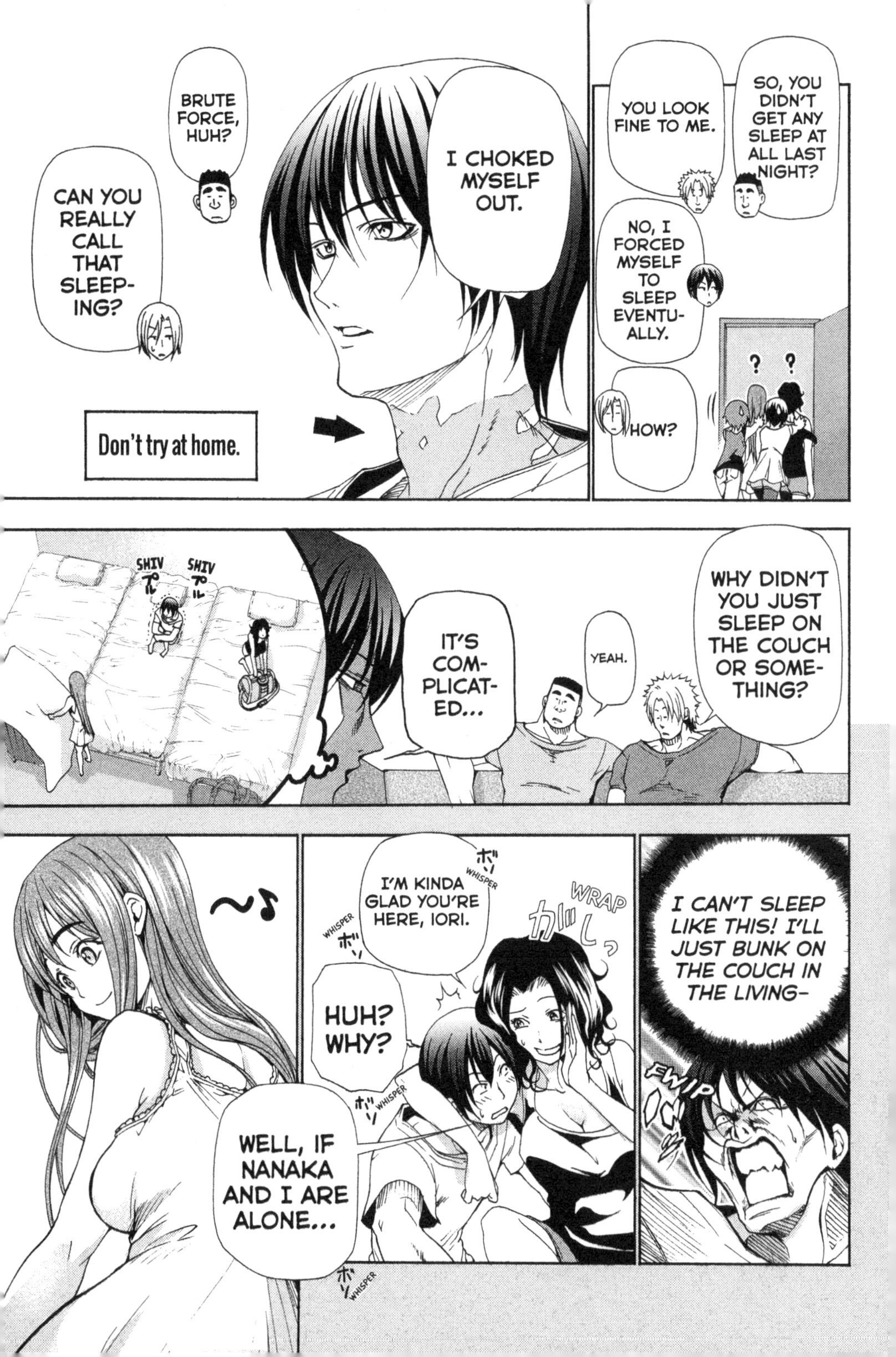
SO, YOU DIDN'T GET ANY SLEEP AT ALL LAST NIGHT?
YOU LOOK FINE TO ME.
NO, I FORCED MYSELF TO SLEEP EVENTUALLY.
HOW?
I CHOKED MYSELF OUT.
BRUTE FORCE, HUH?
CAN YOU REALLY CALL THAT SLEEPING?
Don't try at home.
WHY DIDN'T YOU JUST SLEEP ON THE COUCH OR SOMETHING?
YEAH.
IT'S COMPLICATED...
SHIV
SHIV
I CAN'T SLEEP LIKE THIS! I'LL JUST BUNK ON THE COUCH IN THE LIVING-
FWIP
WRAP
WHISPER
I'M KINDA GLAD YOU'RE HERE, IORI.
WHISPER
HUH? WHY?
WHISPER
WELL, IF NANAKA AND I ARE ALONE...
WHISPER
~♪

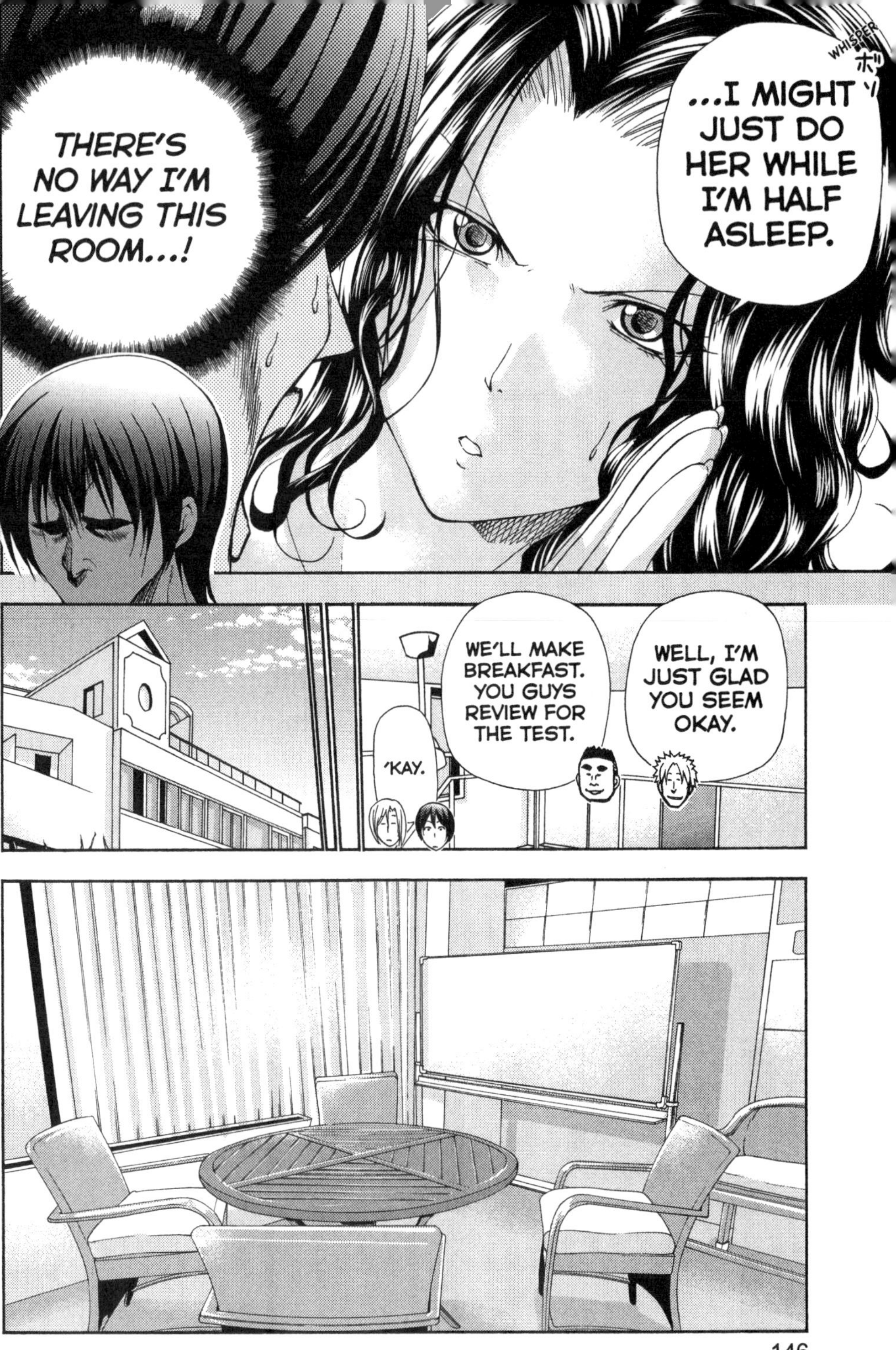
WHISPER
ボソ
...I MIGHT JUST DO HER WHILE I'M HALF ASLEEP.
THERE'S NO WAY I'M LEAVING THIS ROOM...!
WELL, I'M JUST GLAD YOU SEEM OKAY.
WE'LL MAKE BREAKFAST. YOU GUYS REVIEW FOR THE TEST.
'KAY.

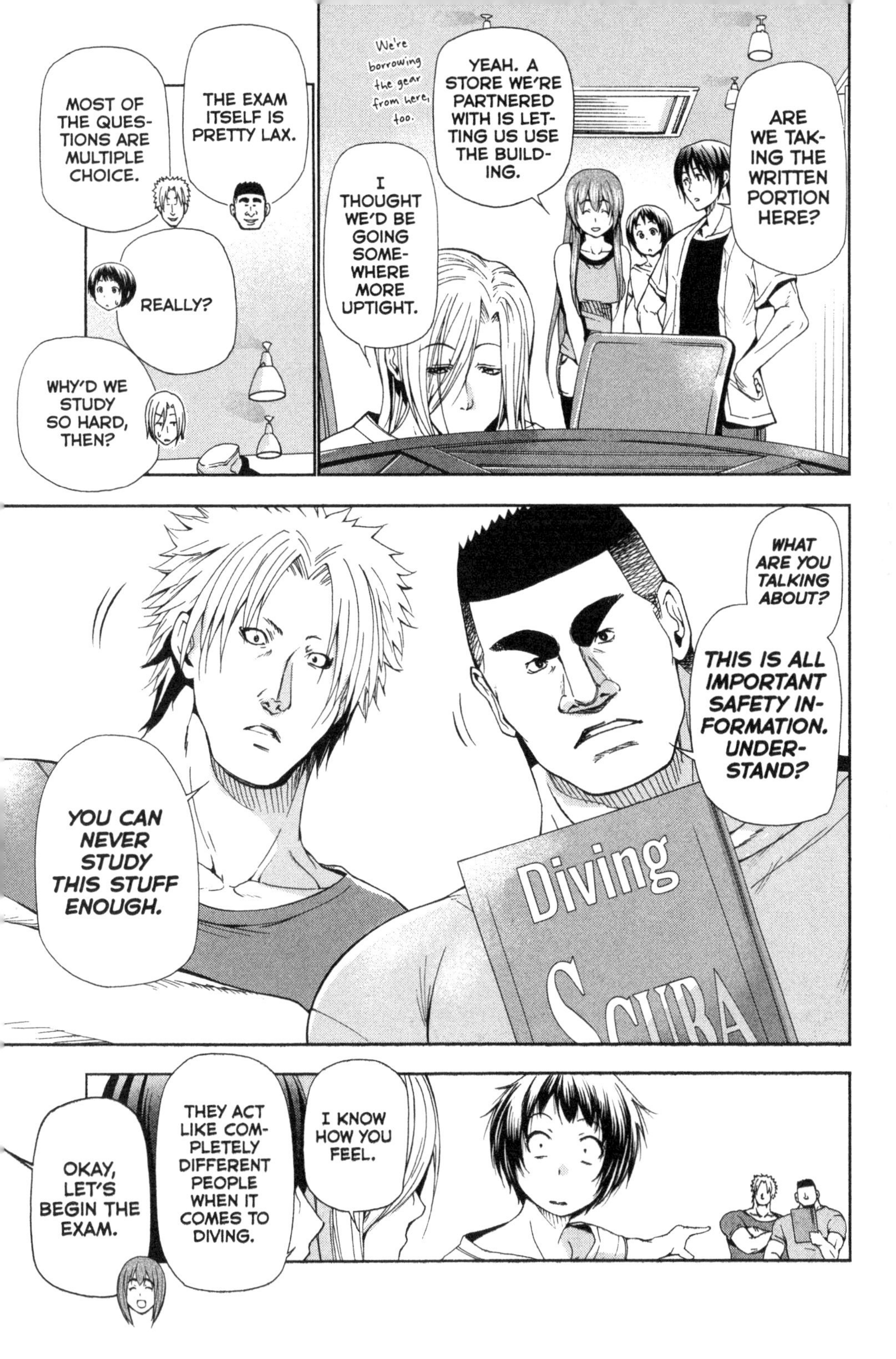
ARE WE TAKING THE WRITTEN PORTION HERE?
YEAH. A STORE WE'RE PARTNERED WITH IS LETTING US USE THE BUILDING.
We're borrowing the gear from here, too.
I THOUGHT WE'D BE GOING SOMEWHERE MORE UPTIGHT.
THE EXAM ITSELF IS PRETTY LAX.
MOST OF THE QUESTIONS ARE MULTIPLE CHOICE.
REALLY?
WHY'D WE STUDY SO HARD, THEN?
WHAT ARE YOU TALKING ABOUT?
THIS IS ALL IMPORTANT SAFETY INFORMATION. UNDERSTAND?
YOU CAN NEVER STUDY THIS STUFF ENOUGH.
Diving
I KNOW HOW YOU FEEL.
THEY ACT LIKE COMPLETELY DIFFERENT PEOPLE WHEN IT COMES TO DIVING.
OKAY, LET'S BEGIN THE EXAM.

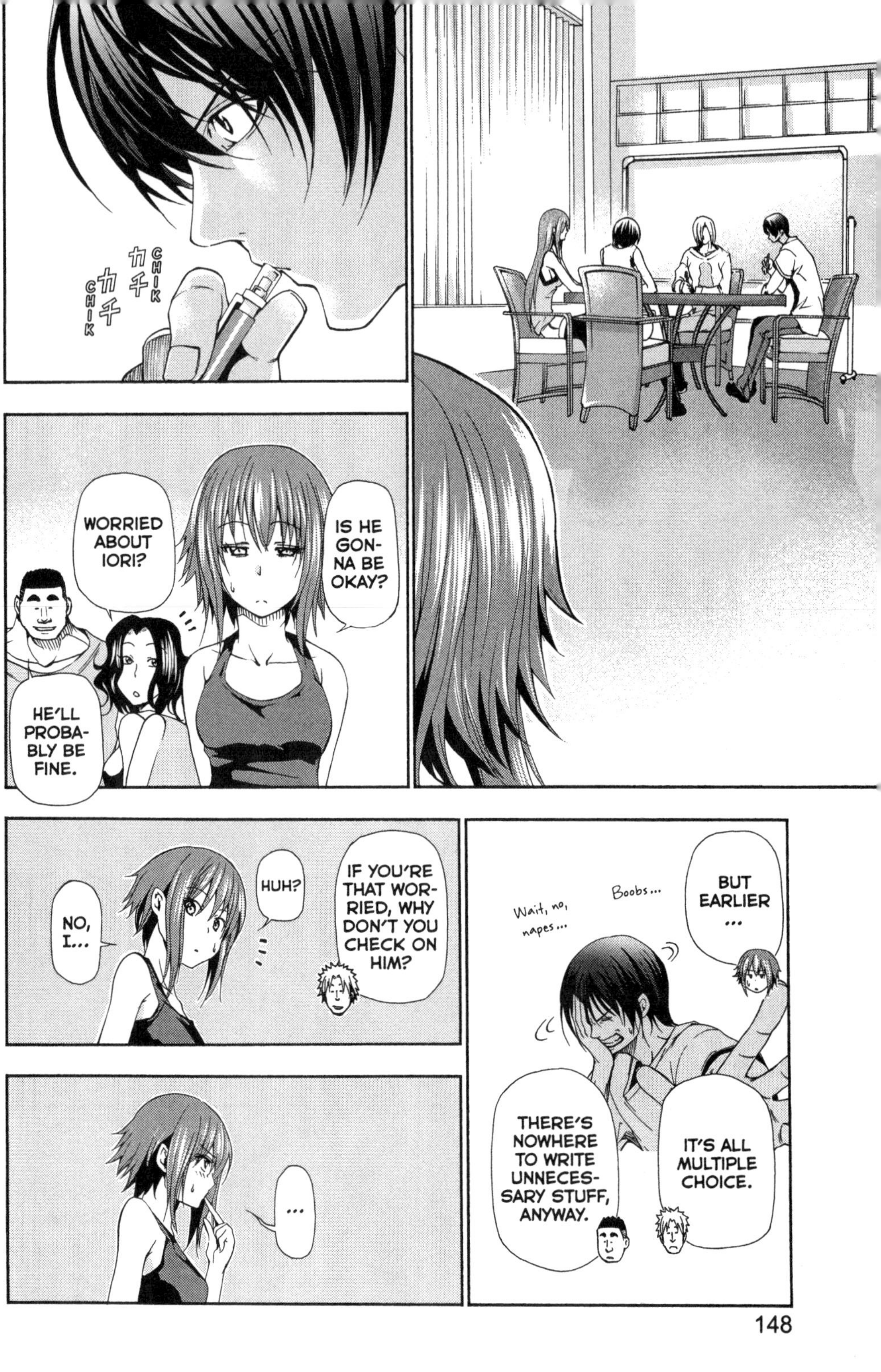
カチ CHIK
カチ CHIK
IS HE GONNA BE OKAY?
WORRIED ABOUT IORI?
HE'LL PROBABLY BE FINE.
BUT EARLIER...
Boobs...
Wait, no, napes...
IT'S ALL MULTIPLE CHOICE.
THERE'S NOWHERE TO WRITE UNNECESSARY STUFF, ANYWAY.
IF YOU'RE THAT WORRIED, WHY DON'T YOU CHECK ON HIM?
HUH?
NO, I...
...

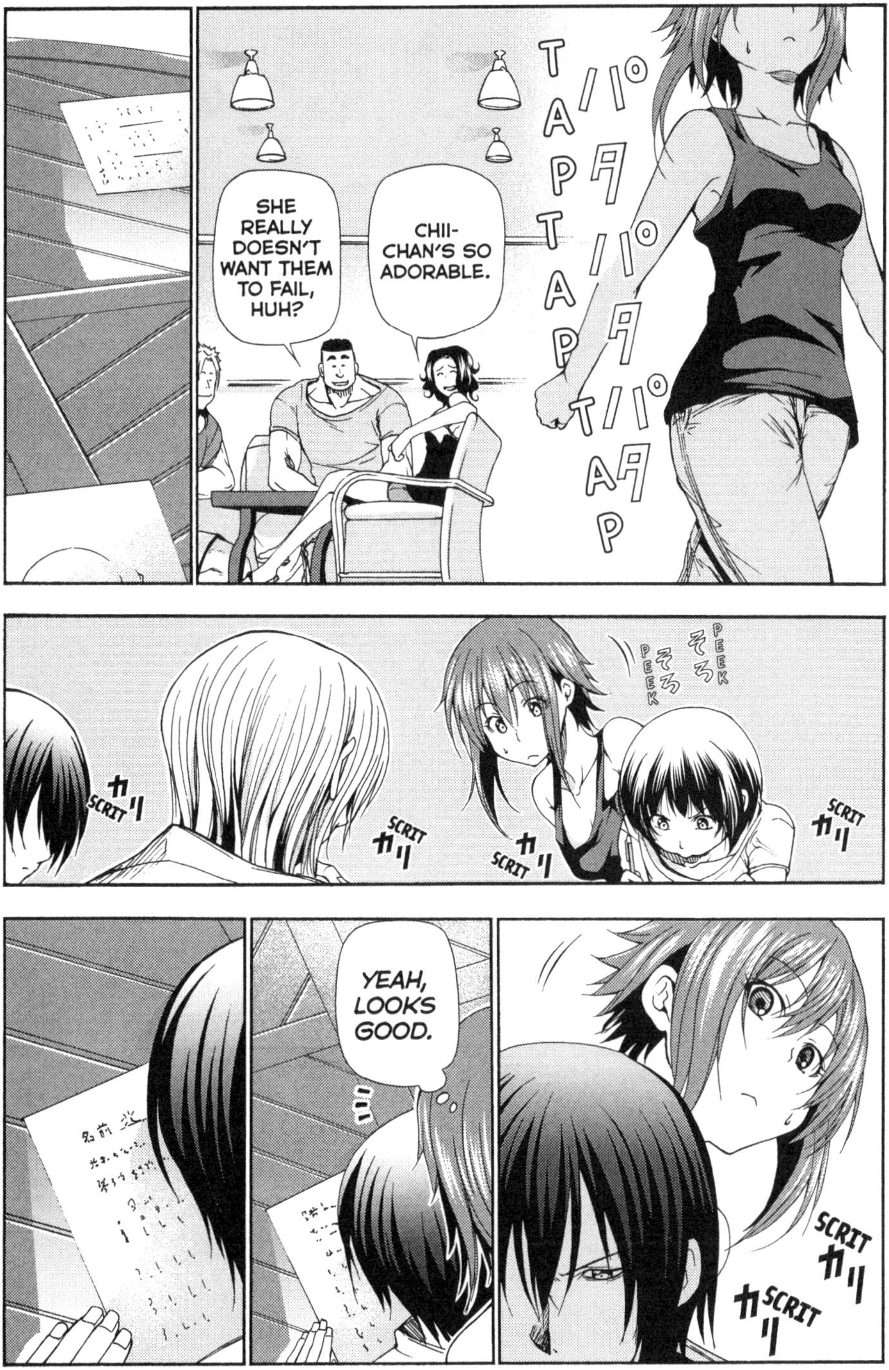
TAP TAP TAP TAP
パタパタパタパタ
CHII-CHAN'S SO ADORABLE.
SHE REALLY DOESN'T WANT THEM TO FAIL, HUH?
PEEK PEEK
そろそろ
SCRIT カリ
SCRIT カリ
SCRIT カリ
SCRIT カリ
SCRIT カリ
SCRIT カリ
YEAH, LOOKS GOOD.
...

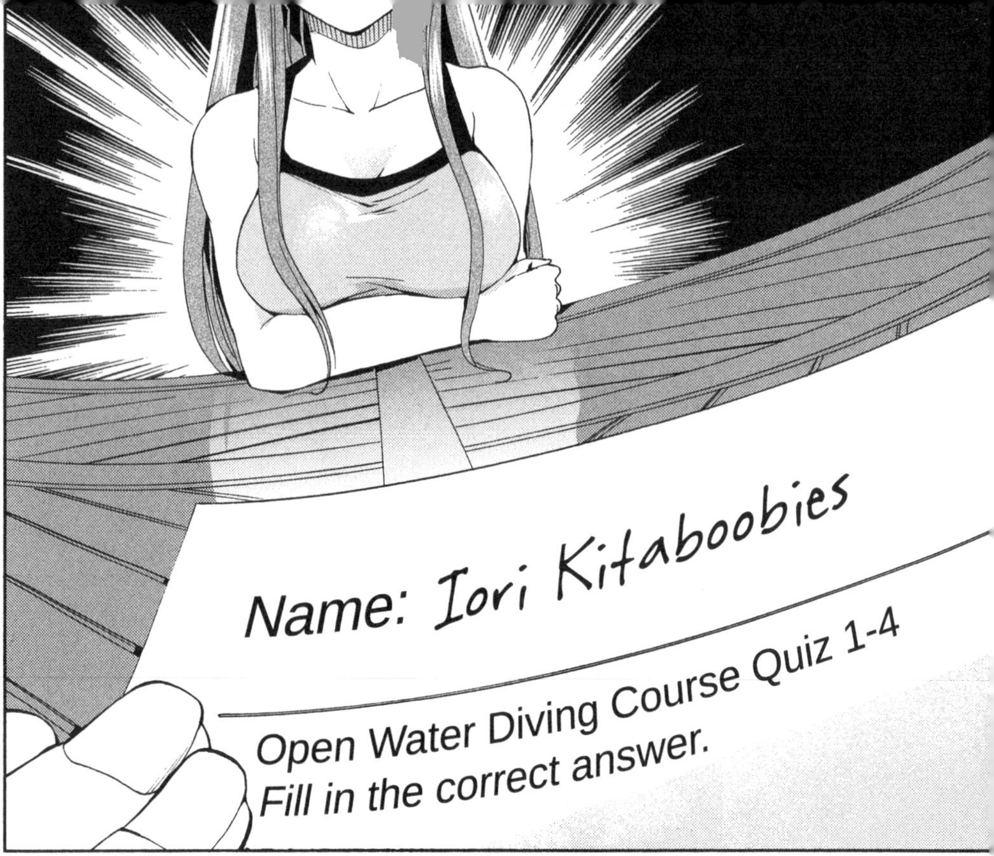
Name: Iori Kitaboobies
Open Water Diving Course Quiz 1-4
Fill in the correct answer.

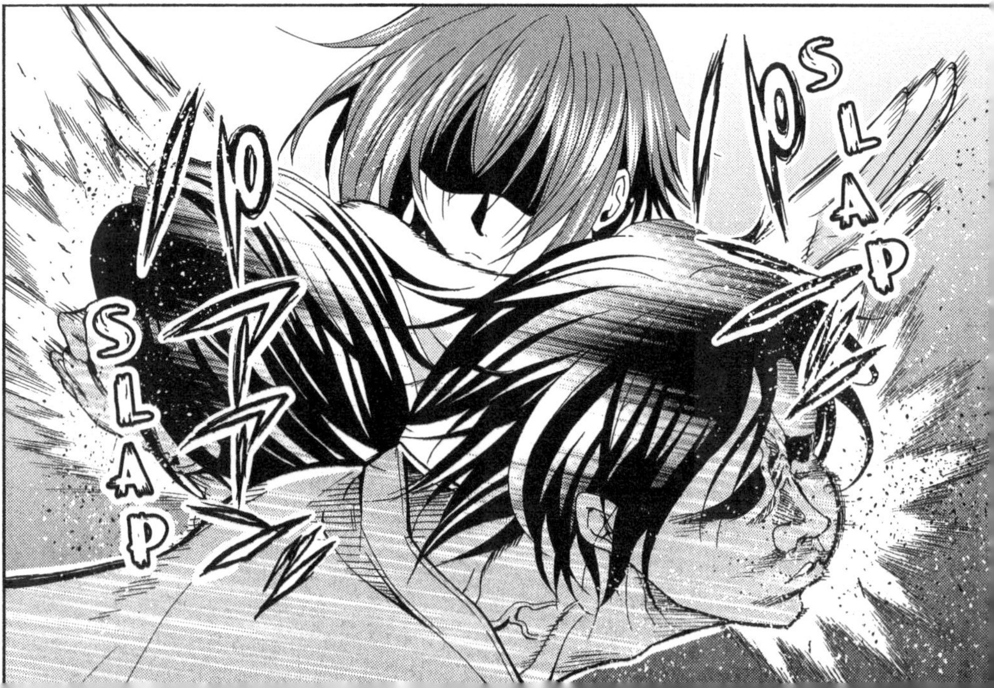
SLAP
SLAP

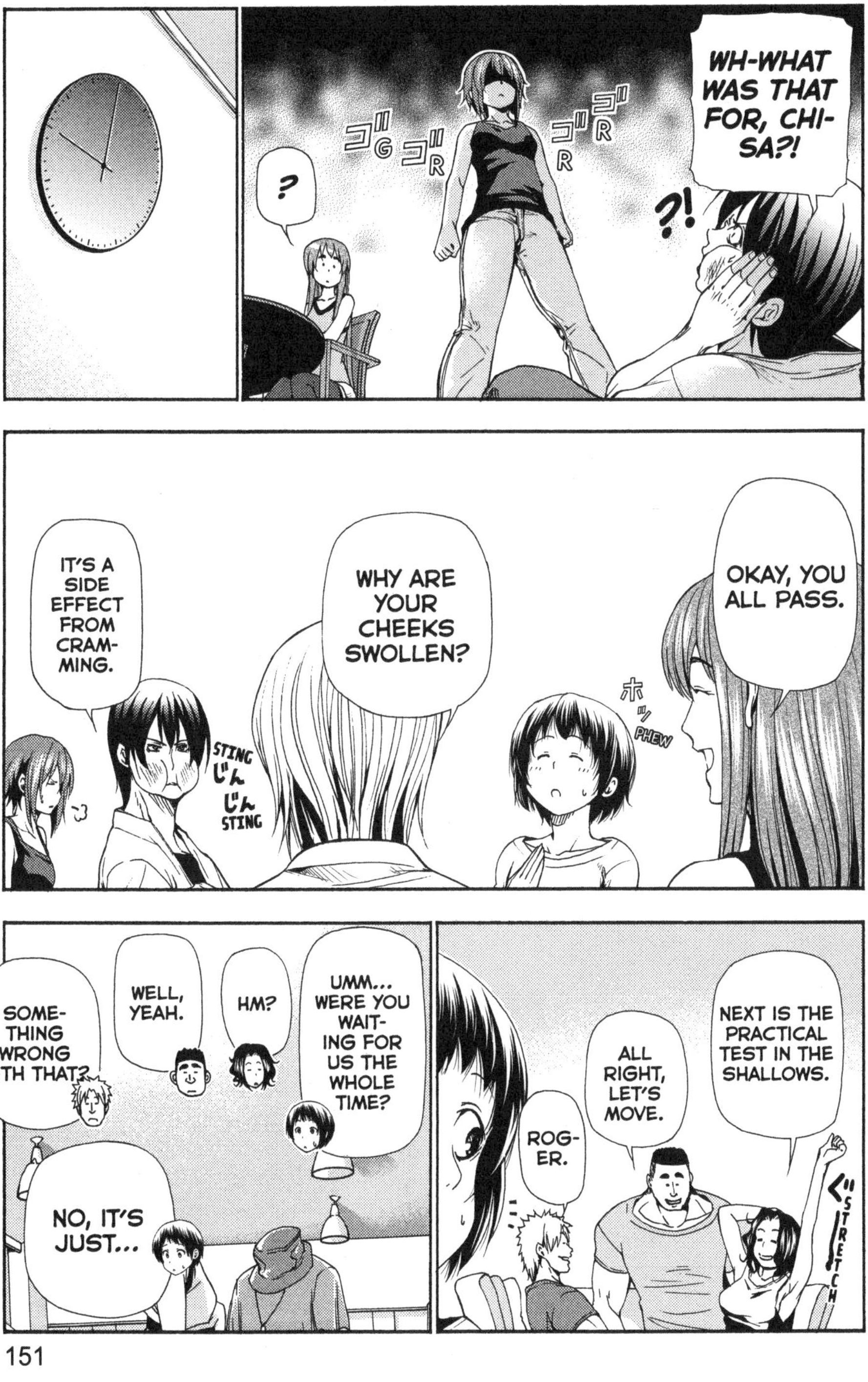
WH-WHAT WAS THAT FOR, CHISA?!
?!
ゴ R ゴ R
ゴ G ゴ R
?
OKAY, YOU ALL PASS.
ホッ PHEW
WHY ARE YOUR CHEEKS SWOLLEN?
STING じん じん STING
IT'S A SIDE EFFECT FROM CRAMMING.
NEXT IS THE PRACTICAL TEST IN THE SHALLOWS.
ぐ STRETCH
ALL RIGHT, LET'S MOVE.
ROGER.
UMM... WERE YOU WAITING FOR US THE WHOLE TIME?
HM?
WELL, YEAH.
SOMETHING WRONG WITH THAT?
NO, IT'S JUST...

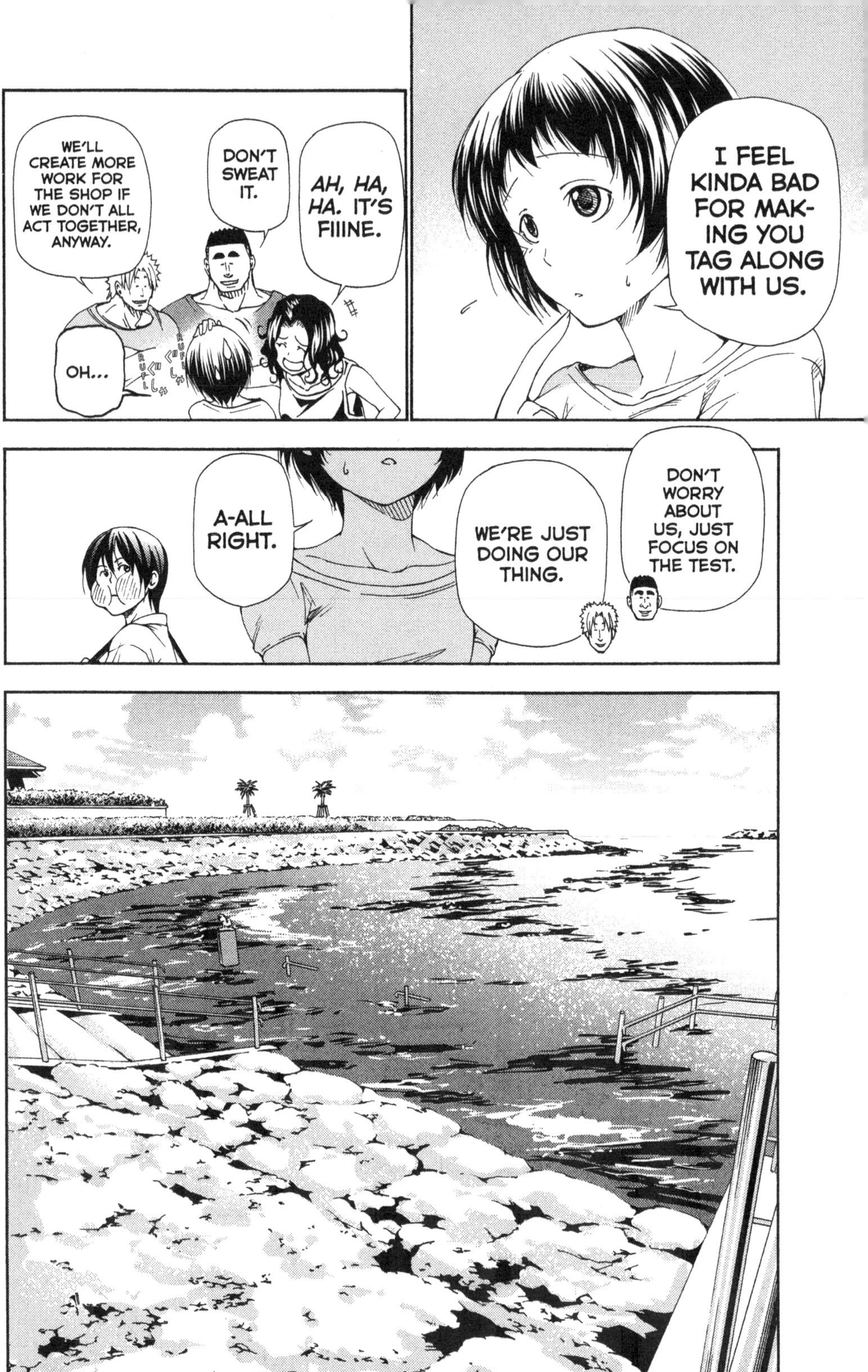
I FEEL KINDA BAD FOR MAKING YOU TAG ALONG WITH US.
AH, HA, HA. IT'S FIIINE.
DON'T SWEAT IT.
WE'LL CREATE MORE WORK FOR THE SHOP IF WE DON'T ALL ACT TOGETHER, ANYWAY.
OH...
DON'T WORRY ABOUT US, JUST FOCUS ON THE TEST.
WE'RE JUST DOING OUR THING.
A-ALL RIGHT.

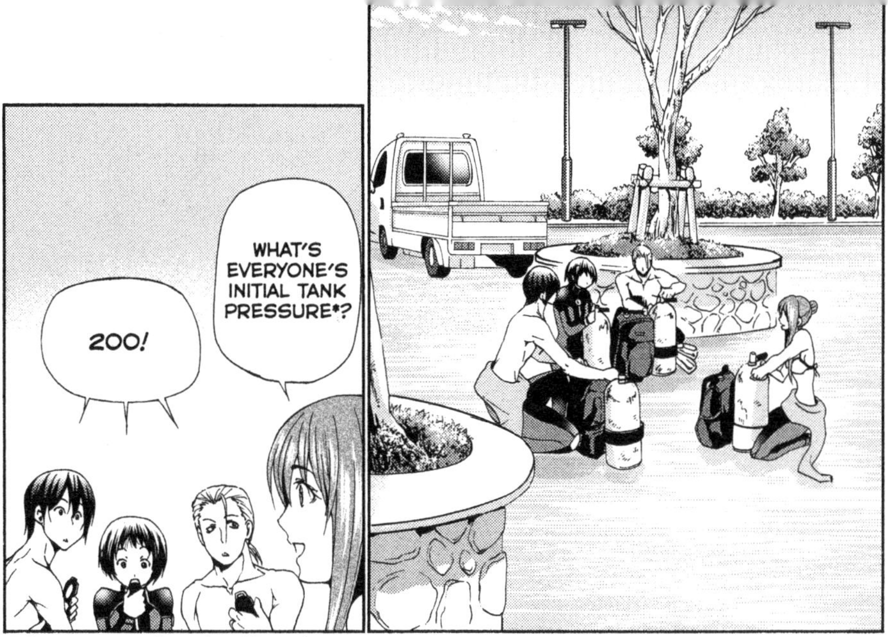
WHAT'S EVERYONE'S INITIAL TANK PRESSURE*?
200!

*Tank Pressure: A measure of how much air is left in a tank.

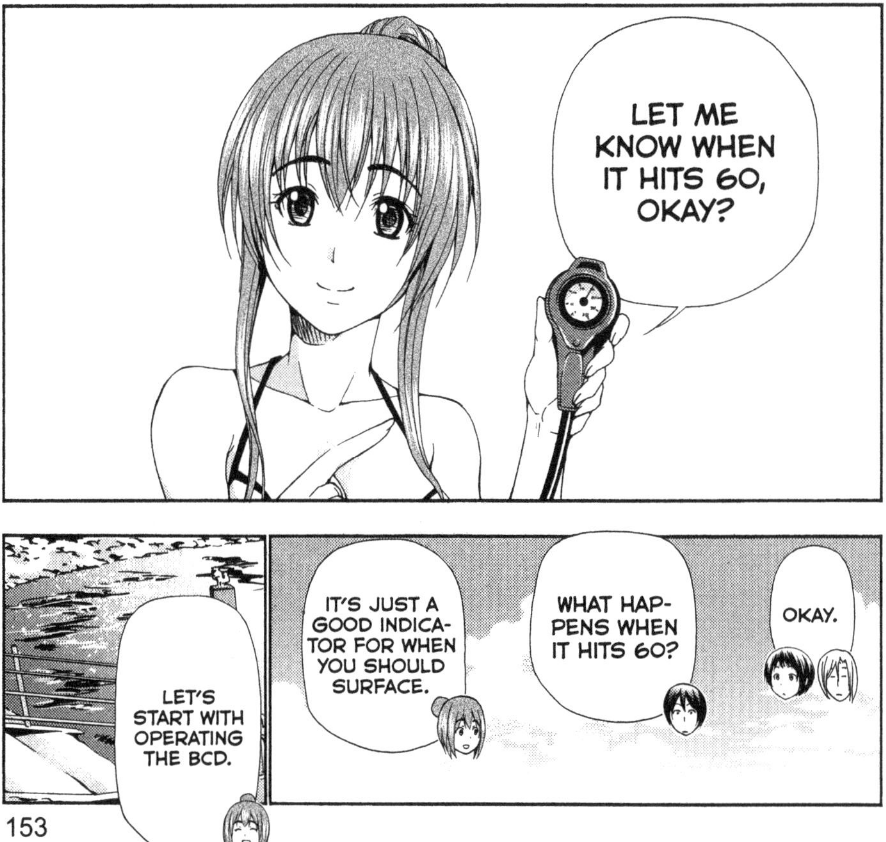
LET ME KNOW WHEN IT HITS 60, OKAY?
OKAY.
WHAT HAPPENS WHEN IT HITS 60?
IT'S JUST A GOOD INDICATOR FOR WHEN YOU SHOULD SURFACE.
LET'S START WITH OPERATING THE BCD.

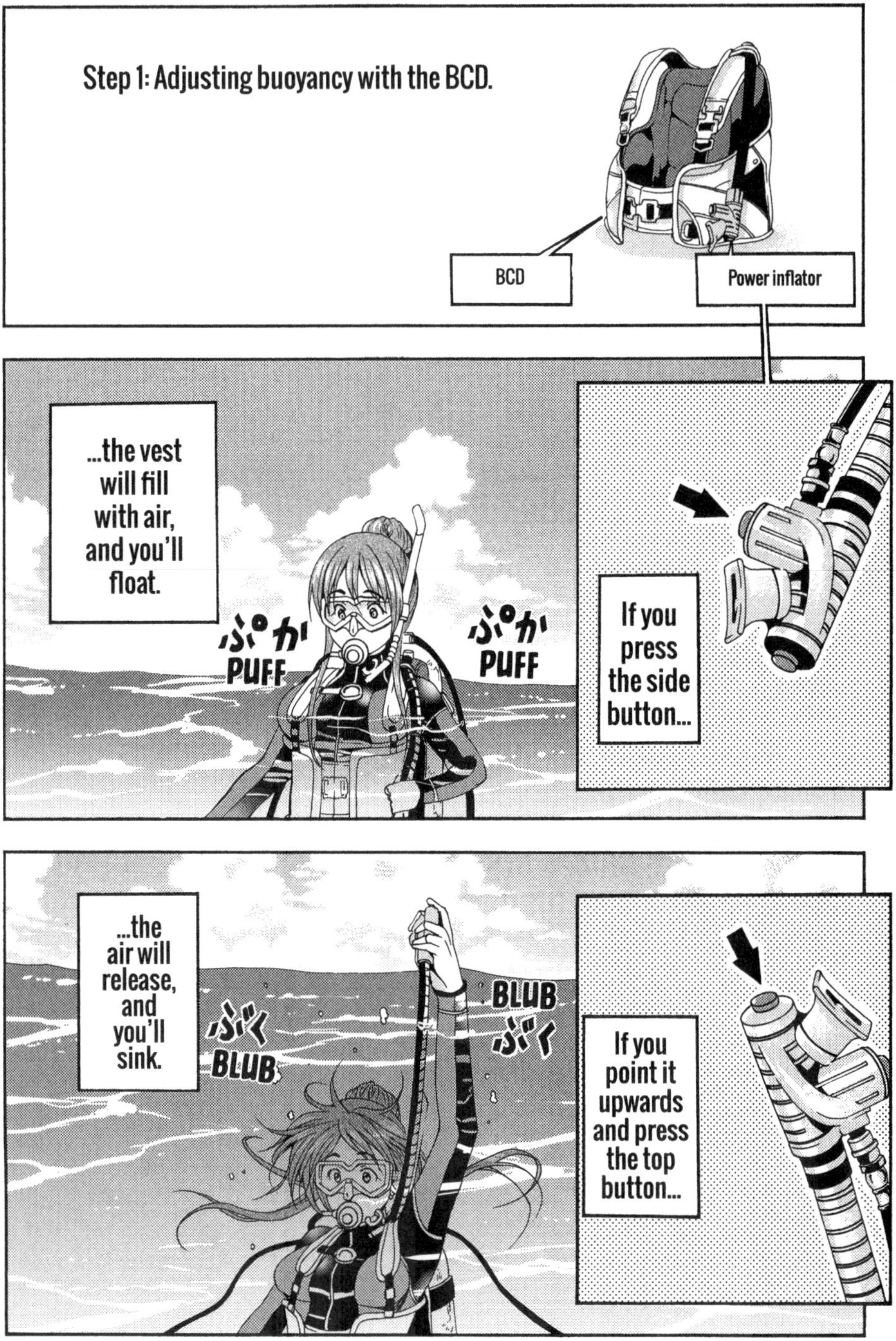

Step 1: Adjusting buoyancy with the BCD.
Power inflator
BCD
If you press the side button...
...the vest will fill with air, and you'll float.
ぷか PUFF
ぷか PUFF
If you point it upwards and press the top button...
...the air will release, and you'll sink.
BLUB ぶく
ぶく BLUB

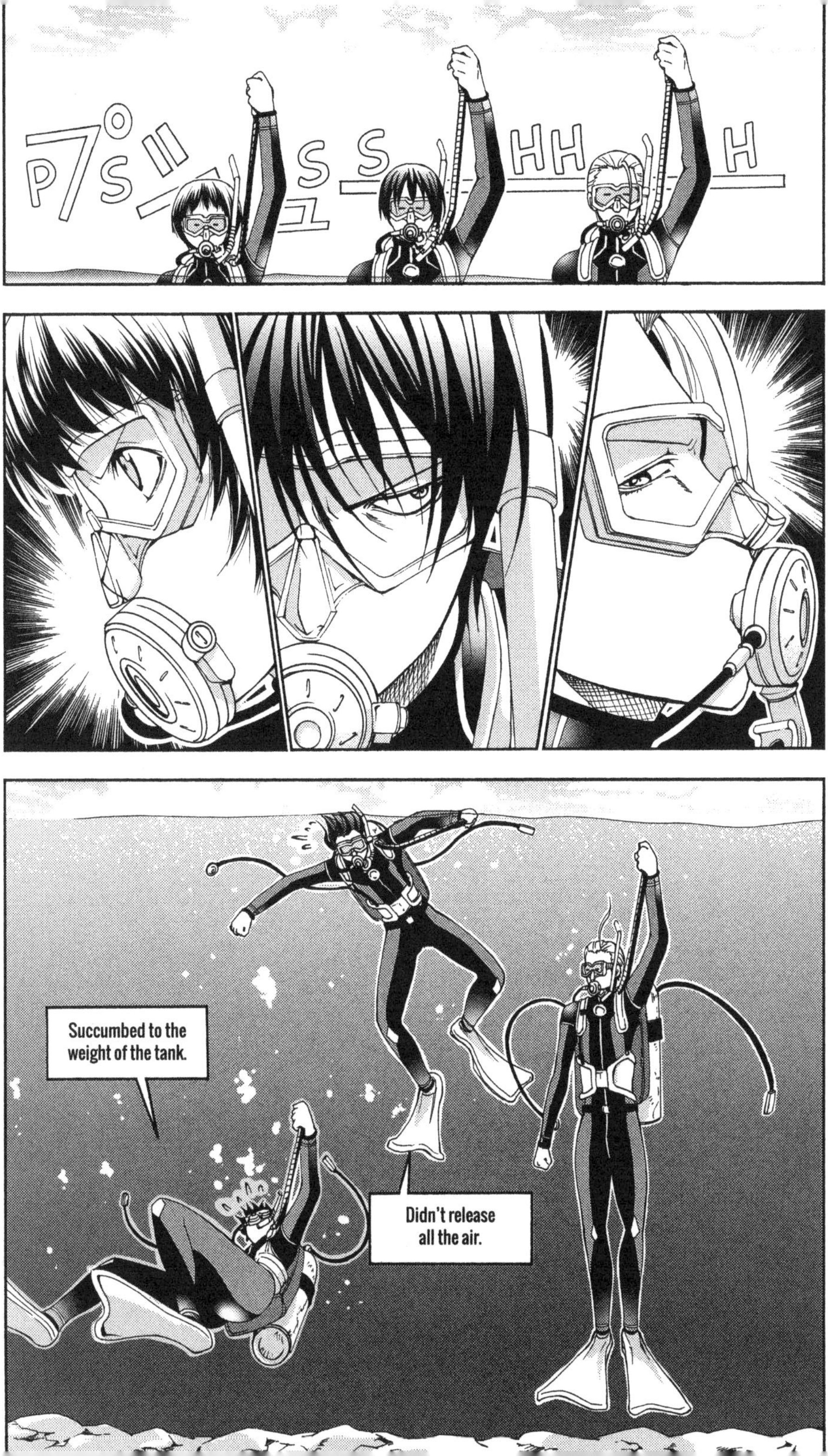
PSSSHHH
Didn't release all the air.
Succumbed to the weight of the tank.

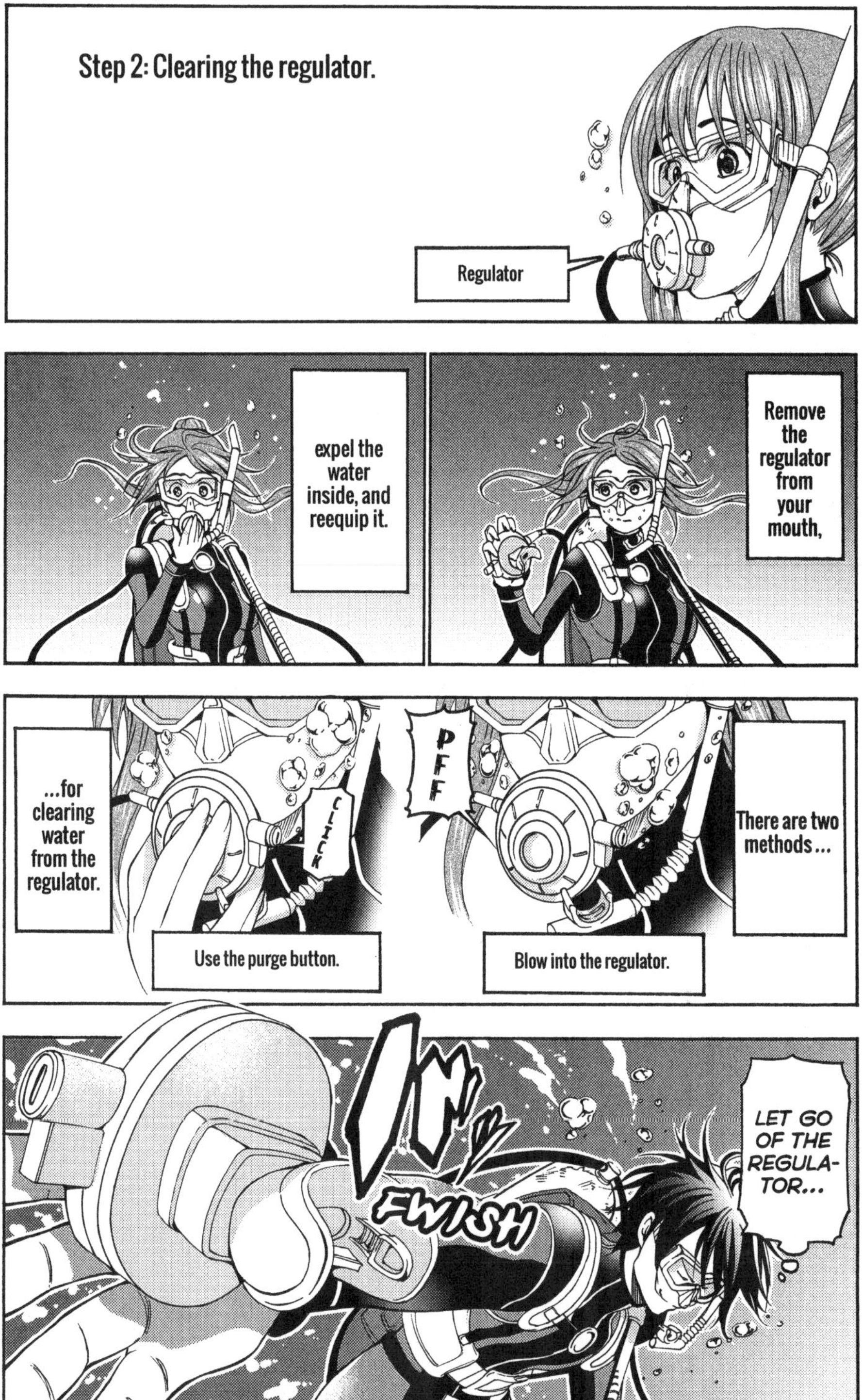
Step 2: Clearing the regulator.
Regulator
Remove the regulator from your mouth,
expel the water inside, and reequip it.
There are two methods...
PFF
Blow into the regulator.
...for clearing water from the regulator.
CLICK
Use the purge button.
LET GO OF THE REGULA-TOR...
FWISH

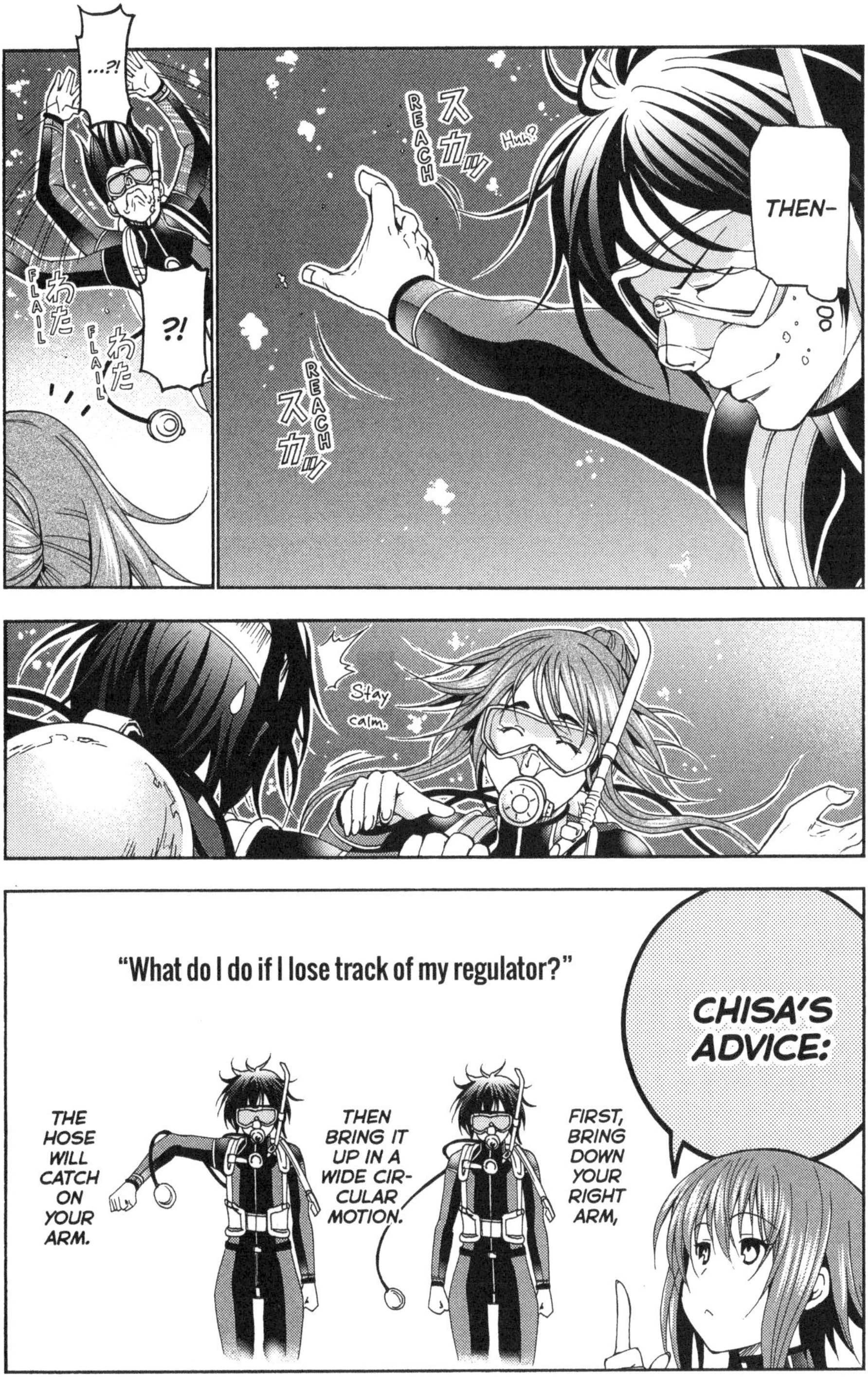
THEN-
Huh?
スカッ REACH
スカッ REACH
...?!
?!
わた FLAIL
わた FLAIL
Stay calm.
"What do I do if I lose track of my regulator?"
CHISA'S ADVICE:
FIRST, BRING DOWN YOUR RIGHT ARM,
THEN BRING IT UP IN A WIDE CIR-CULAR MOTION.
THE HOSE WILL CATCH ON YOUR ARM.

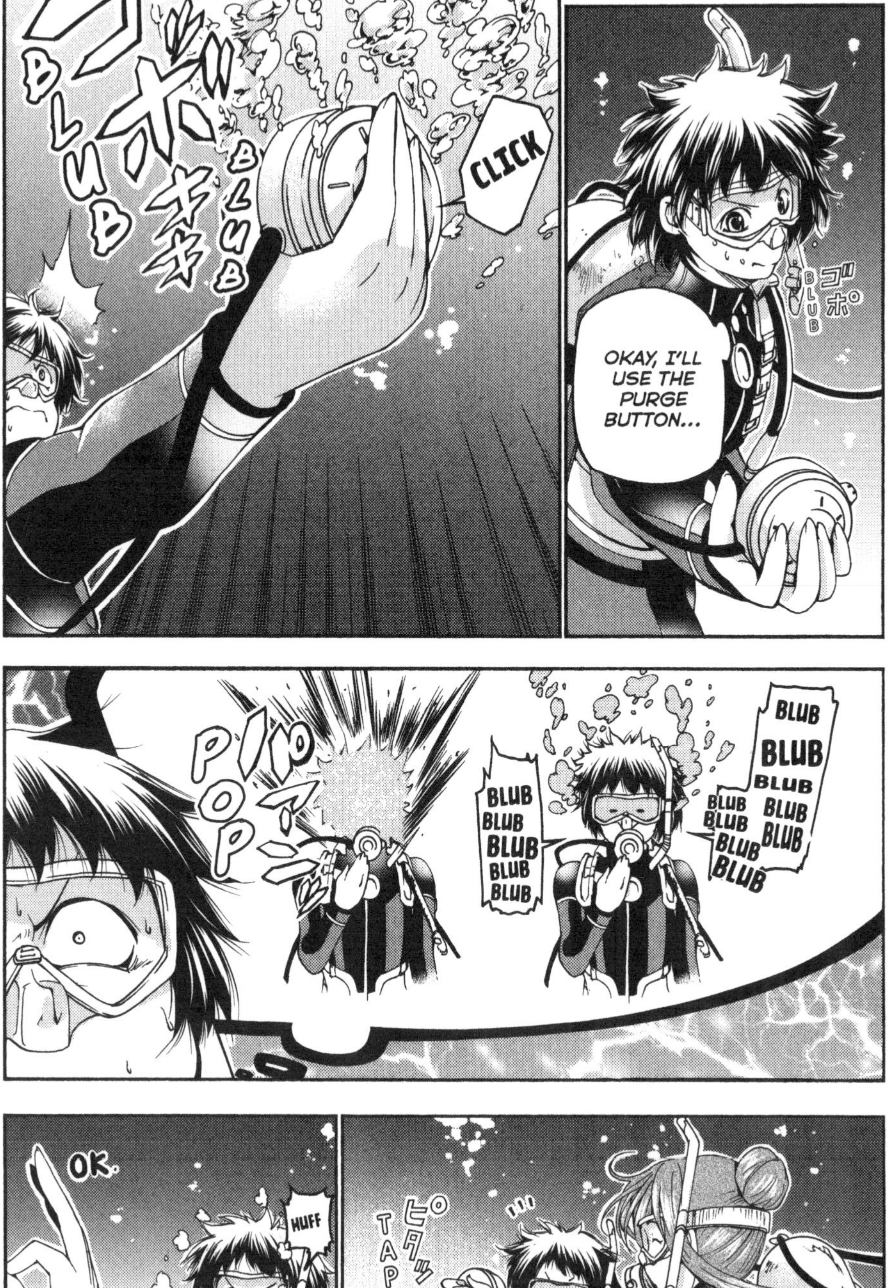
OKAY, I'LL USE THE PURGE BUTTON...
BLUB
CLICK
BLUB
BLUB
BLUB BLUB BLUB BLUB BLUB BLUB
BLUB BLUB BLUB BLUB BLUB BLUB
BLUB BLUB BLUB BLUB BLUB
POP
...
TAP
HUFF
OK.

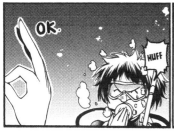

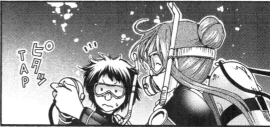

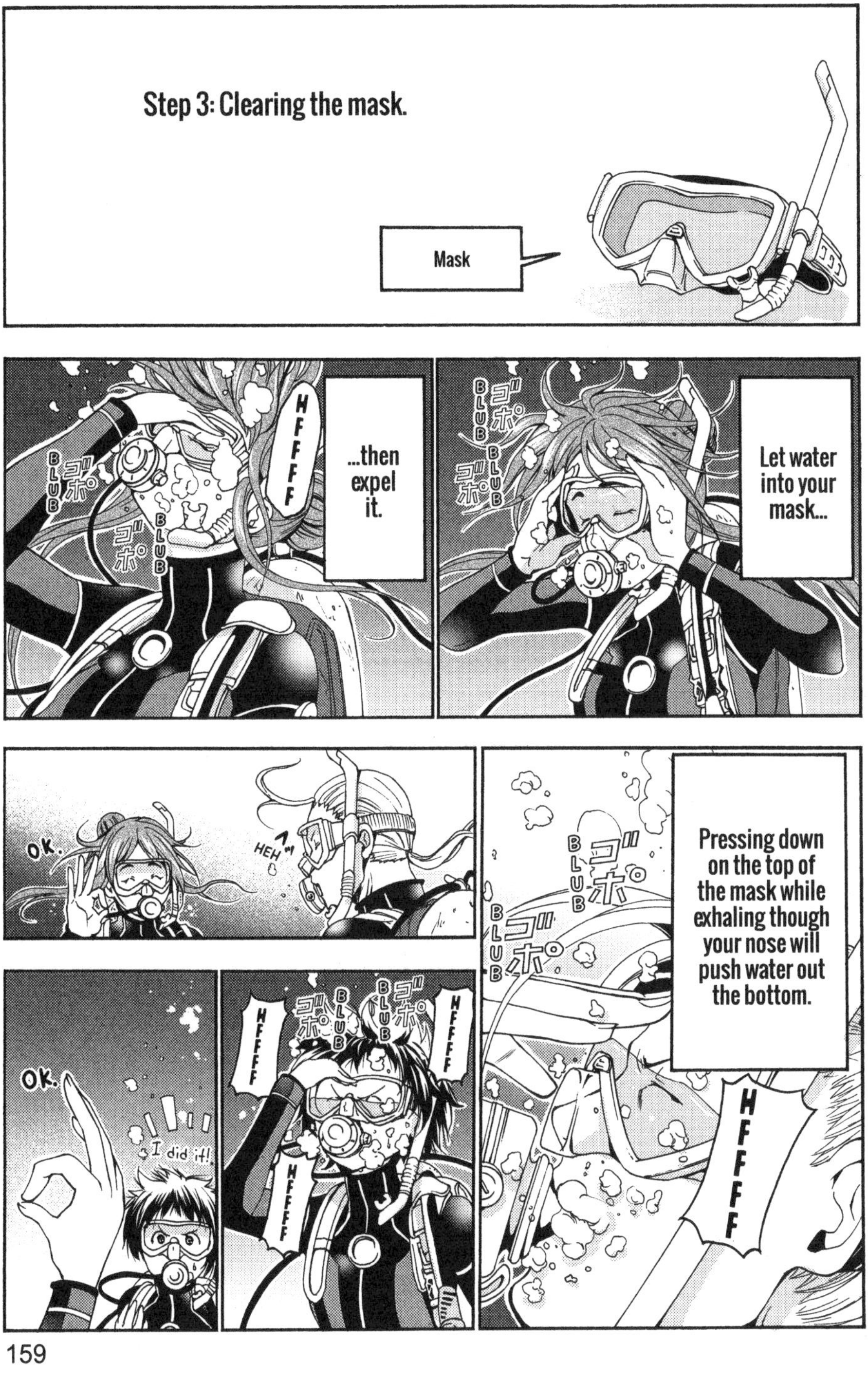
Step 3: Clearing the mask.
Mask
Let water into your mask...
ゴポ BLUB
ゴポ BLUB
...then expel it.
HFFFF
ゴポ BLUB
ゴポ BLUB
Pressing down on the top of the mask while exhaling though your nose will push water out the bottom.
ゴポ BLUB
ゴポ BLUB
HFFFFF
HEH
OK.
HFFFF
ゴポ BLUB
ゴポ BLUB
HFFFF
HFFFF
I did it!
OK.

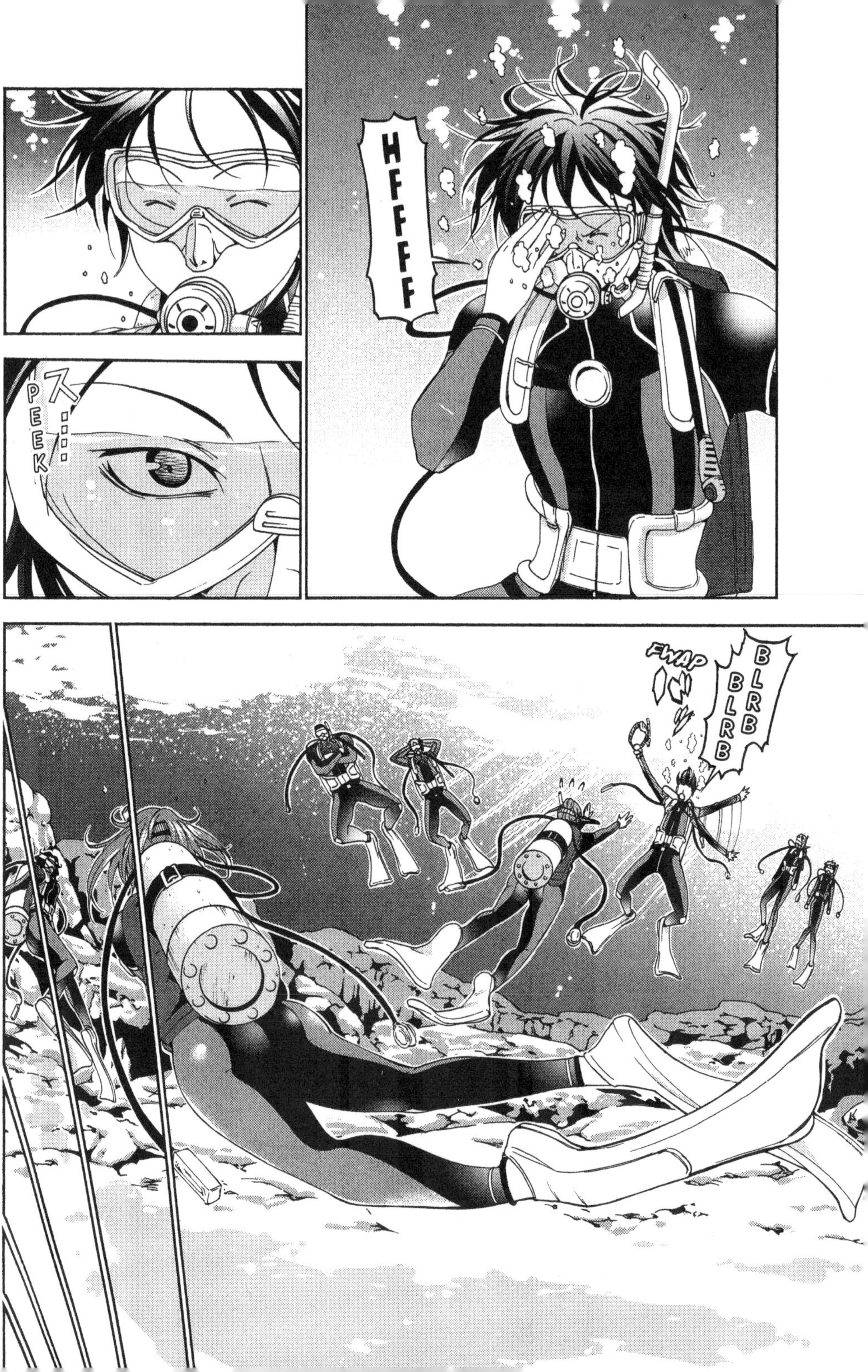
HFFFF
ス....
PEEK
FWAP
BLRB BLRB

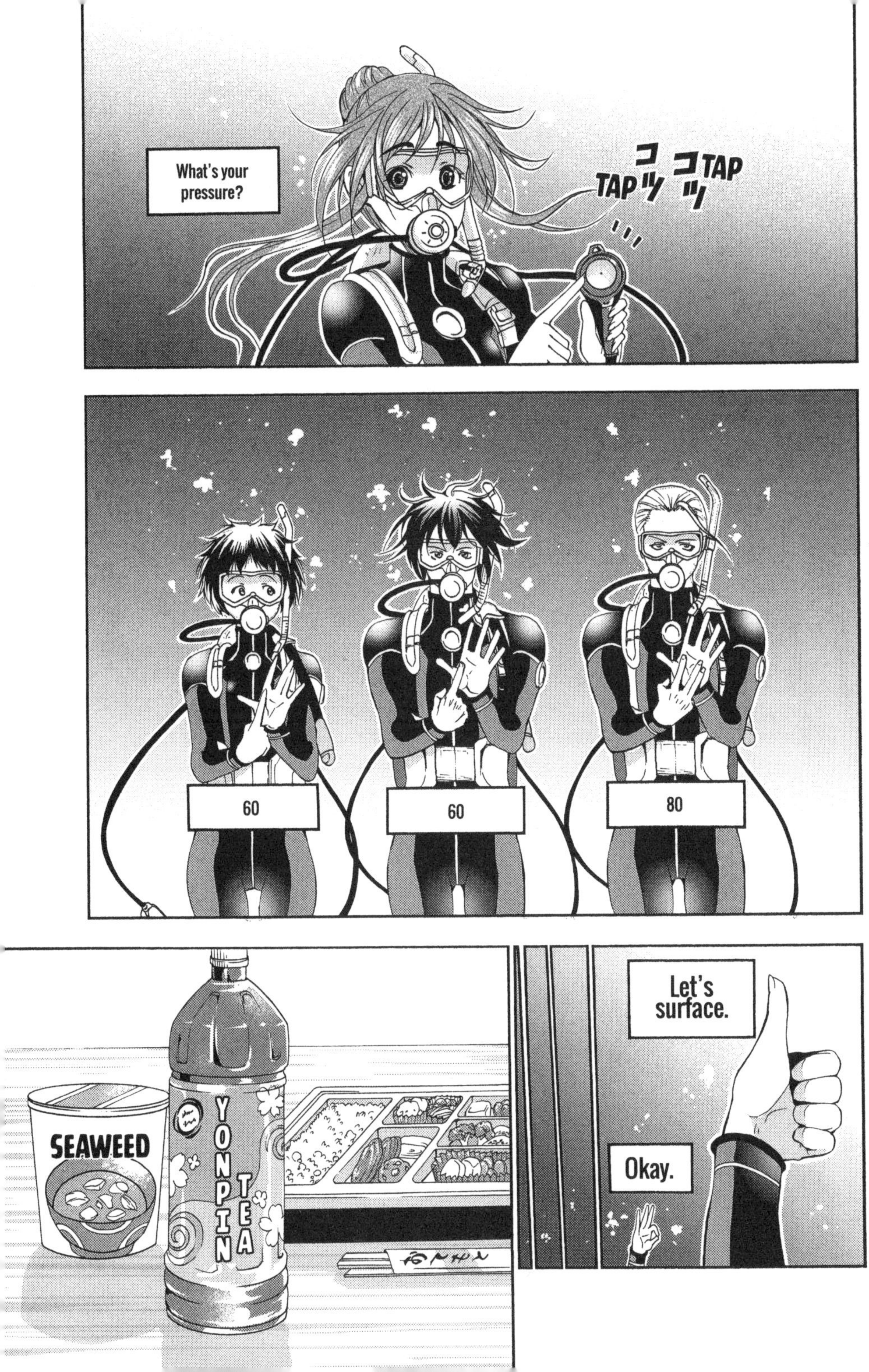
コツ コツ
TAP TAP
What's your pressure?
80
60
60
Let's surface.
Okay.
YONPIN TEA
SEAWEED

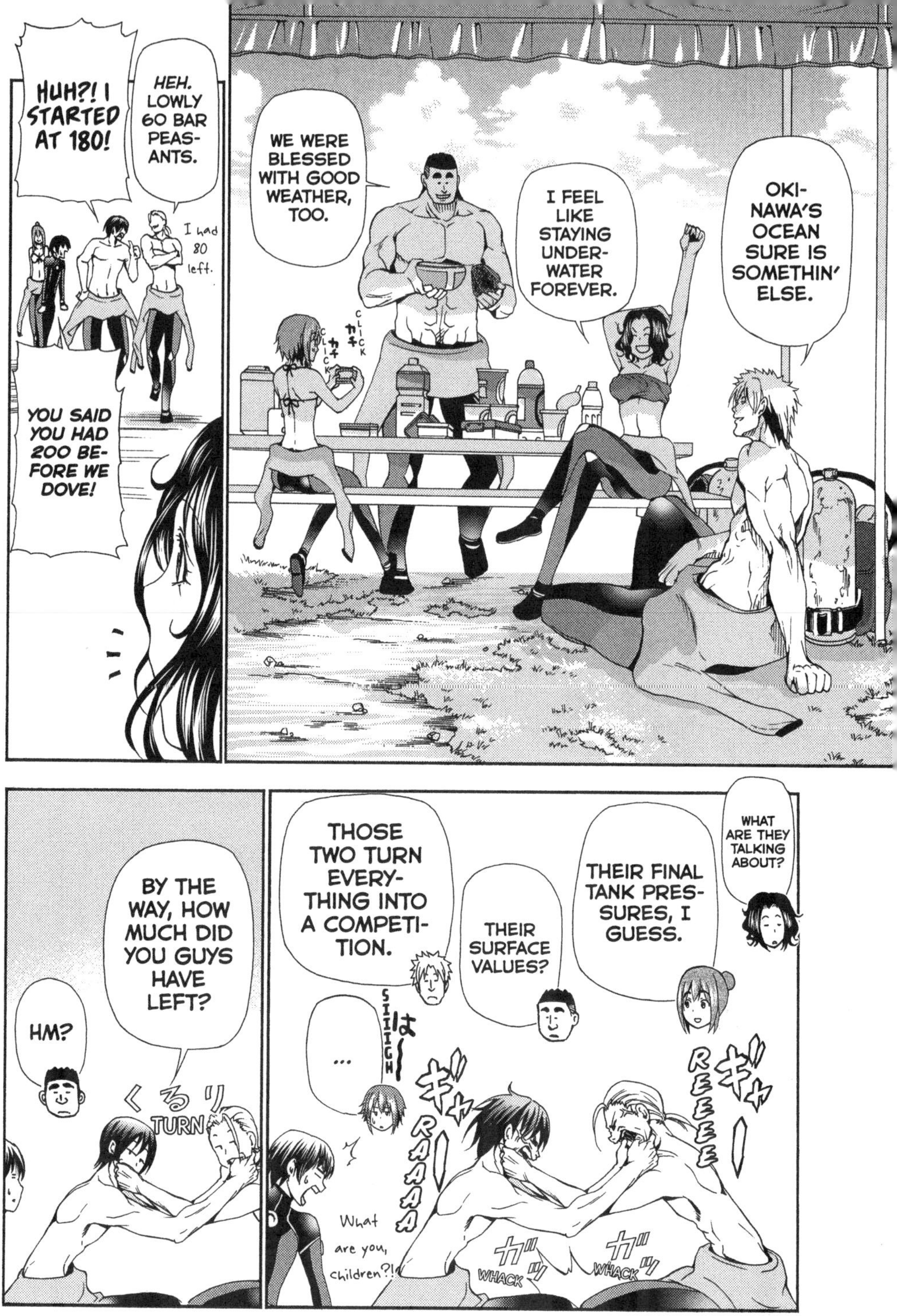

OKI-NAWA'S OCEAN SURE IS SOMETHIN' ELSE.
I FEEL LIKE STAYING UNDER-WATER FOREVER.
WE WERE BLESSED WITH GOOD WEATHER, TOO.
カチ CLICK
カチ CLICK
HEH. LOWLY 60 BAR PEAS-ANTS.
HUH?! I STARTED AT 180!
I had 80 left.
YOU SAID YOU HAD 200 BE-FORE WE DOVE!
WHAT ARE THEY TALKING ABOUT?
THEIR FINAL TANK PRES-SURES, I GUESS.
THEIR SURFACE VALUES?
THOSE TWO TURN EVERY-THING INTO A COMPETI-TION.
ギャー REEEE
ギャー RAAAA
はー SIIIGH
...
What are you, children?!
ガッ WHACK
ガッ WHACK
BY THE WAY, HOW MUCH DID YOU GUYS HAVE LEFT?
くるり TURN
HM?

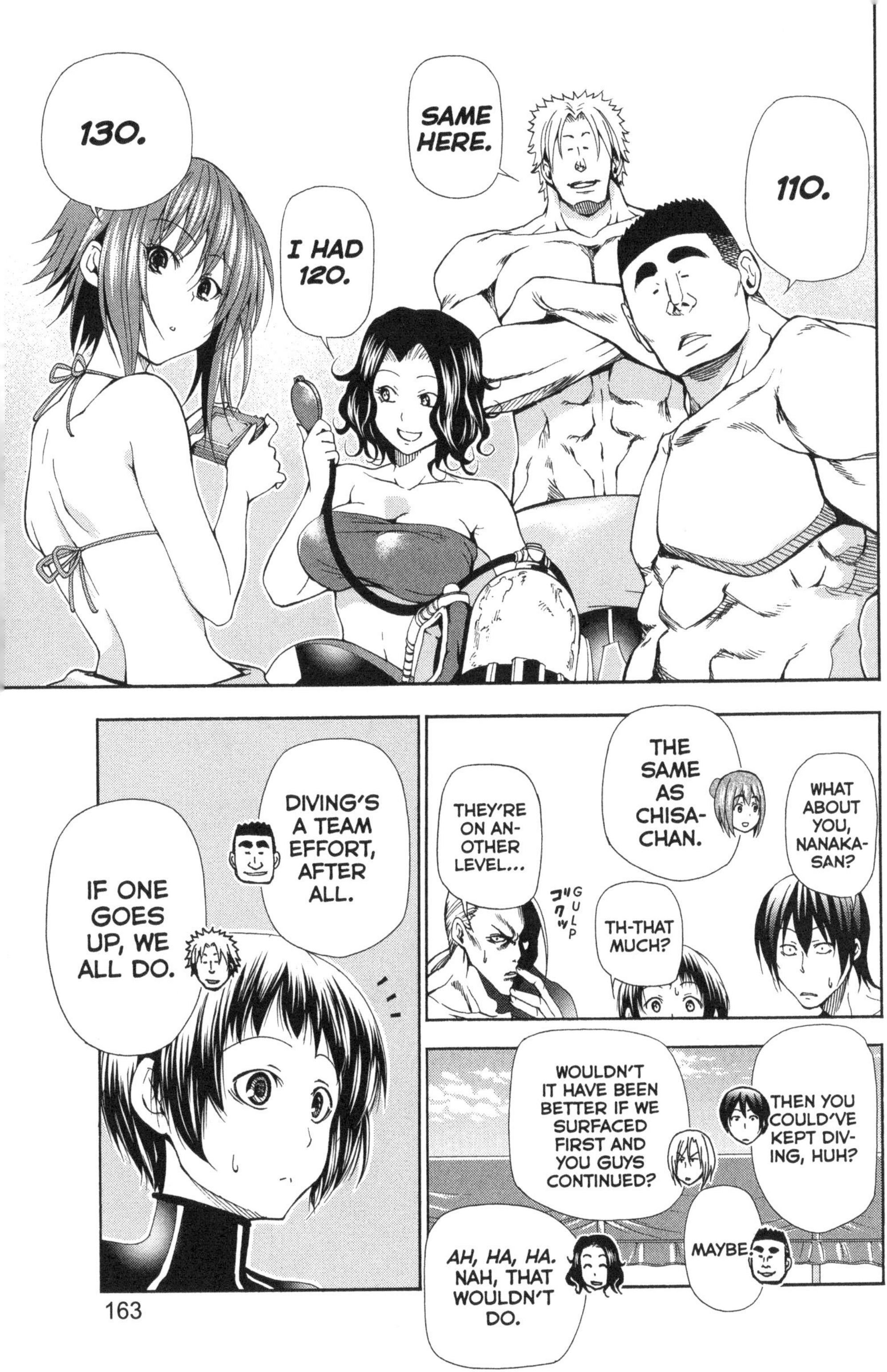
110.
SAME HERE.
I HAD 120.
130.
WHAT ABOUT YOU, NANAKA-SAN?
THE SAME AS CHISA-CHAN.
TH-THAT MUCH?
ゴクッ GULP
THEY'RE ON AN-OTHER LEVEL...
THEN YOU COULD'VE KEPT DIV-ING, HUH?
WOULDN'T IT HAVE BEEN BETTER IF WE SURFACED FIRST AND YOU GUYS CONTINUED?
MAYBE.
AH, HA, HA. NAH, THAT WOULDN'T DO.
DIVING'S A TEAM EFFORT, AFTER ALL.
IF ONE GOES UP, WE ALL DO.

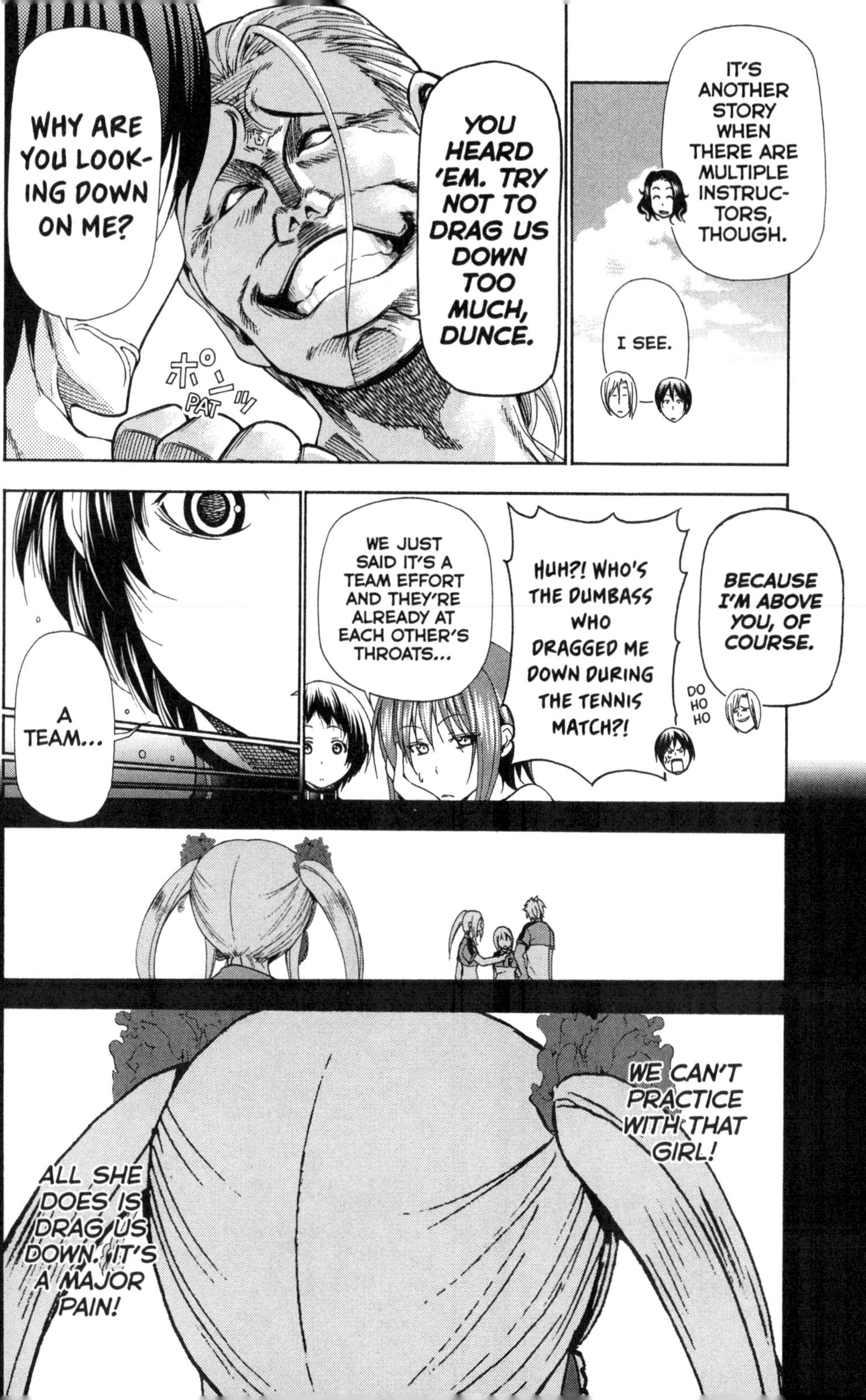
IT'S ANOTHER STORY WHEN THERE ARE MULTIPLE INSTRUCTORS, THOUGH.
I SEE.
YOU HEARD 'EM. TRY NOT TO DRAG US DOWN TOO MUCH, DUNCE.
WHY ARE YOU LOOKING DOWN ON ME?
PAT
BECAUSE I'M ABOVE YOU, OF COURSE.
DO HO HO
HUH?! WHO'S THE DUMBASS WHO DRAGGED ME DOWN DURING THE TENNIS MATCH?!
WE JUST SAID IT'S A TEAM EFFORT AND THEY'RE ALREADY AT EACH OTHER'S THROATS...
A TEAM...
WE CAN'T PRACTICE WITH THAT GIRL!
ALL SHE DOES IS DRAG US DOWN. IT'S A MAJOR PAIN!

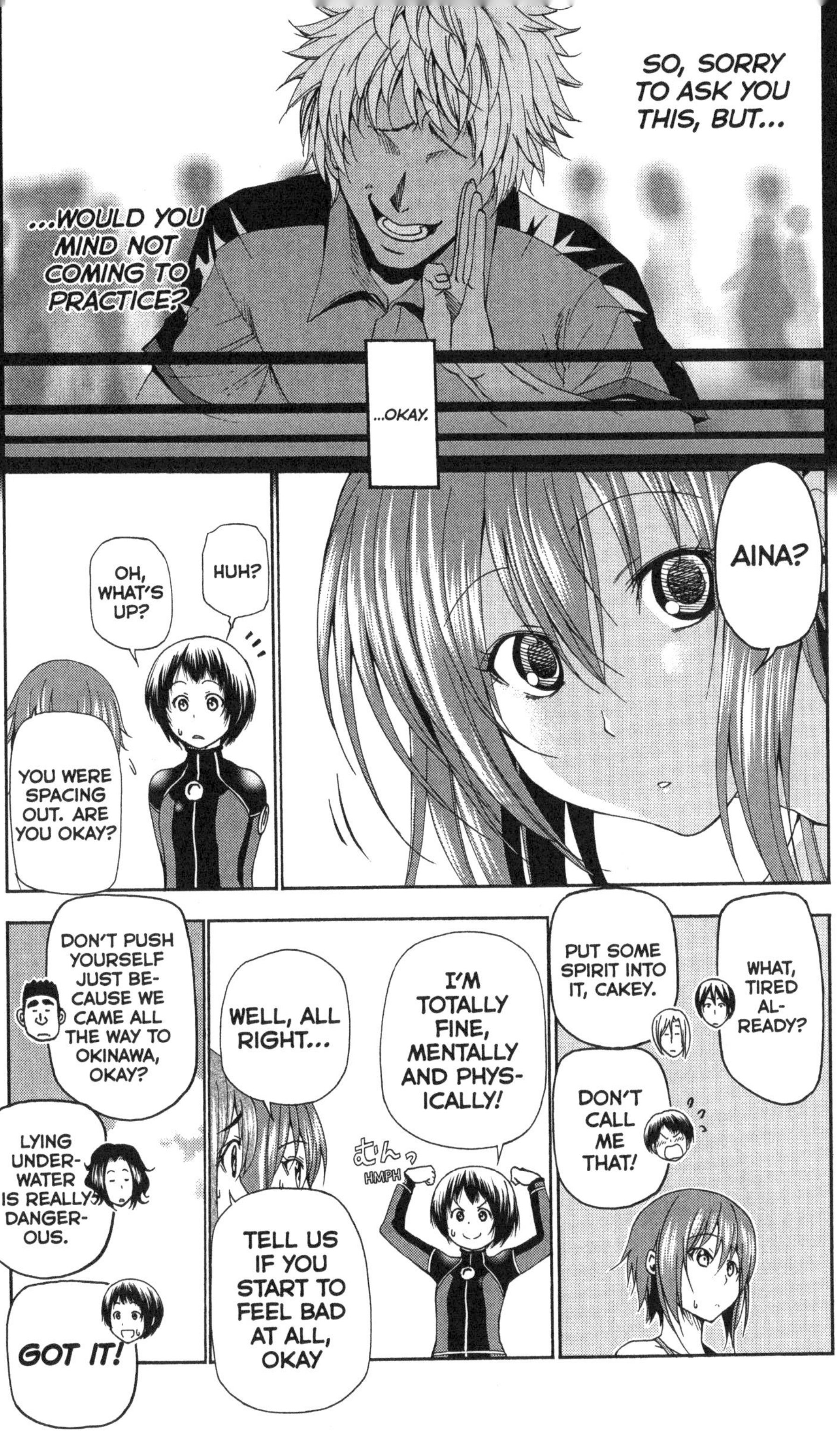
SO, SORRY TO ASK YOU THIS, BUT...
...WOULD YOU MIND NOT COMING TO PRACTICE?
...OKAY.
AINA?
HUH?
OH, WHAT'S UP?
YOU WERE SPACING OUT. ARE YOU OKAY?
WHAT, TIRED AL-READY?
PUT SOME SPIRIT INTO IT, CAKEY.
DON'T CALL ME THAT!
I'M TOTALLY FINE, MENTALLY AND PHYS-ICALLY!
むんっ
HMPH
WELL, ALL RIGHT...
TELL US IF YOU START TO FEEL BAD AT ALL, OKAY
DON'T PUSH YOURSELF JUST BE-CAUSE WE CAME ALL THE WAY TO OKINAWA, OKAY?
LYING UNDER-WATER IS REALLY DANGER-OUS.
GOT IT!

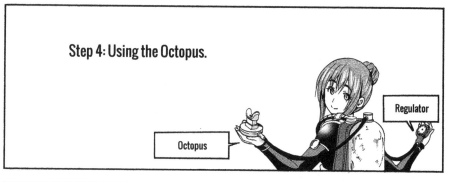

Step 4: Using the Octopus.
Regulator
Octopus
In the event your buddy runs out of air...
I'm out of air.
...hand them your octopus (spare regulator).
While sharing air with your buddy, hold onto each other and gradually surface.
GRAB

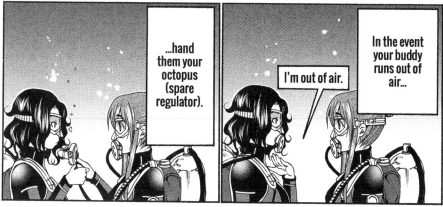

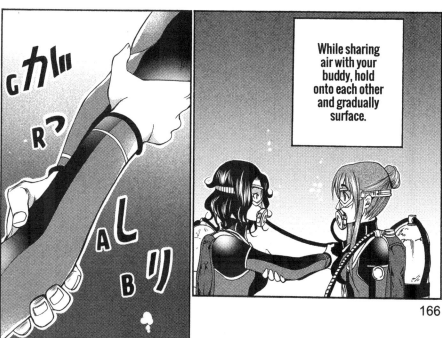

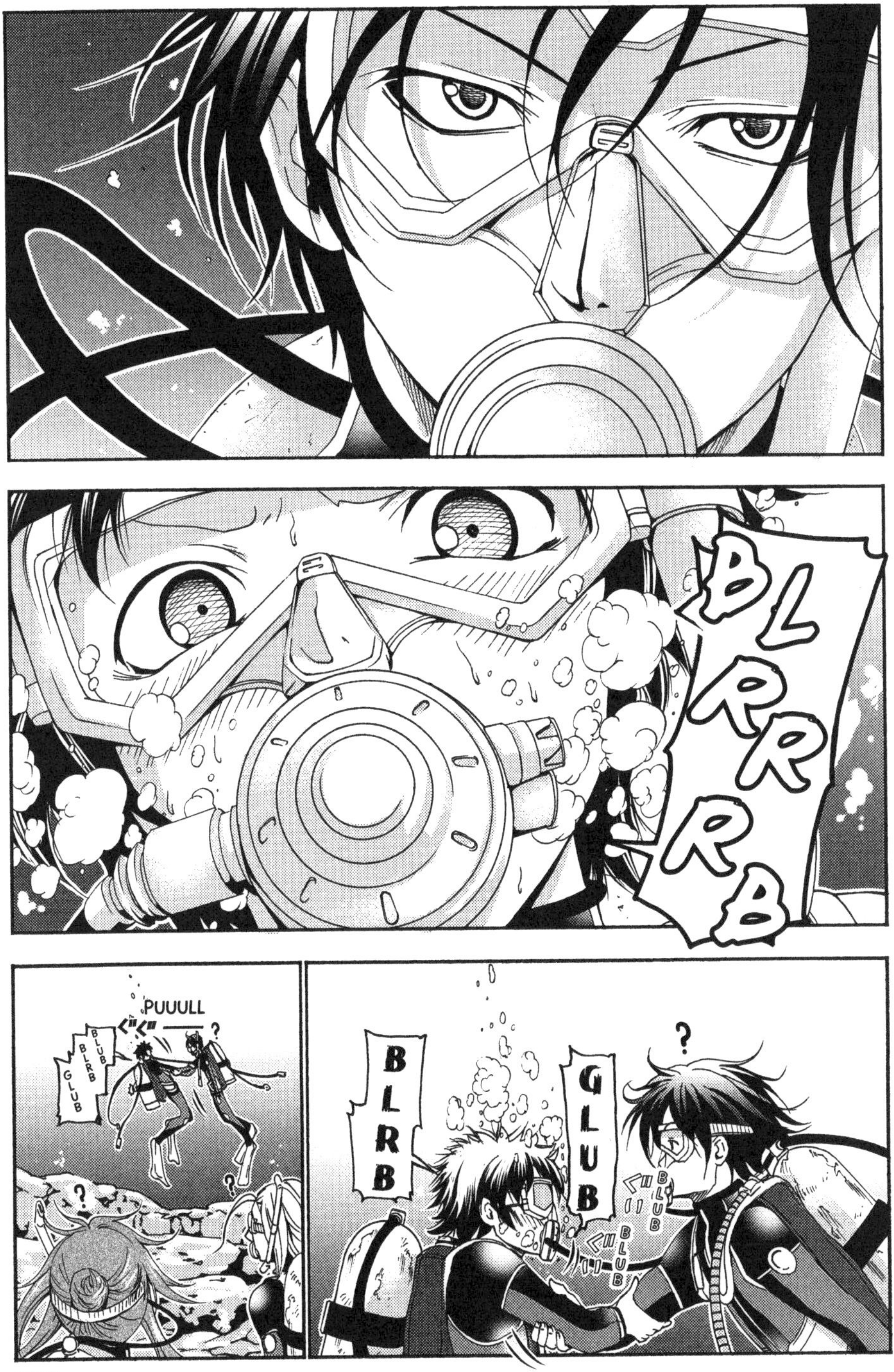
BLRRRB
?
GLUB
BLRB
BLUB
BLUB
PUUULL
?
BLUB
BLRB
GLUB
?
?

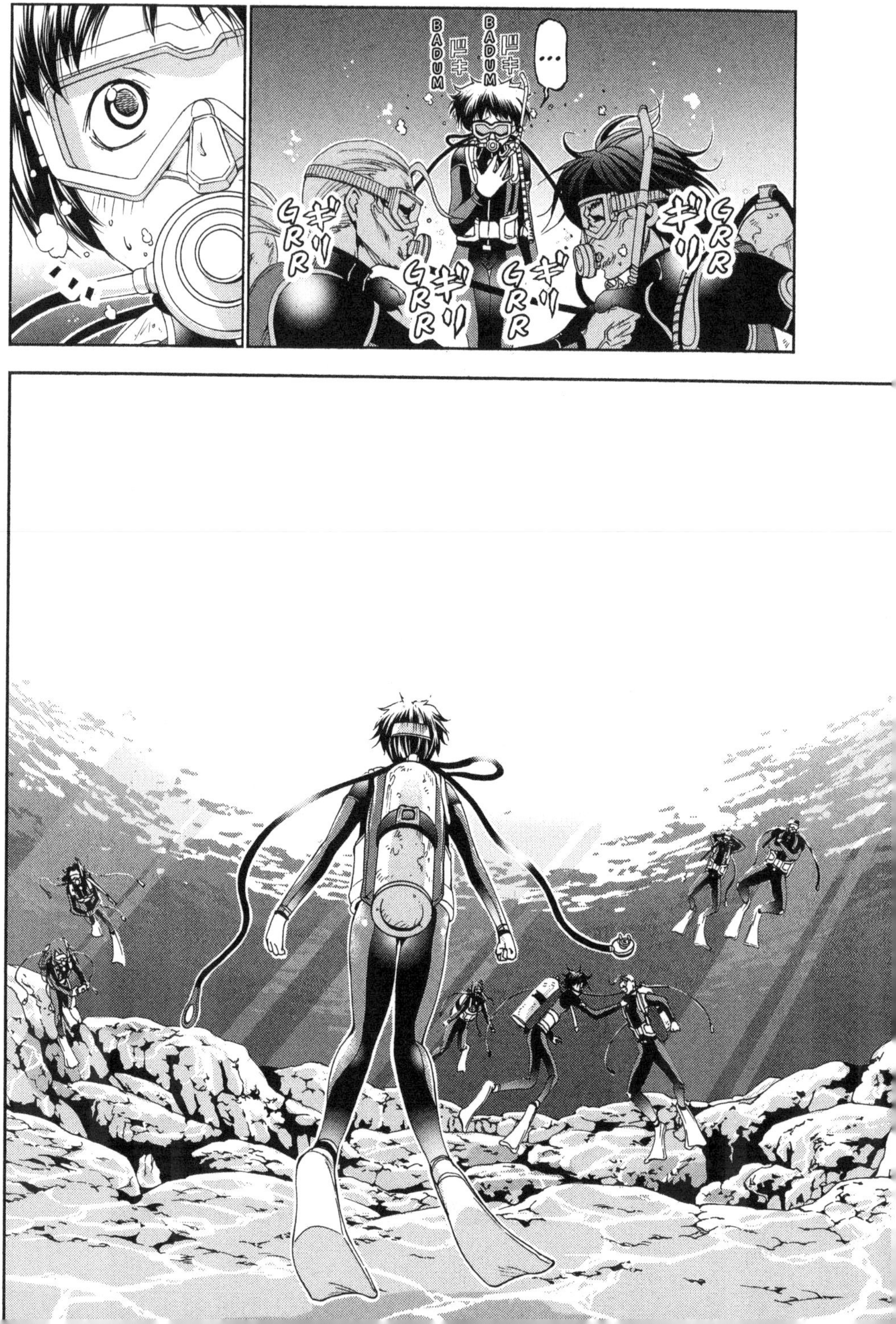
...
ドキ BADUM
ドキ BADUM
ギリ GRR
ギリ GRR
ギリ GRR
ギリ GRR
...

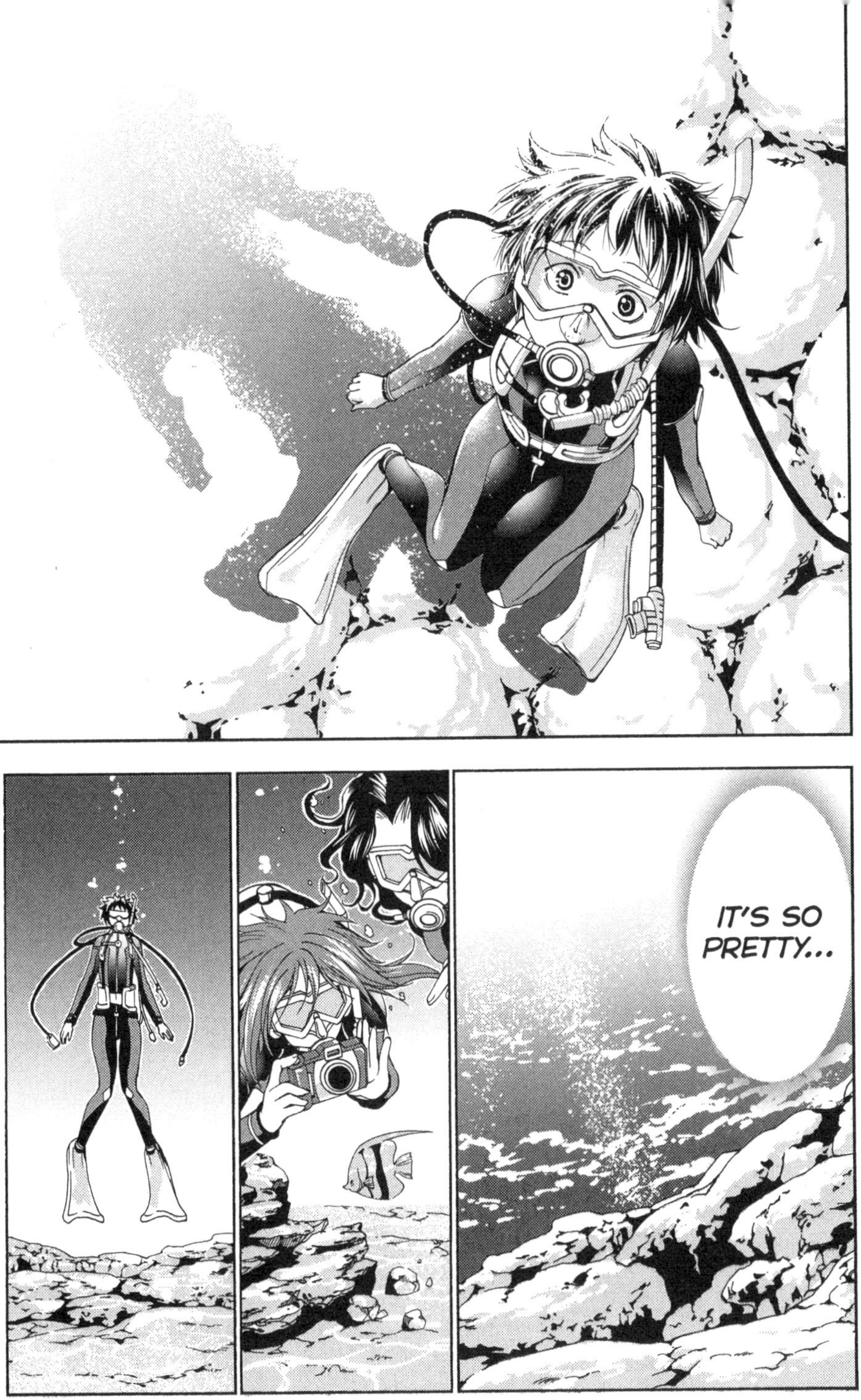
IT'S SO PRETTY...

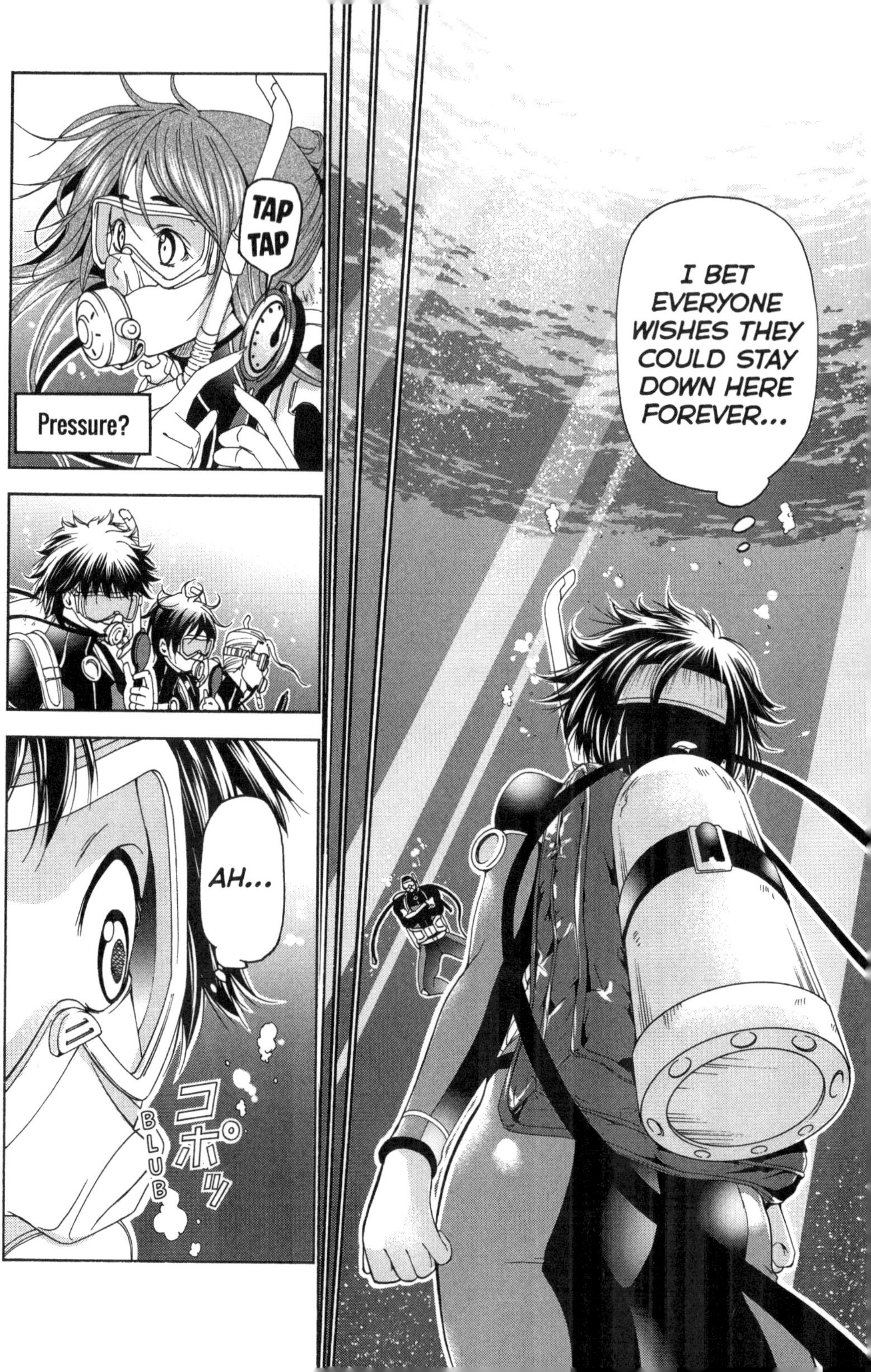
I BET EVERYONE WISHES THEY COULD STAY DOWN HERE FOREVER...
TAP TAP
Pressure?
AH...
コポッ
BLUB

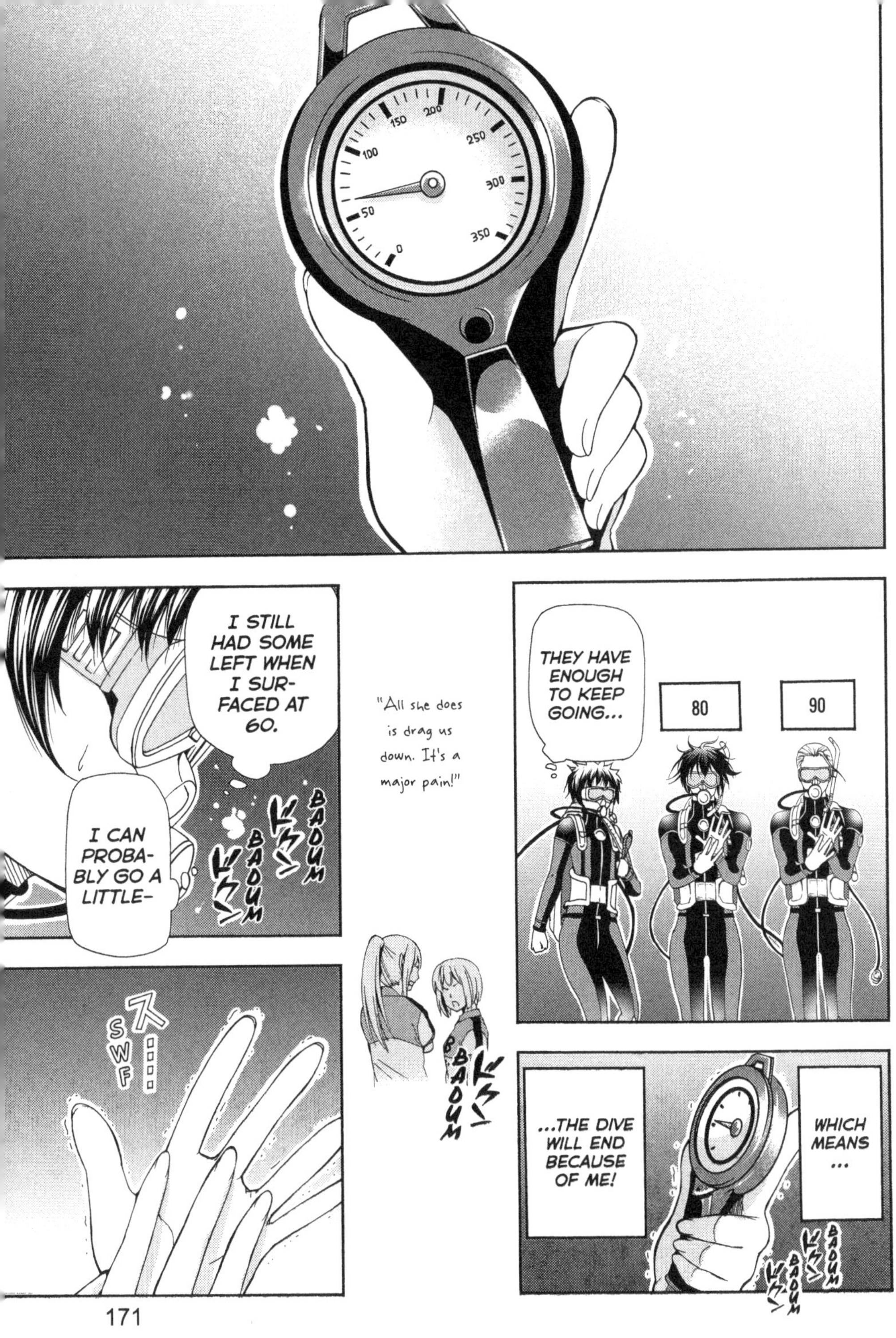
0
50
100
150
200
250
300
350
THEY HAVE ENOUGH TO KEEP GOING...
80
90
I STILL HAD SOME LEFT WHEN I SUR-FACED AT 60.
I CAN PROBA-BLY GO A LITTLE-
BADUM BADUM
"All she does is drag us down. It's a major pain!"
BADUM
WHICH MEANS...
...THE DIVE WILL END BECAUSE OF ME!
BADUM BADUM
SWF

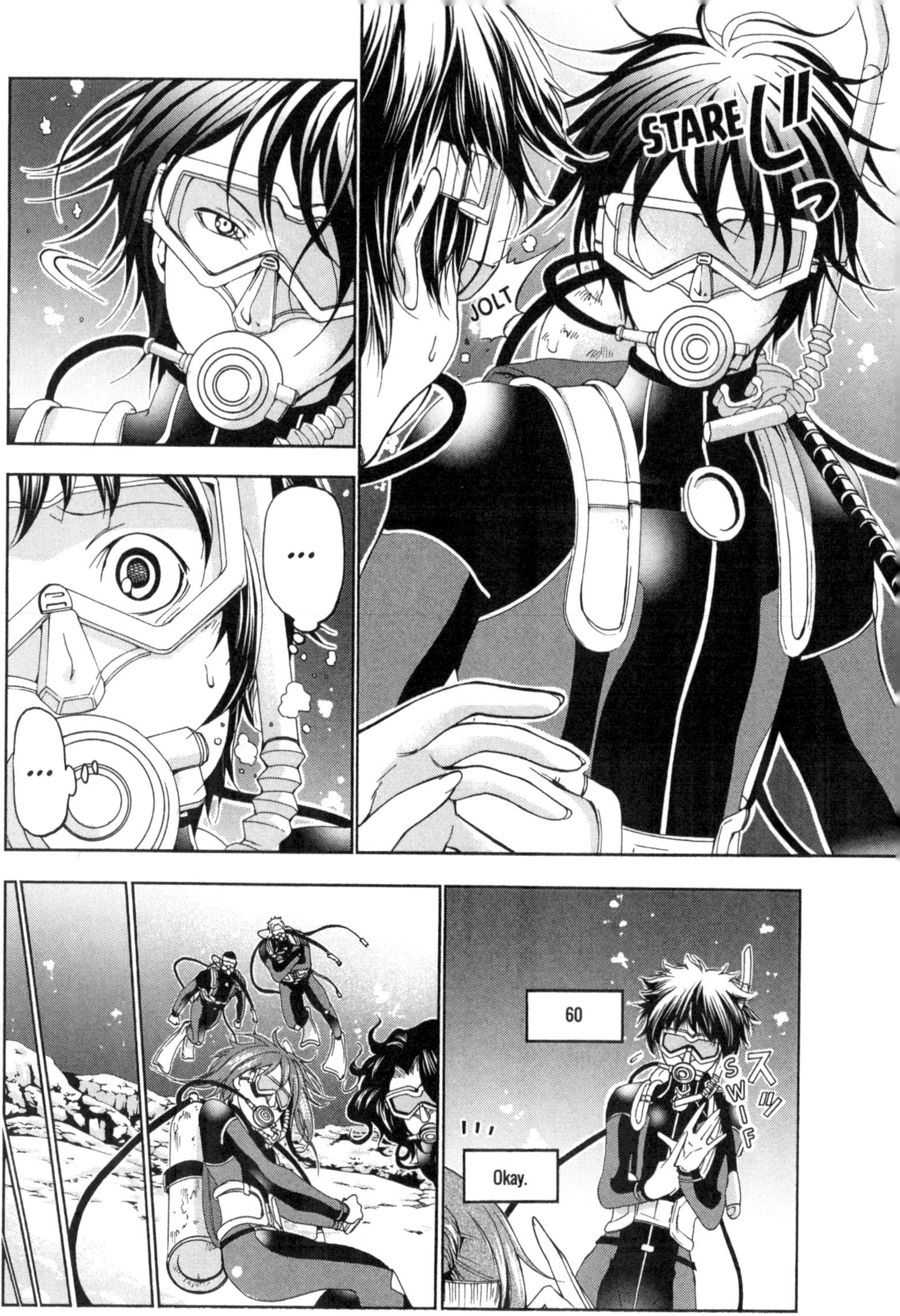
STARE
JOLT
...
...
60
SWIF
Okay.

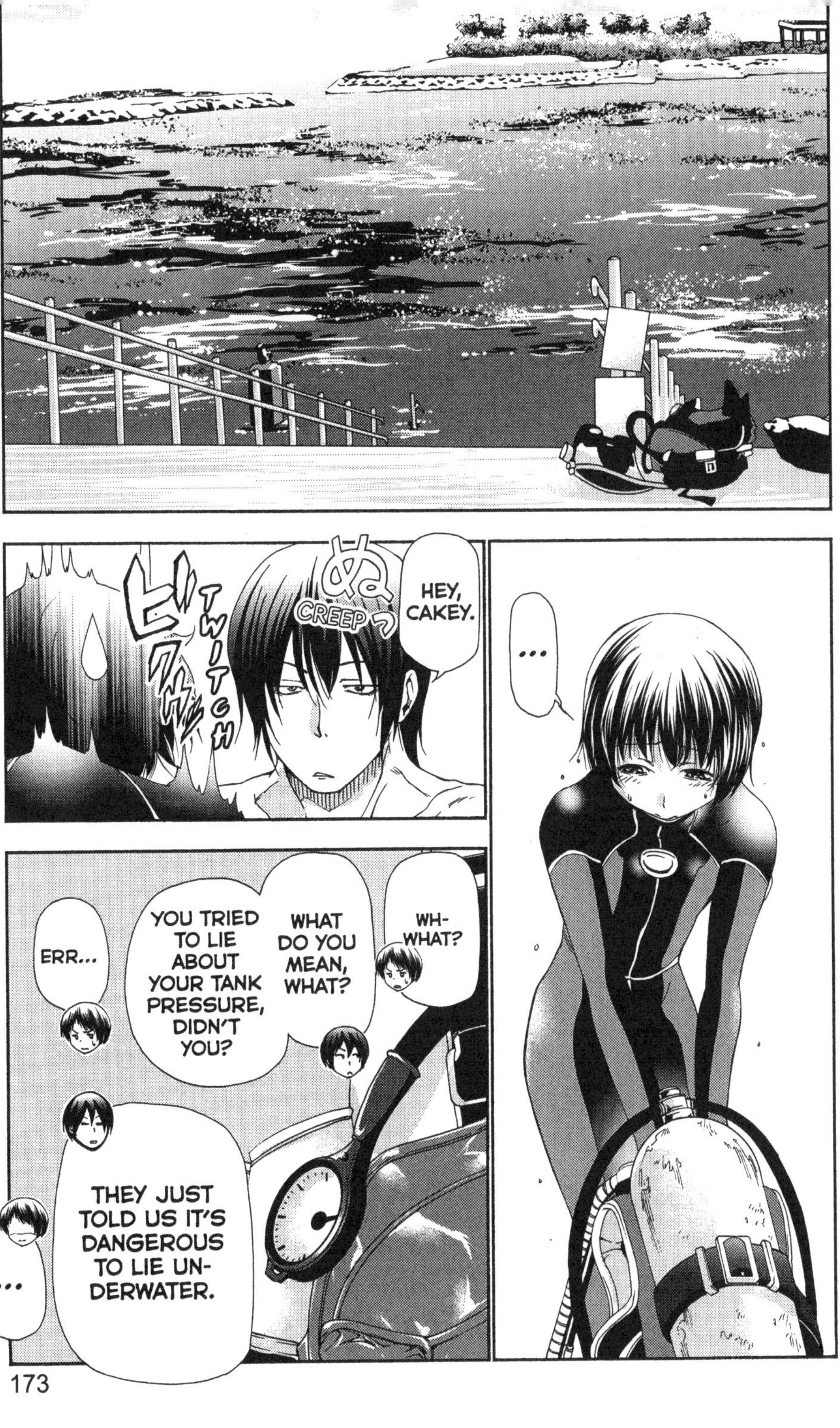
...
HEY, CAKEY.
ぬっ
CREEP
TWITCH
WH- WHAT?
WHAT DO YOU MEAN, WHAT?
YOU TRIED TO LIE ABOUT YOUR TANK PRESSURE, DIDN'T YOU?
ERR...
THEY JUST TOLD US IT'S DANGEROUS TO LIE UN- DERWATER.
...

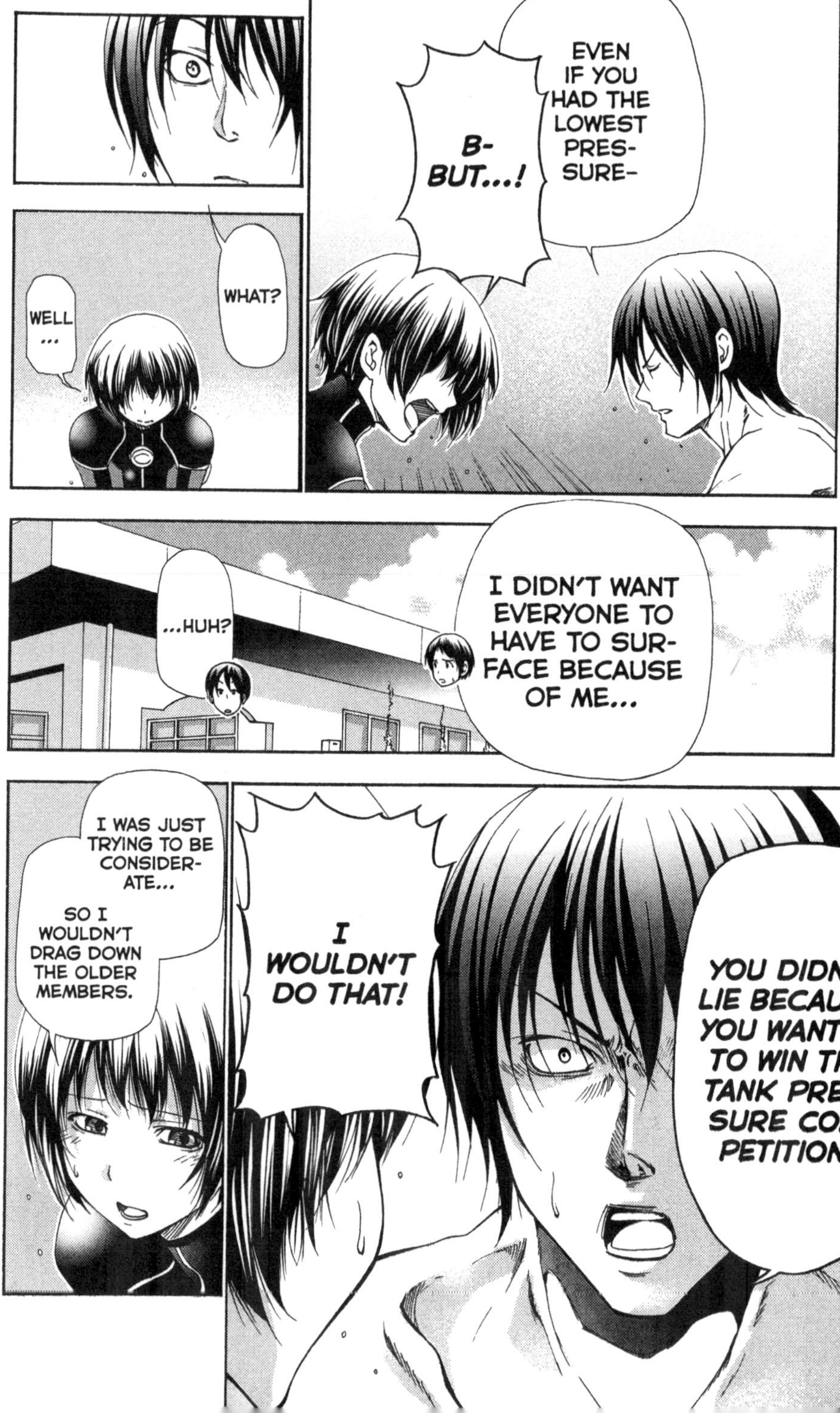
EVEN IF YOU HAD THE LOWEST PRES-SURE-
B-BUT...!
WHAT?
WELL...
I DIDN'T WANT EVERYONE TO HAVE TO SUR-FACE BECAUSE OF ME...
...HUH?
YOU DIDN'T LIE BECAUSE YOU WANTED TO WIN THE TANK PRES-SURE COM-PETITION?
I WOULDN'T DO THAT!
I WAS JUST TRYING TO BE CONSIDER-ATE...
SO I WOULDN'T DRAG DOWN THE OLDER MEMBERS.

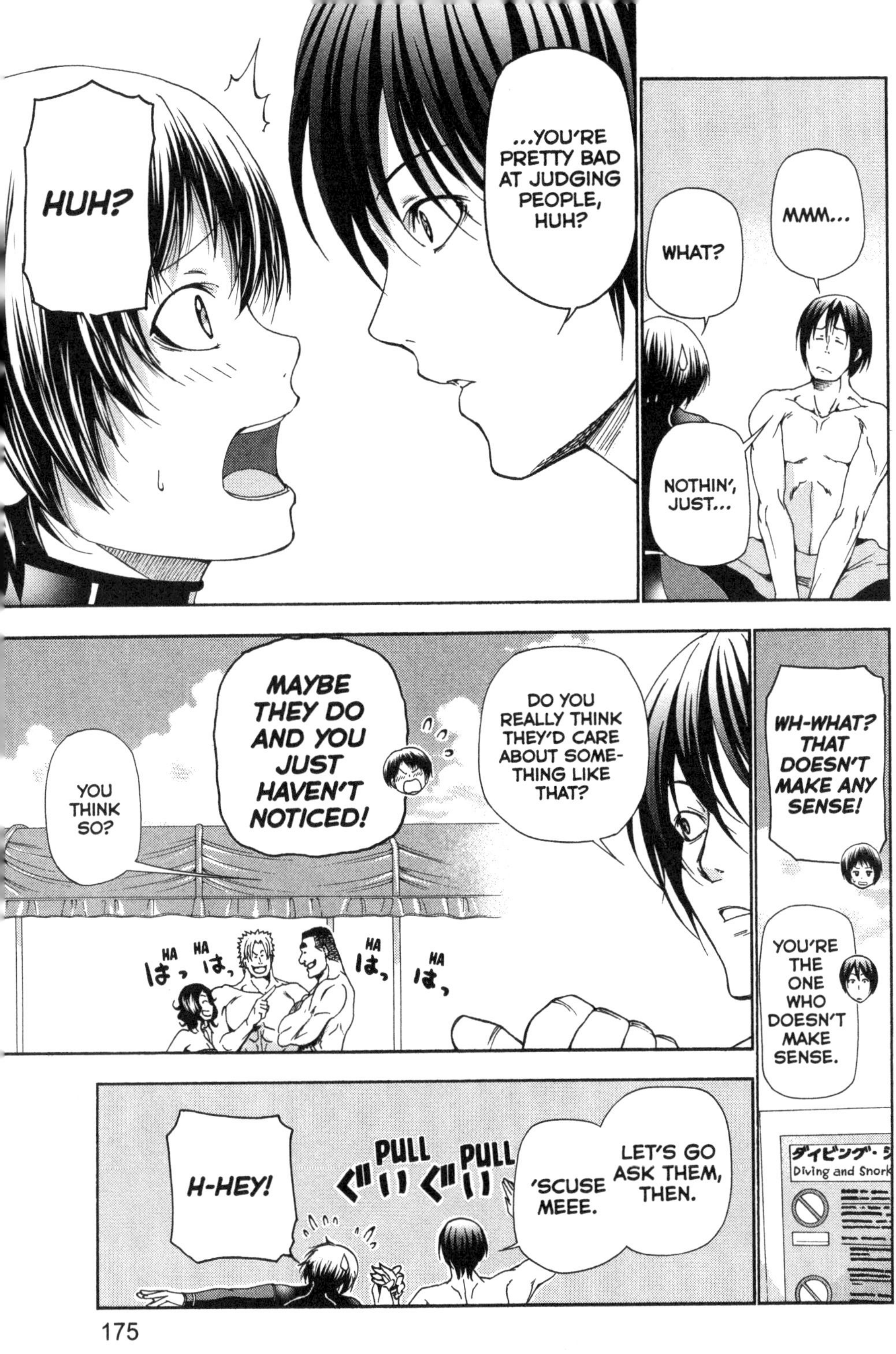
MMM...
WHAT?
NOTHIN', JUST...
...YOU'RE PRETTY BAD AT JUDGING PEOPLE, HUH?
HUH?
WH-WHAT? THAT DOESN'T MAKE ANY SENSE!
YOU'RE THE ONE WHO DOESN'T MAKE SENSE.
ダイビング・シ
Diving and Snork
DO YOU REALLY THINK THEY'D CARE ABOUT SOMETHING LIKE THAT?
MAYBE THEY DO AND YOU JUST HAVEN'T NOTICED!
YOU THINK SO?
HA はっ
HA はっ
HA はっ
HA はっ
LET'S GO ASK THEM, THEN.
'SCUSE MEEE.
PULL ぐい
PULL ぐい
H-HEY!

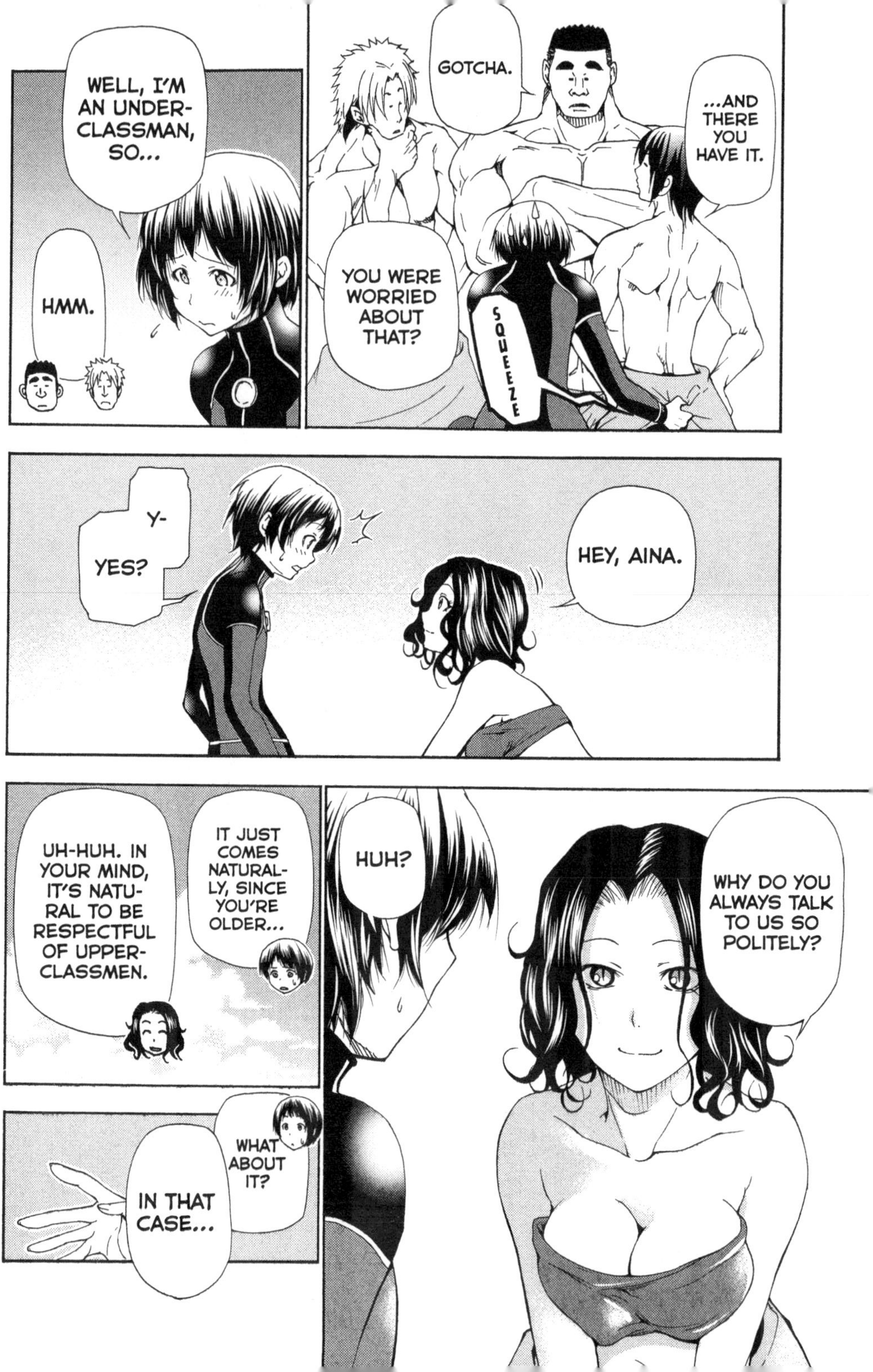
...AND THERE YOU HAVE IT.
GOTCHA.
YOU WERE WORRIED ABOUT THAT?
SQUEEZE
WELL, I'M AN UNDER-CLASSMAN, SO...
HMM.
HEY, AINA.
Y- YES?
WHY DO YOU ALWAYS TALK TO US SO POLITELY?
HUH?
IT JUST COMES NATURAL-LY, SINCE YOU'RE OLDER...
UH-HUH. IN YOUR MIND, IT'S NATU-RAL TO BE RESPECTFUL OF UPPER-CLASSMEN.
WHAT ABOUT IT?
IN THAT CASE...

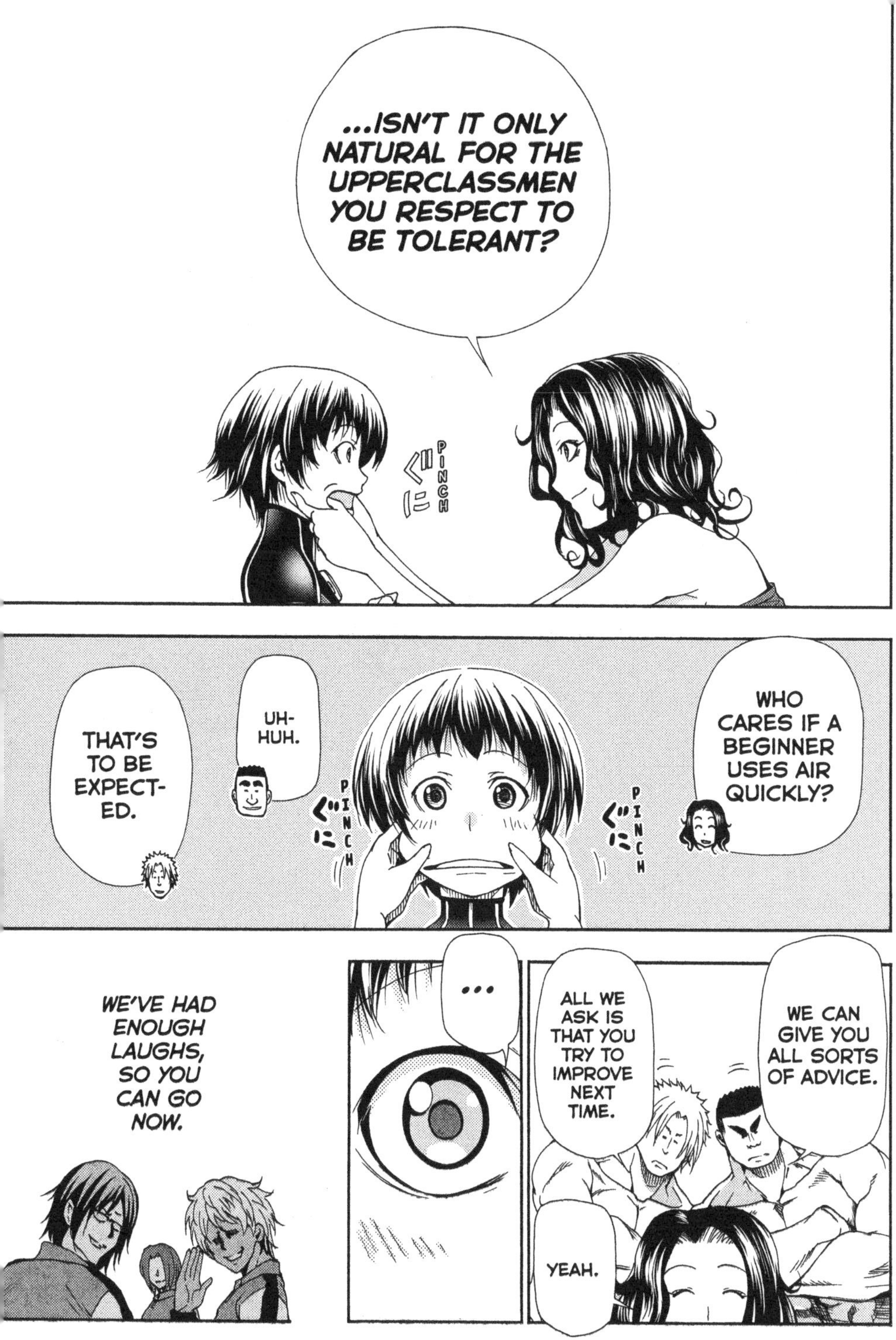
...ISN'T IT ONLY NATURAL FOR THE UPPERCLASSMEN YOU RESPECT TO BE TOLERANT?
ぐに PINCH
WHO CARES IF A BEGINNER USES AIR QUICKLY?
ぐに PINCH
ぐに PINCH
UH-HUH.
THAT'S TO BE EXPECT-ED.
WE CAN GIVE YOU ALL SORTS OF ADVICE.
ALL WE ASK IS THAT YOU TRY TO IMPROVE NEXT TIME.
YEAH.
...
WE'VE HAD ENOUGH LAUGHS, SO YOU CAN GO NOW.

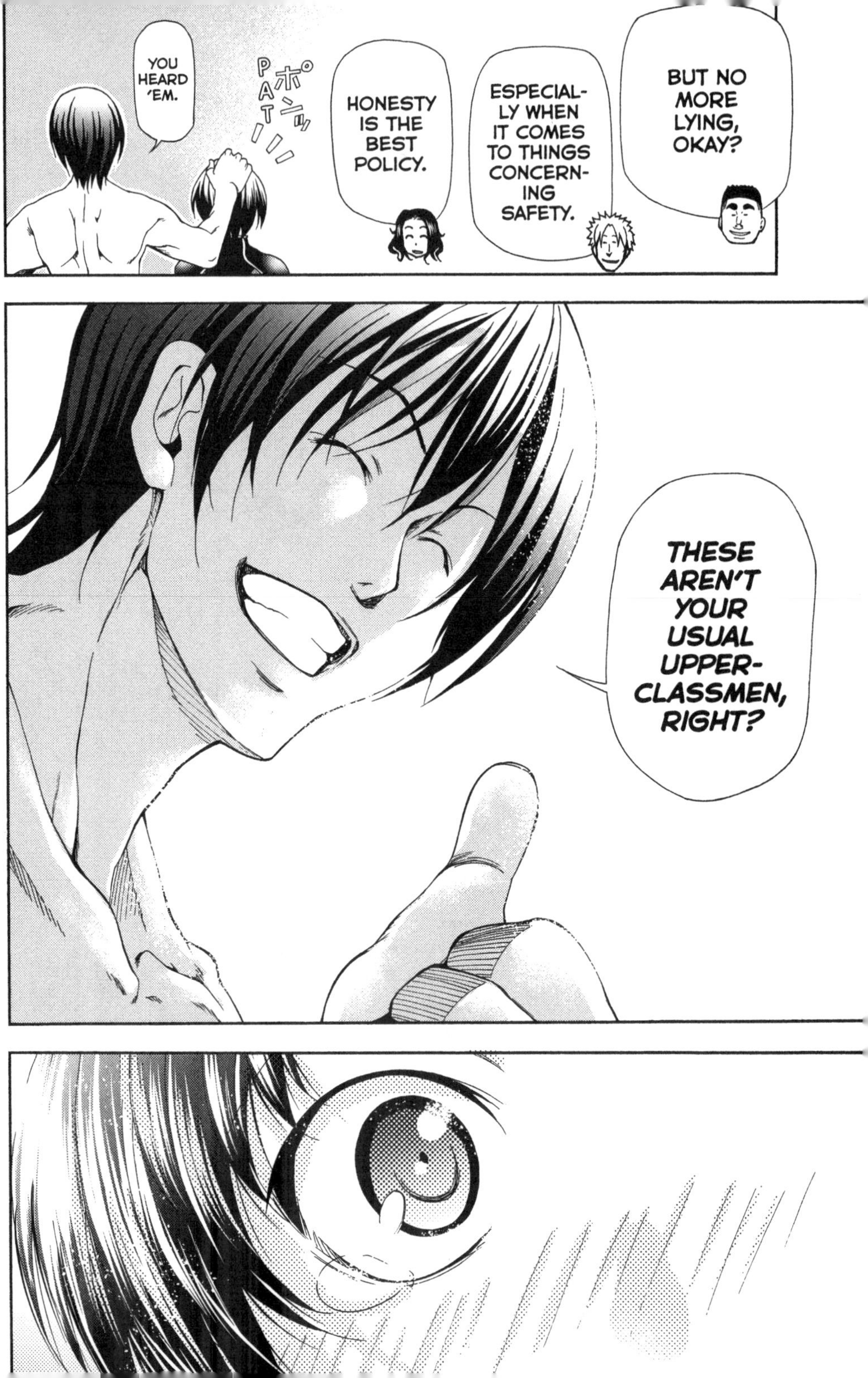
BUT NO MORE LYING, OKAY?
ESPECIAL-LY WHEN IT COMES TO THINGS CONCERN-ING SAFETY.
HONESTY IS THE BEST POLICY.
PAT ポンッ
YOU HEARD 'EM.
THESE AREN'T YOUR USUAL UPPER-CLASSMEN, RIGHT?

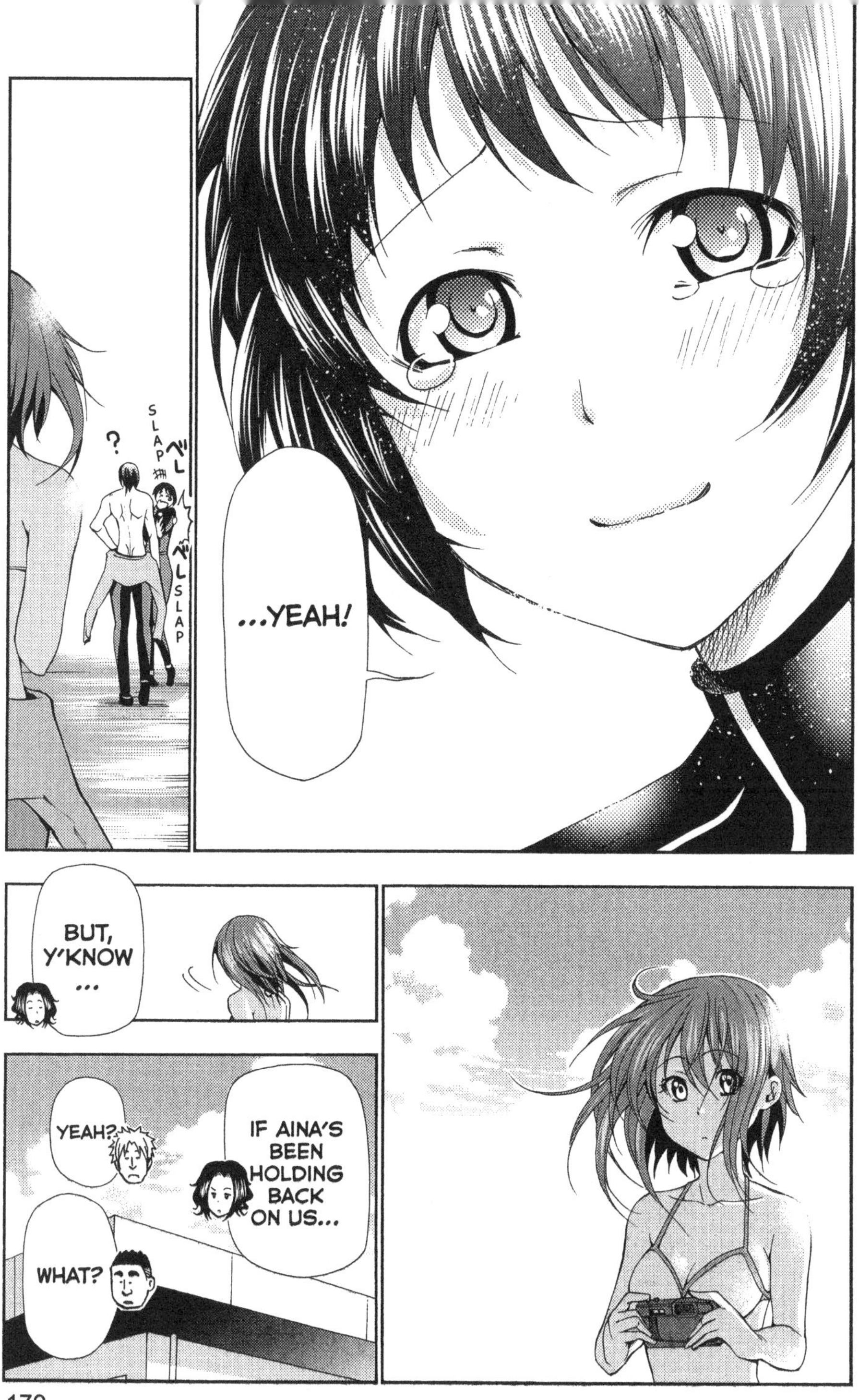
...YEAH!
?
SLAP
SLAP
BUT, Y'KNOW ...
IF AINA'S BEEN HOLDING BACK ON US...
YEAH?
WHAT?

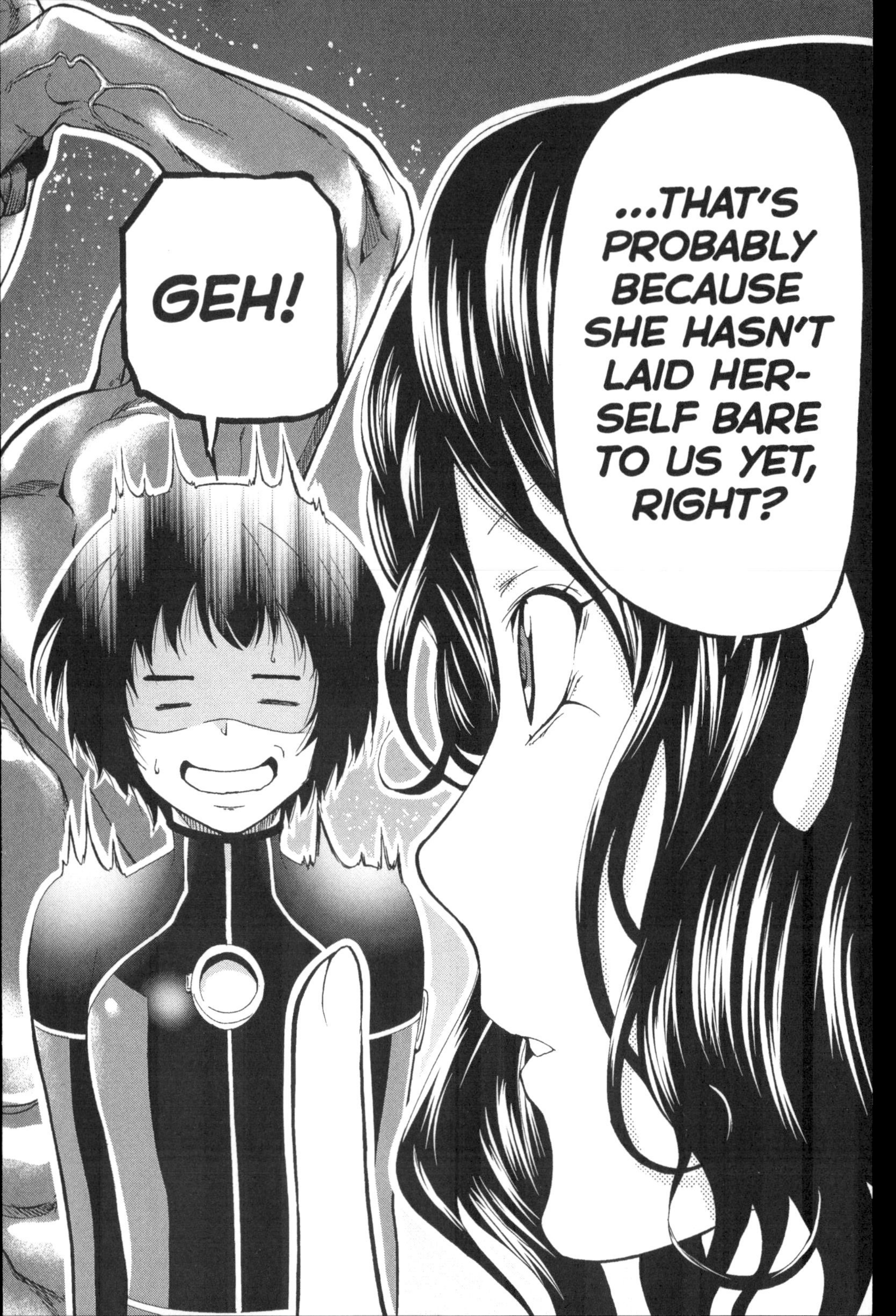
...THAT'S PROBABLY BECAUSE SHE HASN'T LAID HER-SELF BARE TO US YET, RIGHT?
GEH!

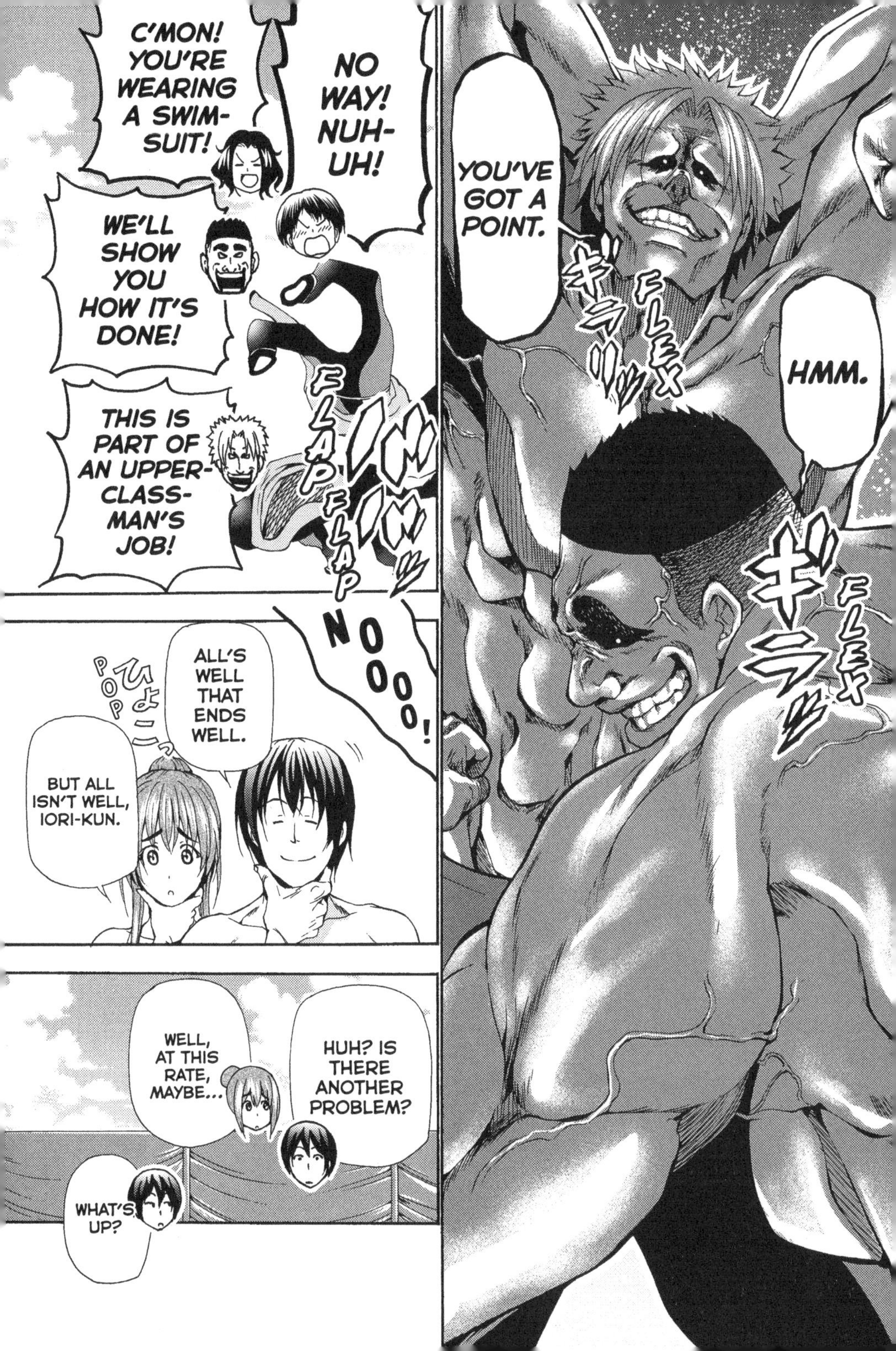
YOU'VE GOT A POINT.
FLEX
HMM.
FLEX
NO WAY! NUH-UH!
C'MON! YOU'RE WEARING A SWIM-SUIT!
WE'LL SHOW YOU HOW IT'S DONE!
FLAP FLAP FLAP
THIS IS PART OF AN UPPER-CLASS-MAN'S JOB!
NOOOO!
ALL'S WELL THAT ENDS WELL.
POP
BUT ALL ISN'T WELL, IORI-KUN.
HUH? IS THERE ANOTHER PROBLEM?
WELL, AT THIS RATE, MAYBE...
WHAT'S UP?

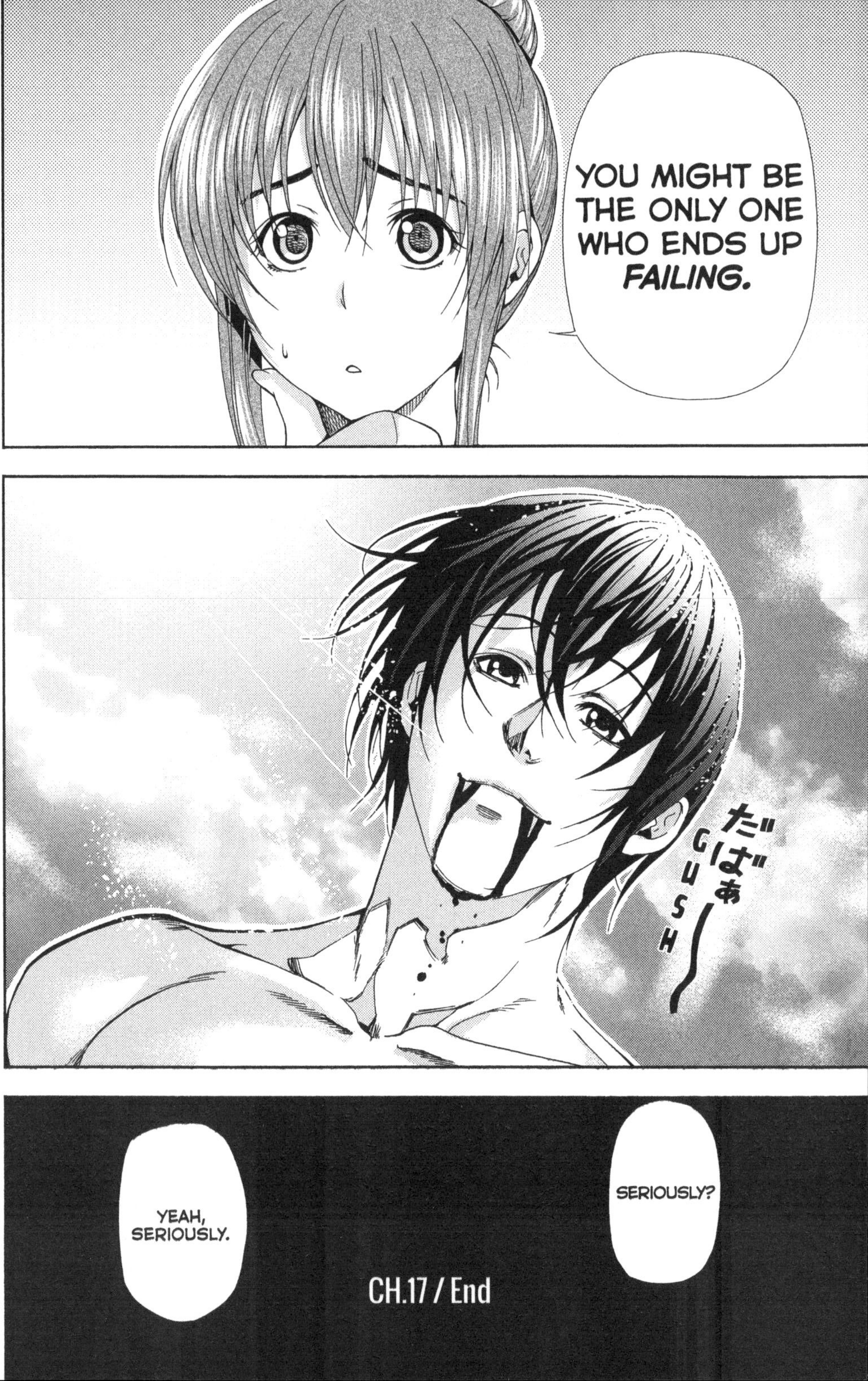
YOU MIGHT BE THE ONLY ONE WHO ENDS UP *FAILING.*
だばぁ〜
GUSH
SERIOUSLY?
YEAH, SERIOUSLY.
CH.17 / End

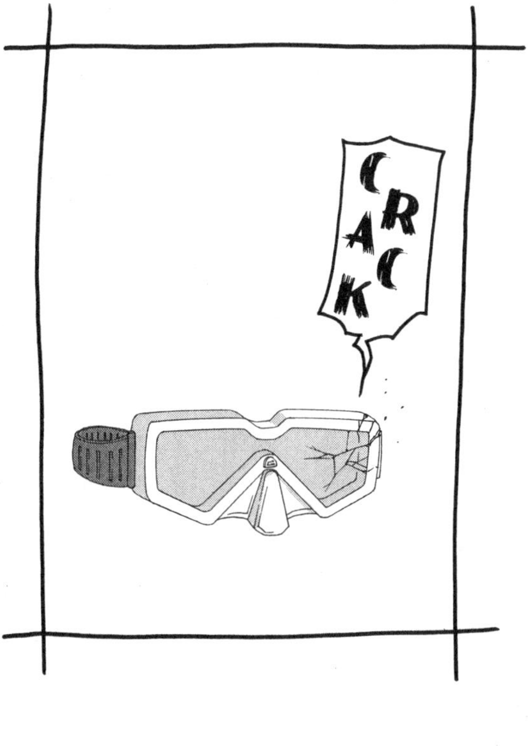
CRACK

COMING UP: A THREE- FOLD TIDAL WAVE OF PREVIEWS!

GO TO NEXT PAGE

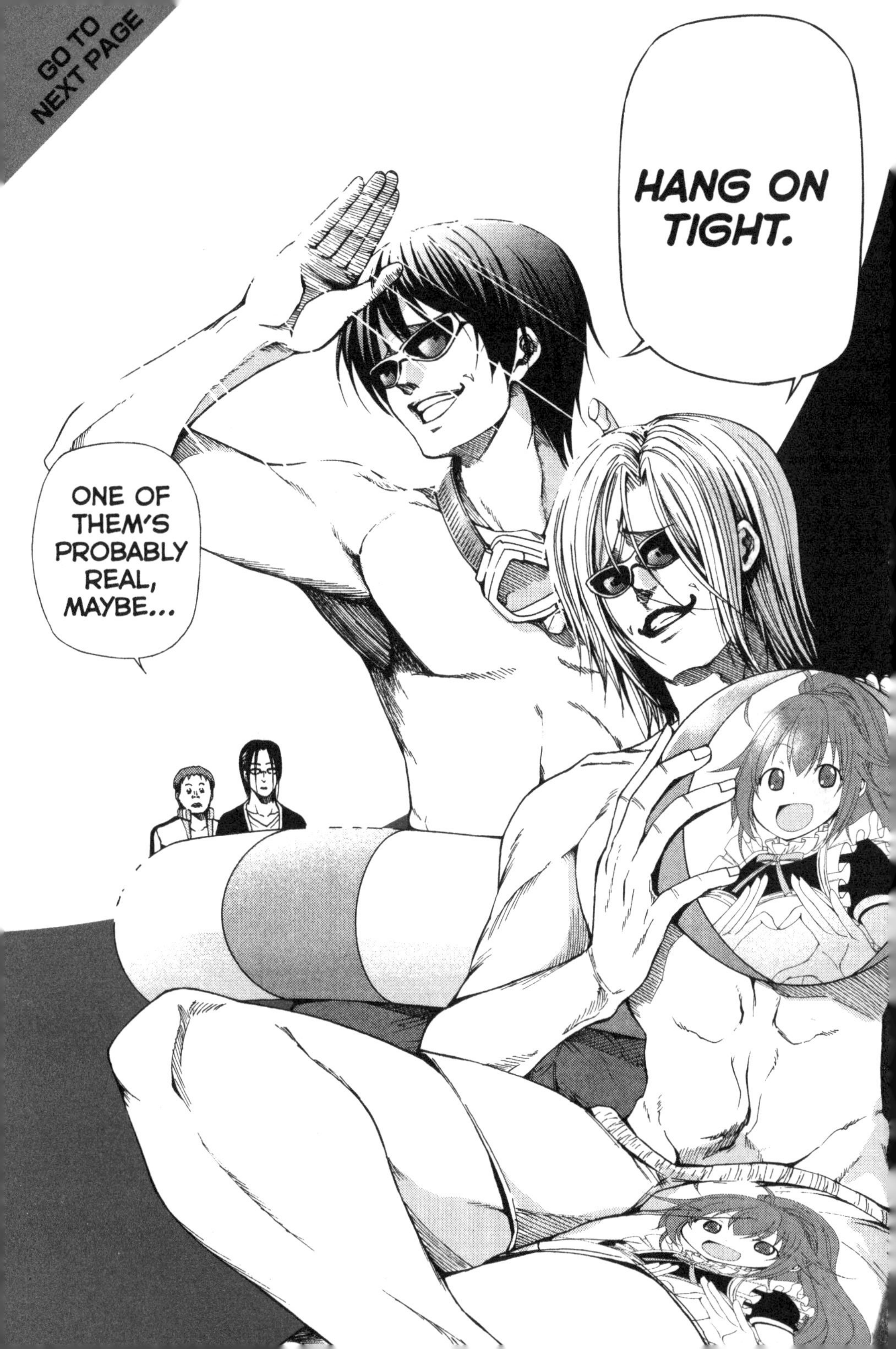
HANG ON TIGHT.
ONE OF THEM'S PROBABLY REAL, MAYBE...

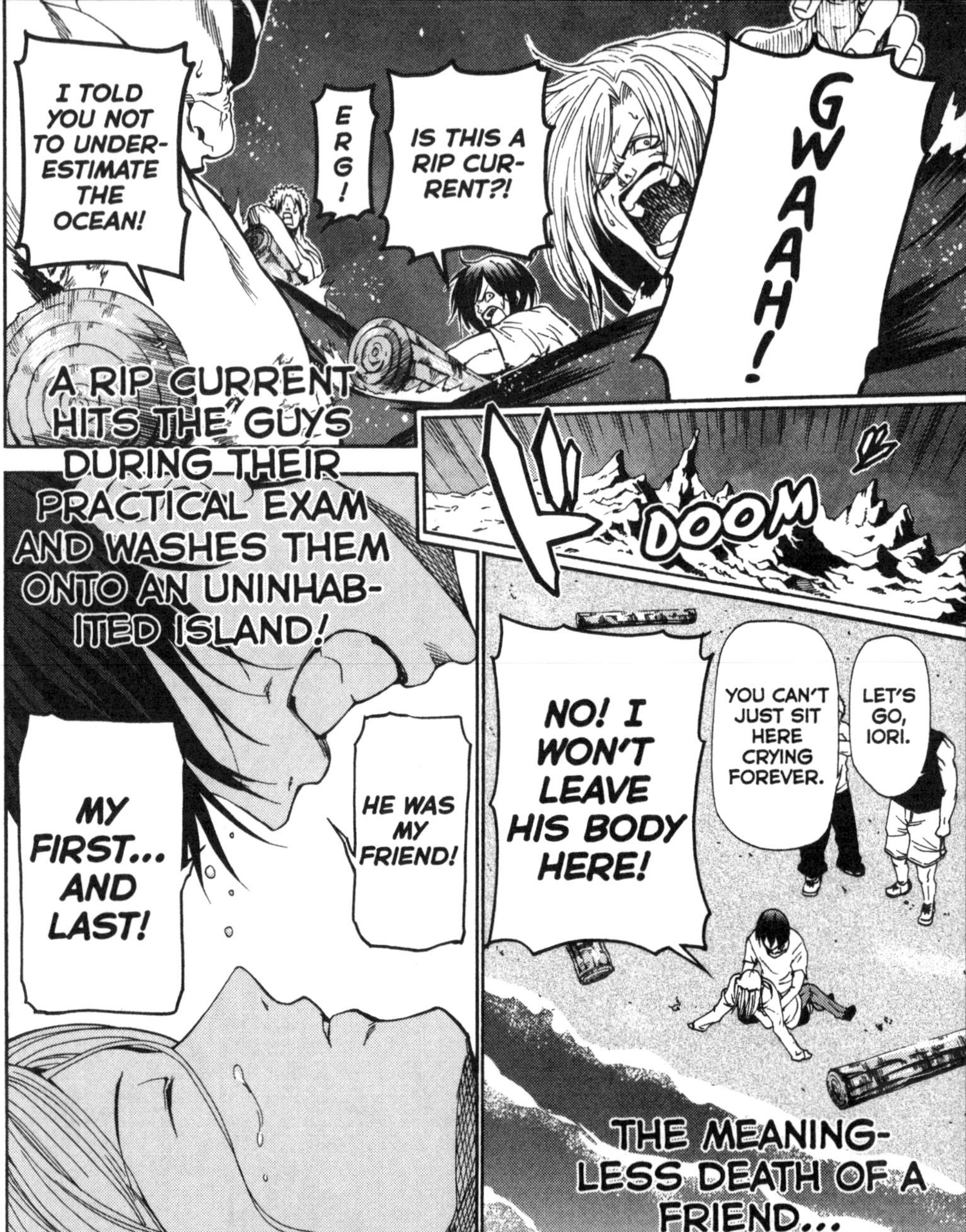
GWAAH!
IS THIS A RIP CURRENT?!
ERG!
I TOLD YOU NOT TO UNDERESTIMATE THE OCEAN!
A RIP CURRENT HITS THE GUYS DURING THEIR PRACTICAL EXAM AND WASHES THEM ONTO AN UNINHABITED ISLAND!
DOOM
LET'S GO, IORI.
YOU CAN'T JUST SIT HERE CRYING FOREVER.
NO! I WON'T LEAVE HIS BODY HERE!
THE MEANINGLESS DEATH OF A FRIEND...
HE WAS MY FRIEND!
MY FIRST... AND LAST!

To be continued in...

*Contents may vary from those portrayed here.

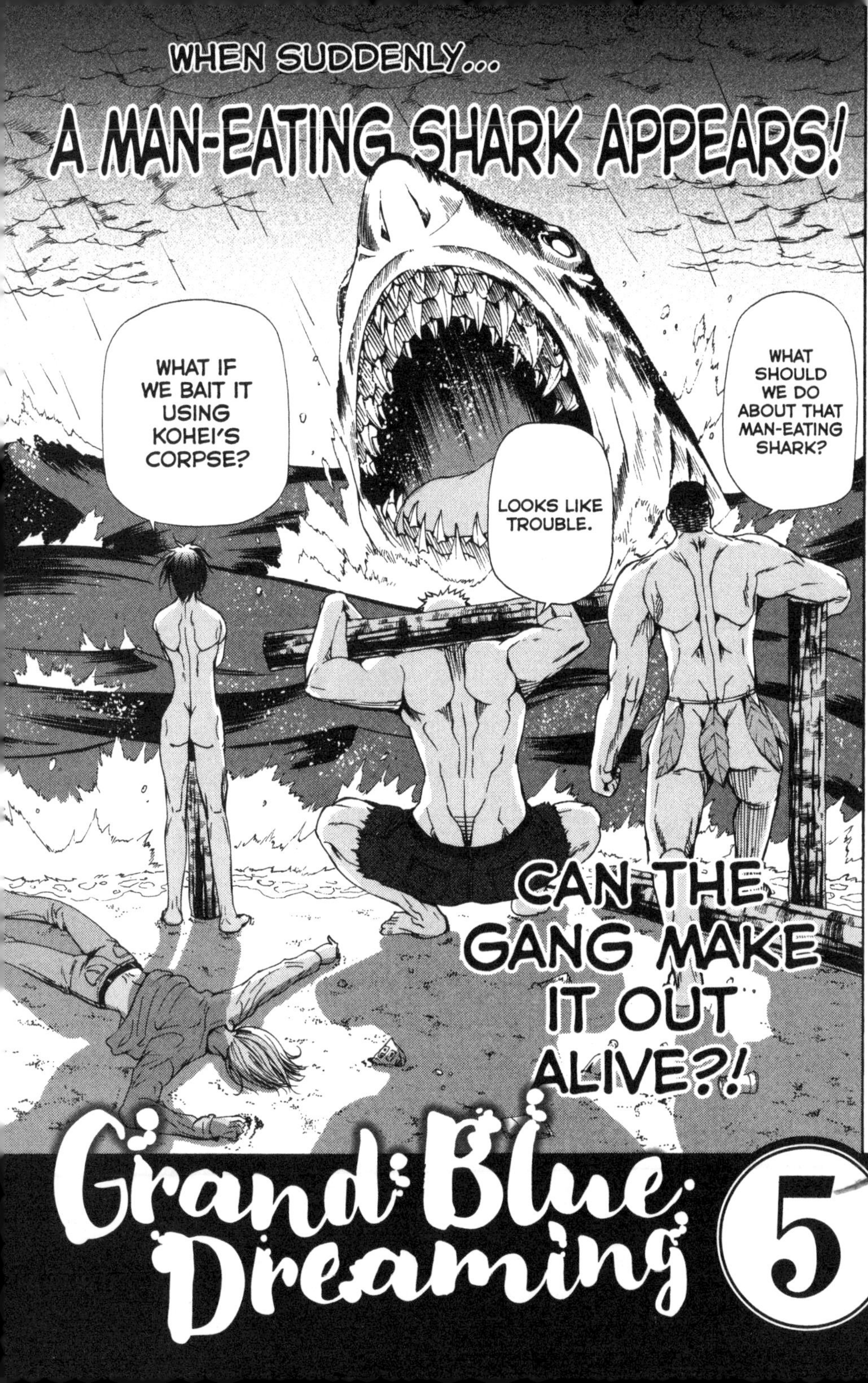
WHEN SUDDENLY...
A MAN-EATING SHARK APPEARS!
WHAT SHOULD WE DO ABOUT THAT MAN-EATING SHARK?
LOOKS LIKE TROUBLE.
WHAT IF WE BAIT IT USING KOHEI'S CORPSE?
CAN THE GANG MAKE IT OUT ALIVE?!
Grand Blue Dreaming
5

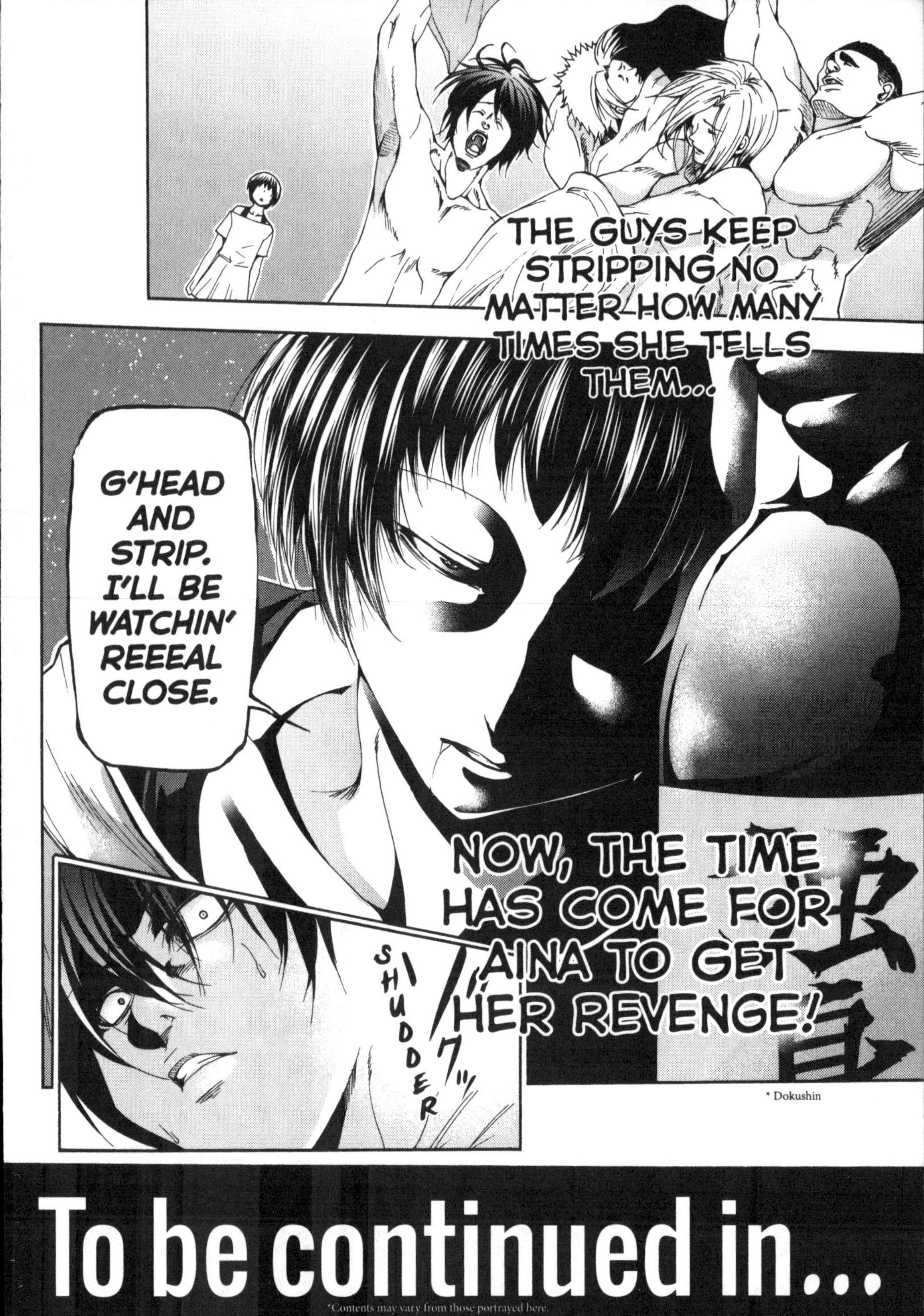
THE GUYS KEEP STRIPPING NO MATTER HOW MANY TIMES SHE TELLS THEM...
G'HEAD AND STRIP. I'LL BE WATCHIN' REEEAL CLOSE.
NOW, THE TIME HAS COME FOR AINA TO GET HER REVENGE!
SHUDDER

* Dokushin

To be continued in...

*Contents may vary from those portrayed here.

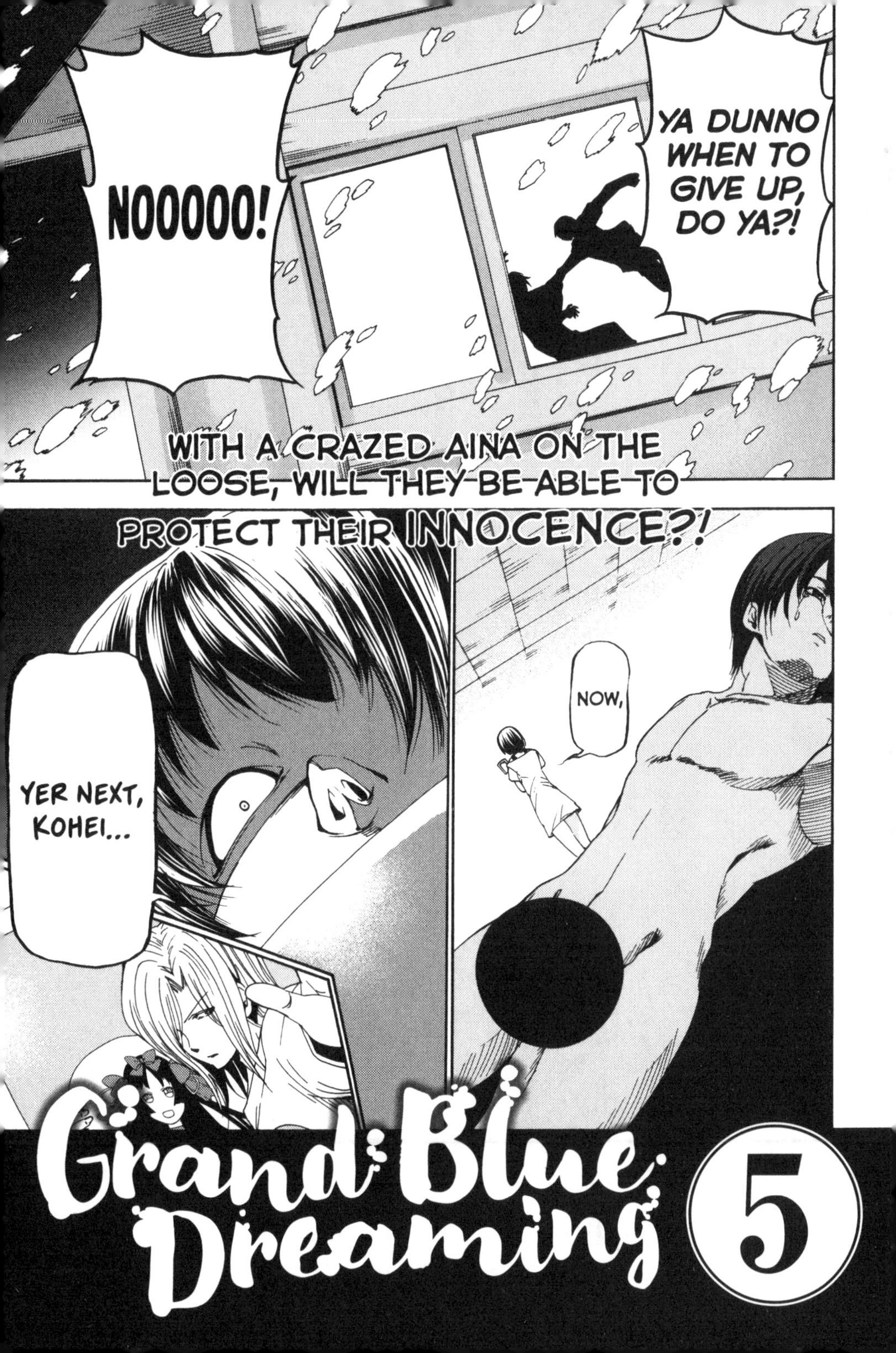
YA DUNNO WHEN TO GIVE UP, DO YA?!
NOOOOO!
WITH A CRAZED AINA ON THE LOOSE, WILL THEY BE ABLE TO PROTECT THEIR INNOCENCE?!
NOW,
YER NEXT, KOHEI...
Grand Blue Dreaming
5

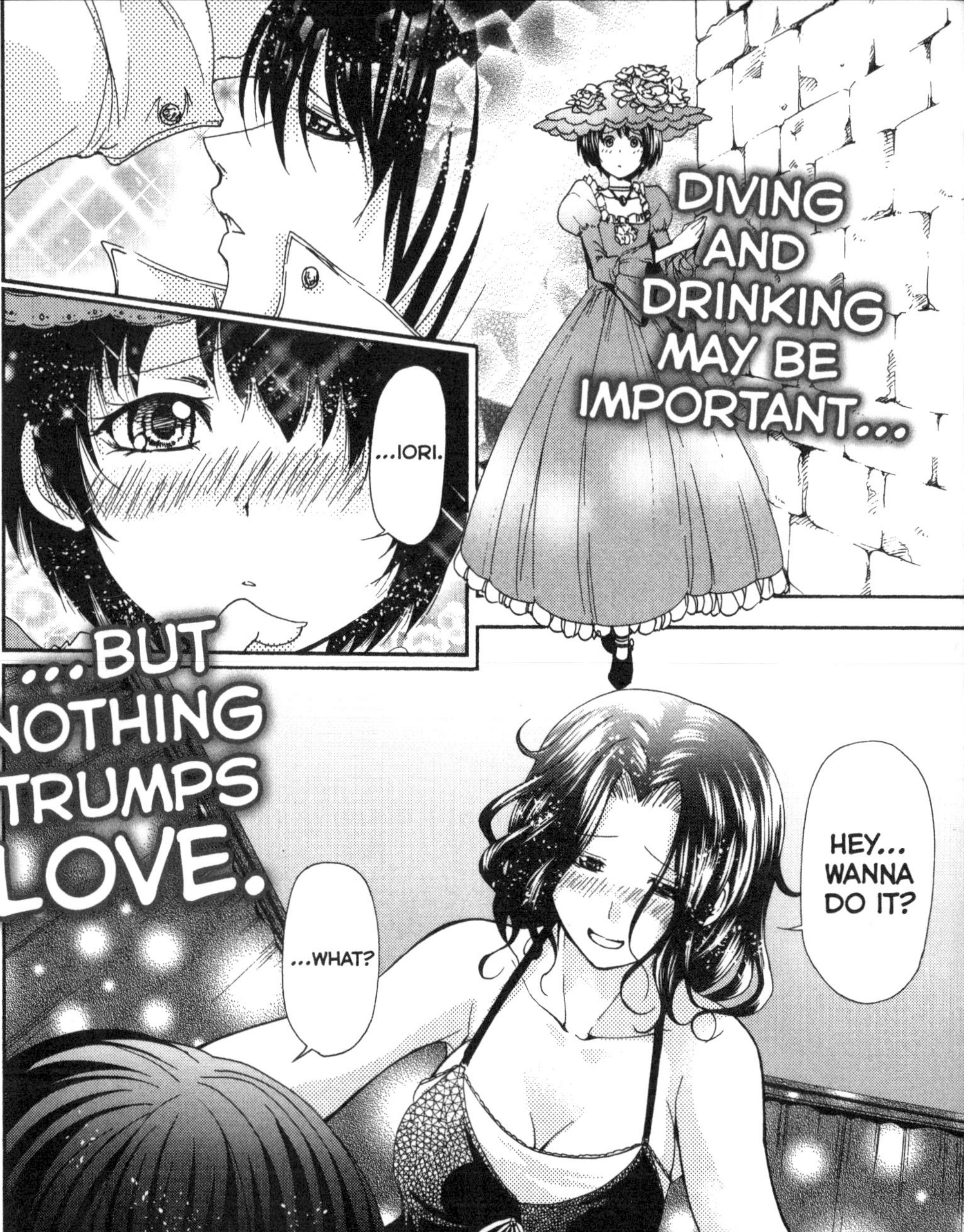
DIVING AND DRINKING MAY BE IMPORTANT...
...IORI.
...BUT NOTHING TRUMPS LOVE.
HEY... WANNA DO IT?
...WHAT?

To be continued in...

*Contents may vary from those portrayed here.

Grand Blue Dreaming volume 4 is a work of fiction.
Names, characters, places, and incidents are the products of the author's imagination or are used fictitiously. Any resemblance to actual events, locales, or persons, living or dead, is entirely coincidental.

A Kodansha Comics Trade Paperback Original.

Published in the United States by Kodansha Comics,
an imprint of Kodansha USA Publishing, LLC, New York.

Publication rights for this English edition arranged through Kodansha Ltd., Tokyo.

First published in Japan in 2015 by Kodansha Ltd., Tokyo.

Cover Design: YUKI YOSHIDA (futaba)

ISBN 978-1-63236-740-2

Printed in the United States of America.

www.kodansha.us

9 8 7 6 5 4 3

Translation: Adam Hirsch
Lettering: Jan Lan Ivan Concepcion
Editing: Sarah Tilson and Paul Starr
Editorial Assistance: YKS Services LLC/SKY Japan, INC.
Kodansha Comics Edition Cover Design: Phil Balsman

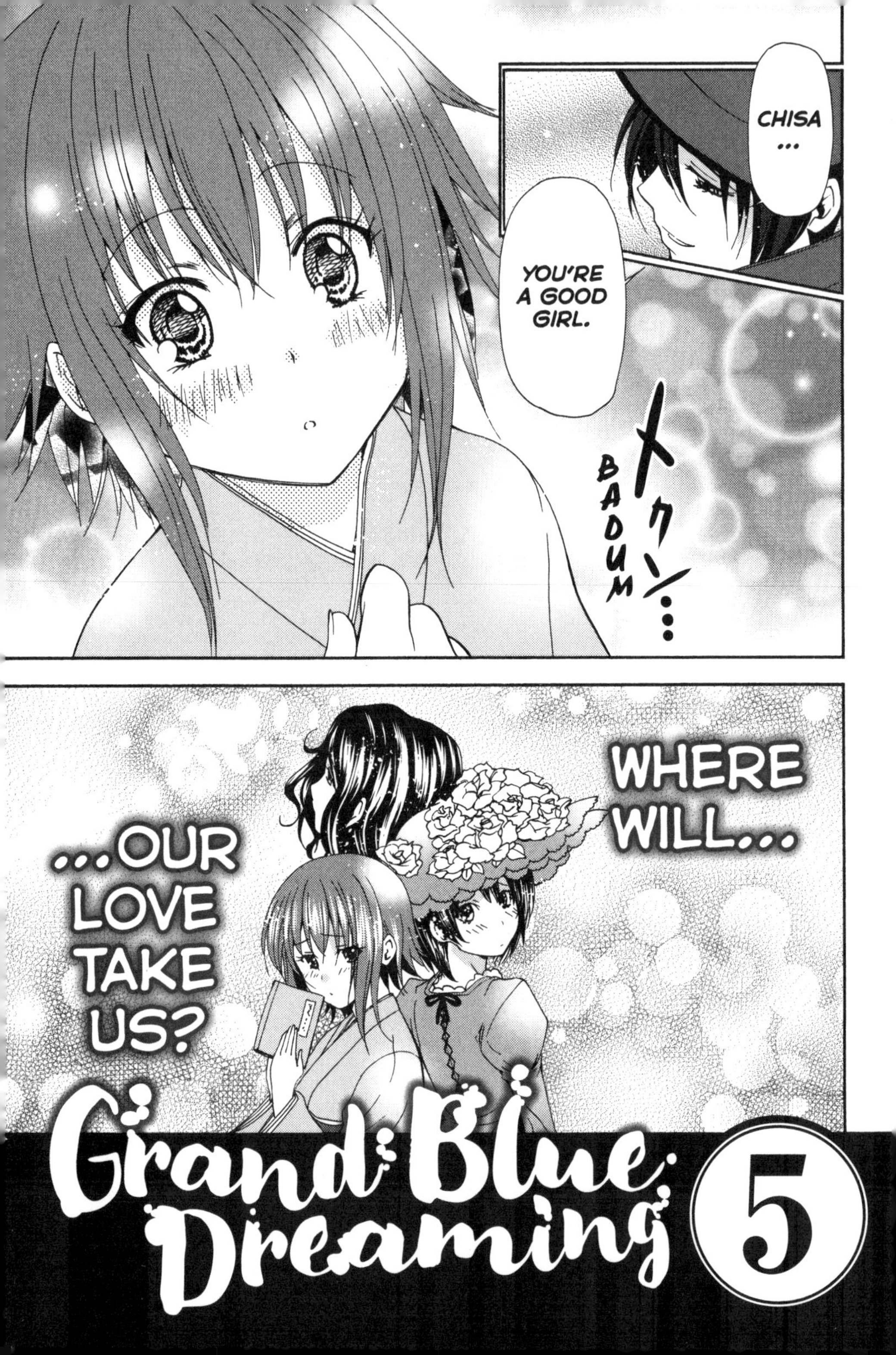
CHISA ...
YOU'RE A GOOD GIRL.
BADUM...
WHERE WILL...
...OUR LOVE TAKE US?
Grand Blue Dreaming
5